the Unofficial Guide® to

Maui

2nd Edition

D1008013

the Unofficial Guide® to Maui

2nd Edition

Marcie and Rick Carroll

WILEY

We are honored to dedicate this book to Wanda Keeble and the late Fred Keeble, who loved Maui longer and better than any other travelers we know.

Please note that prices fluctuate in the course of time, and travel information changes under the impact of many factors that influence the travel industry. We therefore suggest that you write or call ahead for confirmation when making your travel plans. Every effort has been made to ensure the accuracy of information throughout this book, and the contents of this publication are believed correct at the time of printing. Nevertheless, the publishers cannot accept responsibility for errors or omissions or for changes in details given in this guide or for the consequences of any reliance on the information provided by the same. Assessments of attractions and so forth are based on the authors' own experiences, and therefore, descriptions given in this guide necessarily contain an element of subjective opinion, which may not reflect the publisher's opinion or dictate a reader's own experience on another occasion. Readers are invited to write the publisher with ideas, comments, and suggestions for future editions.

Published by:

Wiley Publishing, Inc.

111 River Street

Hoboken, NJ 07030-5774

Produced by Menasha Ridge Press
Cover design by Michael J. Freeland
Interior design by Michele Laseau

For information on our other products and services or to obtain technical support please contact our Customer Care Department within the U.S. at 800-762-2974, outside the U.S. at 317-572-3993 or fax 317-572-4002

Wiley also publishes its books in a variety of electronic formats. Some content that appears in print may not be available in electronic formats.

ISBN 0-7645-7560-0

Manufactured in the United States of America

5 4 3 2 1

Contents

List of Maps

Acknowledgments

Mahalo Nui Loa, Maui . . .

With delight we thank fellow islanders who helped with this second edition of *The Unofficial Guide to Maui*. This guide is not only the result of our personal experiences over three decades but also the latest collective knowledge of many others, including:

- Marsha Weinert and Kelii Brown, Maui Visitors Bureau
- Nane and Candy Aluli, Napili/Kapalua
- Caroline Bhalla, Hana
- Yvonne Biegel, Wailea
- Kathy Dziedzic, Outrigger, Wailea
- Nancy Daniels, Outrigger, Hawaii
- MaryLou Foley, Outrigger, Hawaii
- Bonnie Friedman, Grapevine Productions, Wailuku
- Michele Lee, Sheila Donnelly & Associates, Island of Lanai
- Ruth Limtiaco, The Limtiaco Co., Honolulu.
- Luana Paahana, Kaanapali Beach Hotel, Maui
- Stu Glauberman, Aloha Airlines, Honolulu
- Luly Unemori, Wailea and Makena
- Gigi Valley, Kapalua Resort, Maui
- Caroline Witherspoon, Becker & Associates, Molokai Ranch
- Special thanks to Cheryl Chee Tsutsumi, Honolulu

And we thank editors Molly Merkle and Nathan Lott for enabling us to present this fresh, critical journalistic perspective of Maui, Molokai, and Lanai.

Further, we pay respect to storytellers, interpreters, and authors, living and dead, for their keen observations: Ben Keau Sr., Emmett Aluli, George Kanahele, Katharine Luomala, Duke Kahanamoku, Charmian

K. London, Mary Kawena Pukui and Samuel H. Elbert, Jack London, Isabella L. Bird, Mark Twain, Joana McIntyre Varawa, Robert Louis Stevenson, MacKinnon Simpson, Fletcher Knebel, Michel Tournier, Gian Paolo Barbieri, Charles Nordhoff, and Simon Winchester.

We acknowledge the sources of our personal anecdotes, sidebars, and marginalia: *Great Outdoor Adventures of Hawaii; Chicken Skin True Spooky Tales of Hawaii; Hawaii's Best Spooky Tales volumes 1–6; Aloha, The Magazine of Hawaii and the Pacific; Pacific Connections; Hawaii* magazine; *Outside* magazine; *Successful Meetings* magazine; *San Francisco Chronicle; Seattle Times;* and Oceanic Cable's **http://hawaii.rr.com.**

And, last, we thank you for choosing *The Unofficial Guide to Maui.*

Mahalo nui loa!

Marcie and Rick Carroll
Hana, Maui 2005

About the Authors

Rick Carroll, author of *Madame Pele: True Encounters with Hawaii's Fire Goddess,* is the best-selling creator of *Hawaii's Best Spooky Tales,* the six-volume sequel to *Chicken Skin True Spooky Stories of Hawaii.* He is now writing *In the Path of Night Marchers* online at **www.hawaii.rr.com.** A former daily journalist at the *San Francisco Chronicle,* Carroll wrote award-winning travel and feature stories about Hawaii and the Pacific for the *Honolulu Advertiser* and United Press International. He is contributing editor to *Hawaii Magazine.*

Marcie Rasmussen Carroll, freelance travel writer and former communications director for the Hawaii Convention and Visitors Bureau, earlier wrote political, environmental, and other news for the *San Francisco Chronicle, San Jose Mercury-News,* and UPI in Atlanta. She was a Journalism Fellow in Asian studies at University of Hawaii and in energy studies at Stanford University.

Together, the Carrolls, who moved to Windward Oahu in 1983, collected and edited *Travelers Tales Hawaii: True Stories of the Island Spirit,* an anthology one reviewer praised as "the best collection of contemporary Hawaii travel stories." They are also the authors of the extensively revised and rewritten third edition of the *Unofficial Guide to Hawaii.*

the Unofficial Guide® to

Maui

2nd Edition

Introduction

The Magical Islands of Maui

"Maui No Ka Oi." Anyone who has been to Maui can probably tell you what that means—"Maui is the best!" Not the cheapest, or the most Hawaiian, but the island where culture and nature and golf and beaches come together just right under the tropical sun to create the vacation dream most visitors envision.

For reasons we spell out for you in this guide, Maui is the perennial favorite place to visit in the Hawaiian islands, other than Honolulu, where most visitors by necessity have to arrive and depart because of flight schedules. Not only is Maui the most visited of the Hawaiian islands after Oahu, it has also been voted the best island anywhere, year after year, in multiple travel magazine reader polls. Ever noticed how many people say proudly they're going to Maui? Not just to Hawaii, but to Maui. It's the heart of the Hawaiian islands. Maui's nearby sibling islands, Molokai and Lanai, in contrast, are the least visited of the major islands in the Hawaiian chain. And while a fourth island, mysterious Kahoolawe, beckons on the horizon, this former U.S. Navy bombing range is off-limits for visitors altogether.

Together these islands form the realm of Maui County, jewel of the Hawaiian chain. They could hardly be more different, and yet they are linked by the geologic fundamentals they share under the aegis of towering Haleakala, the "House of the Sun" and largest dormant volcano in the world.

What is it about Maui that makes it so popular? One pilgrim, an Oklahoma restaurateur whose eyes light up just as much today at the thought of a Maui trip as they have every year for the past decade, puts it this way: "On Maui, you just know you're going to have fun."

Myth has it that the demigod Maui, the merry prankster of Polynesian legend, fished up the Hawaiian islands from the middle of the Pacific

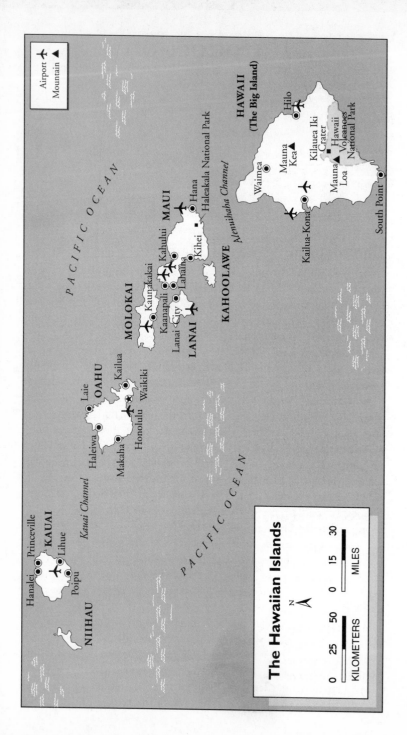

The Hawaiian Islands

Airport ✈
Mountain ▲

PACIFIC OCEAN

PACIFIC OCEAN

KAUAI
Hanalei
Princeville
Lihue
Poipu

NIIHAU

Kauai Channel

OAHU
Laie
Haleiwa
Kailua
Makaha
Honolulu
Waikiki

MOLOKAI
Kaunakakai

Kaanapali
Lanai City
LANAI

MAUI
Kabului
Lahaina
Kihei
Hana
Haleakala National Park

KAHOOLAWE

Menuihaha Channel

HAWAII
(The Big Island)
Hilo
Waimea
Mauna Kea ▲
Kilauea Iki Crater
Hawaii Volcanoes National Park
Mauna Loa ▲
Kailua-Kona
South Point

N

KILOMETERS
0   25   50

MILES
0   15   30

Ocean and lassoed the sun to slow its progress and let it shine longer on his namesake, the island of Maui, thus ensuring long, bright days to accommodate all the things there are to do.

Maui's islands offer experiences of rejuvenation to suit any visitor, from relaxing on a massage table at the spa to careening down the volcano on a specially built bike. And the Pacific is always nearby, offering the thrill of windsurfing, the promise of tanning on the beach, and the wonder of watching giant whales or spinner dolphins frolic in the waves. The important thing is to count on kicking back. This isn't New York, or Kansas, or even Waikiki. These are country islands where tourism is replacing sugar, pineapple, and ranching on huge spreads of land and where clever marketing lent an air of sophistication that somehow became fact.

If the Hawaiian song "Maui No Ka Oi" sounds vaguely familiar, it should. The melody is based on the early American children's song "My Boat Is Sailing," introduced to Hawaii by missionaries in the 1800s. The Rev. Samuel Kapu of Maui took the melody, composed Hawaiian lyrics praising Maui, and changed the title to create the island anthem, according to George Kanahele in *Hawaiian Music & Musicians*. Steel-guitar virtuoso Jerry Byrd and slack-key artists Sonny Chillingworth and Raymond Kane made "Maui No Ka Oi" a local hit.

About This Guidebook

Perhaps the greatest help a guidebook can be is in tailoring your expectations to the reality you are likely to find at your destination. Prepare to enjoy the people of Maui, Molokai, and Lanai and their easy way of living. Lighthearted island attitudes, the surprising generosity of spirit from people who go out of their way for you, and the sense of extended family soon begin to melt even the most hardened urban refugees and suburban road warriors. Remember that this isn't West Coast West, but a former Polynesian kingdom inhabited by a fairly exotic mix of people. Slow down, and be prepared for unfamiliar accents and customs, unexpected pleasures like the sight of a whale breaching as you drive along, and upheavals in your plans. Brief yourself by reading this book, prowling the Internet, and talking to friends. Those who come to the islands with advance knowledge and plenty of patience are bound to have delightful encounters. Bring your *keiki* (kids) and *kupuna* (elders). They'll have a good time in this family-oriented haven.

On the subject of reasonable expectations, know that you won't necessarily find movie-set huts by the sea on Maui's islands, and although there are plenty of beautiful, fanciful resorts, they're not all on the shore.

At the Kahului airport, you're more likely to be met by lines at the rental-car facilities than maidens bearing a lei of flowers, unless you have already paid for the greeting service or are being met by a friend who lives there. However, the welcome at many hotels includes lei of fresh orchids for guests when they arrive to check in.

Last, just because you're on a Hawaiian islands vacation doesn't mean you're immune to misfortune. Maui, Molokai, and Lanai are generally safe destinations, but try not to tempt fate. If you leave valuables unattended on your beach mat or in your rental car, locked or not, chances are they will vanish before you return. If you hike in a waterfall valley, watch out for cloudbursts, or you could be washed away. You can fall off those beautiful seacliffs, so hike *akamai* (wisely). The sea sets its own rules, so keep your challenges within your limits.

We're here to help you make the most of your trip to Maui and perhaps even augment your agenda with some serendipitous experiences. They're really hard to miss on Maui, but we want to help make sure you don't. It's hard for the "official" folks to recommend one of their members or sponsors over another. But it's easy for us to sort through the publicity. We tell you our favorites, and then we try to present a realistic view, pointing out pitfalls as well as don't-miss experiences. We'll provide some important details in advance, so that you'll be free to enjoy your entire vacation.

We aim to help you determine what suits you best among the dizzying array of hotels, condominiums, vacation rentals, and bed-and-breakfasts and find the best deals. You'll get an up-to-date review of the best adventures, attractions, beaches, hotels, clubs, and restaurants. You'll gain insights into local customs and learn a few Hawaiian words and phrases that make you feel more like a *kamaaina* (meaning "child of the land," a longtime or native-born resident).

Along the way, we'll examine questions like these:

- When is the best time to go?
- Where are the best beaches?
- What hiking trails can the family handle?
- Where do we find the best luau?

One Maui hotelier told a guest that a guidebook recommendation for his hotel is equal to a word-of-mouth rave review by a friend. Think of your authors as friends. We've lived in and written about Hawaii for many years and welcomed many friends and strangers as guests. Our own introductions to Maui were unforgettable adventures with family and friends. When we give our recommendations, we tell you what we tell our guests: what we like best and what we think would appeal to your special interests. Seniors, families, singles, honeymooners, European windsurfers, foodies, neo-hippies, and music lovers will all find something to love on Maui.

You want to be at the right place at the right time, enjoying the best Maui, Molokai, and Lanai offer, especially if it is your first trip. For those of you who have been to the Islands of Maui before and are ready to dig deeper, this book will suggest new possibilities. So mix up a mai tai, put on your favorite Hawaiian music, and launch your Maui adventure with *The Unofficial Guide to Maui.*

E komo mai! Welcome. Read on.

How *Unofficial Guides* Are Different

Our goal at *The Unofficial Guides* is to help you make informed decisions on how to pursue the Islands vacation you dreamed about, how to enjoy it best, and perhaps make a new discovery along the way. We try to tell you enough details about Maui, Molokai, and Lanai so that you can decide whether your family will be happier at Kaanapali or Wailea beach resorts, whether you want top-of-the-line hotel accommodations or camping, and whether you want haute cuisine or down-home local fare.

The Islands offer more things to do and see than you could pack into a lifetime of vacations. If you have only a week or two and you really just want to relax on a palm-fringed, gold-sand beach, no problem. We'll suggest—in a concise, easy-to-read format—that perfect beach and provide the information you need to enjoy it.

The Unofficial Guide to Maui, written for repeat and first-time visitors alike, addresses typical planning concerns ("Can I leave my coat and tie at home?" or "Should we visit the Maui Ocean Center?"). You'll find the answers to those questions and more in these pages.

Our Philosophy

If it matters to you, then it matters to us. From the beginning, the people behind *The Unofficial Guides* have worked diligently to deliver honest, straight-up reviews of major destinations and U.S. cities. The authors of this book are former San Francisco daily newspaper journalists who have lived in Hawaii and written about the Islands for two decades. They combine local knowledge with the ability to evaluate experiences from the visitors' point of view.

Special Features

The Unofficial Guide includes these special features:

- Insightful introductions to Maui, Molokai, and Lanai, highlighting the islands' special appeal and character.
- A brief look at the Hawaiian Islands' fascinating history, from discovery by early Polynesians and other explorers, to today's multicultural, mid-Pacific reality.
- Local customs and styles.

- Candid opinions on the best and worst of Maui, Molokai, and Lanai, including accommodations, beaches, restaurants, attractions, shows, clubs, and shops.
- Practical information on driving distances and how to avoid crowds, dodge traffic jams, and park cheaply on Maui. Or, alternatively, how to visit without a car.
- Suggested itineraries for travelers based on their interests.
- A guide to Maui's best golf courses.

Comments and Suggestions from Readers

We welcome your suggestions and comments about all our *Unofficial Guides,* including this book. Should you find any errors or omissions, we would appreciate hearing from you. Some of the best suggestions come from our readers.

How to Write the Authors:

Rick and Marcie Carroll
The Unofficial Guide to Maui
P.O. Box 43673
Birmingham, AL 35243
unofficialguides@menasharidge.com

Be sure to put your return address on your letter as well as on the envelope. And remember, our work takes us on the road for long periods of time, so please forgive any delayed response.

Reader Survey

At the back of this guide you'll find a reader questionnaire that will help you express your satisfaction/dissatisfaction with both this book and your visit to the Maui County Islands. This survey will also help us make improvements to future editions of this guide. Please clip out the survey along the dotted lines and mail it to the above address.

How Information Is Organized

To give you quick access to information about the best of Maui, Molokai, and Lanai, we've organized material in a subject-matter format. Sections of this guidebook are dedicated to:

Hotels   So many hotels, condos, and bed-and-breakfasts seek your business that choosing the right one can be daunting. We offer easy-to-read charts, maps, and rating systems, as well as pertinent information on room size, cleanliness, service, amenities, cost, and accessibility to the beach.

Attractions   There's a lot more to do in Maui County than loll around on the sand—although there are plenty of beaches, and we highlight those, too. Besides thorough descriptions, our attractions overview includes author ratings and ratings by age group to help you determine what to include on your itinerary.

Restaurants   A highlight of every Hawaiian vacation is sampling islands cuisine. The menu is vast, ranging from simple local favorites like plate lunches to extravagant gourmet repasts and Hawaii's own regional cuisine. We take you to the best restaurants, out-of-the-way bistros, and roadside stands.

The Outdoors   Natural splendor is a big part of Maui's appeal. We tell you where to hike, camp, surf, bike, and more—making the Maui outdoors accessible.

Golf   The chance to play the fabled golf courses of Maui and Lanai is a major draw for many visitors. To help you choose the right one, we detail the vital stats of the top courses, including the scenic championship layouts that appear on televised professional tournaments in winter when most duffers are confined to their living rooms, as well as others you might not find without us.

Entertainment and Nightlife   Most visitors want to see live entertainment, Hawaiian style, during their stay. We review shows you shouldn't miss and the nightlife you're likely to find on Maui, Molokai, and Lanai.

The Geographic Regions of Maui County

- West Maui
- Central Maui (and the North Shore)
- South Maui
- Upcountry Maui (and Haleakala)
- Hana (and East Maui)
- Molokai
- Lanai

Kahoolawe

Please note that the Island of Kahoolawe is technically part of Maui County, but we have not listed it as a place you can visit. For decades, Kahoolawe, the red dirt island that seems to be bleeding across the channel from South Maui just beyond the snorkel haven of Molokini Crater, was a target for U.S. Navy bombing practice. Now it is in the process of being transformed into a Hawaiian cultural preserve, but visitors won't be permitted there for a long time to come, for a very good reason: The federal cleanup effort hasn't yet removed all the munition that could still explode in the ground. The uninhabited island is off-limits, except by special invitation. So for now, most of us can only imagine what Kahoolawe Island will be like when all its wounds are repaired.

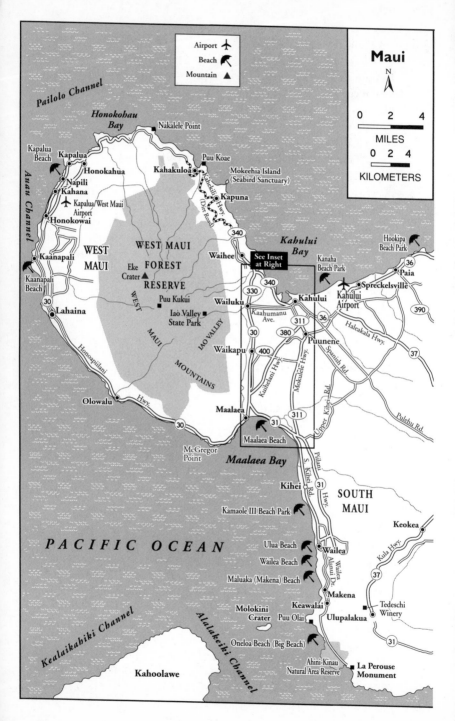

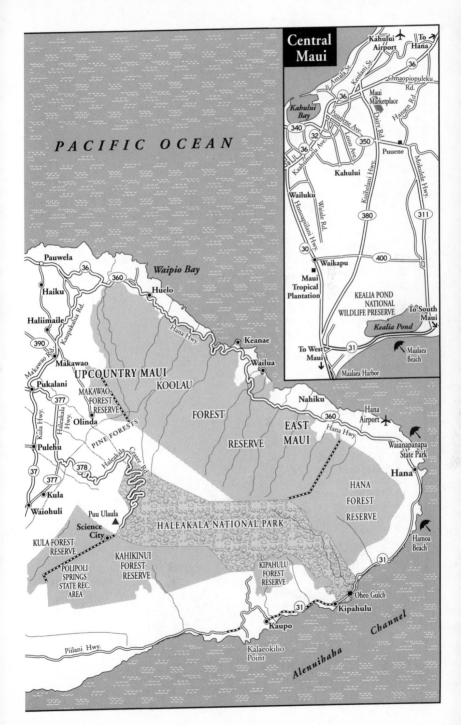

Central Maui

Kahului Airport
To Hana
Omaopiopuleku Rd.
Amala St.
Keolani St.
36
Maui Marketplace
Kahului Bay
36
Puunene Ave.
Dairy Rd.
Hansen Rd.
340
32
36
350
Kaahumanu Ave.
Lono Ave.
Puuene
Kahului
Mokulele Hwy.
Kuihelani Hwy.
Wailuku
Honoapiilani Hwy.
Waiale Rd.
380
311
30
Waiale Rd.
Waikapu
400
Maui Tropical Plantation
KEALIA POND NATIONAL WILDLIFE PRESERVE
To West Maui
31
To South Maui
Kealia Pond
Maalaea Beach
Maalaea Harbor

PACIFIC OCEAN

Pauwela
36
Waipio Bay
Haiku
Huelo
Haliimaile
360
Hana Hwy.
390
Kaupakalua Rd.
Keanae
Makawao
Wailua
Pukalani
UPCOUNTRY MAUI
KOOLAU
377
MAKAWAO FOREST RESERVE
Kula Hwy.
Haleakala Hwy.
Olinda
FOREST
Nahiku
Hana Airport
360
37
PINE FORESTS
RESERVE
EAST MAUI
Hana Hwy.
Pulehu
378
Haleakala Crater Rd.
Waianapanapa State Park
377
Kula
Hana
Waiohuli
Puu Ulaula
HANA FOREST RESERVE
Science City
HALEAKALA NATIONAL PARK
KULA FOREST RESERVE
POLIPOLI SPRINGS STATE REC. AREA
KAHIKINUI FOREST RESERVE
KIPAHULU FOREST RESERVE
Hamoa Beach
31
Oheo Gulch
31
Kipahulu
Kaupo
Piilani Hwy.
Kalaeokilio Point
Alenuihaha Channel

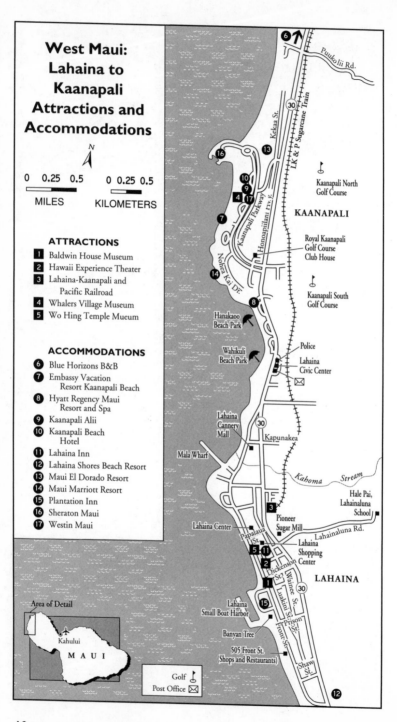

West Maui: Lahaina to Kaanapali Attractions and Accommodations

N

0   0.25   0.5   0   0.25   0.5
MILES   KILOMETERS

ATTRACTIONS

1 Baldwin House Museum
2 Hawaii Experience Theater
3 Lahaina-Kaanapali and
   Pacific Railroad
4 Whalers Village Museum
5 Wo Hing Temple Mueum

ACCOMMODATIONS

6 Blue Horizons B&B
7 Embassy Vacation
   Resort Kaanapali Beach
8 Hyatt Regency Maui
   Resort and Spa
9 Kaanapali Alii
10 Kaanapali Beach
   Hotel
11 Lahaina Inn
12 Lahaina Shores Beach Resort
13 Maui El Dorado Resort
14 Maui Marriott Resort
15 Plantation Inn
16 Sheraton Maui
17 Westin Maui

Puukolii Rd.

Kekaa St.

LK & P Sugarcane Train

Kaanapali Parkway

Honoapiilani Hwy.

Nohea Kai Dr.

Kaanapali North
Golf Course

KAANAPALI

Royal Kaanapali
Golf Course
Club House

Kaanapali South
Golf Course

Hanakaoo
Beach Park

Wahikuli
Beach Park

Police

Lahaina
Civic Center

Lahaina
Cannery
Mall

Kapunakea

Mala Wharf

Kahoma   Stream

Hale Pai,
Lahainaluna
School

Pioneer
Sugar Mill

Lahainaluna Rd.

Lahaina Center

Papalaua
St.

Lahaina
Shopping
Center

Dickenson
St.

Wainee St.

Luakini St.

LAHAINA

Lahaina
Small Boat Harbor

Banyan Tree

505 Front St.
(Shops and Restaurants)

Prison St.

Front St.

Shaw St.

Area of Detail

Kahului

MAUI

Golf
Post Office

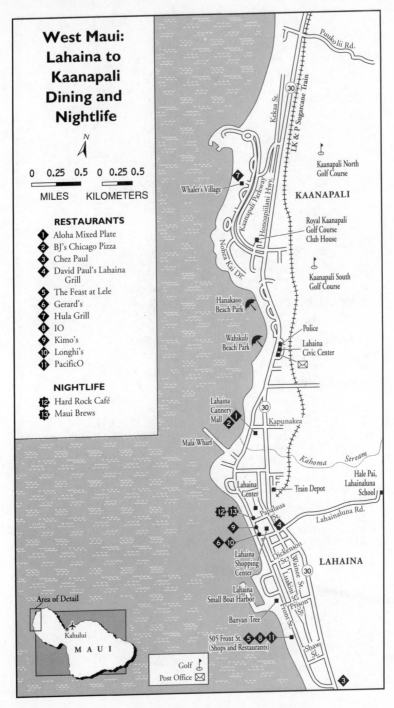

West Maui: Lahaina to Kaanapali Dining and Nightlife

N

0 0.25 0.5   0 0.25 0.5
MILES   KILOMETERS

RESTAURANTS
1 Aloha Mixed Plate
2 BJ's Chicago Pizza
3 Chez Paul
4 David Paul's Lahaina Grill
5 The Feast at Lele
6 Gerard's
7 Hula Grill
8 IO
9 Kimo's
10 Longhi's
11 PacificO

NIGHTLIFE
12 Hard Rock Café
13 Maui Brews

Puuko lii Rd.

LK & P Sugarcane Train

Kekaa St.

30

Kaanapali North Golf Course

Whaler's Village   7

KAANAPALI

Kaanapali Parkway

Honoapiilani Hwy.

Royal Kaanapali Golf Course Club House

Noheakai Dr.

Kaanapali South Golf Course

Hanakaoo Beach Park

Police

Wahikuli Beach Park

Lahaina Civic Center

Lahaina Cannery Mall   1

Kapunakea

2

30

Mala Wharf

Kahoma   Stream

Lahaina Center

Train Depot

Hale Pai, Lahainaluna School

12 13

Papalaua St.

4

Lahainaluna Rd.

9

Dickenson St.

6 10

Wainee St.

LAHAINA

Lahaina Shopping Center

Luakini St.

30

Lahaina Small Boat Harbor

Prison St.

Banyan Tree

Front St.

505 Front St. (Shops and Restaurants)   5 8 11

Shaw St.

Area of Detail

Kahului

MAUI

Golf
Post Office

3

11

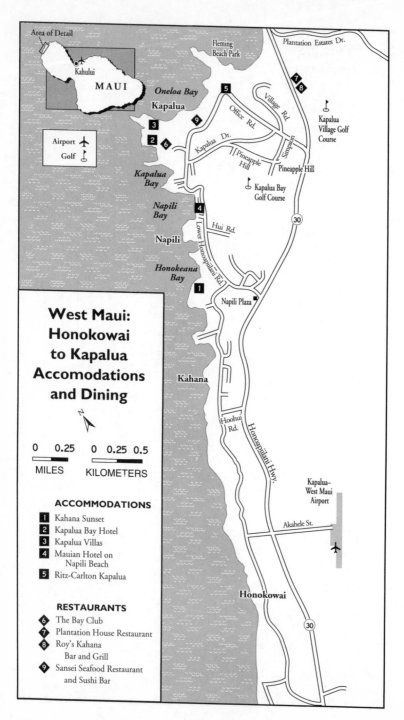

Area of Detail

Kahului

MAUI

Oneloa Bay

Kapalua

Fleming
Beach Park

Plantation Estates Dr.

Office Rd.

Village Rd.

Kapalua
Village Golf
Course

Airport ✈
Golf ⛳

Kapalua Dr.

Pineapple
Hill

Simpson

Pineapple Hill

Kapalua Bay
Golf Course

Kapalua
Bay

Napili
Bay

Napili

Hui Rd.

Lower Honoapiilani Rd.

30

Honokeana
Bay

Napili Plaza

Kahana

Hoohui
Rd.

Honoapiilani Hwy.

Kapalua–
West Maui
Airport

Akahele St.

✈

Honokowai

30

West Maui: Honokowai to Kapalua Accomodations and Dining

N

| 0 | 0.25 | | 0 | 0.25 | 0.5 |
MILES   KILOMETERS

ACCOMMODATIONS

1 Kahana Sunset
2 Kapalua Bay Hotel
3 Kapalua Villas
4 Mauian Hotel on
   Napili Beach
5 Ritz-Carlton Kapalua

RESTAURANTS

6 The Bay Club
7 Plantation House Restaurant
8 Roy's Kahana
   Bar and Grill
9 Sansei Seafood Restaurant
   and Sushi Bar

12

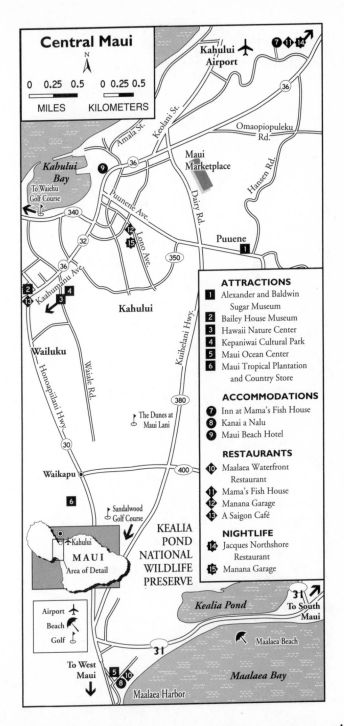

Central Maui

N

| 0 | 0.25 | 0.5 | | 0 | 0.25 | 0.5 |
| MILES | | | | KILOMETERS | | |

Kahului Airport

7 11 14

Kahului Bay

9

To Waiehu Golf Course

340

Amala St.

Keolani St.

Omaopiopuleku Rd.

Maui Marketplace

Hansen Rd.

36

Puunene Ave.

Dairy Rd.

32

12
15

Lono Ave.

350

Puunene

1

36

Kaahumanu Ave.

2
13
4
3

Kahului

Wailuku

Waiale Rd.

Honoapiilani Hwy.

Kuihelani Hwy.

380

▶ The Dunes at Maui Lani

30

Waikapu

400

6

▶ Sandalwood Golf Course

KEALIA POND NATIONAL WILDLIFE PRESERVE

Kahului

MAUI
Area of Detail

Airport ✈
Beach ⛱
Golf ⛳

Kealia Pond

31
To South Maui

To West Maui

31

⛱ Maalaea Beach

5 **10**
8

Maalaea Harbor

Maalaea Bay

ATTRACTIONS

1 Alexander and Baldwin Sugar Museum
2 Bailey House Museum
3 Hawaii Nature Center
4 Kepaniwai Cultural Park
5 Maui Ocean Center
6 Maui Tropical Plantation and Country Store

ACCOMMODATIONS

7 Inn at Mama's Fish House
8 Kanai a Nalu
9 Maui Beach Hotel

RESTAURANTS

10 Maalaea Waterfront Restaurant
11 Mama's Fish House
12 Manana Garage
13 A Saigon Café

NIGHTLIFE

14 Jacques Northshore Restaurant
15 Manana Garage

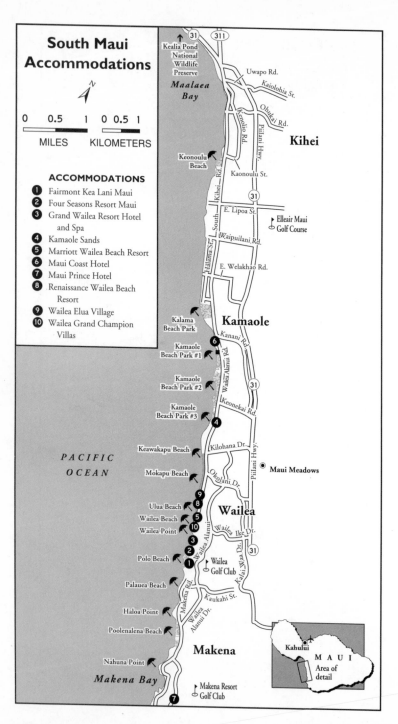

South Maui Accommodations

N

0	0.5	1	0	0.5	1
MILES			**KILOMETERS**		

ACCOMMODATIONS

1 Fairmont Kea Lani Maui
2 Four Seasons Resort Maui
3 Grand Wailea Resort Hotel and Spa
4 Kamaole Sands
5 Marriott Wailea Beach Resort
6 Maui Coast Hotel
7 Maui Prince Hotel
8 Renaissance Wailea Beach Resort
9 Wailea Elua Village
10 Wailea Grand Champion Villas

31 311

Kealia Pond National Wildlife Preserve

Maalaea Bay

Uwapo Rd.

Kaiolohia St.

Kenolio Rd.

Ohukai Rd.

Piilani Hwy.

Kihei

Keonoulu Beach

Kaonoulu St.

Kihei Rd.

31

E. Lipoa St.

South Kihei Rd.

Waipuilani Rd.

Elleair Maui Golf Course

Halama St.

E. Welakhao Rd.

Kalama Beach Park

Kamaole

Kanani Rd.

6 Kamaole Beach Park #1

Wailea Alanui Rd.

Kamaole Beach Park #2

31

Keonekai Rd.

Kamaole Beach Park #3

4

Keawakapu Beach

Kilohana Dr.

Piilani Hwy.

• Maui Meadows

Mokapu Beach

Okolani Dr.

9

8 Ulua Beach

Wailea

5 Wailea Beach

10

Wailea Point

Wailea Ike Dr.

3

2

1 Polo Beach

Wailea Alanui

Wailea Golf Club

Kalai Waa Dr.

31

Palauea Beach

Makena Rd.

Kaukahi St.

Haloa Point

Wailea Alanui Dr.

Poolenalena Beach

Makena

Nahuna Point

Makena Bay

Makena Resort Golf Club

PACIFIC OCEAN

Kahului

MAUI Area of detail

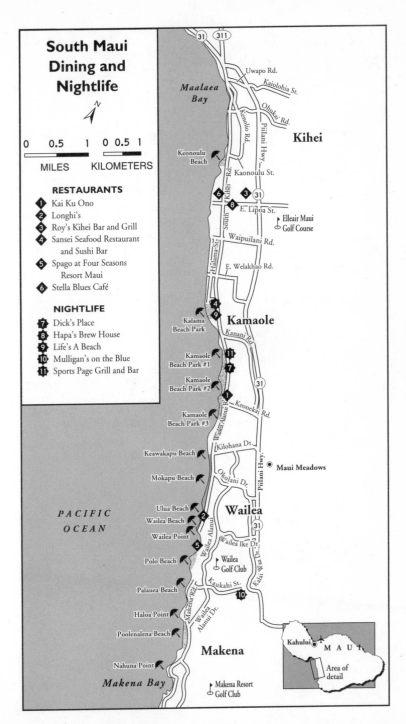

South Maui Dining and Nightlife

N

0   0.5   1   0   0.5   1
MILES   KILOMETERS

RESTAURANTS
1. Kai Ku Ono
2. Longhi's
3. Roy's Kihei Bar and Grill
4. Sansei Seafood Restaurant and Sushi Bar
5. Spago at Four Seasons Resort Maui
6. Stella Blues Café

NIGHTLIFE
7. Dick's Place
8. Hapa's Brew House
9. Life's A Beach
10. Mulligan's on the Blue
11. Sports Page Grill and Bar

Maalaea Bay

Uwapo Rd.

Kaiolohia St.

Ohukai Rd.

Kenolio Rd.

Piilani Hwy.

Kihei

Keonoulu Beach

Kaonoulu St.

South Kihei Rd.

E. Lipoa St.

Elleair Maui Golf Course

Halama St.

Waipuilani Rd.

E. Welakhao Rd.

Kalama Beach Park

Kamaole

Kanani Rd.

Kamaole Beach Park #1

Kamaole Beach Park #2

Keonekai Rd.

Kamaole Beach Park #3

Kilohana Dr.

Keawakapu Beach

Maui Meadows

Mokapu Beach

Okolani Dr.

Piilani Hwy.

PACIFIC OCEAN

Ulua Beach

Wailea Beach

Wailea Point

Wailea

Wailea Alanui

Wailea Ike Dr.

Polo Beach

Wailea Golf Club

Kaukahi St.

Kilani Weha Dr.

Palauea Beach

Makena Rd.

Haloa Point

Wailea Alanui Dr.

Poolenalena Beach

Makena

Nahuna Point

Makena Bay

Makena Resort Golf Club

Kahului

MAUI

Area of detail

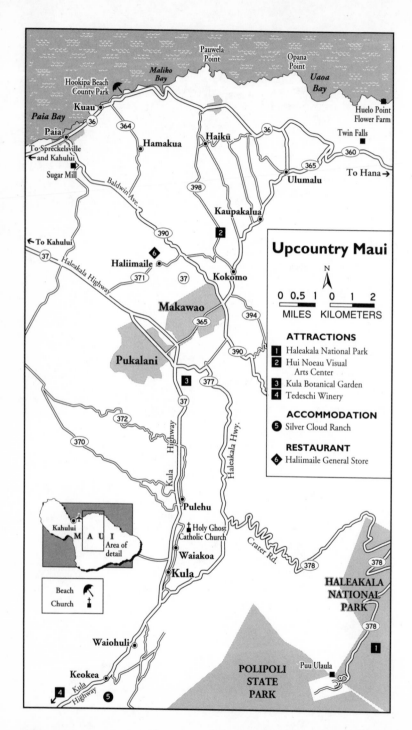

Pauwela
Point

Opana
Point

*Maliko
Bay*

*Uaoa
Bay*

Hookipa Beach
County Park

Kuau

Paia Bay

Paia

36

364

Hamakua

Haikū

36

Huelo Point
Flower Farm

Twin Falls

To Spreckelsville
and Kahului

360

To Hana →

Sugar Mill

365

Ulumalu

Baldwin Ave.

398

← To Kahului

37

Haleakala Highway

390

Haliimaile

371

37

6

Kaupakalua

2

Kokomo

394

Makawao

365

390

Pukalani

3

377

37

372

370

Kula
Highway

Haleakala Hwy.

Pulehu

✝ Holy Ghost
Catholic Church

Crater Rd.

378

378

Waiakoa

Kula

Upcountry Maui

N

0 0.5 1   0 1   2
MILES   KILOMETERS

ATTRACTIONS

1 Haleakala National Park
2 Hui Noeau Visual
   Arts Center
3 Kula Botanical Garden
4 Tedeschi Winery

ACCOMMODATION

5 Silver Cloud Ranch

RESTAURANT

6 Haliimaile General Store

Kahului

M A U I
Area of
detail

Beach

Church ✝

**HALEAKALA
NATIONAL
PARK**

Waiohuli

378

1

Keokea

4

5

Kula
Highway

Puu Ulaula

**POLIPOLI
STATE
PARK**

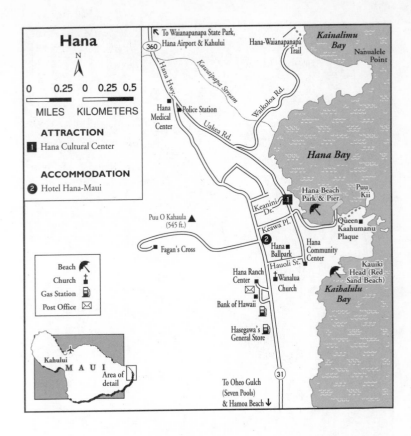

Hana

N

0   0.25   0   0.25   0.5
MILES   KILOMETERS

ATTRACTION
1 Hana Cultural Center

ACCOMMODATION
2 Hotel Hana-Maui

Beach
Church
Gas Station
Post Office

Kahului
M A U I
Area of
detail

To Waianapanapa State Park,
Hana Airport & Kahului
360

Hana-Waianapanapa
Trail

*Kainalimu
Bay*

Nanualele
Point

Kawaipapa Stream

Hana Hwy.

Waikoloa Rd.

Hana
Medical
Center

Police Station

Uakea Rd.

Hana Bay

Puu O Kahaula
(545 ft.)

Keanini
Dr.

1

Hana Beach
Park & Pier

Puu
Kii

Keawa Pl.

Queen
Kaahumanu
Plaque

Fagan's Cross

2

Hana
Ballpark

Hana
Community
Center

Hauoli St.

Kauiki
Head (Red
Sand Beach)

Hana Ranch
Center

Wanalua
Church

*Kaihalulu
Bay*

Bank of Hawaii

Hasegawa's
General Store

31

To Oheo Gulch
(Seven Pools)
& Hamoa Beach

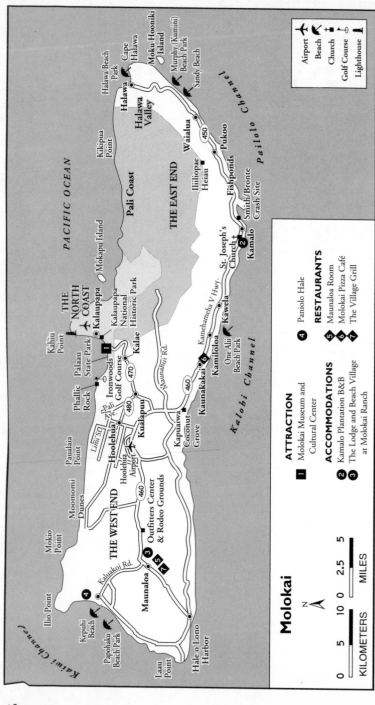

Molokai

N

```
KILOMETERS
0    5    10   0   2.5   5
MILES
```

PACIFIC OCEAN

Kaiwi Channel

Ilio Point

Mokio Point

Kepuhi Beach

Papohaku Beach Park

Hale o Lono Harbor

Laau Point

Kaluakoi Rd.

THE WEST END

Maunaloa

Outfitters Center & Rodeo Grounds

Moomomi Dunes

Paualaia Point

Kahiu Point

THE NORTH COAST

Palaau State Park

Phallic Rock

Ironwoods Golf Course

Hoolehua

Hoolehua Airport

Lihi St.

Pali Ave.

Kualapuu

Kapuaiwa Coconut Grove

Maunaluu Rd.

Kalae

Kalaupapa

Kalaupapa National Historic Park

Mokapu Island

Pali Coast

Kikipua Point

Halawa Valley

Halawa Beach Park

Cape Halawa

Moku Hooniki Island

Murphy (Kumimi) Beach Park

Sandy Beach

Halawa

Waialua

Pukoo

Fishponds

Smith/Bronte Crash Site

Hililiopae Heiau

St. Joseph's Church

Kamalo

Kawela

One Alii Beach Park

Kamiloloa

Kaunakakai

Kamehameha V Hwy.

THE EAST END

Kalohi Channel

Pailolo Channel

Legend

✈ Airport
🏖 Beach
⛪ Church
⛳ Golf Course
🗼 Lighthouse

ATTRACTION

1 Molokai Museum and Cultural Center

ACCOMMODATIONS

2 Kamalo Plantation B&B
3 The Lodge and Beach Village at Molokai Ranch

4 Paniolo Hale

RESTAURANTS

5 Maunaloa Room
6 Molokai Pizza Café
7 The Village Grill

18

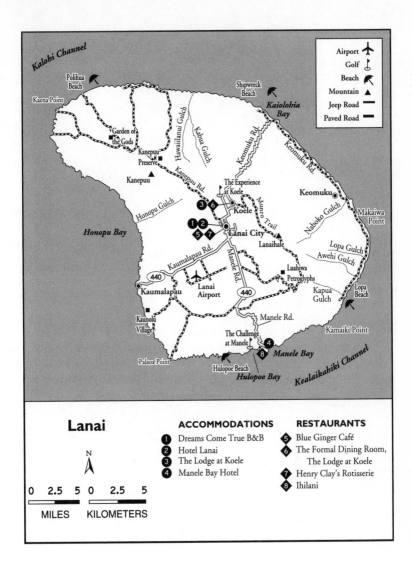

Airport ✈
Golf ⛳
Beach ⚐
Mountain ▲
Jeep Road –
Paved Road —

Kalohi Channel

Polihua
Beach

Kaena Point

Garden of
the Gods

Kanepuu
Preserve

Kanepuu ▲

Honopu Gulch

Honopu Bay

Hawaiilanui Gulch

Kahua Gulch

Shipwreck
Beach

*Kaiolohia
Bay*

Keomuku Rd.

Keomuku Rd.

The Experience
at Koele

❸ ❻

Koele

❶ ❷

❺ ❼

Lanai City

Lanaihale ▲

Monro Trail

Keomuku ◉

Naboko Gulch

Makaiwa
Point

Lopa Gulch

Awehi Gulch

Kaumalapau Rd.

(440)

Kaumalapau ◉

Lanai
Airport ✈

Manele Rd.

(440)

Luahiwa
Petroglyphs

Kapua
Gulch

Lopa
Beach ⚐

Kaunolu
Village

Manele Rd.

The Challenge
at Manele

❹

❽ *Manele Bay*

Kamaiki Point

Palaoa Point

Hulopoe Beach ⚐

Hulopoe Bay

Kealaikahiki Channel

Lanai

N

0   2.5   5   0   2.5   5
MILES   KILOMETERS

ACCOMMODATIONS
❶ Dreams Come True B&B
❷ Hotel Lanai
❸ The Lodge at Koele
❹ Manele Bay Hotel

RESTAURANTS
❺ Blue Ginger Café
❻ The Formal Dining Room,
   The Lodge at Koele
❼ Henry Clay's Rotisserie
❽ Ihilani

Part One

Getting Acquainted with Maui

Maui Nui, Centerpiece of the Hawaiian Feast

The Islands of Maui include Maui, Molokai, and Lanai. All are part of Maui County, politically speaking. This diverse trio comprises one of the best destinations in which to enjoy a Hawaiian holiday.

The Maui County islands are believed to be the tips of a single, sunken island, legendary Maui Nui, or Big Maui. You can see the geologic theory at work on Maui as you fly into Kahului Airport—the two main parts of the "Valley Isle" are mountains linked by a low-lying isthmus or valley, covered with fields of waving green sugarcane and Kahului Airport. If Maui were to sink much more over the coming geologic eons, or if the ocean were to rise dramatically, modern-day Maui could become two islands, one around the base of 10,000-plus-foot Haleakala and the other circling the mile-high West Maui Mountains. Intact and familiar for the foreseeable ages, however, Maui is the second largest of the major islands (next to the neighboring Big Island), at 729 square miles, 48 miles long, and 26 miles across at the widest point, with 81 accessible beaches spread along a shoreline of 120 miles.

They may be joined at the base, but each of the Maui islands is quite different from the next. You can get the big picture from the air, on the descent into Honolulu International Airport from the mainland. Look out the left side of the aircraft during the last 30 minutes, when flight attendants announce the final stage of your trans-Pacific flight. After more than 2,000 miles of open sea, the first sight of land is the two hulking volcanoes of the Big Island, and then across the water after a moment, the cloud-wreathed peak of 10,023-foot Haleakala, the summit of Maui. Sometimes you can see into the crater at the top, a burned and cindery vista that looks like a misplaced chunk of Arizona. Next come Molokai, its steep green slopes continuing out to sea in reefs visible near shore and its flattened, dry West End, ringed with golden beach, and the little red-dirt Island of Lanai, once the world's biggest pineapple plantation and now a luxury retreat. The three islands in the middle of the Hawaiian chain are the core of the archipelago, each with its own appeal. Maui is an island of sophisticated resorts and fine dining, championship golf courses, and great beaches, among other attractions. But its little historic towns add an air of reality and recall the sweet past of sugar plantations and a farming heritage. Molokai is part cattle ranch, part lush valleys and ancient fishponds, part small farm. It is totally laid-back, with little in the way of tourism facilities but plenty to offer visitors who can get along without resorts. Lanai is an exclusive retreat that draws honeymooners and folks with deep pockets who like the great outdoors. From dawn at the summit of Haleakala until the sun sets behind Lanai, your sojourn to Maui's islands can be packed with diversions enough to create a lifetime of memories.

Choosing an Island

The choice depends on what you seek: beaches and water sports, rest and relaxation, action and adventure, hip shops and nightlife, historic homes and ruins, romantic evenings with champagne and chocolate, nature and culture, hiking and camping, championship golf, or just lazy days under the tropic sun.

A stay on Maui promises warm beaches, great golf on championship courses, winter whale-watching, snorkeling and sailing, hikes, sunrise at Haleakala Crater, and quiet nights, outside of Kihei and Lahaina. People come to Maui to have fun—with their lovers, their families, their business associates, their school friends and cruise mates, their best pals and fellow travelers. But all that popularity means you will share Maui with lots of others. If you're looking for a getaway, consider those other little-known islands across the water, Molokai and Lanai.

Maui offers the most action, hotels, shopping, restaurants, golf, and beaches and is most accessible. Molokai offers the least of those features and the most undisturbed tropical landscape. Lanai, a secluded luxury retreat, offers some of both: great hotels, golf, dining, and wide-open spaces to explore.

The following passages give an overview of each island, describing Maui in keeping with the geographical divisions used throughout the book: West Maui, Central Maui, South Maui, Upcountry Maui, and Hana. Besides providing an introduction to the physical and cultural geography of Maui County's distinct regions, the passages will help you determine where to focus your vacation. All of Maui County will be within reach during your stay (though interisland travel can be costly and time-consuming). However, if you know you want to spend your time at the beach, it doesn't make sense to stay Upcountry. Targeting your vacation to a resort, city, or region can save you lots of transit time, thus leaving more play time. More important, it helps ensure that you encounter the side of Maui that most appeals to you. This is especially true if you're planning to stay at one of the major resorts and spend a lot of time on site.

Maui, Island of Adventure

Maui is Hawaii's most famous island, thanks to the popularity of the sunny resorts and golf courses on its southern and western coasts. Maui's two volcanic masses are joined by a slender valley and ringed with golden beaches and blue sea. Haleakala Crater's sheer bulk anchors the isle. Its slopes covering more than half Maui's land, Haleakala towers like a guardian spirit above the whole, particularly the South Maui resort coast, which it shields from wind and rain. What draws everyone to Maui, we suspect—besides its natural diversity, great beaches, and endless summer weather—is location: smack dab in middle of the inhabited Hawaiian chain with a clear view of five nearby islands. Mainlanders and people who live land-locked lives somehow feel comforted by the presence of other islands in plain sight. We don't know why this is; we only know that to be all alone on the vast Pacific is an isolation only solo sailors crave. In the empty ocean, even migratory whales seek out Maui. The West Maui Mountains are mysterious, a series of steep valleys that lead to peaks lost in clouds, lending haunting beauty to the sloped fields of cane and pineapple behind the seaside West Maui resorts. Maui combines a hint of Honolulu's cosmopolitan flash, the genuine country pace of a rural plantation island, and the sophisticated influence of its luxury spreads and the people who frequent them.

With nearly 19,000 visitor units, ranging from less than $100 to more than $10,000 a day, and 16 golf courses, Maui accommodates wide-ranging tastes. Elegant luxury hotels cater to the wealthy and free-spending corporate incentive winners, but Maui also offers some affordable bargains for budget travelers.

This island delights people who like living it up at swanky beach resorts and those who prefer bedding down in rustic park cabins and camps, people who like hiking upland trails or kayaking with the windy sea and those content to watch from the beach, people who like to shop international boutiques in shorts and those who crave the awesome beauty of natural vistas. Getting rowdy in Lahaina is a century-old tradition, and young visitors line up nightly to keep the whalers' heritage alive in their own way. More than a few Maui travelers are drawn by the mystic powers attributed to Haleakala, "House of the Sun," and then find themselves caught by the misty magic of the West Maui Mountains. Whatever the draw, visitors with myriad interests regularly return to Maui, and Maui eagerly embraces its tourists, more than two million a year from around the world. They mean jobs and prosperity for a large share of Maui residents and Molokai commuters, many of whom would otherwise find it rough to make ends meet on these tiny dots in the middle of the vast North Pacific.

MAUI FACTS

Flower: Lokelani (rose)
Color: Pink
County Seat: Wailuku
Area: 729 square miles
Length: (east–west): 48 miles
Width: (north–south): 26 miles

Population: 128,094
Highest Point: Haleakala (10,023 feet)
Coastline: 120 miles
Airports: Kahului Airport, Central Maui and Kapalua, West Maui

---

West Maui

A world to themselves, the towns and resorts of West Maui ring the mountains around **Eke Crater.** It's a leisurely hour's drive from Kahului Airport (longer if you stop to watch the passing whales in winter) south to **Maalaea** and on to **Lahaina,** with a final 20 minutes along Honoapiilani Highway (Route 30) through open country, dry slope on one side and ocean and beach on the other. From bustling, historic Lahaina town, it's three miles farther to the manicured park-like setting and mid-rise hotels and condos of **Kaanapali Beach Resort.** The developed coast continues north seven more miles to elegant **Kapalua Resort.**

Central Maui

Maui's upland **Iao Valley** flanks the West Maui Mountains on the east, dipping to the slender lowlands that connect Maui's two massive mountain structures. This low, flat stretch is Central Maui. To most visitors, Central Maui is just a corridor through which they travel after landing at **Kahului Airport** on the North Shore en route to resorts in West Maui (via Kuihelani and Honoapiilani Highways) or the island's southwestern shore (via Mokulele and Piilani Highways). If and when you traverse Central Maui, through fields of waving sugarcane from the island's northern to southern shores, you'll see the smokestack of the **Puunene**

Sugar Mill, still at work even though sugar mills have shut down across most of the Islands.

South Maui

Beginning at the southeastern end of the isthmus valley at **Kihei,** South Maui spills down around the base of Haleakala like a newly unfolding map. The area lines up much like West Maui, minus the 20-minute drive through volcanic badlands. First comes the resort town, Kihei, home to an array of shops and restaurants centered around **Kamaole Beach Parks I, II,** and **III,** which draw aspiring surfers and whale-watchers alike. South of Kihei is the famous, manicured resort **Wailea,** where boutiques and three golf courses await visitors willing to splurge. Then come the least known, most remote **Makena Resort,** and finally **Makena State Beach Park,** before the road runs out around the bend in lava-flow wilderness at **La Perouse Bay.**

Upcountry Maui

Haleakala National Park is the centerpiece of Upcountry Maui and its primary draw. The park stretches from the sea (at Oheo Gulch) in the east to the crater's summit, though most visitors arrive from the west via **Kula.** Upcountry offers a respite from Maui's tropical heat, and there's even a winery, **Tedeschi Vineyards,** at Ulupalakua Ranch south of Kula. Pineapple wine and other vintages, including sparkling wines, are available to sample and buy at the tasting room. To the north, surrounded by cane and pineapple fields, are **Makawao,** a ranching and rodeo town with colorful Western-style storefronts; the working plantation village of Haliimaile, home to the deceptively named restaurant, **Haliimaile General Store;** the rural hamlet of **Haiku;** and **Paia,** a former plantation town now a bustling, picturesque tourist shopping village. Few visitors will spend a night in Upcountry Maui, unless they do so in a tent on the slopes of Haleakala. However, Kula offers the quaint **Upcountry Kula Lodge** and a variety of bed-and-breakfast rooms or vacation rentals. Also, rentals and bed-and-breakfasts in **Haiku** and the vicinity are favorites of the windsurfing jet-setters who come for the waves at Hookipa.

Hana

The twisty road to Hana takes you winding by magnificent sea views, waterfalls, and botanical gardens on a skinny lane for 52 miles, away from the here-and-now and deep into old Hawaii. The old times are relatively intact in the remote village of Hana, even though celebrities live there, too. The **Hotel Hana-Maui,** a comfortable veteran of many owners and facelifts, is again being brought back to glory as a luxurious tropical retreat. It has the only restaurant for dinner, although takeout food is available across the way at the **Hana Ranch** headquarters. A few condos and vacation rentals offer shelter, but most visitors return at night to the brighter lights on the other side of the mountain.

Count on two to three hours each way for the drive to Hana on Maui's most famous road, depending on how many times you stop to swim in waterfall pools or admire the view. The rich and famous fly to Hana in small planes, and you can, too. There is a small airport served by planes from Kahului.

HANA REDUX

We spent our first summer in Hana 30 years ago. We stayed in a big old beach house near the police station, where Keith Keau then served as one of Hana's two policemen. Their chief mission seemed to be rescuing tourists in rental cars who had missed a turn while admiring the scenery. That summer, we swam in five icy pools, with one eye on the sky in case of a cloudburst, shook breadfruit out of trees, ate poi pancakes with tree-ripe bananas from our yard, dug an *imu* (pit) for a *luau* (barbecue party) of kahlua pig, picked opihi on the reef, hiked to the white cross on the hill, visited Lindbergh's grave, learned half a dozen old Hawaiian songs, made lei of flowers so big they looked unreal, attended Sunday services sung in Hawaiian, hiked to Red Sand beach, body surfed at Hamoa Bay, set reef nets at sunset and plunged into the sea at sunrise to pick *pupu* (appetizers) of bright, tropical fish, and, of course, shopped Hasegawa's General Store.

It was the best of times in Hawaii, that summer in the 1970s in Hana. And, wonder of it all, three decades later this vestige of old Hawaii is as it was. Oh, there have been a few changes—Hasegawa's burned down and rose from the ashes at a new location. The Hana Hotel closed and reopened and closed and reopened. There's a paved parking lot at Kipahulu now, and by noon it resembles a rental-car lot. Wild pigs don't run across the road as often, but you can still buy those juicy mangoes for giveaway prices at roadside stands, and everyone smiles if you do. Life in Hana is still wonderful.

Molokai: Friendly Isle, Accidental Destination

People go to Molokai to wrap themselves in its abundant, unencumbered nature and Hawaiian ways, or possibly by mistake, since the history of Molokai tourism seems to involve unintended, serendipitous stops. Some of its first Western visitors were two daring airmen who flew from the mainland bound for Honolulu, 26 more miles across the sea, and almost made it. When they ran out of fuel and crashed on Molokai, they discovered a gentle island, now somewhat lost from view compared to its neighbors. Look for the historic plaque along Kamehameha V Highway on the island's East End, denoting the 1927 Smith-Bronte flight. Molokai, content with relative obscurity, suffered tourism rather than seeking it, and even in the face of spiraling welfare and agricultural setbacks an anti-tourism contingent continues to fight any proposal that opens the island more. Formed by two volcanoes, the long, narrow island is the result of a merger that didn't quite work out. One side is hot, dry, and flat; the other is lush green and steepled like Tahiti. It's a schizophrenic island that's always described in negatives: Molokai has no Disneyesque fantasy resorts, no fancy-pants restaurants, no stoplights, no malls nor Golden Arches, and no buildings taller than a coconut tree. And that's all to the good, for less is more on Molokai, Hawaii's last raw outpost (if you don't count Niihau or Kahoolawe—and we don't). The simple life and absence of contemporary American landmarks is what attracts those in search of the "real" Hawaii. The majority of the 7,000 residents display warm hospitality, willingness to share their culture, and friendly low-key attitudes. The few facilities devoted to visitors are interesting and different, such as the switchback mule ride down a steep seacliff to a historic former leper colony and the dude rodeo for visiting riders at Molokai Ranch.

MOLOKAI FACTS

Flower: White kukui blossom

Color: Green

Villages: Kaunakakai and Maunaloa

Area: 260 square miles

Length: 38 miles

Width: 10 miles

Population: 6,717

Highest Point: Kamakou Peak (4,961 feet)

Coastline: 88 miles

For better or worse, Molokai has avoided the usual definition of "progress." The island has sustained a number of economic hits over recent years—sugar and pineapple production ceased, residents opposed new hotels and tourism, and on an island where one ranch alone has more than 54,000 acres devoted to cattle ranching, federal officials in the mid-1980s ordered all the cows killed to stamp out an obscure ailment that had been around for decades.

Islanders grow prized produce, such as watermelons, sweet potatoes, boutique miniature veggies, honey, coffee, and macadamia nuts. Molokai folks are uncommonly friendly and down-home. And honest. Once we inadvertently left a usable airplane coupon ticket at the rental car counter in Molokai's tiny airport. Three days later, it was still there—not far from the sign reminding passengers not to carry watermelons in the overhead racks.

The island is not a destination for everyone, especially those who crave creature comforts, although there are some. The beaches are wild and empty, but not generally safe or desirable for swimming. The greatest natural features, the world's tallest sea cliffs and the jungle valleys of the North Shore, are virtually inaccessible wilderness. The most famous, and poignant, attraction is **Kalaupapa National Historic Park,** where leprosy victims were banished by royal edict in the 1860s.

Adventurers, families, and those who love the great outdoors: This island's for you. There's plenty to do: mountain biking, trail riding, snorkeling, diving, kayaking, fishing. The Nature Conservancy runs preserves and hike programs at **Moomomi Dunes** and at **Kamakou** in the high country, a cloud forest filled with rare native plants. Hikers have been known to trek through scenic **Halawa Valley** wilderness on the East End, although the ancient Hawaiian settlement was declared off-limits to visitors by the private owner. Ask locals about its status when you visit.

Sightseers find an odd assortment of natural and historic sites like ancient fishponds, **Mapalehu Mango Grove,** and **Iliiliopae Heiau,** temple ruins of an ancient school of sacrificial rites. The frontier-like town of **Kaunakakai** is a sleepy crossroad with a handful of stores and a bakery.

Lanai: The Plantation Island

Smallest among the main islands, Lanai is a world removed. Your arrival at Lanai Airport after a short hop by air from Honolulu or Maui will prove it. The plane touches down in **Palawai Basin** on an empty, bright landscape of rusty earth and green scrub that truly looks like the middle of nowhere, no trees or buildings in sight except for the cheery little terminal, the state's newest. Then you are met by the unlikely sight of uniformed hotel staff who guide you to a shuttle bus and whisk your bags aboard for the short ride through fallow fields to your lodging. You hear echoes in your mind, "Da Plane! Da Plane!" But this fantasy island is real.

At your hotel, you are wrapped up in a Hawaiian welcome and presented with a glass of pressed pineapple cider. Soon you are itching to shed travel clothes, jet lag, and your adult years and get out there to discover freedom in this compact near-wilderness playground—on foot, horseback, golf cart, off-road four-wheel drive, rental car, resort shuttle, or boat. Unlike most destinations, there are few places here you cannot go, whether or not you use one of the three paved roads, and it's all within the secure confines of a nearly private island.

Lanai is no tropical wonderland, however; its deep gorges and eroded plains speak of a hard agricultural life. But there's beauty to its hinterlands, headlands, and wide-open red valley touched only by blue sky and puffy white clouds. While prowling the 100 miles of four-wheel roads, explorers can find historic sites like a crumbled sugar town, an ancient king's summer fishing residence, strange rock formations, and petroglyphs etched into lava rocks by ancient artists. On a clear day, from **Lanaihale** summit, you can see most of the main Hawaiian islands. Hunters come to pursue wild (introduced) game: turkeys, pigs, Mouflon sheep, and small Axis deer, which outnumber people on this island.

LANAI FACTS

Flower: Kaunaoa
Color: Orange
Village: Lanai City
Area: 141 square miles
Length: 18 miles

Width: 13 miles
Population: 2,800
Highest Point: Lanaihale (3,366 feet)
Coastline: 47 miles

Lanai, in Maui's rain shadow, is dry and hot around the lower edges but cool and misty on the slopes of 3,366-foot Lanaihale, thanks to a unlikely crown of pines planted on the mountain ridge long ago to snag passing clouds. The genius responsible was an early manager, George Munro from New Zealand. The summit trail is named for him.

Lodging on the island is available from two fabulous luxury hotels, a charming old lodge, and a few rentals. If the sky's the limit, reserve a buttered suite. You'll find them at both the **Manele Bay Hotel** and the **Lodge at Koele.** As your personal concierges, butlers will ease your arrival and departure and greet you personally, make your reservations, bring you anything you like, take care of any wrinkles in your trip, and send you a good-bye note when you leave.

With access reined in by luxury rates and limited rooms, the island remains secluded. The people of Lanai still enjoy a quiet plantation lifestyle that is rapidly vanishing throughout Hawaii. It is an island of anomalies, isolated and yet worldly. Former immigrant fieldhands who retrained as hotel workers and old Hawaiian families are neighbors now with celebrity travelers and wealthy residents who wanted to stay longer under their own tin roofs. It's red-dirt rural with a good supply of fine champagne. In former times, the days started with a plantation whistle at 5 a.m. Now, days in the sun begin with more discreet wake-up calls.

Shopping's a bit limited, but you can catch the Expeditions ferry over to Lahaina to shop and play. Nightlife is nonexistent except for evening entertainment performed by island dancers and musicians at the hotel lobbies and a lecture series for visiting scholars and artists. A very few less pricy alternatives exist for visitors, including the Manele Bay Hotel and vacation rental prospects. Day-long snorkel-sail trips from Maui are a good way to see Lanai overland and underwater, without paying dinner prices for breakfast. Hats off to Lanai's new owners for figuring out how to turn its riffed, rutted, abandoned plantation roads into adventure trails for the gentry.

Hawaii's Privately Owned Islands

In Hawaii, where land is finite and costly, it may seem odd that any one person could own an island in the chain. Yet it is possible, because Hawaii once was a kingdom, and the king sold land (sometimes a whole island) when he needed cash. Both Lanai and Niihau are privately owned, one by heirs of a New Zealand family, the other by a self-made California tycoon. Dry, barren Niihau, once known as the "forbidden" island because travel there was once prohibited, is owned by the Robinson family, who raise sheep and cattle and otherwise keep the island (and its Hawaiian-speaking residents) unchanged. There are no telephones, no jail, no paved roads, and no tourists in Puuwai (population 226), the island's lone settlement. The Robinsons are descendants of Eliza Sinclair of New Zealand, who traded her piano and $10,000 in gold in 1864 to acquire the island from King Kalakaua. Her grandson, Charles Gay, paid $200,000 for Lanai in the late 1800s, but his farming enterprise failed.

Lanai was eventually sold to James Dole, who turned the island into the world's largest pineapple plantation. In the 1980s, entrepreneur David Murdock gained control of Dole Food Corporation in a merger acquisition, and he discovered that as majority stockholder he now owned Lanai. He closed the moribund pineapple plantation and opened two ritzy resorts.

So, How's the Weather?

Maui enjoys one of the world's most agreeable climates. The norm is blue skies, tradewinds, temperatures in the 70s and 80s, and almost 12 hours of daylight every day of the year. The reason is geographic. Maui sits in the middle of the Hawaiian chain, in the middle of the Pacific, 1,700 miles north of the Equator and just inside the Tropic of Cancer (between 154° 40' and 179° 25' west longitude and 18° 54' to 28° 15' north latitude, to be precise).

AN ILL-FATED ISLAND?

Lanai is perhaps most interesting because of its history of defeating nearly all who set foot on the island—early Polynesians, fierce Hawaiian kings, European explorers, even Mormons, among the most steadfast Pacific missionaries. Ancient Hawaiians believed Lanai was haunted by "spirits so wily and vicious that no human who went there could survive," according to Ruth Tabrah, author of the aptly titled history *Lanai*.

In 1778, Big Island King Kalaniopuu invaded Lanai in "the war of loose bowels." His men slaughtered every warrior, and set fire to everything except a bitter root that gave them dysentery. When, 14 years later, Captain George Vancouver sailed by what he wrongly termed "Ranai," he noted in his journal: "It seems thickly covered with shriveled grass in a scorched state." King Kamehameha the Great had a summer house on Lanai in the early 1800s; yet only stacked rocks remain. In 1802, Wu Tsin tried to harvest wild sugarcane on Lanai, but failed. New England missionaries arrived in 1820 and used Lanai as a prison for women convicted of adultery. Walter Murray Gibson looted the Mormon treasury, bought half the island, and founded a cult in 1866; it lasted three years. Charles Gay subsequently acquired 600 acres of Lanai at auction and planted pineapple; a three-year drought bankrupted him. Others tried cotton, sisal, sugar beets, a dairy, sheep, and pig farms. All failed.

Harry Baldwin, a missionary's grandson, may be the island's lone success story. He bought Lanai for $588,000 in 1917, developed a 20-mile water pipeline, and five years later sold the island to Jim Dole for $1.1 million. Dole planted 18,000 acres of pineapple and enjoyed great success for a half century. However, even Dole was eventually vanquished; cheaper pineapple production in Asia ended Lanai's heyday.

The island today seems to be slipping back in time, resembling old photographs of itself in the glory days of Dole, except, of course, for two notable exceptions: a pair of hotels built for $400 million. The engines of Lanai's new tourism industry are so deliberately nostalgic they appear to have been here all along. Any minute now, you half expect to look up and see old Jim Dole himself rattling up the road in a Model T truck with a load of freshly picked pineapples. Only now there is a new lord of the manor, and his name is David Murdock. He's gambling you will pay big bucks to visit his "private island." And, maybe, buy one of his $1 million vacation retreats, too.

Cold northeast winds, which propelled New England whalers and sailors to Lahaina from the West Coast and earned the name "tradewinds," still sweep down the North Pacific, softening as the water warms, so that the tamed breezes arrive as natural air-conditioning. All the islands have a cooler, wetter "windward" side, which receives the trades and their showers first, and a hotter, drier "leeward" side where the sun bakes the land. The line between is a northeast–southwest diagonal echoing the tradewind flow.

On Maui, the hottest spot is Lahaina, named for its oven-like heat. The coolest place on the resort coast is Kapalua, where the trades blow in directly. On Molokai, the East End gets the welcome showers to nourish its green landscape, while the West End is drier. Lanai, situated in the rain shadow of Haleakala, is lucky to get any rain. Long ago, an insightful plantation manager planted the signature pines of Lanai in the uplands to snag the passing clouds and hold them long enough to drop their mist on the little island.

Cooling tradewinds are always welcome. But on the Island of Maui, they are often blustery, especially in the isthmus valley in the afternoons and on the windward northwest coast. Now and then, the winds die off in what is called *kona* (leeward) weather, hot and still and fretful, and the smudgy haze off the volcano, called "vog," creeps northward, obscuring the normally clear views.

Reflections on Water

We once spent a summer away from Hawaii, traveling in Asia, and what we came to miss most was not the singular beauty of the place, or the soft tropical air, but the water. It wasn't only the cobalt-blue Pacific Ocean surrounding the islands that we missed, but rather the embracing wetness of the place. You might say we missed the climate, but our yearning went beyond that. We missed the waterfalls and the ceaseless waves, the light rain everyone calls a blessing, and the sudden summer squalls. We missed what Hawaiians call the *wai* and the *kai*. They call fresh water "wai" and salt water "kai." Sitting in Tokyo on a gray day that summer in Asia, we found ourselves dreaming of the soft, warm rain that drizzles down on Hana. We could close our eyes and see all the great bays (Kaneohe, Kailua, Mamala, Kealakekua, Hilo, and Hanalei) and the little pretty ones (Hanauma, Kahana, Hamoa, Wailea, and Kapalua). Our eyes ached to see again the amazing variations on the color blue, from turquoise to deep purple, with shades of sapphire, cobalt, mulberry, and indigo for effect. We could almost feel the foggy dew of Manoa and the fine mist raised by Akaka Falls. We could hear the roar of North Shore surf in winter. We yearned to snorkel the green tidepools on Maui's black lava coast. Out there in Asia, it all seemed like a dream, and we suppose in a way it is. The wonderful waters of Hawaii—the wai and kai—are so otherworldly that we suspect they must be two of the essential elements of paradise.

Maui's year-round average temperature of 77°F is one of the most agreeable anywhere. The difference between winter and summer, and between night and day, is about 5–10°F on the islands' shorelines, with normal daytime highs in the 80s, although they can be lower in winter, when storms hide the sun, or rise into the low 90s in steamy August and September. Nights are in the 70s in summer and 60s in winter, with rare dips into the 50s. The rest of the thermometer seems superfluous, until you travel up. Temperatures drop as the altitude rises—about 3.5°F for every 1,000 feet, meteorologists estimate. Each of these islands has at least one mountain in the middle, so if the heat gets you down, go up and cool off. You may need a jacket or sweater and a blanket at night at Kula, Maui, and Lanai City, Lanai, even in the warmer months. The weather atop Haleakala can be downright alpine; a winter dusting of snow is not unusual.

A word about showers: Don't worry too much about getting wet in the tradewind showers that often blow through. It's just more of the natural air-conditioning system. If it rains while you're on the beach, jump in the water or get under a beach mat or Hobie cat trampoline. The shower will probably be gone in a minute or two. With the ubiquitous Hawaiian "pineapple juice" showers that drift over while the sun shines brightly, everyone just gets wet one moment and dries off the next. Showers are considered blessings.

Colorful History

Once you touch the *aina* (land) of the Valley Isle, you will begin to see why more than two million people find their way here each year. It isn't only the sea breezes and golf greens that bring them back again. They come to roam the volcanic peaks, gaze at the spectacular scenery, and draft dream messages announcing they won't return as planned. A whole parade of adventurers, entrepreneurs, heroes, and scoundrels have done so throughout Island history. Since the Hawaiian Islands were settled in about A.D. 650 by Polynesian seafarers, all kinds of people have washed ashore.

Born of fire in the middle of the sea, the Island of Maui has a most interesting history, with tales of legendary gods, fierce kings, and fabled explorers, whalers, missionaries, sugar planters, immigrants, and travelers from around the world.

The island gets its name from the demigod Maui, a multitasking Polynesian superman.

THE FIVE GREAT FEATS OF MAUI

We once read in Katharine Luomala's *Voices on the Wind: Polynesian Myths and Chants* about the five great feats of the god Maui, who overwhelmed the gods of the air, sea, and underworld to make the world a better place. Maui, according to legend, lassoed the sun with a rope of his sister's pubic hair, used a fishhook carved from his grandmother's bones to catch the fish that he transformed into islands, and stole the secret of fire from the fire god so people could cook their own fish. But his singular achievement, we think, is this: He lifted the sky so people could stand and walk upright.

The first Hawaiians most likely sailed to the Big Island from the Marquesas. Some later crossed the Alenuihaha Channel to Maui, where they settled coastal villages and farmed taro in narrow stream valleys like those at Iao and Kahakuloa. They built *heiau,* or temples to worship their gods, including massive Piilani Hale, now the site of an archeological dig on the Hana coast. They buried their dead in sand dunes in places like the Kapalua and Wailuku shores and held sacred the jumping-off places for the spirits of the deceased, like Black Rock on Kaanapali Beach. These adventurers from the South Pacific, seeing the Island of Molokai a short distance across the Pailolo Channel from northwest Maui, probably set sail for the island's calm south shore, where they built a complex of fishponds that still line the coast and constructed Iliiliopae Heiau, a kind of early university for sorcerers. Molokai gained a reputation for sorcery. According to some historians, Molokai was also the island where the Hawaiian dance was first performed on the summit of Mount Kaana, known today as "the birthplace of the hula."

Adventurers also wandered to neighboring Kahoolawe, which served as a prison for a time, and to Lanai, which gained a reputation of being haunted by cannibal spirits so fearsome no mortal man could survive a night there—until a brave prince proved them wrong. Bad spirits continued to plague the island. Lanai was the scene of one of the first and bloodiest battles in the royal effort to unify the islands into one kingdom in the late 1700s. Most of the residents were killed, and the island was burned by a raiding party from the Big Island that included the future king Kamehameha. The battle was decisive, but Lanai never quite recovered its Hawaiian populace or its original landscape.

Captain Cook and La Perouse

In 1778, British explorer James Cook reported sighting Maui and Molokai but sailed on by, bound for the Big Island, where he was later killed. Cook's explorations inspired many others, including Jean Louis de Galaup, known as Admiral La Perouse, the first recorded European to land on Maui. In 1785, the king of France commissioned La Perouse to head an expedition to explore Pacific whaling and fur prospects, map the islands more precisely, and establish French claims. With two ships, the *Astrolabe* and the *Boussole,* and a crew of 114, including scientists, draftsmen, naturalists, and a mathematician, La Perouse sighted the peak of Haleakala on the morning of May 28, 1786. As the French ships sailed past Maui, La Perouse was "enchanted by its beauty" and fascinated to find waterfalls and coastal villages of grass houses built in "the same shape as the thatched cottages found in certain parts of France."

"Imagine the feelings of the poor sailors, who, in this hot climate, had been reduced to a water ration of one bottle a day, when they saw the mountains clothed in vegetation, the homes surrounded by green banana trees," he added in his journal. But the surf was too strong to land, and they sailed on to a safe anchorage on "a shore made hideous by an ancient lava flow." That was the tip of South Maui, a place now known as La Perouse Bay.

... when we were in sight of Maui about two hundred canoes came out from the shore to meet the frigates. All the canoes were loaded with pigs, fruits, and fresh vegetables which the natives conveyed to us on board and forced us to accept as gifts. The wind then became stronger and speeded us on our way, preventing us from further enjoying the picturesque view of the island and the great gathering of canoes, which as they moved about, provided us with the most exhilarating and exciting scenic spectacle imaginable.

—The Journal of Dr. Rollin, ship's surgeon aboard
Boussole, Voyages & Adventures of La Perouse, 1786.

Now that Maui was on the map, the inevitable began to occur: Others found the island, including lusty New England whalers spoiling for shore liberty and soon after, prim Boston missionaries. They found themselves at odds in, of all places, Lahaina.

In 1812, the first whalers sailed into Lahaina. They found eager women and ready grog, and their behavior gave Lahaina a wild reputation as word spread that there was "no God West of the Horn." Presumably, Pacific humpbacks they hunted elsewhere were right offshore breeding and raising their young and cruising as they do today, but it seems the whalers went to the strategic mid-Pacific stop for other reasons—to restock their ships and go ashore in search of rowdy times. They did, however, begin to kill whales in Maui waters, a practice that died off when the whales stopped coming around.

In the whalers' heyday, 1840 to 1860, several hundred whaling ships anchored in Lahaina Roads. The sailors preferred Lahaina to Honolulu because of its easy-access harbor, low fees, and, most of all, the warm embrace of the local folks. When 20 or more whaling ships dropped anchor at once and the whalers went ashore, the people of Lahaina prospered. The whaling era gave rise to tourism with all the usual good and bad results. Missionaries took a dim view of the whalers' onshore diversions, which involved alcohol, gambling, and sexual excess.

Thriving Lahaina became the royal capital of the Hawaiian kingdom in 1840, only to surrender political clout to Honolulu four years later. In 1871, whaling was halted by the discovery of petroleum oil in Pennsylvania. Whale oil for lamps became obsolete. Lahaina, once the wealthy port of call, dozed in the hot sun, safe in the hands of Bible-toting missionaries. The now-civilized seaport began to trade with merchant ships. The missionaries stayed on and acquired land and power.

Maui is very foreign and civilized, and although it has a native population of over 12,000, the natives are much crowded on plantations, and one encounters little of native life.

—Isabella L. Bird, Six Weeks in the Sandwich Islands

Kalaupapa's Sad Legacy

Over on Molokai, authorities conducted a forced immigration to remote Kalaupapa Peninsula, 5,000 acres at the foot of imposing seacliffs that served as a natural prison for victims of leprosy. The only ways in or out of Kalaupapa were by sea or on foot, via the three-mile trail down a 1,664-foot cliff with 26 switchbacks—still one of the most spectacular, if daunting, hikes in the Pacific. Leprosy victims were hunted throughout the Islands, rounded up, and exiled to live and die on Kalaupapa. Some 800 sufferers were there in 1873 when a Belgian priest, Father Damien de Veuster, was dispatched to tend to the ailing souls. He stayed until his own death on April 15, 1889, after he contracted the disease. Leprosy, or Hansen's disease, was eradicated decades ago with sulfa drugs, and Kalaupapa is now a lonely National Historical Park. Father Damien is a candidate for sainthood.

Sweet Success

In 1876, a German immigrant named Claus Spreckels arrived on Maui from San Francisco and changed life on the island. He became pals with King Kalakaua, bribed him with $10,000 cash, loaned him $40,000, plied him with champagne, and acquired vast tracts of Maui. He irrigated the land, planted it with sugarcane, and made a fortune refining the sugar in California.

"Never in the history of the Hawaiian kingdom had money been used to procure official favors from the king," according to Ralph Kuykendall, author of *The Hawaiian Kingdom*. The idea of "owning" land was a Western concept, not understood by Hawaiians until foreigners introduced it to the royalty earlier in the 1800s. Hawaiians' family-held lands, uncertain in title and boundaries, were often simply taken by the enterprising foreigners to amass the acres needed for sugar plantations.

Not enough Hawaiians could be found to tend the sugar, so owners like Spreckels imported immigrants from Japan and China, and later Korea, the Philippines, Portugal, Puerto Rico, and other areas of Europe and Asia, who worked cutting and hauling cane for a pittance and a home. They lived on plantations, tied to the company house and the company store in a kind of contracted servitude. Samuel Alexander and Harry Baldwin, descendants of New England missionaries, later acquired the Spreckels plantations and pioneered an island company that continues today.

Sugar governed the Hawaiian economy from the 1860s to the 1980s, with Wailuku and Paia/Makawao among the major centers. Life was sweet, and sugar was king of the Hawaiian economy, drawing thousands of immigrants who saw it as a way to escape harsh conditions in their homeland and seek a new life. As soon as many of them could work off their debt, they started to leave the plantations and pursue their fortunes in other endeavors. Other nationalities were recruited to take their place.

In another, perhaps more surprising saga of royal patronage with a sugary episode, the arid Island of Lanai passed from the pocket of one foreign lord after another through history and is still largely owned by one man's company. It may seem odd that a private owner could control a whole island in the chain. But when the Islands were a kingdom, the king sold land when he needed cash. In 1864, New Zealander Eliza Sinclair traded her piano and $10,000 in gold to acquire the Island of Niihau from King Kalakaua. (She decided not to purchase Waikiki, then a mosquito-choked swamp.) Then in the late 1800s, her grandson, Charles Gay, paid $200,000 for Lanai. But his farming enterprise there failed, as had cultivation attempts 30 years prior by Mormons, who came to the island in the 1850s but were thwarted by insects and droughts. Lanai eventually was sold to a young American named James Dole, who dug into the rich red dirt and, in a sense, struck gold.

Dole turned the island into the world's largest pineapple plantation, some 20,000 acres fenced by an ocean, featuring the golden fruit that became Hawaii's icon. But competition from other nations' pineapples eroded the market and Lanai's influence dwindled. In the 1980s, southern California entrepreneur David Murdock gained control of Dole Food Corporation—and discovered that as majority stockholder, he owned the Island of Lanai. He closed the pineapple operations, an institution for 65 years, recycled Filipino fieldhands into chambermaids and waiters, and opened two ritzy resorts, The Lodge at Koele and Manele Bay Hotel, with two remarkable golf courses. He built new tracts of million-dollar estates and began cultivating well-heeled tourists. The world's richest man, Microsoft billionaire Bill Gates, got married here; Oprah Winfrey stayed a week with her personal fitness trainer and hairdresser in adjoining private suites.

I have visited Haleakala, Kilauea, Wailuku Valley—in a word, I have visited all the principal wonders of the Island, and now I come to speak of one which, in its importance to America, surpasses them all. A land which produces six, eight, ten, twelve, yea, even thirteen thousand pounds of sugar to the acre on unmanured soil! There are precious few acres of unmanured ground in Louisiana—none at all, perhaps—which yield 2,500 pounds of sugar; there is not an unmanured acre under cultivation in the Sandwich Islands which yields less. This country is the king of the sugar world as far as astonishing productiveness is concerned.

—Mark Twain, September 10, 1866

Wartimes

The American Civil War officially ended in 1866. Meanwhile in Hawaii, sugar mills began to falter, but the industry stumbled on, through crippling strikes and the rise of competing imported sugar at cheaper prices. Eventually, the plantations closed on several islands, ending a way of life that created the Hawaii of today in several ways. However, Maui's cane fields are still producing and being harvested, even after those of other islands long since went fallow or became housing tracts. Above Kapalua Resort, Maui pineapples are still harvested as well.

When the Japanese attacked Pearl Harbor on Oahu in 1941, Maui County turned out the lights and pulled down the blinds. All islands were placed under martial law, and blackouts were mandatory so the enemy could find no easy targets. Many Japanese Americans on Maui volunteered for army duty and served heroically in Europe and the Pacific. On the day after the Pearl Harbor attack, the U.S. Navy began dropping bombs on Kahoolawe, across the Alalakeiki Channel from South Maui. (Target practice continued into the mid-1990s, when President George H. W. Bush finally stopped it.)

Maui became a major training ground for jungle fighters during the war. Thousands of American troops came to Maui, marching off navy ships to prepare to fight the bloody battle of Okinawa in April 1945. Maui boomed while the troops bivouacked, but when World War II ended and the military camps closed, the island economy sank. Many postwar Mauians left the island to seek jobs on the West Coast.

But in 1946, a new wave of people flooded the Islands: The last major immigration of 6,000 new plantation workers came from the Philippines aboard the *SS Maunawili,* a converted U.S. troopship. They were brought in from Ilocos Sur by the Hawaii Planters Society to work the cane fields of Maui and other islands. It was an effort to bring the fields back to life. Immigrants from Japan and China had been outlawed, and would-be recruits from Korea, Puerto Rico, Spain, Portugal, and other European countries were too scarce. Filipino plantation workers went to all the islands, including Lanai in more recent times.

The Hawaiian Islands boomed again as an R&R destination for Vietnam warriors and their wives and sweethearts. Tour buses began to rumble on island roads, and jets brought in a new age of tourism. While condos began to sprout all along Kihei's scalloped beaches, a group of West Maui sugar planters decided to devote a chunk of unprofitable coastal scrub land to create Hawaii's first master-planned resort, Kaanapali Beach Resort. They drew up plans for golf courses, shops, lodging, and restaurants, all along a picturesque beach. First came the Royal Lahaina in 1962. In 1963, the Sheraton Maui opened as the first luxury hotel on Maui, on the very site where Maui's King Kahekili took daredevil leaps off *kapu* (forbidden) Puu Kekaa (Black Rock) almost two centuries prior. As more and bigger chain resort hotels, like Marriott, Hyatt, and Westin, opened on Kaanapali Beach, Maui began to entertain a new breed of visitor who spent small fortunes in upscale fantasy resorts full of exotic macaws, parrots, and swans.

Golden People

One outstanding feature of Hawaii is the diversity of its people. Throughout the 50th state, no ethnic group comprises a majority of the population. People who declare themselves of mixed race are the largest group, followed by Caucasians, Japanese, and Filipinos. Pure Hawaiians are in short supply, but part-Hawaiian heritage is shared by many.

Each ethnic group has made its mark on Island culture, contributing foods, arts, music, and customs to Hawaii's melting-pot community.

The Chinese were the first immigrants. More than 200 workers from southeastern China came to the Islands in the mid-nineteenth century after signing five-year contracts to work the sugar plantations. These laborers were provided food, clothing, shelter, and a salary of $3 a month. Most of the Maui Chinese lived in Lahaina.

The first Japanese immigrants arrived in 1868. By the beginning of the 20th century, more than 60,000 Japanese laborers and their families lived in Hawaii. Like all immigrants, Japanese faced racial prejudices, but far more so after Japan's attack on Pearl Harbor. Many Japanese Americans were taken away to internment camps on the mainland, and many more lost their family businesses, even though not a single case of Japanese American treason or sabotage was ever documented. But they rebounded strongly in Hawaii after the war, gained prominence in politics and education, and integrated Japanese customs and design into everyday life. Today, Japanese Americans are a major presence in Hawaii, and most residents embrace at least a degree of Japanese custom, including removing shoes before entering a home. Rice, sushi, sashimi, mochi, and miso soup are staples at the Hawaii local table.

In 1903 the first Koreans arrived to work on the plantations. Ambitious and hardworking, Koreans have the highest education and income level per capita of any ethnic group in the Islands.

A group of 15 Filipino laborers began working on Island plantations in 1906; by mid-century, that number had swelled to 125,000. Every summer, the Filipina Fiesta festivals held throughout the state celebrate the colorful traditions and customs of the Filipino culture. Dishes such as chicken adobo, pancit, and lumpia are favorites on any local menu.

Later immigrants included Southeast Asians, some of them refugees of the Vietnam War, and Pacific Islanders from throughout Polynesia, mostly Tonga and Samoa.

Endangered Species

Hawaiians are a vanishing minority in their own land. When Cook "discovered" Hawaii in 1778, the native population was estimated at 20,000 to 30,000, although some historians believe the population may have reached 800,000. Today, there are fewer than 8,000 pure Hawaiians left. Diseases brought by foreigners, destruction of habitat, broken spirit, and changing times contributed to the decline. Reflecting the plantation immigrations of the past, the resident population of Hawaii today is a cosmopolitan cultural mix of Pacific Islander, Portuguese and other Caucasian, Japanese, Filipino, Chinese, Korean, and Southeast Asian. No one race achieves a majority rank. Most modern Hawaii natives are *hapa*—half Hawaiian and half Caucasian or something else—or, more often, a sum of many racial ingredients. It's a heritage often referred to locally as "chop suey." Many Hawaii residents believe the most important contribution the Islands make to humankind is not the promise of unparalleled vacation beaches but the reality of a multiracial culture where, by and large, people get along.

Things the Locals Already Know

The Lei Tradition

A Hawaiian flower lei is one of the most extravagant presents in the world. Some lei take more than a thousand flowers and quite a bit of time and artistry to make. They fade and perish within hours or days of their creation. Often they are worn only once.

Lei giving is one of the most colorful traditions in Hawaii. You'll see it first at the airport. But it isn't an embarrassing designation of a newly arrived tourist. Lei are a sign of honor, for a family member, friend, or special guest, of either gender.

Having a garland placed around your neck is a special welcome, farewell, or congratulations, usually followed by a hug or kiss on the cheek, especially if you know the donor. A lei greeting remains Hawaii's most tangible expression of aloha. Local tradition is to drape loved ones up to their noses with lei at graduations; they are also given for anniversaries, birthdays, and other special celebrations. They're great ice breakers with local strangers who want to admire the lei and congratulate you on your special occasion. It's also customary to share the lei around after you wear it for a while (take it off and give it to someone else to wear).

Hawaiian language advisory: The word, *lei,* is singular and plural; there is no "s" in the Hawaiian language.

The tradition of lei giving may have originated with Hawaii's earliest settlers, who brought flowering plants to use for adornment. Early Hawaiians offered lei to their gods during religious ceremonies.

Today, long lei are also draped over the statues or images of important people in Hawaiian history, or over the bows of victorious racing canoes, or on anything worthy of commemoration. Each June, the King Kamehameha Day celebration kicks off with a colorful lei-draping ceremony at the King Kamehameha statue in downtown Honolulu.

Writer-poet Don Blanding initiated Lei Day, an annual May 1 celebration held since 1928. The biggest event is held at Kapiolani Park in Waikiki, where floral creations by the state's top lei makers are displayed.

Before World War II, I never saw lei presented to all and sundry accompanied by a kiss. True, our greeting was the honi, kiss, almost like the hongi of the Maoris of New Zealand, but we did not greet everybody that way with a lei—and so I wondered how a kiss with lei giving began. One day, I wondered out loud at the Waikiki Camouflage Unit where I worked shortly after the beginning of World War II. A worker who was a cutter in the Camouflage Unit by day and a USO entertainer at night, heard me and laughed. She then told me that while entertaining one evening, her fellow musicians dared her to kiss a homely officer sitting nearby. She could not just barge up to kiss him, so she sat thinking a while until an idea came. When there was a little recess, she walked up to him, removed her lei, placed it on his shoulder, and said loud enough for those about to hear, "This is a Hawaiian custom," and implanted a kiss upon the man's cheek. Thus a neo-Hawaiian custom was born.

—Mary Kawena Pukui, *Aspects of the Word Lei, Directions in Pacific Traditional Literature* (Bishop Museum Press)

Fresh flower lei can be purchased throughout Hawaii, at every major airport and many supermarkets as well as florists. Home style is to make your own, and many families still do. You'll find lei made of all kinds of flowers, including plumeria, gardenias, ginger, orchids, pakalana, roses, ilima, and carnations, as well as fragrant maile leaves, braids of ti leaves, kukui nuts, seashells, flowers made of dollar bills, and, for the kids back home, even candy and gum.

Lei costs range from a few dollars for a simple crown flower or sweet-smelling tuberose lei to $40 for an intricately crafted rope lei. One of the most popular new lei is the cristina, an expertly sewn garland made of purple dendrobium orchids ($25–$30).

Often people try to keep a lei alive by refrigerating it. Here's another suggestion: Drape it over a doorknob or lampshade in your hotel room or some other place where it cheers you to see the flowers and smell the fragrance.

A Tip about Tipping

Many service workers in Hawaii depend on tips for their living. At the airport, tip a porter a dollar or two per bag. Taxi drivers receive a 15 percent tip of the total fare plus 25¢ per bag or parcel. At the hotel, tip the bellhop $5 for transporting your luggage to and from your room, and give the parking valet a couple of dollars. Tip your room housekeeper $1 for each day of your stay. For dining, tip 15 to 20 percent of the bill.

Local Customs and Protocol

- When going to the *lua* (restroom) make sure you know the difference between *kane* (man) and *wahine* (woman), since many restrooms are only identified in Hawaiian.

- Here's a sign of friendship: Close your middle three fingers of either hand while keeping your thumb and pinky finger fully extended. Shake your hand a few times in the air. That's the *shaka*, a gesture expressing acknowledgment, goodwill, or appreciation, suitably made to children and adults. That, and maybe the universal thumbs-up, are the only finger signals we suggest you make.

- Technically speaking, Fridays are Aloha Friday throughout Hawaii and in the Maui Islands, a tradition like casual Fridays on the mainland except it calls for wearing aloha shirts and muumuu or other colorful island wear. But actually, on rural islands where shorts and sandals are de rigeur, aloha wear is dressing up. Many invitations to weddings and other events call for "aloha attire" or even sometimes "evening aloha attire." It's what to wear to the luau, along with flowers in your hair. Women, if you don't have a muumuu or plan to buy one, that colorful *pareo* (sarong-like wrap) makes a great aloha skirt. If you can't get a plumeria or other small flower to stay in your hair, try sticking a toothpick down the throat of it and pinning or placing the toothpick base. The first aloha shirt was sold in the mid-1930s in Honolulu, where boys wore shirts made from Japanese prints, and the idea caught on. The origin of the muumuu traces to missionary days when the missionary wives sewed "Mother Hubbard" nightgowns to hide the bodies of half-dressed Hawaiian women.

- If you are invited to a kamaaina home, remember to bring a small gift and, in most cases, remove your shoes before entering the house. The tangle of loose shoes in front of the door is your first clue.

- Local people of all kinds share a deep reverence for the *aina* (land), although all that litter along Hawaii's roads can't be from visitors alone. This is a beautiful place that deserves respect. Please don't trash it.

State Holidays

In addition to all major U.S. holidays, Hawaii celebrates three state holidays.

- Kuhio Day (March 26). This holiday honors Prince Jonah Kuhio Kalanianaole (1871–1922), a statesman and member of the royal family who served in the U.S. Congress in the early 1900s.

- King Kamehameha Day (June 11). Hawaii's great king, Kamehameha I, united the islands into a kingdom under one rule. An imposing figure—some reported him as tall as eight feet—the Big Island–born monarch died in May 1819, when he was believed to be in his early 1960s, and his bones were hidden at a secret location, perhaps on the Kona Coast. Modern islanders celebrate the life of Kamehameha with colorful festivities, including lei-draping ceremonies, parades, and *ho'olaule'a* (public parties).

- Admission Day (third Friday in August). On August 21, 1959, U.S. President Dwight D. Eisenhower signed the proclamation welcoming Hawaii as the 50th state, following a long, often emotional campaign for statehood that originated more than a century earlier. Many expected Hawaii to be named the 49th state, but that distinction went to Alaska in 1958. Today, "Hawaii—49th State" memorabilia, ranging from record labels to buttons, is highly prized by collectors.

A Word about Directions

We try to orient you somewhat with the familiar directions of north, east, south, and west. But these words won't be terribly helpful in Hawaii. Local usage has little to do with the compass. The words you want to know are *mauka* (uphill, inland, toward the mountains) and *makai* (toward the sea). The other directions are known by a bewildering variety of local landmarks.

Saying It in Hawaiian

In Hawaii, English and Hawaiian are both official languages.

The Hawaiian alphabet has only 12 letters—the vowels a, e, i, o, and u and the consonants h, k, l, m, n, p, and w. A diacritical mark called the okina, pronounced as a glottal stop, is almost as vital as a letter, so that those vowels can do extra duty. The language takes practice and patience. The most authoritative Hawaiian language book is the *Hawaiian Dictionary*, by Mary Kawena Pukui and Samuel H. Elbert.

Here are some general rules of thumb for you to remember:

- Vowels are pronounced this way: a as "uh," as in "lava"; e as "ay," as in "hay"; i as "ee," as in "fee"; o as "oh," as in "low"; and u as "oo," as in "moon."

- All consonants are pronounced as in English except for w, which is usually pronounced as "v" when it follows an i or e. Example: Ewa Beach is pronounced as "Eva" Beach. When following an u or o, w is pronounced as "w." When it is the first letter in the word or follows an a, there is no designated rule, so the pronunciation follows custom. Which means Hawaii and Havaii are both acceptable.

- Some vowels are slurred together in a diphthong, forming single sounds. Examples: ai as in "Waikiki," au as in "mauka," ei as in "lei," oi as in "poi," ou as an "kou," and ao as in "haole."

TEN WORDS EVERYBODY ALREADY KNOWS (DON'T YOU?)
You may not know a papaya from a puakenikeni (one's a juicy fruit, the other's a sweet-smelling South Pacific flower), but everybody knows these Hawaiian words and expressions. Test your vocabulary here:

aloha (ah low hah) noun, verb: All-purpose Hawaiian word, hello, good-bye, I love you. Not to be shouted like a tour bus driver, but said softly with feeling.

mahalo (mah haw low) noun, verb: Appreciative Hawaiian remark, thanks, thank you. *Mahalo nui loa* means "thank you very much."

ohana (oh hahna) noun: Old Hawaiian for family or kin group, da gang.

keiki (kay kee) noun: Old Hawaiian word meaning child, offshoot, youngster, tot, little one. *Keiki o ka aina,* literally means "a child of the island."

mele (mehl lay) noun: Old Hawaiian for song, anthem, or chant. Also merry, as in Mele Kalikimaka, "Merry Christmas."

talk story (tawk sto ree) noun, verb: Pidgin expression for story telling, the oral tradition of Polynesia. "Let's talk story."

kaukau (cow cow) noun: Food, though often referred to more specifically using *ono, grinds,* or *pupu.* **ono** (oh-no) is a Hawaiian/pidgin hybrid, adjective or noun meaning good or good food. Ono appears on local menus as onolicious (oh no lish uss), Hawaiian/haole for "real good." **grinds** (grines) means meal, entree, breakfast, plate lunch, or a dinner less than a luau. Derived from the act of mastication, chewing, or grinding food. "Dis mahi ono grinds, brah." **pupu** (poo poo) means finger food, snacks, small bites of kaukau, Hawaiian for hors d'oeuvres. Plenny pupu may amount to grinds, but grinds typically moah kaukau than pupu.

alii (ah lee ee) noun: Old Hawaiian king, monarch, chief, or commander. Also meaning haimaukamauka kine folks, or uncommon people.

kupuna (coo poo nah) noun: Old Hawaiian for grandparent, ancestor, elder. Similar to **tutu** (too too), someone who's supposed to know all the answers.

kane/wahine (kah nay/vah hee nay) nouns: Old Hawaiian terms for male and female, respectively, often seen on public bathroom signs. If you don't know the difference by now, plenny pilikia, but that's one 'nother story, brah.

All pau, now. Live aloha. For more information and definitions, see *The Hawaiian Dictionary* by Mary Kawena Pukui and Samuel H. Elbert.

- Some are separated by a glottal stop, or okina, an upside-down and backward apostrophe that emphasizes a separate vowel sound, acting like another consonant, and keeps identically spelled words from being confused. For instance, *pau* means "finished," but *pa'u* is a skirt worn by women horseback riders. *Pau* is pronounced as "pow," and *pa'u* is pronounced as "pah-oo."

- A macron, or kahako, designates a long vowel. A macron is marked as a line directly over the vowel. Logically enough, long vowels last longer than regular vowels. The macron however, is used less frequently than the okina, in part because it isn't as often needed to distinguish between words. This book, like most English publications from Hawaii, excludes macrons. However, don't be surprised if you see them over the "i"s in Waikiki. They indicate that the word is correctly sounded "why-kiki" rather than "why-kee-kee."

- Every Hawaiian syllable ends with a vowel. Thus, every Hawaiian word ends with a vowel. Which means the word "Hawaiian" isn't a Hawaiian word.

- If a word contains no macrons, the accent usually falls on the next-to-last syllable. Examples: a-LO-ha, ma-HA-lo, ma-li-HI-ni, and 'o-HA-na.

Pidgin

You may hear people talking in what sounds like abbreviated English, except that it's more colorful. Hawaii-style pidgin, the local patois, is the third language of the islands. It combines words and syntax of several languages and was developed so that multicultural plantation people could communicate. Although it is a true creole language and not simply slang, it's definitely not an official tongue.

The term aloha used either in music, poetry, or social behavior, is regarded as, perhaps, the singularly most important word in Hawaii today. The idea of love, affection, openness, generosity—all connoted by the term—is most readily associated with Hawaiians; that is, ethnic Hawaiians and their culture, of which the songs of aloha are a part.

—George Kanahele, *Hawaiian Music and Musicians; An Illustrated History*

The pros and cons of pidgin have long been debated by local educators and cultural experts. Some say that the practice should not be encouraged because it is not an acceptable manner of speech, whereas others insist that pidgin is a treasured cultural asset that should not be looked down on. In Hawaii, it's not uncommon for a kamaaina to speak perfect English in an office setting, then pick up the phone and speak pidgin to a friend. Following are some commonly used pidgin words and phrases you might hear during your stay.

Twenty Words Every Hawaii Visitor Should Know

If you can pronounce Aiea, Keeaumoku, and Anaehoomalu correctly, know hapa from hapai, then you are akamai, brah. No need to read da kine. If you no can understand a word up there, mo bettah you read da kine.

Da kine is one of 20 words or phrases every Hawaii visitor should know. So are *akamai* and *pau*. When you go pau reading da kine, you will be akamai, li'dat.

Welcome to Hawaii, the linguistically rich and confusing Islands with not one but two official languages—Hawaiian and English—where the 12-letter alphabet has 7 consonants and 5 vowels, and everybody speaks a little pidgin. No other archipelago has such an eclectic array of words that look and sound so foreign. You probably can get by with a now-and-then aloha and a mumbled mahalo, but to understand what's really going on in Hawaii, you need to know a few basic words like: huhu, da kine, humbug, owzit, and mo' bettah.

Everyone knows wahine from kane and mauka from makai, but what about akamai, kokua, and holoholo? Most haoles (that's you seestah and blahlah) have trouble saying Hawaiian words because they are repetitive, have too many vowels, and look like the bottom line of an eye chart, e.g.: Kaaawa, Kuliouou, and Napoopoo. A good example of all the above is humhumunukunukapuaa, the state fish. To haole eyes, honed on brittle consonants, Hawaiian looks impossible. Once spoken, the way Hawaiian was intended, the soft, round, soothing vowels are music to your ears.

Banned by New England missionaries, who crudely translated into English what they thought they heard, the native tongue survived underground to carry a nation's culture down through generations in warrior chants, hula lyrics, and talk story. And then there is pidgin, the local patois originated by Chinese immigrants to do business with an easy-to-understand lingo. The root word of pidgin is, in fact, business. A caveat: Before you go to Hawaii and put your foot in your mouth, it's probably a good idea to clip and save this lexicon for future review. Or, as any local might put it: Good t'ing, brush up on da kine, brah, so no make A.

Here are 20 words, common in everyday Hawaiian usage, that you should know. Fo' real. They will also help you make sense of the passage above.

    I. kokua (ko-coo-ah) *verb:* Help, as in help, assist, (please kokua), or contribute (kokua luau), a gentle reminder. "Your kokua is appreciated."

COMMONLY USED HAWAIIAN WORDS AND PHRASES

aina	Land, earth
aloha	Love, kindness, or goodwill; can be used as a greeting or farewell
e komo mai	Welcome!
hale	House
hana hou	Do again, repeat, or encore
haole	Formerly any foreigner, now primarily anyone of Caucasian ancestry
holoholo	To go out for a walk, ride, or other activity
hoolaulea	A big party or celebration
hooponopono	To correct or rectify a situation
ikaika	Strong, powerful
ilima	A native shrub bearing bright yellow or orange flowers; used for lei
kahuna	Priest, minister, expert
kala	Money
kamaaina	Native-born or longtime island resident
kanaka	Person, individual
kane	Male, husband, man
kapu	Taboo
keiki	Child
kohola	Humpback whale
kokua	Help, assistance, cooperation
kolohe	Mischievous, naughty; a rascal
kupuna	Grandparent

2. **pau** (pow) *noun:* All gone, no more, time's up. Used every Friday (when you go pau hana), finish work, when you finish kaukau ("All pau"), when your car or other mechanical object breaks down ("Eh, dis buggah pau"). Not to be confused with **make** (mah kay), which means dead, a permanent form of pau.

3. **malihini** (mah ly hee nee) *noun:* Nonderisive old Hawaiian word, meaning the opposite of kamaaina, or local. If first time come Hawaii, that's you, brah: a stranger, tourist, someone who wears socks and shoes instead of rubbah slippahs and eats rice with fork not chopsticks. You remain a malihini until you use "used to be" landmarks as directional aids.

kuuipo	My sweetheart
lanai	Porch, verandah
lua	Toilet, bathroom
luau	A Hawaiian feast
luna	Foreman, boss, leader
mahalo	Thank you
makahiki	Ancient Hawaiian harvest festival with sports and religious activities
makai	Toward the ocean; used in directions
malihini	Newcomer
mana	Spiritual power
mauka	Inland direction, toward the mountain
me ke aloha pumehana	With warm regards
mele	Song
Menehune	Legendary small people who worked at night, building fishponds, roads, and temples; according to legend, if the work was not completed in one night, it was left unfinished
muumuu	Loose-fitting Hawaiian gown
ohana	Family
ono	Delicious
pau	Finished, done
pupu	Hors d'oeuvre, appetizer
tutu	Grandmother
wahine	Female, wife, woman

4. **mo' bettah** (mow bedder) *adjective:* A contemporary pidgin self-descriptive term meaning excellent, outstanding, the best. Often used for comparison of ideas, objects, or places, as in "Dis beach mo bettah." Sometimes spelled "moah bettah."

5. **no ka oi** (nok caw oy) Hawaiian phrase, a sequence of words that serves as an *appositive,* can only follow nouns as in "Maui no ka oi" (Maui is the best), a superlative expression, bragging rights, the best, similar to mo' bettah.

6. **hana hou** (hah nah ho) *interjection:* Hawaiian expression of joy, a cry for more, the local equivalent of encore. Most often heard at music concerts after Auntie Genoa Keawe sings.

COMMONLY USED PIDGIN WORDS AND PHRASES

an den?	So? And then?
braddah	Brother or friend
brah	Short for "braddah"
bumbye	Do it later
bummahs!	That's unfortunate!
da kine	The kind of, that thing
fo real?	Really?
garans	Guaranteed
geev um!	Go for it!
go fo broke	Give it your all (famous motto of the 442nd Battalion in WW II)
how you figgah?	How do you think that happened?
howzit!	How are you?
laytahs	See you later

7. **to da max** (to dah macks) *interjection:* Pidgin expression of boundless enthusiasm, meaning no limits, to the moon, give it your all, knock yourself out. Also, the partial title of a popular book, *Pidgin To Da Max* by Douglas Simonson, Ken Sakata, and Pat Sasaki.

8. **akamai** (ah kah my) *noun:* Smart, clever, locally correct in thought, common sense as opposed to intelligence, or school smarts. "Many are smart but few are akamai." Also the name of a high-tech mainland computer outfit.

9. **chance 'em** (chants em) *verb:* Take a chance, go for it, try. Also a rally cry. Often heard in Las Vegas at blackjack tables and in Aloha Stadium late in fourth quarter when the Warriors are behind. "Fourth and inches on the five. Coach June Jones says, 'chance 'em.'"

10. **chicken skin** (chee kin skeen) *noun:* Descriptive pidgin term, the local version of goosebumps, for a frisson or shiver of excitement. Also the title of best-selling local spooky book by favorite author. "Oh, dat spooky kine stuff gives me chicken skin."

11. **laters** (lay derz) *noun:* Salutary remark, often substituted for goodbye, pidgin for see you later, sayonara, adios, after a while crocodile.

12. **howzit?** (house it) *adverb, interjection:* A greeting, always a question, friendly contraction of "How is it?" The inquiry is directed at

lidat	Like that
minahs	Minor; no problem; don't worry about it
mo bettah	Better
no shame	Don't be shy or embarrassed!
nuff already!	That's enough!
shaka	Greetings; good job; thank you
small keed time	Childhood
soah?	Does it hurt?
stink eye	Disapproving glance, a dirty look
talk story	Converse, talk, or gossip
tanks, eh?	Thank you
whatevahs	Whatever
who dat?	Who is that?
yeah, no?	That's right!

your state of mind at the time. The preferred response is, "It's good, brah!" Or, maybe "I'm feeling junk" (pidgin for poorly).

13. **shaka brah** (shah kah brah) *interjection, noun:* A contemporary pidgin phrase similar to hang loose, used as a casual form of agreement that everything is cool. The first word, *shaka,* refers to a hand signal made with thumb and pinkie extended, index, middle, and ring fingers closed, and a brisk horizontal flip of the wrist. This public sign that all is well often follows the phrase "life is good, brah," and is seen nightly on local TV news sign-off. The second word, *brah,* is a truncation of *brother.*

14. **holoholo** (hoe low hoe low) *verb:* An old Hawaiian word meaning to go out for pleasure on foot or in a car or boat, a stroll to check things out, with emphasis on going out for fun. Not to be confused with similar sounding *halohalo* (hah low hah low), the classic Filipino desert made with ice cream and chopped fruit.

15. **wikiwiki** (wee key wee key) *adjective, noun:* An old Hawaiian word and the name of the Honolulu International Airport shuttle bus, originally meaning to go fast, move rapidly, hurry (a concept missing on the islands of Molokai and Lanai). Not to be confused with *hele* (hell lay), which means to go, or let's go, as in "Hele on."

16. **mauka/makai** (mao cah/mah kigh) *noun:* Two of the four key directions on Oahu, *mauka* and *makai* are used on all Hawaiian Islands. *Mauka* means inland or toward the mountain, and *makai* means toward the ocean. Other Oahu directions are Ewa (eh vah) and Diamond Head (die mohn hed) meaning toward the Ewa plain or Waikiki's famous crater, known in Hawaiian as *Leahi* (lay ah hee) or tuna brow. On Maui, Upcountry same t'ing mauka, brah.

17. **kapu** (kah poo) *noun:* An old Hawaiian word meaning taboo, off limits, no trespassing, keep out, forbidden, sacred. Often seen on signs in high-crime areas, danger spots, and geothermal plants.

18. **hapa-haole** (hah pa-howl ee) *noun, adjective:* If you're not *kanaka* (kah nah kah), that's you: literally a person with no breath. *Ha* is breathe, *ole* is nothing. Haole is what early Hawaiians called the first European visitors, who looked pale as death, or breathless. *Hapa* is Hawaiian for half, not to be confused with *hapai* (hah pie), meaning one and a half, or pregnant. *Hapa-haole* is half white. When used derogatorily, *haole* is generally prefaced by adjectives like "stupid" or "dumb."

19. **da kine** (dah khine) *adjective, interjection:* Pidgin slang literally meaning "the kind," implying something perfectly understood but not exactly defined. A one-size-fits-all generic expression used when two or more people know what they are talking about but nobody can think of the right word, as in "Cannot explain, you know, da kine."

20. **li'dat** (lye daht) *adverb:* Existential pidgin phrase meaning that's the way it is, from "like that." Agreement or confirmation that an idea, concept, or statement is what it is. Similar to English "uh-huh,"and Japanese "honto des."

Problems in Paradise?

None of these potential difficulties would keep you from coming, but be prepared.

Winds The same gusty trades that make North Shore Maui an international windsurfers' joy can rock your landing jet and sting your skin with sand at the beach, not to mention kicking up the channel waters under your snorkel cruiser. It's a natural phenomenon. Nearly constant tradewinds accelerate when they funnel through Maui's isthmus valley or whistle down the interisland channels. If you are an iffy sailor, go in the mornings when it's calmer.

Clouds Takeoffs and landings can be delayed on the Island of Lanai by low cloud conditions.

Sunburn Don't underestimate the power of tropical sun. It's strongest from 9 a.m. to 3 p.m. Do what you want when you want, but slather everyone with high-potency waterproof sunscreen, before you go out and often during your activity, and use sunglasses and hats as well. If you do get scorched, slather even more with aloe vera gel.

Sharks Shark attacks are rare in Hawaii, but sharks are not. Attacks have occurred off Maui beaches. Those clear blue waters harbor a variety of the creatures, which, by Hawaiian legend, are more revered than feared as *aumakua,* or family guardian spirits.

Foods Maui's cornucopia of restaurants and food stores dries up on the smaller islands. Molokai is one of those places where you don't nap into dinnertime, or you might miss it if you wait too late. Molokai receives milk and staples by once-a-week barge from Honolulu. If you shop the island markets and cook your own meals, plan dinner around what there is to buy. Although U.S. Department of Agriculture rules restrict movement of fresh produce between Hawaii and other places, anything goes interisland. If you're renting a condo for a family of fussy eaters, you may want to consider buying some groceries on Oahu or Maui and carrying them to Molokai. In Lanai City, limited groceries are available in the plantation general stores, and a couple of restaurants serve breakfast and lunch. Otherwise, you eat at the hotels only, which are excellent.

Water Maui, Molokai, and Lanai are fragile, isolated ecosystems with few resources and little margin for error in tight times. Even the abundant rainfall of wetter areas drains away quickly, leaving water problems for the increasing population of Maui.

Now and then, water gets out of control. Rogue waves and riptides can sweep you out to sea, and occasionally threats are posed by rough surf and even tsunami, or tidal waves, as well as flash-flooding that occurs when tropical rainstorms, usually brief and intense, meet mountains. The runoff down steep slopes poses flash-flood dangers in a downhill waterfall valley or across a road that briefly becomes a raging waterfall course. If you get caught in a storm while hiking by a stream, go immediately to high ground. If driving, park before you get to deep water on a road and wait an hour or two. It will all be gone soon as the water flows out to sea.

Pests Bugs love the climate, too. You may see huge red or black centipedes and smaller blue ones (they bite, painfully); delicate, small scorpions (their sting is like a bee sting, according to one victim); several species of terrorizing cockroaches that don't bite; fast, hairy cane spiders (harmless); several sizes of ants; your average fly and superfly; little black pineapple bugs; and mosquitoes that seem to prefer tender flesh fresh from the mainland. Mosquitoes will breed in vases of flowers and the rain held by a leaf overnight. Imported and hitchhiking plants and animals also thrive in the tropical air, usually at the expense of a former arrival. The history of the Islands is a tale of one species crowding another toward extinction—particularly risky for the rare and delicate native inhabitants, including the vanishing race of pure Hawaiians.

Traffic This is not a problem on Molokai or Lanai, but the Maui roads are inadequate for large crowds, as you'll discover if you land on a loaded jumbo jet flight at local commute time. One of the traffic problem areas is the three miles between Lahaina and Kaanapali Beach Resort. Allow extra time on airport runs or plan to take a breather if the traffic is bugging you.

You'll also encounter crowds at rental-car stands when big jets arrive. The best policy is to slow down and cool off. Allow more time. Strike up a conversation. Hawaiia time just isn't as *wikiwiki* (speedy) as you're used to, so relax and enjoy it.

Population Maui County grew by 28 percent in the decade before the 2000 census, to 128,000 people. The influence of new residents, many of them from California, and increasing economic reliance on tourism has changed the once-insular social culture of islands formerly devoted to agriculture, mostly sugar and pineapple plantations. The multicultural populace of Maui County, like the rest of Hawaii, is a harmonious racial rainbow most of the time, but clouds do appear.

Cost of Goods Prices are relatively high for food, gas, and other items. On the other hand, the advent of big discount stores and increased retail competition has helped diminish the high costs and increase the choices, at least on Maui. In populations as small as Molokai and Lanai, shoppers are limited to what the ships bring in once a week and what they can make, grow, or catch at home.

These remote islands share many of the same problems that burden other American communities: drugs, crime, and traffic. But open-hearted strangers are welcome, and local people largely rely on kindness, respect, and humor to get along. The skies and seas are truly blue way out here, and there is plenty of spectacular scenery to soothe the soul.

Important Phone Numbers

Here's a list of phone numbers that may come in handy during your stay. For interisland calls, use the area code (808) before the number. Be aware these calls generally are charged long-distance rates.

- Police, fire, ambulance 911

- Directory assistance 411
- Weather forecast 877-5111
- Marine conditions 877-3477
- Time of day 242-0212 (Maui), 553-9211 (Molokai), 565-9211 (Lanai)
- Kahului Airport 872-3803, 872-3893
- Kapalua Airport 669-0623
- Hana Airport 248-8208
- Molokai Airport 567-6140
- Kalaupapa Airport 567-6331
- Lanai Airport 565-6757
- Office of Consumer Protection 984-8244

Safety Tips

Hawaii is a peaceful state with few violent crimes. Much is invested in the safety of tourists, the state's biggest industry, but the state is not crime-free. We urge you to use the same common sense and self-protective measures you would at home.

- Carry only as much cash or travelers checks as you need for the day.
- Never leave your luggage unattended until you arrive at your hotel.
- Never display large amounts of cash during transactions, such as at automated teller machines.
- Beware of pickpockets, especially in crowds.
- Carry your purse close to your body.
- Carry your wallet in a front pocket rather than a rear pocket.
- Avoid waiting alone at a bus stop after dark.
- Never leave valuables in your rental car.
- If your vehicle is bumped from behind at night, do not stop; instead, proceed to the nearest public area and call 911 for assistance.
- Leave your hotel room key with the front desk when going out.

Part Two

Planning Your Visit

When to Go

You can go to Maui whenever you feel like it—when you see the best bargains, when your frequent-flyer mileage has to be claimed, when school's out, or if you live on the West Coast, when you can get away for a long weekend with your sweetie.

There is no "tourist season" on these islands, because nothing shuts down for the winter or even for the weekend. This is the land of eternal spring, according to some poets, or perpetual summer, according to others. Tourism is the most important business, and you are always welcome. So timing your trip will depend on other factors.

Travel industry experts in Maui report that the "booking window," or the period between reservations and actual travel, has narrowed dramatically since the events of September 11, 2001, accelerating a trend that emerged over recent years. Not as many people are traveling, and more people are taking advantage of last-minute deals offered by airlines, hotels, and rental-car firms anxious to fill empty spaces. This greatly improves your chance of getting what you want, when you want, at the price you want to pay.

Weather, or Not

More people want to head for Hawaii, the only American tropical state, when their weather at home is awful or when they can bring the family, so that relatively speaking, rates go up and availability goes down in winter and summer. That makes spring and fall the easiest and best value seasons. As for the weather on Maui, Molokai, and Lanai, temperatures around the shoreline vary only slightly from one time of year to another, with winter months being the coolest and wettest. In a real cold snap, daytime highs can sometimes dip below 80°F at beach level. Cool night winds and higher elevations can inspire you to seek out a sweatshirt. The winter storms that sweep across America often visit the 50th state first, making winter the rainiest time of year.

Perhaps the strongest argument for visiting Maui in winter is the migration of Pacific humpback whales to Hawaiian waters, with the peak time being January through April and the peak place the federally protected waters off Maalaea Bay in the center of Maui's resort coast. Winter is also the season for big surf, major golf events, visually stunning squalls rolling across the horizon, and sometimes snow dusting the top of Haleakala. It's the rainier, often less breezy time between the holidays in late November or December, and in late March, when the hills are particularly green. Winter isn't brown or leafless in the Islands, although there are some deciduous trees that drop their leaves for six weeks and grow them right back. Some tropicals bloom and ripen any time of year, on their own schedules—bananas and orchids, for example.

Summer in the Islands, on the other hand, is the time of ripe mangoes (the Yee Orchards in Kihei grow an incredible variety), the sweet scent of jasmine, calmer seas on north shores and bigger surf on south shores, hurricanes and tropical storms marching west across the Pacific yet generally warmer and drier weather, and an explosion of flowers, not that there weren't plenty in winter. The Southern Cross and Perseid meteor showers appear in the skies in late summer. Rates for airfare and accommodations may or may not be lower, since summer weather in the Islands is often kinder and gentler than the steamers at home and it's a time when school's out and families head West for fun in the sun.

If you just want to kick back, watch travel ads and the Internet and catch the next plane that suits your budget and schedule.

Get a Head Start

The fact that you're reading this *Unofficial Guide* suggests you're a savvy traveler who already recognizes the value of planning ahead. Though most people arranging a Maui vacation plan to enjoy the famous laid-back Islands attitude, preparedness is still important. In fact, there's nothing more frustrating than sitting in traffic or standing in line at a car-rental counter when you expected to be lounging on the beach. And wouldn't you rather read a novel on the beach than luau brochures from the hotel lobby? A few hours' research in advance of your trip will really pay off in Maui, helping you relax and get the full value of your vacation.

Get a Map

The best maps of Maui, Molokai, and Lanai are created by cartographer James A. Bier and published by the University of Hawaii Press. Each topographic map includes island highways, roads, and trails as well as large-scale inset maps of towns with significant populations. They include points of natural, cultural, and historic interest; parks and beaches; sea channels; peaks and ridges (with altitudes); and Hawaiian words spelled with all their accent marks. The maps, printed on heavy paper, cost $2.95 for Maui and $3.95 for Molokai and Lanai and fold to fit easily into a carry-on bag or backpack.

If your bookstore doesn't carry these maps, you can order them directly from the Marketing Department, University of Hawaii Press, 2840 Kolowalu Street, Honolulu, HI 96822. Specify which island map you want. You can also request a free catalog of great books about Hawaii and the Pacific. Call the University of Hawaii Press at (808) 956-8255 for more information.

Recommended Reading

Every traveler to Maui, Molokai, or Lanai should read about these fascinating destinations before going. Check your local bookstore or library (you can also visit Booklines, the biggest distributor of books in Hawaii, on the Internet: **www.booklines.com**). Here are some suggested titles.

- *Beaches of Maui,* by John R. K. Clark; published by University of Hawaii Press, 1999. Guide to 50 of Hawaii's best beaches.

- *Camping Hawaii,* by Richard McMahon; published by University of Hawaii, Press, 1997. The only guide to 120 campgrounds in the Aloha State.

- *Hawaiian Heritage Plants,* by Angela Kay Kepler; published by Fernglen Press, 1998. Thorough presentation of Hawaii's native plants. Full-color photos.

- *Hawaii Pono: An Ethnic and Political History,* by Lawrence H. Fuchs; published by Island Book Shelf, 1997. This book covers how Hawaii came to be the "melting pot of the Pacific" and America's most cosmopolitan state.

- *Hawaii: True Stories of The Island Spirit,* edited by Rick and Marcie Carroll; published by Travelers Tales, San Francisco, 1999. This is an anthology of essays by a divergent group of contributing authors, some famous, others unknown, but all insightful.

- *Hawaii's Best Golf,* by George Fuller; published by Island Heritage Publishing, 1999. Hawaii's best golf courses, profiled and photographed in full color.

- *Maui Hiking Trails,* by Craig Chisolm; published by Fernglen Press, 1999. Detailed look at 50 of the best hiking trails on Hawaii's six major islands.

- *Molokai: An Island in Time,* by Richard Cooke III, photographer and long-time resident; published by Beyond Words, Honolulu, 1984.

- *Shoal of Time: A History of the Hawaiian Islands,* by Gavan Daws; published by University of Hawaii Press, 1994. This history book reads like a novel.

Newspapers and Magazines

Maui News is Maui's daily newspaper, published in Wailuku. Call (808) 244-3981 or visit the Web site, **www.mauinews.com** for information.

Maui No Ka Oi Magazine, a quarterly celebrating Valley Isle personalities, local issues, restaurant reviews and events, is published by Haynes Publishing Group on Maui. Call (808) 871-7765 to subscribe. The magazine's Web site is **www.mauinokaoi.net.**

Maui, Molokai, and Lanai are featured often in travel magazines like *Condé Nast Traveler, National Geographic Traveler, Travel + Leisure,* and *Arthur Frommer's Budget Travel Magazine* and airline in-flight magazines, but only a few feature magazines devote full coverage to the Islands.

Hawaii magazine, a bimonthly featuring articles on Island people, culture, arts, history, and travel is published by Fancy Publications in Irvine, California. It's available at major news stands, or call (800) 365-4421 to subscribe.

Surf the Internet

Search for the word "Maui" and you'll find a virtual tsunami of matches, too much to surf in a lifetime. More Maui Web sites appear every day.

Visit Maui   The Maui Visitors Bureau Web site, **www.visitmaui.com,** makes you want to pack right now. It offers lots of solid information and useful links, including seven remote cameras (one focuses on Hookipa windsurfers) with island scenes. You can check out the surf report and daily temperatures, order a free Maui Vacation Planner, book a B&B, and tour beach resorts. It links to **www.hawaii.com,** a new commercial Web site that provided information about the Islands to an estimated six million Internet users in 2002. Check out **www.maui.net** too, for an independent round-up of Maui information put together by Maui's primary Internet service provider.

Surf Molokai   Going to Molokai is like "landing in rural Arkansas sometime back in the 1930s or 1940s," novelist Fletcher Knebel once said. "I've had the feeling that if I turned on a radio, I'd hear Eddie Duchin on the piano, FDR in mid-fireside chat, or perhaps the Japanese bombing Pearl Harbor." Things haven't changed that much since Fletcher's day. However, old-fashioned Molokai has a big Internet presence: at least 54 home pages, from Molokai Ranch (**www.molokai-ranch.com**) to Monkey Pod Records (**www.monkeypod.com**), which promotes local musicians. One site details the somber history of the Kalaupapa National Historic Park, where victims of leprosy were once banished, and the way to get there—the Molokai Mule Ride (**www.muleride.com**).

Look at Lanai   Find lots of details about a little island at **www.lanaion line.com,** a broad perspective on what there is to see and do and where to eat and sleep on the old plantation isle. At **www.lanai-resorts.com,** you can get a peek at the exclusive resorts of Lanai, plus the real estate for sale in several high-end developments. Another site features Hotel Lanai, the small historic and unpretentious lodge in Lanai City, owned and operated by Henry Clay Richardson, the chef at Henry Clay's Rotisserie, and family (**www.hotellanai.com**). Check out **www.lanairental.com** to see a vacation rental property, the Captain's Retreat.

Find Kahoolawe   The devastated Island of Kahoolawe presents quite a challenge to the Hawaiians working to restore it and create a cultural preserve, because the U.S. Navy used it for bombing practice for half a century. You can learn more at **www.kahoolawe.org.** Or look up "virtual tour of Kahoolawe" to find a fascinating log by researching students who went there several years ago and documented what they found (**www.saftp.soest.hawaii.org**).

Maui Visitors Bureau

In the early 1900s, several of Hawaii's hoteliers created the world's first tourist bureau to attract travelers and foster dreams of visiting the Islands. The boosters later hired Mark Twain to extol the virtues of a Hawaii vacation and sent entertainers on the road, a practice that continues today as the next best thing to being here. Now, the Hawaii Visitors and Convention Bureau spends millions of dollars globally to promote Hawaii as a top world destination. Part of that job belongs to its offspring, the Maui Visitors Bureau, which spreads the word about Maui, Molokai, and Lanai activities, accommodations, restaurants, and events. The statewide HVCB Web site is another source of information and links (**www.gohawaii.com**).

Hawaii Visitors and Convention Bureau

2270 Kalakaua Avenue, 8th Floor
Honolulu, HI 96815
(808) 923-1811 or (800) GO-HAWAII
www.gohawaii.com

Request a free copy of *The Islands of Aloha,* the Hawaii Visitors and Convention Bureau vacation planner.

Maui Visitors Bureau

1727 Wili Pa Loop
Wailuku, HI 96793
(808) 244-3530 or (800) 525-MAUI
www.visitmaui.com, www.gohawaii.com

Call or write for a free copy of *Maui, The Magic Isles,* travel planner featuring the Maui, Molokai, and Lanai.

Destination Lanai

P.O. Box 700
Lanai City, HI 96763
(808) 565-7600 or (800) 947-4774
www.aloha.net/~dlanai/lanaitour, www.gohawaii.com

Molokai Visitors Association

P.O. Box 960
Kaunakakai, HI 96748
(808) 553-3876 or (800) 800-6367
www.molokai-hawaii.com, www.gohawaii.com

International

Australia

Hawaii Visitors and Convention Bureau
c/o The Sales Team
Suite 2, Level 2
34 Burton Street
Milsons Point, NSW 2061
61 (2) 9955-2619
rlane@thesalesteam.com.au, www.gohawaii.com

New Zealand

Hawaii Visitors and Convention Bureau
c/o Walshes World
18 Shortland Street, Level 6
Auckland
64 (9) 379-3708
darragh@walwor.co.nz, www.gohawaii.com

United Kingdom

Hawaii Visitors and Convention Bureau
P.O. Box 208
Sunbury on Thames
Middlesex TW165RJ
England
44 (208) 941-4009
xcd16@dial.pipex.com www.gohawaii.com

Canada

Comprehensive Travel Industry Services
1260 Hornby Street, Suite 104
Vancouver, BC V6Z1W2
(604) 669-6691 or fax (604) 669-6075
compre@intergate.bc.ca

Pack Light

No matter what the season, pack light. Think summer casual, without the chilly nights of California. The most you'll need at lower elevations is a light (not wool) sweater or windbreaker. In the cooler high country, the temperatures will seem like spring, so dress accordingly. If you have colorful aloha shirts and sarongs, bring those. If you yearn to hike those green trails, bring appropriate shoes and light socks.

Golfers, Island pro shops sell great tropical-weight duds for the links, and you can play in shorts on many courses. Windsurfers, you'll probably want to bring money for the new gear you'll be tempted to buy. If you're planning to ride horses, bring covered footwear and jeans and hang onto your hat. If you're going camping, you can bring or rent gear, according to your preference and the amount of time you plan to camp. A night or two? Rent. A month? You might prefer your own.

A word to the wise: besides sands of many colors on the beaches, these Islands are full of red dirt that stains clothing such as white tennies and shorts. Bring clothes that won't get in the way of a good time.

What men need: Shorts, T-shirts and informal tops, a favorite Hawaiian shirt, swim trunks, lightweight slacks, a light jacket or sweatshirt for Upcountry, and sandals, sports shoes, or loafers. No ties or suits needed, unless your trip will involve a funeral or full-dress wedding. Most restaurants' dress codes run to requiring footwear rather than formal wear.

What women need: Sundresses or shifts, swimsuits, bathing-suit coverups, shorts or cropped pants or skirts, tops, light sweater or jacket, sandals, sports shoes, and maybe a muumuu for the luau. Hemlines and styles vary at will here, and skin is in. No urban power-wear. Unless you're staying in butlered digs, minimize high-maintenance clothes, although many hotel rooms do come equipped with iron and board.

If you pack wisely for the tropical climate you can put all your lightweight clothes in one case and bring an empty one for all the gifts you'll bring back.

Staying in Touch

If a laptop computer is attached to your arm, bring it. The airport security process requires you to take it out of its carrying case and put it through the scope in a basket; then be sure to recover it at the other end. Most hotels in the Islands have phones and dataports in the rooms. Most also charge for making phone calls, even toll-free or local calls—but they are certainly a cheaper option than long-distance calls, so check with your Internet service provider to see if there is a local number to call on Maui, Molokai, or Lanai. Many hotels also provide high-speed Internet access, for your computer or on the room's television screen, for a fee, usually $10 a day. And some have rentable computer game gear.

What Not to Bring

Don't bring live animals or plants. Forget illegal drugs, including marijuana. Drug-sniffing dogs at baggage claims have sensitive noses, well trained to find such drugs; carriers are taken into custody on the spot.

Certain animals and plants are banned, and most are restricted from entering Hawaii. Inbound pets like dogs and cats end up in month-long, expensive quarantine. Snakes end up in the zoo or dead (the Islands have no wild land snakes and want none).

Exotic flora and fauna have a negative impact on Hawaii's fragile ecosystem. By the same token, the U.S. Department of Agriculture bans shipping of certain fruit, plants, and other items from Hawaii to prevent the spread of fruit flies and other insects. Pineapples and coconuts are okay. Bananas, avocados, and uncertified papayas are not. For specific information, call the USDA's Plant Quarantine Branch at (808) 586-0844 or the Animal Quarantine Branch at (808) 483-7171.

What Time Is It in Hawaii?

Hawaii has its own time zone, known as Hawaii Standard Time or HST. On standard time, noon in San Francisco is 10 a.m. in Honolulu. Hawaii time is two hours earlier than the West Coast and five hours earlier than the East Coast. During Daylight Savings Time on the mainland, April to October, Hawaii is three hours behind the West Coast and six hours behind the East Coast.

With an average 12 hours of sunshine daily, year-round, Hawaii has lots of daylight—and no need to "save" it. Hawaii's longest day, on June 21, is 13 hours and 26 minutes long. Its shortest day, on December 21, is 10 hours and 50 minutes.

Worth the Long Flight

The flight to Hawaii is about five hours from the West Coast, eight from Dallas, nine from Atlanta, and eleven hours in the air from New York. Most major U.S. and several international airlines serve the Islands regularly, as do charters. Hawaii-based Aloha Airlines and Hawaiian Airlines connect the Islands with various West Coast cities and Phoenix and Las Vegas (a frequent destination for Hawaii residents).

Honolulu International Airport (HNL) on Oahu is one of the nation's busiest airports, with 1,400 daily operations, many of them international, and more than 24 million passenger arrivals and departures annually. Most mainland-to-Hawaii flights touch down in Honolulu, and passengers for Maui, Molokai, or Lanai then must transfer to the Interisland Terminal for short hops to those islands. Maui County airports are

Kahului Airport, Hana Airport, and Kapalua–West Maui Airport on Maui; Hoolehua Airport on Molokai; and Lanai Airport on Lanai.

Some scheduled flights do go nonstop to Kahului Airport on Maui. Hawaiian Airlines flies nonstop to Maui from Seattle, Los Angeles, and San Francisco. United Airlines has daily Maui flights from Los Angeles and San Francisco. Delta Airlines and American Airlines fly nonstop to Kahului from Los Angeles. Aloha flies to Maui from Burbank, Oakland, and Orange County, California, with links to Phoenix and Las Vegas, as well as from Vancouver, British Columbia.

All schedules are subject to change. Call toll-free numbers below for updated information.

If you had a bumpy flight, consider, please, the flight of Commander John Rodgers, the first pilot to almost fly to Hawaii. A 1908 Naval Academy graduate, Rodgers, the grandson of Commodore Matthew Peary, learned to fly from Wilbur and Orville Wright in 1911. On August 31, 1925, Captain Rodgers, age 44, lifted off from San Francisco in a Boeing PN9-1 seaplane named the *Flying Dreadnought* with 40 ham sandwiches and a crew of four. The seaplane's twin Packard V-8 engines ran out of gas 25 hours and 23 minutes after takeoff, and Ridges downed at sea about 300 miles off Maui. When no rescuers arrived, the crew rigged a sail and made 50 miles a day in their "mutant square rigger"—as historian MacKinnon Simpson wrote—until they spotted Oahu's jagged Koolau peaks but were unable to stop. Wind and sea set them sailing on to Kauai, where they arrived September 10, after a nine-day sea leg. Total voyage: 1,870 miles by air, 450 by sea. Rodgers's feat is memorialized in a bronze plaque at Honolulu International Airport, which is officially named for him.

AIRLINES

Air Canada	(800) 776-3000	Continental Airlines	(800) 523-3273
Air New Zealand	(800) 262-1234	Delta Airlines	(800) 221-1212
Aloha Airlines	(800) 367-5350	Hawaiian Airlines	(800) 367-5320
American Airlines	(800) 433-7300	Northwest Airlines	(800) 225-2525
British Airways	(800) 247-9297	United Airlines	(800) 241-6522

How to Book

Booking your vacation through a travel agent may save you time and money, since the agent can plow through myriad fares and rates to find you the best airfares, lodgings, and car rentals and take advantage of specials offered just to agents. But you may also have to pay a fee, because more and more agents are charging customers these days. You can book your vacation yourself on the Internet or the telephone, although it consumes time and tries your patience. Internet fares are often discounted. The best plan is to do research on your own to acquaint yourself with what's available and also find out what an agent can do for you, and then decide.

If you make the arrangements on your own, here are some tips and advisories on finding a good deal on airfares, hotels, and travel packages:

- Check out the travel-booking Web sites: **expedia.com, travel.yahoo. com, travelocity.com, hoteldiscount.com, cheaptickets.com,** and others. Several Island providers will also book your whole trip if you choose. Look up hotels, cars, and airlines by name if you prefer or plan to cash in mileage awards.

- Be flexible in your travel plans. The best airfare deals are usually for travel on certain days of the week or hours of the day. Ask the reservations agent how you might save money by leaving a day earlier or later, or taking a different flight. Check carefully into fare restrictions and penalties if you change plans after purchase. Check the Internet to see if you can find cheaper fares. You can hold your telephone reservation on most airlines for a day or so before you commit finally to the ticket. In some cases you have to call to cancel. In others you have to call to activate the reservation. Once you're ticketed, changes can be costly.

- If your travel itinerary falls into a busy flight period, book early. Flights during holidays may sell out months ahead of time.

- Many discount fares are nonrefundable and usually nontransferable. (One exception is the books of coupons offered by local airlines). If you want to change your discounted booking, you will pay more if that fare is not available on the new flight.

Plan to Camp?

If you intend to camp at national parks and other popular spots, you may have to compete long before you arrive for inexpensive reservations for rustic cabins and tent sites. (See camping section, page 249.)

How to Avoid Jet Lag

Start before you depart to combat jet lag, circadian desynchronization in scientific terms. Whatever its name, it is that zonked feeling, which occurs after flying across several time zones, especially when flying East. It is a physical and mental condition lasting a few hours to a few days. You are sleepy, disoriented, and a little out of synch.

Here are some practical tips:

- Avoid coffee for a day or two before and after your flight and drink water, lots of it, rather than coffee, sodas, or alcohol on the plane. Alcohol can intensify jet lag. Drink water to prevent dehydration—an eight-ounce glass for each hour of flight, according to our doctor. This will also combat the colds passengers often give one another.

- During flight, remove shoes to improve circulation. Flex your feet, ankles, and legs often. If possible, stroll through the cabin and stand for awhile.

- Adjust your watch to Hawaii Standard Time when you board the plane. This prepares you mentally to adjust to Hawaii time. Think of time as it is where you're going, not where you've been. Then, on the ground, get acclimated to local time as soon as possible. Stay up until bedtime in the Islands if you can, even though you may feel extremely tired.

- Go for a swim or a long soak. It will replenish moisture lost during your flight and soothe tired muscles and nerves.

Travel Advisory

Honolulu's International Airport is currently undergoing a $200 million improvement project to add an efficient security checkpoint, new people movers, and an information center. While renovations are under way, travelers may experience disruption, confusion, and construction noise. The project is scheduled to be completed by 2006.

Interisland Flights

Maui is linked by frequent, efficient jet service all day from sunrise to late evening by the two full-service Honolulu-based airlines, Aloha Airlines and Hawaiian Airlines, which share the Interisland Terminal at Honolulu Airport. Fewer flights, often on small aircraft, serve Molokai and Lanai from the commuter terminal at Honolulu Airport.

Aloha's sister small-craft, interisland airline, Island Air, flies twin-engine planes to smaller airports, including Kapalua and Hana on Maui and Hoolehua Airport on Molokai. Hawaiian no longer flies aircraft smaller than jets and thus no longer serves Kapalua, and offers only a few commuter-hour flights to and from Lanai and Molokai.

Both Aloha and Hawaiian have small first-class seating areas, but the flights take only 25 minutes, so the chief advantage, besides bigger seats and more service, is that you can board and deplane first. Check with the airlines for their carry-on baggage rules. Boogie boards, surfboards, coolers, skateboards, and strollers are not allowed in the cabin.

When booking your interisland flight, ask about special promotions that may lower fares. Or check the Aloha and Hawaiian Web sites.

CONTACTING HAWAII'S AIR CARRIERS

Aloha Airlines
Toll-free: (800) 554-4833
Oahu: (808) 484-1111
Maui: (808) 244-9071
Big Island: (808) 935-5771
Kauai: (808) 245-3691
www.alohaair.com

Hawaiian Airlines
Toll-free: (800) 367-5320
Oahu: (808) 838-1555
Maui: (808) 871-6132
Big Island: (808) 326-5615
Kauai: (808) 245-1813
Molokai: (808) 553-3644
Lanai: (808) 565-7281
www.hawaiianair.com

Island Air
Toll-free: (800) 652-6541
Molokai: (808) 567-6115
Lanai: (808) 565-6744

Molokai Air Shuttle
Oahu: (808) 567-6847

Pacific Wings
Toll-free: (800) 575-4546
Maui: (808) 873-0877
www.pacificwings.com

Paragon Air
Toll-free: (800) 428-1231
Maui: (808) 244-3356
www.maui.net/wing

Trans Air
Toll-free: (800) 836-8080

Car Rentals

It's possible to enjoy Maui, Molokai, and Lanai without rental cars. The larger Maui resorts have free shuttles to link your lodgings with airports, beaches, and golf courses, as well as a full array of other amusements. But to explore Maui and Molokai the way they deserve, you have to rent a vehicle.

Likewise on Lanai: A resort shuttle will take you to most sites, but one of Lanai's more popular activities is to explore the back roads in a four-wheel-drive rental, allowing you to discover wild country and island history on your own. People talk of driving "around the island," but you can't really do that around the entire coastline of any of the islands. Yet, given their relatively small size, each island can be traversed in a matter of hours.

Carry as little as possible in your rental car that might appeal to thieves. We usually leave ours empty and open; no sense paying for a broken window.

Car rentals are available on all islands. The cost averages around $30 per day, with taxes (rates tend to be higher on Molokai and Lanai, where there are fewer cars and customers). Rental-car rates are lower in the Islands than the nation as a whole. Shop for rates by telephone or on the

Internet, if making your own arrangements. Try Expedia, Priceline, Travelocity, and other Internet travel discounters. We've had the best luck with Priceline.com a few days before departure, but only during a less busy, nonholiday period.

Most major car-rental firms offer special rates and include car rentals in money-saving travel packages with airfare and accommodations. Check with a travel agent or call the car-rental agencies for details before you go. Again, be sure also to try the Internet travel discount sites for special package deals. When making interisland flight reservations, ask the airlines for any special deals on rental cars. They often partner with car agencies in promotional fly/drive packages. All sorts of discounts can lower your rates: You may get a break of 5–15 percent for association memberships, credit cards, frequent-flyer clubs, and coupons. Agency Web sites (provided below) can offer up to 20 percent off regular rates.

All the major car-rental agencies are located at or near Maui's airports, and many have reservations desks at various resorts or stores. Keep in mind however, that Budget and Dollar are the only car-rental agencies at the Molokai Airport, and Dollar is the only car-rental option at Lanai Airport. On Maui, besides Kahului Airport and the hotels, many car-rental agencies operate near Kapalua Airport in West Maui at the Kaanapali Transportation Center (30-1 Halawai Drive), a five-minute free shuttle ride from the Kapalua terminal.

Maui is just the kind of place you might want to splurge and rent a convertible or a fancy sports car. Most car-rental agencies have a fleet of vehicles, ranging from economy cars and luxury sedans to four-wheel-drive Jeeps and shiny red roadsters. Luxury wheels like Ferraris and Vipers and Harley Davidson motorcycles are also available for rent on Maui.

As with car rentals in any destination, you can rent a car after you arrive, presuming one is available, but you'd do better to reserve a car before you go. Courtesy phones and free shuttles in airport terminals connect you to their nearby offices. Rental rates are based on the number of cars available, so they constantly fluctuate. Since you don't have to pay up front, you can always book one early and recheck rates later.

Expect to see that rental fee jump by the time you sign for the car, since several costs will be added on. Car rentals are subject to a $2-per-day state road tax and a nominal vehicle license tax (17–45¢ per day). In addition, transactions that take place at an airport are subject to an airport concession fee of 7.5 percent.

Optional insurance rates vary by car rental agency. It's a hard-sell situation when you're picking up the car, but remember that your own car insurance, and often your major credit card, provide insurance coverage on you while driving rental cars. Check before you leave. Hawaii is a no-fault insurance state.

Gas prices will look astronomical on Maui, Molokai, and Lanai, compared to almost any mainland location. But think about where you are. Fortunately, rental cars today are rarely gas-guzzlers, and the Islands are small enough that you seldom rack up major mileage.

About Island Driving: These islands don't have a lot of roads. Most roads are two lanes and speed limits are lower than in other states. Island driving manners are such that people will let you merge into their lane, turn left in front of traffic, or stop briefly to pick up or dispatch a rider, without protest. Take it slow, signal, look, smile a lot, and wave your thanks. Leave your aggressive driving habits at home.

CONTACTING HAWAII'S CAR RENTAL AGENCIES

Alamo Rent-A-Car
Toll-free: (800) 327-9633
www.goalamo.com
Maui:
Kahului Airport: (808) 871-6235
Kaanapali Transportation
  Center: (808) 661-7181

Avis Rent-A-Car
Toll-free: (800) 331-1212;
www.avis.com
Maui:
Kahului Airport: (808) 871-7575
Kaanapali: (808) 661-4588
Renaissance Wailea Beach
  Resort: (808) 879-7601
Ritz-Carlton Kapalua:
  (808) 669-5046

Budget Rent-A-Car
Toll-free: (800) 777-0169;
www.budgetrentacar.com
Maui:
Kahului Airport: (808) 871-8811
Kaanapali: (808) 661-8721
Molokai:
Molokai Airport: (808) 567-6877

Dollar Rent-A-Car
Toll-free: (800) 367-7006;
www.dollarcar.com
Maui:
Kahului Airport: (808) 877-2731
Hana: (808) 248-8237
Kaanapali Transportation
  Center: (808) 667-2651
Molokai:
Molokai Airport: (808) 567-6156
Lanai:
Lanai Airport: (808) 565-7227

Hertz Rent-A-Car
Toll-free: (800) 654-3011;
www.hertz.com
Maui:
Kahului Airport: (808) 877-5167
2580 Keka'a Dr.: (808) 661-7735
Westin Maui: (808) 667-5381
Maui Marriott: (808) 667-1966

National Car Rental
Toll-free: (800) CAR-RENT;
www.nationalcar.com
Maui:
Kahului Airport: (808) 871-8851
Kaanapali Transportation
  Center: (808) 667-9737

Island-Hopping: Pro or Con?

On paper, it looks easy to hop at will between Maui, Molokai, and Lanai, as well as Honolulu, and it used to be. But today's increased airport security requirements, reduced flight schedules, and insufficient ticket counters and staff, especially in the case of Kahului Airport, make for airport traffic jams that can consume hours of your precious vacation time. If you're staying on Maui and want to see Lanai, one pleasant way to go is by boat. The cruises are fun, and some include an island tour. The passenger ferry that links Lanai and Lahaina is inexpensive and scenic.

When you do fly between islands, the flights are only half an hour or so and the airlines are efficient, but the transfers are time-consuming and plane tickets are expensive, well over $100 per round-trip. (One hint: from within Hawaii, you can buy one-way Hawaiian Air coupons at certain Bank of Hawaii ATMs, for a discounted rate).

Most interisland flights are to or from Honolulu, which means that you often have to go back to Honolulu to connect to other islands. Before you leave, ask your agent or airline about discounted interisland rates. After you arrive, ask the airlines about discounted coupon books, where you can buy six one-way flights' worth of coupons in advance for a cheaper rate.

Expect to spend several hours commuting from place to place—to pack, check out, get to the airport, return your rental car if you have one or go earlier in a transit vehicle, stand in line to check in for your flight, go through security, wait for the plane, board the plane, fly, deplane, get your luggage, get another rental car, drive to another hotel, register your room, and unpack. Phew.

You can save money by staying longer on each island. Some major hotels offer a free night's stay when you book four or more consecutive nights, or two rooms for the price of one when traveling with the family.

The quickest way to see the Islands is a scenic flight on a helicopter or twin-engine airplane. Several companies offer low altitude half-day and full-day scenic tours over the main islands. One is **Pacific Wings:** (808) 873-0877; **www.pacificwings.com.**

Norwegian Cruise Lines offer one-week Hawaiian cruise, aboard the *Norwegian Star,* with port calls on several islands. Call (800) 327-7030, or visit **www.ncl.com/fleet/02/star.**

Suggestions for Travelers with Special Interests

Singles

Best Island to Visit Maui

Things to See and Do Ride with a bike tour down Haleakala or take a snorkel cruise to Molokini or Lanai. Drive to Makawao and Paia and poke around the villages. If you're a golfer, pro shops are often looking to fill up a foursome on the links. Head Upcountry to Kula and stop to taste

Tedeschi Wines at the winery at Ulupalakua Ranch. The best places to party are Lahaina and Kihei, where the few bars with live music and dancing are easy to find and the action commences after 10 p.m.

Comments If you're traveling solo, Maui has the most social appeal, the most single visitors of various ages to meet, and the most places to meet them. You won't feel uncomfortable eating alone in restaurants or signing up by yourself for activities.

Couples

Best Islands to Visit Lanai and Maui

Things to See and Do On Lanai, divide your time between the seaside Manele Bay Hotel, where you can wake up warm to spinner dolphins in the waters out front, and the inland Lodge at Koele, where evenings are chilly enough to cuddle and after dinner, not much else is on the agenda. Hike to Sweetheart Rock, or take a four-wheel-drive vehicle out to the secluded hinterlands, or ride horses through the woods. Paddle a kayak for two through snorkel-garden waters.

On Maui, get up early to see the spectacular sunrise over Haleakala, then relax with massages for two in tents by the sea and take a stroll on Wailea Beach. If you seek solitude, just go to Hana to see how romantic Maui really is.

Comments If you love the one you're with, you won't need our help for suggestions on romance and entertainment. Maui will do it for you, and Lanai is so indulgent of privacy that the world seems to fall away, leaving just you and the soft tropical nights and the starry skies.

Families

Best Island to Visit Maui

Things to See and Do Lanai and Molokai have great appeal for families as well, but Maui is the place the kids most want to go. It has the most family-oriented attractions designed to educate as well as entertain, such as the Maui Ocean Center and the Whale Museum at Whalers Village Shopping Center in Kaanapali Beach Resort. That is, if you can tear them away from the water-park pools at hotels throughout Kaanapali and Wailea resorts—the most elaborate being the Grand Wailea Resort Hotel and Spa water complex, with pools, canyons, slides, and a water-driven elevator. Smaller kids can learn about the Islands and make new friends at supervised hotel children's programs while their parents enjoy some adult time. Hawaii Nature Center programs in Wailuku offer a chance for kids to discover denizens of the rain forest.

Comments Kaanapali Beach in West Maui is considered the most popular family destination, but all three islands are excellent family choices. Maybe the best thing about Islands vacations *en famille* is that they happen *en famille*—rather than as simultaneous individual vacations—because Hawaii's activities and attractions have broad appeal. Bring everybody, from tots to nephews to grandparents, and spend some real quality time together. If the family group is one parent and child, exploring Maui, Molokai, and Lanai together will be the experience you hoped for. Plenty of discoveries await families on these islands, and you'll be surprised how many the children make first.

Bikers

Best Islands to Visit Maui and Molokai

Things to See and Do You won't forget the thrill of coasting down 10,000-foot high Haleakala on a specially built bicycle, 38 miles to the sea on a guided cruise. The air is cold in the early morning at the summit, but warms as you descend the slope. There are frequent stops to shed clothes and admire the scenery that starts with alpine rockscape and ends up with tropical wonderland. You are awed by the majesty of the sleeping volcano. If your notion of bike cruising runs to Harleys, your ride awaits at the nearest rental spot. Be forewarned: The biker bars have already been discovered, largely by prowling CEOs who like to hang incognito with the folks. Bicycles are available to guests at several hotels, including the Hana-Maui, where the grounds have gentle slopes and shady paths. Mountain bikers, head for the wild open spaces of Molokai Ranch, where some of the 54,000 acres of ranchland is ribboned with challenging trails just for you. Mountain biking is one of your options on a long list of inclusive ranch activities that come with overnight stays at Lodge at Molokai Ranch (upland, upscale) and Beach Village (ecotourism tent camping by Kaupoa Beach). Lanai activities also include mountain biking.

Comments Equipment rentals are readily available, the terrain is challenging and scenery mesmerizing. What a terrific way to experience the Islands.

Nature Lovers

Best Islands to Visit Molokai and Maui

Things to See and Do On Maui, go directly up—to Haleakala National Park to look for rare Silversword plants and the endangered Hawaiian Nene goose, or to hike in the cloud forest at Polipoli State

Park. Or head along the north shore toward Hana; the crooked road leads through some of the most beautiful scenery waterfalls and exotic plants can produce. Stop at Waianapanapa State Park for a short stroll to a jet-black beach. Go for a guided hike in any of the forested hills. Drive on your own on the Upcountry road through Kula and continue past Ulupalakua Ranch for a few miles on a new road that takes you through an incredible variety of mini-climate zones without a building in sight.

Molokai has more nature than man-made scenery. It varies from verdant fern valleys and coconut groves on the east end to vast empty stretches of dryland ranch on the west end. Investigate the Nature Conservancy preserves in the high-country bog and lowland sand dunes, and sign up for a guided tour to hear about the extraordinary nature of Hawaii's rare species that abound there.

Lanai's landscape is wild and open, and nature is reasserting itself after nearly a century of pineapple plantation agriculture. The pine-lined uplands offer forest trails up the flank of Lanaihale, the old volcano that anchors the island.

Comments Hawaii's natural beauty is legendary; its native wildlife (Monk seals, Nene geese, and native Hawaiian birds) may be endangered, but you will not be disappointed by the great outdoors. Maui's fabled Hana is a prime destination for people who like to feel overwhelmed with the majesty of nature. If you're lucky, you may win admission to the Puu Kukui nature preserve atop the West Maui Mountains. For details, see "A Rare Hike between Heaven and Earth," page 240.

Golfers

Best Islands to Visit Maui and Lanai

Things to See and Do On Maui, 19 golf courses beckon to you, so how can you lose? Your choices include the world-famous sites of pro golf classics telecast each winter, such as the Mercedes PGA championship Tournament at Kapalua, and courses relatively obscure to all but the Island golfer. The newest is Maui Lani near Wailuku. Lanai has only two, but what a pair—upland, The Experience at Koele, with its signature hole in the middle of a forest, across water, between trees, and 200 yards from the tee, and the oceanfront Challenge at Manele, its very beauty a hazard to the distractable golfer.

Comments Golf doesn't get much better, or more beautiful, than the Golf Coast of Maui and the courses of Lanai.

Gays and Lesbians

Best Islands to Visit Maui and Molokai

Things to See and Do Tolerant attitudes, a Polynesian tradition that recognizes a "third sex" (*mahu*) and plenty of outrageous beauty makes Maui equally popular with gay as straight. Few places cater specifically to gay travelers, but most places accept visitors of all persuasions. Try a few days on Molokai, quiet, private, and low-key, with a local gay tradition. The Islands had a brief moment of fame for allowing same-sex marriages in the late 1990s, but voters and judges threw out the law that permitted them. Now same-sex marriages are illegal in Hawaii, but gay couples planning commitment ceremonies on Maui will find assistance from Forever Maui Productions, online at **www.gayonmaui.com** and **www.lesbians onmaui.com.**

Ocean Swimmers

Best Islands to Visit Maui and Lanai

Things to See and Do Maui's best swimming/snorkeling beaches include Kapalua Beach, fronting the Kapalua Bay Hotel, and Napili Bay Beach, fronting the Mauian and other small hotels and condos, on the northern end of the resort coast and Wailea Beach, fronting the Four Seasons Resort Maui, on the southern end. In the center, surfers and swimmers head for Kamaole Beach County Park III in Kihei. The black- and-white sands of Hamoa Beach in Hana are scenic and the waves just right for body surfing much of the time. Maluaka Beach in Makena, across a small sand hill from the Maui Prince Hotel, is another satisfying choice.

We like these beaches because the waters are clear and buoyant, the bottoms sandy, the waves gentle and fun, and the swimming safe. The bay and cove beaches with finite edges of lava reef, such as those at Kapalua and Wailea resorts, lure swimmers to do laps, particularly on calm mornings. Snorkeling is good off the lava rocks that form the bays.

At Lanai's scenic, palm-shaded Hulopoe Beach, below Manele Bay Hotel, the waters are usually fine for swimming and snorkeling. There is also a pool carved into the lava on one side just right for little kids to splash around safely.

Comments Oddly enough, a lot of visitors and residents alike don't go in the ocean waters. It's a shame, for there's no finer place to swim in the sea.

Active Seniors

Best Island to Visit Maui

Things to See and Do Seniors can do anything they like on Maui's islands, often at a discounted rate. Able elders find most Maui facilities are easily accessible, including view points. Van groups will have the most sightseeing choices on Maui. Attractions include the Maui Tropical

Plantation, where visitors ride trams through sample fields of island crops, which they can then pick up at the produce market. The National Tropical Botanical Gardens, the only such federally chartered research gardens, are definitely worth a visit near Hana, where the 125-acre Kahanu garden of Pacific Island plants also includes the state's largest archeological site, Piilanihale Heiau. Plenty of privately operated botanical gardens are sprinkled throughout the Islands, too.

Comments Anyone with gray in their hair tends to be viewed with respect in the Islands. You are considered a wise *kupuna* (elder), especially if you take advantage of senior discounts that shave the costs of activities, attractions, meals, and even merchandise in some stores—sometimes but not always on certain days of the week. For instance, Outrigger Hotels Hawaii offers a substantial break from published room rates for visitors over 50 years and members of the American Association of Retired Persons (AARP), a group that also offers organized tour travel packages to members. Hawaiian Airlines offers a discount and one-way ticketing options for passengers 60 and over. Elder Hostel stages affordable, stimulating educational travel programs in Maui County and elsewhere for travelers 55 and older. The healthy seniors who live in the Islands surf, dance, play golf, and swim daily—and so can you.

Visitors with Disabilities

Best Island to Visit Maui

Things to See and Do Haleakala National Park, Maui Tropical Plantation, and Maui Ocean Center on Maui—all of which accommodate disabled visitors.

Comments The *Aloha Guide to Accessibility,* published by the Commission on Persons with Disabilities, provides detailed information on accessibility features of Island hotels, attractions, beaches, parks, theaters, shopping centers, transportation services, and medical and support services. Write the commission at 919 Ala Moana Boulevard, Room 101, Honolulu, HI 96814, or call (808) 586-8121. You can visit their Web site at **www.hawaii.gov/health/cpd.**

Hawaii Centers for Independent Living also has a Web site that provides useful information for the disabled at **www.assistguide.com.**

Business Travelers

Best Islands to Visit Maui and Lanai

Things to See and Do Business does happen on Maui's islands, even though they seem devoted to pleasure. Most hotels offer fitness and business centers, in-room dataports for laptop computers or high-speed Internet access, and complete understanding when it comes to 24-hour business anxiety, even on vacation. Corporate meeting groups flock to the luxury resorts of Maui and Lanai whenever the economy permits. Situated in the middle of the Pacific, the Aloha State is the only place in the world where you can talk and transact live with New York, Japan, China, and Hawaii all on the same business day.

The Maui County islands are favorites for corporate groups meeting for fun and profit, rewarding top performers, top customers, and top prospects. The extensive choice of luxury resorts and outdoor sports, imaginative team-building events, al fresco parties, and other features draw groups back year after year. The remote setting, extensive international air service in nearby Honolulu, and controlled access (nearly everyone flies in or out), plus the relatively safe and secure environment add to the appeal of the Maui for diplomats, scientists, politicians, and economic leaders, among others.

Comments Technology is up and running on Maui, where the fiber optics system linking the island to the West Coast is one of the best in the world, thanks to the presence of an air force supercomputer. This supercomputer complex at Kihei includes a program where businesses and scientific groups and other organizations can use the computer's research and data-banking powers for a fee.

Art Aficionados

Best Island to Visit Maui

Things to See and Do Maui has a thriving arts and crafts community, with galleries in Lahaina, Wailea, and Kahului as well as Hana, Paia, Upcountry, and in the northwest area of Kahakuloa. Not to mention the Maui Arts and Cultural Center and Hui Noeau Visual Arts Center. The quality, popularity, and price of Island art has increased in recent years, and works by artists from other places are also featured in several galleries.

Comments Crafts fairs and crafts booths at other fairs are a good place to see and buy local handicrafts. Fairs are held frequently on the Maui Islands, and local artisans demonstrate and display their work at resorts and hotels as well. For instance, you don't have to go to the Kingdom of Tonga to find examples of Tongan basketry, some of the best in the Pacific, because a friendly Tongan family participates in the weekly crafts "fair" at Napili Shopping Center, to the right of the market.

Hawaiian Culture Seekers

Best Islands to Visit Maui and Molokai

Things to See and Do Hawaiian cultural arts, dances, music, and crafts are in the spotlight year-round in the resorts and communities of Maui, Molokai, and Lanai. Perhaps the most emphasis on Hawaiiana comes in the fall during the annual Aloha Festivals. Colorful parades and pageantry and special performances of music and dance are among the features. The islands each have their own programs during the statewide Aloha Festivals, September through October. Resorts support Hawaiian culture, hosting traditional performances and showcasing arts and crafts. Hawaiiana is the way of life on Molokai, where the annual spring festival celebrating the birth of the hula is particularly festive. Maui Arts and Cultural Center, the island's premier showcase, presents a rich cultural array of talent from local hula halau to world-class entertainers. Check the schedule at **www.mauiarts.org.**

Comments Look for *hula halau* (school) fundraisers, church and community luau, music festivals, holiday festivities, and talk story events for a real look at the Hawaiian culture. Or just tune the radio to a Hawaiian music station and get in the groove.

Gourmets

Best Islands to Visit Maui and Lanai

Things to See and Do Superb fine dining is abundant on Maui. Hawaii Regional Cuisine chefs Bev Gannon, Roy Yamaguchi, and Peter Merriman have restaurants on the island, but they are not the only creative chefs in action on the Valley Isle. Make room on your agenda for less formal dining in a variety of indoor and outdoor locations, where you will enjoy fine, funky, and fusion versions of Japanese, Chinese, Thai, Vietnamese, Swiss, Korean, French, Italian, American, and even Nuevo Latino (Manana Garage in Kahului) cuisines. There's a gourmet luau, The Feast at Lele, where chef James McDonald applies his skill to Pacific Island dishes you're unlikely to have anywhere else. Lanai's two hotels offer first-rate restaurants, and the village of Lanai City offers some popular alternatives, notably Henry Clay's Rotisserie, with Cajun accents at the Hotel Lanai. The only fine dining on Molokai is found at the Maunaloa Room of the charming Lodge at Molokai Ranch. The setting is an open-air perch looking out over the ranchlands, the service is truly hospitable, and the fare a very tasty blend of fresh ingredients in dishes that reflect the chef's expertise and local background.

Comments Be sure to treat your palate to a Hawaii Regional Cuisine dinner. (See Part Eight, "Dining and Restaurants.")

History Lovers

Best Island to Visit Maui

Things to See and Do Maui's historic preservation plum is Lahaina. Not only have missionary-era homes, a Chinese temple, and other buildings been restored and granted National Historic Landmark status, but plans are under way to unearth and restore an ancient royal Hawaiian palace site currently buried beneath a ball field. Don't miss the Bailey House Museum in Wailuku, housing a collection of artifacts that help tell Maui's story in a restored missionary home. The Piilanihale Heiau dig near Hana will appeal to archeology buffs.

On Lanai, you can drive and hike to petroglyph rocks on a hill over Palawai Basin, or pilot a vehicle over rough roads to Kaunolu, King Kamehameha I's summer fishing camp, or Keomoku, a deserted sugar village.

Comments Buildings crumble rapidly under the assault of tropical sun, rains, bugs, and verdant jungle, so the few that have been restored and maintained are all the more precious. All you'll find of ancient Hawaiian buildings are the lava-rock foundations of homes and temples, but these are revered.

Going to Maui to Marry?

Maui has long been one of America's favorite honeymoon destinations. But increasingly, couples choose to hold wedding ceremonies on the Valley Isle as well. Sometimes, the whole entourage comes for the wedding, meaning a Maui vacation for all. Sometimes, just the lucky pair appears for the ceremony, escaping the family dynamics back home. As soon as the vows are spoken, the couple is already on their honeymoon. Weddings have become a thriving business on Maui and Lanai. Lots of planners are available to handle the details. Hotel concierges and wedding consultants can be helpful. Plenty of Internet sites offer information and services. Lovers can get married at sunset on a scenic golf course overlooking the sea, barefoot on the beach at dawn (**www.beachweddingshawaii.com** specializes in this popular option), on a knoll by a tumbling waterfall, under water amid tropical fish, in special wedding chapels and churches old and new, on sailboats, and even in midair while sky diving. Or, pick your favorite location when you get there. Your selection runs from free-of-charge at public beaches to $10,000 to rent a popular chapel, such as the Grand Wailea's.

Today, thousands of couples are wed each year on Maui. Some hotel chapels average multiple weddings daily. But in old Hawaii, marriage ceremonies were reserved only for high-ranking *alii* class. The first Christian marriage took place in 1822, two years after the arrival of the American missionaries. For a time, it was illegal for non-Christian marriages to be held in the Islands.

Lanai is another prized wedding location, famous as the place where Bill and Melinda Gates were married some years ago. Its elegant resorts, great outdoors to explore at will, private and secure atmosphere, and scenic backdrops comprise a dream setting for a bride and groom.

MUSING ABOUT MAUI: ROMANTIC SUGGESTIONS

He: Remember our first trip to Maui? When we were young, in love, and spontaneous?

She: What you are is mature, married, and in trouble. What makes you think you have to be young to be in love and spontaneous?

He: Well, you don't, but it helps.

She: So does going to Maui.

He: You're absolutely right. Even the climate is right for romance—steamy days, soft breezes, warm seas.

She: Cool waterfalls and red sunsets and the sweet perfume of flowers in the air ... and the hula, and of course, the aloha spirit. Aloha means love, doesn't it?

He: I thought it meant hello and good-bye.

She: I wonder why there aren't more romance novels set on Maui? And movies? Hollywood should love Maui because it's so gorgeous—and all the stars like to go there.

He: Forget the movies, let's go see the real thing.

She: Great idea. Our anniversary's coming up. We can start by finding a secluded beach ... there's that secret snorkeling cove near Makena.

He: Or we could fly to Lanai and laze under the palms at Hulopoe Beach, or search for fishing floats at Shipwreck Beach.

She: Let's go to Molokai. We could find that little golden beach on the East End, have a picnic and watch the moon rise over the West Maui Mountains across the water ... and swim in the moonbeams.

He: What about skinny-dipping at Kaihalulu, the red sand beach at Hana on Maui?

She: Sunburned and arrested, too? I'll just wait for you in our private hot tub at the Hotel Hana-Maui. Now, there's a romantic spot.

He: You know, if I really wanted to impress a girlfriend, I'd charter a yacht and take her out to watch the whales ... and then head for the Grand Wailea Resort Hotel and Spa. We'd stay in the biggest suite, dance half the night, and have massages by the sea.

Molokai isn't fancy, but it offers picturesque historic chapels and natural settings for couples who enjoy ecotourism activities or find comfort in the homey atmosphere.

How to Get Married in the Islands

Getting a marriage license is relatively easy in the Aloha State, since there are no residency, citizenship, or blood-test requirements. The legal age to marry is 18 years. However, with the written consent of both parents or

She: Girlfriend!?

He: It's entirely theoretical, anyway, since that suite runs about $10,000 per night. Where would you want to go to enjoy a romantic dinner?

She: Can we afford dinner at Wolfgang Puck's showplace at the Four Seasons Wailea? I can hear the waiter now: "More champagne, Mrs. Carroll?"

He: We'd have to eat plate lunches the rest of our trip.

She: I thought money was no object when it came to our anniversary? A candle-light dinner for two at Swan Court at the Hyatt Regency Maui Resort and Spa would do fine. Or the Wailea Renaissance, dinner for two on the oceanfront lawn, breeze ruffling my linen dress, stars peeking through the trees.

He: The prices aren't really coming down.

She: Okay, affordable, but it has to be oceanfront with a sunset view.

He: I think Hula Grill at Kaanapali Beach would be perfect. So beachfront you can dig your toes in the sand at the Barefoot Bar.

She: Or, we could skip the view for once and concentrate on the food—put a little spice in our life, compliments of Sansei at Kapalua.

He: Nothing like some wasabi to bring a romantic tear to your eye. And for dessert, fresh Kula strawberries dipped in Hawaiian Vintage Chocolate. Or we can just have a romantic picnic under the wild avocados at Tedeschi Vineyard. Did you know it used to be called Rose Ranch?

She: Perfect.

He: Then we can go for a mai tai or two at Hula Moons, that seaside shrine to Don Blanding at the Wailea Marriott. The next day, we could rent a Harley and ride around the lonely side of Haleakala.

He: Or, we could ride horses down into Haleakala crater and spend the night. In a rustic cabin or even in a tent, by a campfire, just the two of us in the wilderness.

guardians and a family court judge, bride and groom may be married at 15. Consent forms may be obtained from a marriage license agent. Teenagers 18 and under must bring a certified copy of their birth certificates, and people over 19 should have proof of age in the form of a military ID or driver's license. Cousins may legally marry. Formerly married participants should be prepared to provide the date and location of divorces or deaths of prior partners on their new marriage license application. The names of each partner's parents and places of birth must also be provided.

You can review the rules and download a marriage license application from the State Department of Health (**www.state.hi.us/health/records/ vr_marri**) before you arrive or pick up an application at a marriage license office after you get to the Islands.

Both bride and groom must be present to file the application for a license with a Maui County licensing agent. The fee is $50 in cash. Once approved, the license is issued then and there, good for getting married within 30 days anywhere in Hawaii.

To plan the actual event, you have a choice of more than three dozen wedding coordinators on Maui. You can find out what several have to offer on the Internet—just search for "weddings" in combination with Maui, Molokai, and Lanai.

After the wedding, your officiator will file the necessary paperwork and you will get a copy of the marriage certificate, the document that proves your legal marriage, but be advised that it may take two or three months to receive your certificate at home by mail. If you need a copy faster, or additional copies in the future, the State Health and Human Services/ Vital Records division offers specific instructions online at the above Intenet address.

You can obtain a license in Honolulu at the State Department of Health's Marriage License Office, 1250 Punchbowl Street, Honolulu, HI 96813. A free "Getting Married" pamphlet is also available from Hawaii's Marriage License Office. Write to the address above or call them at (808) 586-4544. The Marriage License Office is open Monday to Friday from 8 a.m. to 4 p.m. (closed on holidays).

Call the registrar on these Maui County islands for information on contacting a marriage agent:

- Lanai: (808) 565-6411

- Maui: (808) 984-8210

- Molokai: (808) 553-3663

You can also ask your hotel concierge or wedding coordinator to help you find the nearest agent.

The Hawaii Visitors and Convention Bureau has a list of wedding planners on all islands at **www.gohawaii.com**.

Romantic Wedding Settings

Maui

Hamoa Beach, Hotel Hana-Maui, Hana   Down on the sands, with ocean breezes teasing your veil and waves for your soundtrack: Make it Hawaiian-style wedding in Hana, with wedding lei, a traditional service, hula, and a luau to celebrate with your family and friends. Then later, steal away to your Sea Ranch Cottage with its private hot tub on the deck and contemplate your future. Contact Hotel Hana-Maui, (800) 321-4262.

Overlook at Kapalua Beach, Kapalua Bay Hotel Picture this: Watching the sun set on a grassy point overlooking the sea, Molokai in the background, beautiful beach below, pineapple fields forever up the slopes behind the gracious hotel with its lush tropical gardens and huge trees. If it's wintertime, look for the spouts of party-crashing humpback whales out in the channel. Nature's done all she can. The rest is up to you. Contact Kapalua Bay Hotel, (800) 367-8000.

Wailea Golf Club High on a hill, with a breezy view and a fiery sun setting into the sea, or outdoors on the course, or on the clubhouse deck: Scenic grandeur adds an element to your wedding preparations that could even upstage the loving couple. Contact Wailea Golf Club, (800) 888-MAUI.

Waterfall Garden, The Maui Prince Hotel, Makena Resort The peaceful waterfall pool garden in the open-air atrium, a patch of green surrounded by black lava tide pools where golden Japanese carp splash, is a popular wedding site in South Maui for local and visiting brides-to-be. Contact Maui Prince Hotel at Makena, (808) 874-1111.

Molokai

Molokai Ranch High noon or sundown, a wedding way out West on the Molokai Ranch is the way to go when both of you love horses. You can choose a hilltop, a cliffside, or a beach for the main event before moseying back to the romantic Lodge at Molokai Ranch for a reception overlooking the pastures and the sea. Contact Molokai Ranch, (808) 552-2791.

Lanai

The Conservatory at Koele Exchange vows amid thousands of exotic orchids in the glass-paned Conservatory, then dance your wedding waltz in the Lodge at Koele, a most romantic setting for weddings and honeymoons. Contact Lodge at Koele, (808) 565-7300.

A CALENDAR OF FESTIVALS AND EVENTS

Maui County loves a party, and the list of annual cultural, sports, food, and entertainment events gets longer every year, making it much easier to include a local event in your travel plans.

Following is a sampling of what's coming up in the future. Ongoing cultural activities with changing programs and dates also merit attention— for instance, programs at the Maui Arts and Cultural Center (phone (808) 242-7469) and continuing resort programs, such as The Fairmont Kea Lani Maui Food and Wine Masters series in Wailea (call (800) 659-4100) and the monthly Lanai Visiting Artists Program (phone (800) 321-4666). Maui Ocean Center has a summertime schedule of special events for children (call (808) 270-7000).

Please note: The event timing in our calendar is approximate, based on traditional and advance schedules, but future events may have different dates. We've tried to include community celebrations with the flavor and culture of the Islands. If you plan your trip around a special interest or a specific event, or just want to see what's happening during the time you want to be on Maui, Molokai, or Lanai, confirm dates with event organizers or look at the online calendar maintained by Maui Visitors Bureau, **www.visitmaui.com.**

January

Annual Festival of Hula   Lahaina Cannery Mall, Lahaina, West Maui. Here's a chance to see local hula schools perform in an annual competition. (808) 661-5304.

Mercedes Championships Professional Golf Association Tournament   Kapalua Resort Plantation Course, West Maui. A $4 million purse attracts the world's best golfers in the PGA Tour season opener, held the first weekend after New Year's. (808) 669-2440.

Molokai Makahiki Festival   Kaunakakai, Molokai. This cultural celebration of hula, Hawaiian arts and crafts, games, and food re-creates the spirit of the ancient makahiki harvest festivals. (808) 553-3673.

February

Chinese New Year and Lion Dance   Lahaina, West Maui. Dance with the lion at historic Wo Hing Temple on Front Street in Lahaina, center of the annual celebration, which includes fireworks, food booths, and arts and entertainment. (808) 667-9175.

Hula Bowl Maui Football All-Star Classic   War Memorial Stadium, Wailuku, Central Maui. College football stars excel to earn the right to play in this annual classic and enjoy a week of festivities, in early February. Ticketing starts the previous April. (808) 874-9500 for information, (888) 716-HULA for package trips.

Whale Week   Wailea-Kihei, South Maui. South Maui honors its biggest, most famous visitors, the humpback whales, in mid-February at the height of their winter migration. Events include parade, run, regatta, and annual Whale Day Celebration in Kalama Park in Kihei, with Hawaiian entertainment, gourmet food booths, a craft fair, and a carnival. If you want to watch whales for a reason, volunteer to join Pacific Whale Foundation's annual count from shore. (808) 879-8860.

March

Art Maui   Maui Arts and Cultural Center, Kahului, Central Maui. The annual juried spring show features works by Maui artists, displayed in March and April. (808) 242-7469.

Prince Kuhio Celebration   Kaunakakai, Molokai. March 26, a statewide holiday in the Islands, is the birthday of Prince Jonah Kuhio Kalanianaole, one of Hawaii's last royals and first congressman in the early 1900s. Molokai celebrates a bit earlier in March, a one-day cultural event with food, arts and crafts, and entertainment. (808) 553-3876.

April

Celebration of the Arts   Ritz-Carlton, Kapalua, Kapalua Resort, West Maui. Celebration of the people, arts, and culture of the Islands; workshops, demonstrations, and entertainment, on Easter weekend. (808) 669-6200.

Da Kine Hawaiian Pro Am Wavesailing Championship   Hookipa Beach, Central Maui. Top wave sailors compete on the Maui stop of the Professional Windsurfing Association's World Tour. (800) 827-7466.

David Malo Day   Lahainaluna High School, Lahaina, West Maui. Try attending this community luau with hula performances in late April, which celebrate Hawaii's most famous scholar, in lieu of the commercial ones down the road. (808) 662-4000.

East Maui Taro Festival   Hana Ball Park, Hana. Ancient Hawaiians believed man descended from taro (*kalo* in Hawaiian), so essential was the plant to the culture. This festival celebrates the taro tradition with exhibits, lectures, demonstrations, food booths, and entertainment, in mid-April. (808) 248-8972.

A CALENDAR OF FESTIVALS AND EVENTS *(continued)*

April (continued)

Ulupalakua Thing Maui Agriculture Trade Show and Sampling, Upcountry Maui. Tedeschi Vineyards at Ulupalakua Ranch is the picturesque setting for this colorful annual food show, with chef demos, an ultimate picnic contest, plus a floral competition, in late April. $10 entry supports Maui 4-H and agriculture students. Free parking with shuttle. (808) 878-6058.

May

Annual Wailea Open Tennis Championship Wailea Golf and Tennis Club, South Maui. Free to spectators, this tournament features players of world renown in several divisions. (808) 879-1958.

In Celebration of Canoes Front Street, Lahaina, West Maui. The mighty oceangoing canoe is the star of this week-long cultural festival featuring master canoe carvers from around the Pacific carving canoes from logs throughout the event, a parade of canoes, cultural demonstrations, and a concert. (888) 310-1117.

Kaiwi Challenge One Man Canoe Race Kaunakakai, Molokai. International relay teams paddle a tough route from Molokai to Oahu in a race of one-person outrigger canoes. (808) 969-6695.

May Day, Annual Lei Festival and Competition Marriott Wailea Beach Resort and Fairmont Kea Lani Maui, Wailea, South Maui. The Marriott Wailea sponsors a flower lei competition with Hawaiian entertainment and an appearance by the Aloha Festival Royal Court to mark the statewide floral explosion. (808) 879-1922. At the southern end of Wailea, the Fairmont Kea Lani Maui displays flower, feather, and kukui nut lei, also with Hawaiian entertainment. (808) 875-4100. A Hawaiian musical concert and hula by the Brothers Cazimero with Leinaala Heine follow May 2 at the Maui Arts and Cultural Center in Kahului (because the Caz, as they're known, perform every May 1 at the Waikiki Shell).

Molokai Ka Hula Piko Papohaku Beach Park, Molokai. Annual cultural festival celebrates the hula, which by legend was born on Molokai, with pageantry, hula performances, lectures, storytelling, Hawaiian food, games, and crafts. (808) 658-0662.

Mother's Day Orchid Show Queen Kaahumanu Center, Kahului, Central Maui. Savor this profusion of blooms in the Maui Orchid Society's juried show and sale of exotic award-winning orchids and custom corsages, sure to please Mom. (808) 877-3369.

June

Japanese Summer Festival Market Street, Wailuku, Central Maui. Here's a good excuse to spend some time on Market Street in quaint Wailuku, complete with cultural festivities, food, crafts, and displays, early June. (808) 270-7414.

King Kamehameha Day Floral Parade and Hoolaulea Front Street, Lahaina, West Maui; Molokai Civic Center, Kaunakakai, Molokai. June 11 is a statewide holiday honoring King Kamehameha I, who united the Islands into a kingdom two centuries ago. Colorful flower floats and elaborately costumed riders in parade, cultural performances, entertainment, food, and crafts festivals in Lahaina, (888) 310-1117, and Kaunakakai, (808) 567-6027.

Maui Film Festival Wailea Resort, South Maui. Cinephiles give it two thumbs up as one of the best small film festivals, for independent film premieres and location, location, location: outdoors under the stars at Wailea. The week-long mid-June event draws celebrity guests and Hollywood directors and producers (like part-time Wailea resident Clint Eastwood). One popular event at the film festival is the Wild on Water Awards, which honors extreme sports athletes and filmmakers with the Wowwy Award. Categories include: Best Big Wave Surfer, Best Surfer, Best Windsurfer, Best Kite Surfer, Waterman and Waterwoman of the Year, Video of the Year, and Living Legend (like Laird Hamilton, who crossed the English Channel in a paddle board, pioneered toe-in surfing, and first surfed the 40-foot barrels of Maui's Jaws). (808) 572-3456 or (888) 999-6330.

Upcountry Fair Eddie Tam Community Center, Makawao, Upcountry Maui. Annual country fair features a 4-H livestock auction, farmers market, games, crafts, plants and flowers, ethnic dances, entertainment, and food, in early June.

July

Fourth of July Kaanapali Beach Resort and Lahaina, West Maui. Kaanapali celebrates the Independence Day with live music and children's special activities throughout the day. After dark, look to the Lahaina skies for fireworks. (808) 661-3271.

A CALENDAR OF FESTIVALS AND EVENTS *(continued)*

July (continued)

Kapalua Wine and Food Festival   Kapalua Resort, West Maui. Wine-makers from around the world conduct formal tasting seminars and panels, then pair their wares with the creations of local and visiting chefs to create tasty informal events as well. Restaurant professionals attend the sessions at the Ritz-Carlton, Kapalua, and Kapalua Bay hotels and wine lovers will learn interesting things from the discussions as well as the tasting, four-day weekend in late June or early July. (808) 669-0244.

Lantern Boat Ceremony/Bon Dance   Lahaina Jodo Mission, West Maui. Colorful Buddhist ceremony honors ancestors by symbolically setting their spirits free to float to sea in tiny lantern boats; accompanied by a traditional O Bon celebration and dance. (808) 661-4304.

Makawao Rodeo and Annual Paniolo Parade   Makawao, Upcountry Maui. You'll never see another July Fourth parade like this one, replete with flowers trimming the cowboy hats, horses, and riders of all ages—definitely worth getting up early on Parade Day (rarely on the actual 4th) to go Upcountry, park at the Rodeo Grounds, and shuttle to town to celebrate Independence Day, downhome Maui style. Rodeo follows at Oskie Rice Arena, usually after the Fourth. (808) 572-2076.

Pineapple Festival   Lanai City, Lanai. Lanai's heritage as home of the golden fruit is celebrated with pineapple eating and cooking contests, entertainment, arts and crafts, food, and fireworks. (808) 565-7600.

Quicksilver Cup Windsurfing Contest   Kanaha Beach Park, Kahului, Central Maui. This favored windsurfing area is just beyond the airport, on Maui's north shore. The contest draws top pro and amateur men and women board sailors in July, followed by a state championship meet. (808) 877-2111.

August

Admissions Day   August 21 is Admissions Day, a statewide holiday marking Hawaii's anniversary as a state. The Aloha State was admitted to the United States on August 21, 1959.

Annual Maui International Jazz Festival   Maui Arts & Cultural Center, Kahului, Central Maui. Jazz fans, you're in luck. Dream setting, fine music by an assortment of musicians from the Islands, such as big-band sax player Gabe Baltazar and ukulele jazz viruoso Jake Shimabukuro and guest stars from the mainland. (808) 242-7469.

Maui Onion Festival   Whaler's Village Shopping Center, Kaanapali Beach Resort, West Maui. Behold the Maui onion, so sweet and good you could just eat it like an apple (kula apple is its Upcountry nickname). Or you could cook it in a dozen different ways, such as they do in this annual celebration with chef demonstrations, entertainment, and onion-recipe contest. (808) 661-4567.

Maui Writers Conference and Retreat   Marriott Wailea Beach Resort, South Maui. So you've always wanted to write that novel and you've always wanted to go to Maui. Do both in this retreat, six inspiring days, learning the art and craft of writing with top authors and agents in workshops, lectures, and panel talks, in late August. (888) 974-8373 or (808) 879-0061; **www.mauiwriters.com.**

Red Bull Cliff Diving World Championships   Kaunolu, Lanai. Ancient daredevils dove off cliffs to the sea at this historic site, a royal summer camp. Modern divers echo the feat, no less a test of skill and nerve today. (808) 565-7600.

September

Aloha Festivals   Maui, Molokai, and Lanai. A cultural celebration of the music, dance, and history of Hawaii, with observances on every island between late September and mid-October. Check on Molokai, (800) 852-7690; Lanai, (808) 852-7690; and Maui, (808) 878-1888.

Annual Na Wahine O Ke Kai   Papohaku Beach, Molokai. One of the Islands' two biggest paddling events, the wahine (women) race 40 miles from Molokai to Oahu in six-person outrigger canoes, late September. (808) 259-7112.

Hana Relays Race   Kahului to Hana. Relay teams take on Maui's famous, 52-mile crooked Hana Highway in this annual mid-September run. (808) 871-6441.

Maui Marathon   Kahului to Lahaina, Central and West Maui. This annual late September race begins at Queen Kaahumanu Center and heads 26.2 miles to Lahaina, with a prize purse of $10,000. (808) 871-6441.

A Taste of Lahaina   Lahaina Civic Center, West Maui. Annual food festival shows off the talents of local chefs, beginning with an elegant dinner and continuing with cooking demonstrations, wine tasting, entertainment, and a kids zone, in mid-September. (888) 310-1117 or (808) 667-9194.

October

Halloween in Lahaina   Lahaina, West Maui. Everyone takes to Front Street in search of fun, masked and costumed, for the so-called Mardi Gras of the Pacific. (888) 310-1117 or (808) 667-9194.

A CALENDAR OF FESTIVALS AND EVENTS *(continued)*

October *(continued)*

Maui County Fair   War Memorial Complex, Wailuku, Central Maui. Parade, arts and crafts, ethnic foods, amusements, rides, and a grand orchid show highlight this tropical fair. (808) 270-7626.

Molokai Hoe Canoe Race   Molokai. The men's version of the annual 40-mile Molokai to Waikiki championship race in six-person outrigger canoes, an October classic. (808) 259-7112.

November

Christmas House   Hui Noeau Visual Arts Center, Makawao, Upcountry. Shop for handcrafted items, made on Maui, for your holiday gift list. (808) 572-6560.

Hula O Na Keiki   Kaanapali Beach Hotel. Young hula students from throughout the Islands compete each year for solo honors in this children's dance festival at Kaanapali Beach Hotel. Awards are given for language, music, costume, adornment, and *oli* (traditional chant). (808) 661-0011.

December

Christmas Light Parade   Kaunakakai, Molokai. A light parade launches the holidays on Molokai with Santa's arrival. (808) 567-6180. Wailea Resort, South Maui. Santa doesn't find too many chimneys in Hawaii, so he tends to show up by other means, such as paddling onto Wailea Beach in an outrigger canoe in early December. You can explain that one to your *keiki* (children). (808) 879-1922.

Gala Tree-Lighting Ceremony   Ritz-Carlton, Kapalua, West Maui. Launch the holiday season early with special dinners, brunches, a life-size gingerbread house, children's hula performances, and lighting the tree. Held December 1. (808) 669-6200.

Mele Kalikimaka! Hauoli Makahiki Hou!   Merry Christmas! and Happy New Year! What better present could you want than spending the holidays on Maui, Molokai, and Lanai?

Na Mele of Maui (The Songs of Maui)   Kaanapali Resort, West Maui. Festival to perpetuate Hawaiian culture includes children's song contest and holiday arts-and-crafts fair. (808) 661-3271 or (800) 245-9229.

Part Three

Accommodations

Where to Stay

Your choices run the gamut from top of the line to bare basics among the nearly 19,000 visitor units in the Maui County islands. Most are on or near a beach, but others beckon from the cool uplands and forests.

The Maui Visitors Bureau counts 61 hotels, with 10,664 rooms, 103 vacation condos, with 7,343 units, 40 bed-and-breakfasts, and 2.3 million visitors a year to stay in them all.

Many famous hotel management and marketing firms—such as Starwood, Westin, Hyatt, Marriott, Prince, Sheraton, Ritz-Carlton, Four Seasons, Fairmont—are well represented on Maui, as well as locally owned Aston and Outrigger hotels and family-owned independents. Time-share operations are moving into established hotels such as the Maui Marriott and Westin Maui.

You know what to expect from the Four Seasons and the Ritz-Carlton, and these luxury establishments will not disappoint you. But if your budget has limits not recognized by your taste in vacation spots, we've included the hotels or condos we consider to be hidden jewels among the better known and more expensive options at each resort.

Chances are your choice of resort defines your experience as much as the individual hotels within it. So here is a recap of each of Maui County's regions and the resorts that make each distinct.

West Maui

The classic planned resort, **Kaanapali Resort,** first emerged in the 1960s and is still a pacesetter for others to follow. It is the engine that has driven Maui tourism for decades, just past **Lahaina,** the historic party town. Further north is the condo land of the **Honokowai** and **Kahana** areas, mid-rise units. They are newer and nicer for the most part than their counterparts around Kihei, although beach and swimming conditions are better in Kihei. Finally, West Maui resorts end with the little-known **Napili Bay** resort cluster and superlative **Kapalua Resort,** shared by Kapalua Bay Hotel, the Ritz-Carlton, Kapalua, and a number of luxury condos dating from the mid-1970s.

Lahaina

Lahaina, the old whaling capital, missionary outpost, and former center of the ancient royal kingdom from 1820 to 1845, is a colorful waterfront village with a lively past, echoed in its quaint preserved buildings. Lahaina has gone to some effort to recapture its history, which lends charm to a raffish collection of shops, bars, and restaurants along the shoreline, along with a few hotels and other visitor lodgings. It offers a shopping frenzy of art galleries, jewelry boutiques, souvenirs, T-shirts, and fine Hawaiian crafts, mixed in with bars, restaurants, and show-rooms along tiny, crowded streets and in small malls.

You can elect to stay at the century-old **Pioneer Inn** for a real taste of history. It was once the hangout of lusty whalers on R&R, until disap-proving missionaries prevailed. Lahaina also offers lodging in the **Lahaina Inn** and **Plantation Inn** and hotel-like condo resorts, the **Maui Islander** and the beachfront **Lahaina Shores,** as well as bed-and-breakfasts and vacation rentals.

But Lahaina is primarily a fun zone, where everybody congregates to shop, eat, drink, and meet. The Lahaina area is also filled with residential neighborhoods, an old sugar mill, and an active harbor with a large fleet of tour vessels. Sheltered by neighboring Lanai across the waters of Auau Channel, the Lahaina shoreline is protected and calm, not much of a place to swim, but a safe anchorage—which is why the Lahaina Roads has been a favorite mooring spot for centuries. Once upon a time, whal-ing ships and sailing barques anchored offshore for the winter. Nowa-days, winter cruise ships stop here in such abundance that a new kind of traffic jam has developed: Shoregoing passengers may have to wait a little while for the lighter vessels that ferry them between ships and shore. Lahaina is a place to stop and watch the sunset, memorable when the sun starts dropping like a fireball behind Lanai and the boats in Lahaina har-bor. It's a welcome moment in Lahaina, which is by nature hot and dry. Its name means "cruel sun," and its streets can swelter in the daytime. Perhaps that's why it has always been a popular nightspot. Most of West Maui's nightlife is situated here. Other amusements are also found in Lahaina, notably the best live theatrical show in the Islands, *Ulalena,* at the Maui Myth and Magic Theater, other productions, some noteworthy restaurants, and a couple of good luau, the **Old Lahaina Luau** and **The Feast at Lele.**

Kaanapali Beach Resort

Kaanapali is the prize-winning role model for an Islands master-planned resort, invented in the 1960s by a group of visionaries as a promising way to develop some excess sugar lands along the beach. Like most of its successors, the resort is a cluster of individual hotels, all thriving on the same beaches, restaurants, shops, and golf courses. You'd never guess its age. The success of the resort stemmed from the brilliance of its early marketing. No one outside Hawaii could master the name, Kaanapali. So instead, the resort was promoted in campaigns that aimed to make a household word out of a name much easier to pronounce: Maui. As in "Here today, gone to Maui" and other catchy slogans. By promoting the Island of Maui, the resort at the heart of local tourism flourished, and everyone else did, too.

Kaanapali is three miles north of Lahaina, but when the traffic is heavy, the drive can take more than half an hour. Once you get there, the resort is a pleasing parklike spread of lawns, trees, a curving boulevard, and mid-rise beachfront hotels separated by trees and gardens of lush tropical plants. After nearly 40 years and prizes for its pioneering design, Kaanapali continues to reinvent itself and remains a most popular destination at the center of Maui tourism. Its southernmost hotels are popular with corporate groups, as well as families, honeymooners, and all who like the active resort atmosphere. Kaanapali mid-rise beachfronts include **Hyatt Regency Maui Resort and Spa, Maui Marriott Resort, Kaanapali Alii** (condos), **Westin Maui,** and **The Whaler** (condos). North of Whalers Village Shopping Center, **Kaanapali Beach Hotel** and **Sheraton Maui** share the beach on the southern end of the resort, all linked by a beachfront promenade. A lava headland called **Black Rock** at the Sheraton divides the beach. The **Royal Lahaina** commands the principal setting to the north, followed by a nearby cluster of hillside condos, including the **Maui Eldorado,** and nearby the beachside condos, **Maui Kaanapali Villas, Aston Kaanapali Shores,** and **Aston Mahana at Kaanapali.**

The 600-acre resort has two golf courses, executive resort homes, restaurants with a full range of open-air, ocean-view, and oceanfront dining, and the beachfront **Whalers Village Shopping Center.** The center houses upscale European and American boutiques in addition to merchants specializing in Maui goods, art galleries, and a whale museum. Kaanapali also has beachfront tennis courts, public accessways, and beach parks, and a shuttle that connects to **Kapalua/West Maui Airport.** It's convenient to visit except for the off-putting practice of charging for parking in hotel lots that once were free. Guests are charged for parking and issued cards to get in and out during their stay. Public beach-access parking is very limited. Three entries from the highway lead to parts of Kaanapali Beach Resort, but they don't all connect. The southernmost entry leads to the lion's share of facilities, including lodging, restaurants, golf, and shopping.

Kaanapali is an ideal place to bring a family, especially one with teenagers. They can find plenty to check out, without needing a car or driving parent, but little real trouble to get into unless they have a credit card. Activities *en famille* are easy and fun, from Hawaiian crafts at the **Kaanapali Beach** and water slides at the Hyatt to cruise excursions that leave from the beach. You can jump on a resort shuttle and go off to Lahaina to play. Kaanapali succeeds because it still fills the bill, providing visitors a good value and memorable experience. It's not the newest, swankiest, or most serene resort, but it is one of the best maintained, and it far exceeds the normal American definition of vacation resort.

The smaller-craft Kapalua/West Maui Airport is a few miles further north, about ten minutes away from either Kaanapali to the south or Kapalua Resort to the north and an alternative to the commute to busy, understaffed Kahului Airport.

Kahana/Napili Beach/Kapalua Resort

Farther still to the north, the coastal route, Lower Piilani Highway, leads past a dizzying forest of midsized condo towers from Honokowai to Kahana—some of them with beachfront access but otherwise hard to distinguish, except for attractive low-profile standout the **Kahana Sunset**— along with restaurants, some shops, and beach parks mostly used by surfers. Then without fanfare, after a series of residential oceanfront neighborhoods, comes one of Maui's great little secrets—Napili, a handful of affordable small hotel and condo complexes along a golden beach and its rocky lava promontories. Comfortable, if not fancy, properties located on the beach or rocky reefs include the **Napili Beach Club,** the smaller **Mauian Hotel** on the beach next door (with studio units about half as expensive), and the smaller-still **Hale Napili,** plus a collection of condo resorts. For a change of scene, you can walk north to Kapalua's **Bay Club** fine-dining restaurant or just beyond it, to the public accessway for **Kapalua Beach.**

Kapalua Resort

The signature Cook and Norfolk Island pines marching along roads and ridges denote luxurious Kapalua Resort. Kapalua is more edge-of-the-world than end-of-the-road, situated at the lowest edge of a 23,000-acre pineapple plantation whose spiky gray-green plants carpet red-dirt hills on up to the high forests below the summit of 5,871-foot-high Puu Kukui, the tallest peak in the West Maui Mountains. To the north, an open vista stretches for miles. This is the most beautiful part of West Maui, a setting framed by wild lands and open seas, with Molokai in the backdrop.

Kapalua is home to two grand hotels—the **Kapalua Bay Hotel** and the **Ritz-Carlton, Kapalua**—plus postcard beaches, several clusters of luxury condo villas and homes, three standout golf courses, a small shopping complex, and several restaurants, including **Sansei,** one of Maui's brightest fusion-food stars. For contrast, the tidy, prim red buildings of the adjacent still-functioning plantation share this hilly setting at the base of Puu Kukui. The general store, church, and plantation managers' home have been restored for resort use. Kapalua-bound guests can fly from Honolulu to West Maui Airport in smaller aircraft and avoid the congestion of Kahului. Your hotel will send a shuttle to meet you at the airport. Shuttles also go to Lahaina, ten miles away. At Kapalua, especially at the Ritz and northward beyond the sheltering influence of Molokai across the water, the weather is more windward, meaning gustier trades, cooler temperatures, and more passing showers than at the resorts to the south.

Beyond Kapalua, development stops and the road leads along Maui's great northwest coast. Still undiscovered by most visitors, this is some of the island's finest territory, with huge ranches spreading from mountains to sea; popular surfing beaches and sheltered snorkeling bays; coastal lookouts like **Nakalele Point,** where you might see the great pod of spinner dolphins that pirouette and play in these waters; and the tiny settlement at **Kahakuloa Head,** the 636-foot-high coastal rock landmark where you'll find a gallery of made-on-Maui works. The road is not for the fast-paced or faint-hearted, with stretches of crooked one-lane track clinging to the coastal slopes and few pullouts for passing, but it is interspersed with better pavement and engineering at some places. Eventually, the coastal ranches give way to mini-estate subdivisions and residential communities around Wailuku and Kahului.

Our Choices in West Maui

Best on the beach at any price Kapalua Bay Hotel has the best blend of old-fashioned grace and elegant new appointments, but most important, the best beach and waterfront location.

Best value on the beach Kaanapali Beach Hotel, known for its true Hawaiian spirit, enjoys lush gardens and a less noisy setting on the best part of the beach.

Best condo on the beach Kaanapali Alii, situated in a garden setting front and center on Kaanapali Beach, has luxury units in which families enjoy the same great views with more room and privacy than at surrounding hotels.

Best condo value on the beach Kahana Sunset, on a secluded cove beach surrounded by neighborhoods, is charming in setting and architecture; its 79 units are stepped down a hillside with lower units on the sand.

Best-kept secret The 44-unit Mauian Hotel on Napili Beach, Maui's Hawaiian family–owned and operated hotel, is intimate and low key, right on the sand, and so popular with return guests that some families rent several units at a time.

Central Maui

The Wailuku/Kahului/Paia stretch of the **North Shore** in Central Maui isn't a resort at all, but there are a few interesting places to stay for a different kind of Maui experience, and plenty of outdoor adventures at your fingertips. Budget beachfront hotels on the Kahului waterfront are good for tight airplane connections and thrifty business stays. On the other end of Maui's central valley, nearly a dozen condo resorts are clustered on the beach and reef at **Maalaea,** near the Maui Ocean Center and harbor area, with restaurants and cruises galore. Everybody who drives from Kahului to the southwestern shore sees them, but most drive on, much further, to seek a more crowded and expensive version of much the same thing. Those who stop tend to stay a while; ask about the monthly rates. Keep in mind that Maui's famous winds funnel through the Central Valley most afternoons and may sandblast your exterior on that five-mile beach.

Kahului/Wailuku

Departing Kahului Airport, you run a gauntlet of familiar commercial landmarks (Costco, Wal-Mart, Barnes & Noble). But there is a Maui, if you persist. Wander farther into Kahului and you'll find more interesting shops around the harbor, where the interisland cruise ship makes a port call weekly. Across the boulevard, look for the trendy **Manana Garage** restaurant (the best reason to visit Kahului). Close at hand are the **Queen Kaahumanu Mall,** with more than 100 shops (see Shopping, page 327), a number of smaller malls, and the neighborhoods of Kahului, a waterfront town with a busy port and three small, clean, affordable bayfront hotels frequented by budget travelers. They are the **Maui Beach, Maui Palms,** and **Maui Seaside,** and while you won't want to spend your vacation there, they are close to the airport and handy for early-morning and late-night departures.

The famous windsurfing beach areas, **Kanaha and Hookipa Beaches,** are beyond the airport, on the North Shore road toward Hana.

In the opposite direction, up beyond Kahului, is the county seat of **Wailuku,** historic and quaint, and the scenic rain forest at **Iao Valley State Park.** *Akamai* (in-the-know) travelers check into **The Old Wailuku Inn at Ulupono,** a 1920s-vintage former plantation manager's house that offers ten private rooms, well appointed with plush towels, clawfoot tubs, Aveda room amenities, and a breakfast to rival any five-star hotel.

Maalaea

Maalaea, on the resort coast at the other, southwest, end of Maui's central valley, is home to the island's best pay attraction, the **Maui Ocean Center,** and principal harbor of the snorkel-sailing, whale-watching, reef-cruising fleet. Migrating Pacific humpback whales spout and breach and spy-hop everywhere around Hawaii January through April, but nowhere more abundantly than in Maui's **Maalaea Bay,** once a whale-hunting ground and now a national marine sanctuary. Clusters of condos rise up along the shore of Maalaea and across the isthmus, at **Sugar Beach,** where families enjoy an affordable waterfront location, just before the congestion of Kihei. Swimming is better at Kihei beaches, but the waters here are popular for surfing.

Our Choices in Central Maui

Best place to stay at any price   Old Wailuku Inn is far from a beach but handy to Iao Valley, the airport and North Shore, the road to Hana and Upcountry, and old Wailuku. A true inn, its rooms are charming and well appointed, and breakfast is delicious, but it's the hospitality of Janice and Thomas Fairbanks that puts it at the top of our list.

Best value on the beach   Maui Beach Hotel on Kahului Bay.

Best condo on the beach   Units at the Kanai A Nalu, designed so that all face the sea, or at Hono Kai are hard to beat for price and proximity to the beach, both among several picks at Maalaea Bay Village.

Best condo value on the beach   Punahoa Condos have beachfront *lanai* (patios) and views of Lanai, Kahoolawe, and Molokini. They are located close to shops and restaurants on a quiet, beachfront street near Kihei. One and two bedroom units start at $85. Call (808) 879-2720.

Best-kept secret   Mama's Fish House, near Paia's Hookipa Beach on the windy North Shore, has built Mama's Beachfront Cottages, six units in a small space next to the restaurant, under coco palms looking out to a sandy beach. The neighbors are pretty close by—restaurant on one side, residences on the other, highway behind—but attractive appointments and a discount at the pricy fish house make this appealing.

South Maui

Development in South Maui runs from **Kihei** in the north, south to La Perouse Bay, where the road terminates. In the busy beach town Kihei, condo-dwelling vacationers and local residents share shopping, restaurants and bars, golden beaches, good swimming, and rolling surf.

Below Kihei, **Wailea Resort** is emerging as the premier Maui resort. Developed mostly during the 1980s, this luxurious spread of green contains five hotels and several condo complexes of varying settings. Wailea enjoys easy access at the end of a bypass highway, reliably good weather, the new Shops at Wailea (the largest, newest, and fanciest of the resort shopping areas), three notable golf courses, a tennis complex, homes, and other condo choices for varying budget levels.

Just down Wailea Alanui Drive is **Makena Resort,** home of the Maui Prince Hotel, two condo resorts, and two golf courses. The resort, located near a former ranching village, has a laid-back air, perhaps owing to the fact that road ends nearby and few visitors, save guests, pass through.

Kihei

If you're after sun on a budget, go straight to Kihei. It is a sprawling beachside shopping, dining, and entertainment strip, lined with some 50 vacation condo complexes—first popular in the 1960s with visiting Canadian snowbirds who would bunk in for four months at a time to escape winter—and new residential neighborhoods. A newer hotel, the **Maui Coast Hotel,** is located across the street from **Kamaole Beach Park I** and an older (and unfortunately neglected) one, the **Maui Lu,** at the western end of Kihei. Many of the condos are pretty basic shelter, but **Hale Kamaole** is recommended, especially for its location across from **Kamaole Beach Park III,** as well as the **Aston at the Maui Banyan, Kihei Kai Nani,** and the **Mana Kai Maui,** all of which enjoy good beach access.

Kihei suffers the ill effects of strip zoning and sometimes seems like one long traffic tie-up, easily avoided now that a highway bypasses the whole place. But Kihei has beautiful swimming/surfing beaches with public parks, not to mention good restaurants, some of them located on the beach, and fun bars. It is the nightlife district for South Maui. In the daytime, its surfing breaks call to a burgeoning number of surfing-school students, so that visiting kids can learn to be surfa' guys and surfa' girls and get out there with the locals. Outrigger canoe clubs practice in Kihei waters, and humpback whales winter there. Just like the Canadians who first put affordable Kihei condos on the map, the whales leave the cold north each year and head for Maui waters to spend several months lolling about and cavorting in the tranquil seas.

Kihei is also the home of many people who work in the neighboring resorts, as well as the **Air Force Super Computer** technology complex nearby, which gives it an air of reality as opposed to the too-good-to-be-true refined resort atmosphere of neighboring Wailea. The town fronts a ten-mile coast indented by black lava reefs that frame some excellent pocket beaches and broad beach parks alike. Most popular is **Kamaole Beach III,** in the heart of Kihei, with a tree-shaded grass picnic area and park, views of Lanai and Kahoolawe, and free parking. Canadians and Europeans still come to Kihei to stay as long as they can. Families like the freedom and extra space of condo units by the beach. We have California friends who have loved Kihei for many of their nearly 90 years of age and won't stay anywhere else. Judging by the crowded bustle of Kihei, in good tourism times or bad, they are not alone.

Wailea

While verdant **Wailea Resort** used to be "the other" resort on Maui, other than Kaanapali that is, it now claims status as the top destination for the luxury resort crowd. Created mostly since the 1980s, this is a groomed green oasis on the sunny coast, where lavish hotels and condos, and public accessways, share five desirable beaches defined by lava headlands. The mid-rise structures are largely hidden by landscaping and their beachcliff setting, on the last leg of Haleakala's southern slope before it runs into the sea. Other features are a new high-end boutique shopping center with galleries, shops, and restaurants, a competition tennis stadium complex, and three velvety golf courses, plus off-beach condo complexes and executive homes. When money's no object, or the boss is paying, or you're pining for a spectacular golf fix, Wailea is the place to be.

A 1.5-mile coastal walking and jogging trail along the waterfront affords stunning views of Kahoolawe, Molokini, and Lanai and occasionally whales, outrigger canoe races, and other marine travelers. The trail's southern end features thriving native-plant gardens and an ancient village ruins. On its north end, the two original hotels, the **Renaissance Wailea Beach** (formerly Stouffers) and **Marriott Wailea Beach Resort** (formerly the Inter-Continental), lead the beachfront lineup, followed by **Grand Wailea Resort Hotel and Spa, Four Seasons Maui Resort,** and, finally, the Arabian fantasy–styled **Fairmont Kea Lani Maui** at the trail's southern terminus. Along the route are plushy waterfront condo homes and resorts. The most established, the Marriott and Wailea Renaissance hotels, have great charm and a relaxed atmosphere, plus the oceanfront units are closest to the beach. The same is true of the oldest condos, the **Ekahi** units. Behind the Marriott, the **Shops at Wailea,** with architecture every bit as grand as the hotels, is a collection of retail shops that range from esoteric European boutiques to the ubiquitous **Lapperts Ice Cream,** plus galleries with exceptional wares and something Wailea used to lack, a choice of good restaurants.

Grand Wailea features a multimillion-dollar art collection, much of it commissioned for the hotel, a renowned spa, a busy wedding chapel, and an elaborate water complex with miniature river canyons, slides, dives, waterfall caves, and a water-powered elevator so swimmers (and they're not just kids) don't have to walk back up to the top to start over. Despite the theme-park appointments, Grand Wailea has earned AAA five-diamond distinctions, just like the elegant neighbor with which it shares Wailea's best beach, the Four Seasons. Beyond Four Seasons, the luxury condos of **Wailea Point** occupy the top of an ocean cliff. Though not exactly condos, Fairmont Kea Lani Maui is all suites and villas fronting a fine beach. **Diamond Resort** is an all-suites resort, too, higher up the slope, set apart from the others on the southern end of the resort.

In some ways, Wailea perfects the master-planned resort trend that Kaanapali started in the 1960s. Its beaches are better, its location closer to Kahului airport, its setting less dominated by cars, and it is more than twice as large, at 1,500 acres. Wailea properties are also linked by a resort shuttle, which also serves to bring customers to the new The Shops at Wailea from neighboring Makena.

Makena

Want more solitude and less bustle? That would be serene **Makena Resort** at Maui's southern end. On its 1,800 mostly natural acres, the **Maui Prince Hotel** rises among the scrubby kiawe and other greenery like a mirage. It is ringed by splendid, underpopulated wild beaches and two excellent golf courses. South Maui is punctuated by Puuolai, a cinder-cone peninsula that juts into the sea just beyond the Prince. Some residential development is occurring at the border between Wailea and Makena, but that's far from sight of the hotel.

Makena is actually an old village where cattle from the upland Ulupalakua Ranch, directly above, were once herded down the mountain and into the water to swim for the ships that would take them to market. They were hoisted aboard in giant slings. Cowboys flapped their hats to ward off sharks. The tiny community today has a picturesque Hawaiian-language church, **Keawalai Congregational,** by the sea.

The road ends where Haleakala's last eruption spilled lava down to the sea south of Makena, more than 200 years ago. Horseback riding, a sporting-clay shooting range, and hiking add to Makena's appeal. But it is isolated from the rest of the island, making dinner out an expedition. Fortunately the food in the hotel is good.

Our Choices in South Maui

Best on the beach at any price Four Seasons Resort Maui is classy from top to bottom without being ostentatious, quiet without being deadly. Rooms, food, setting, and service are all great.

Best value on the beach Marriott Wailea Beach Resort is less expensive than most at Wailea, with a prime location that is part beach, part headland, all shady, and parklike in the gracious old Hawaiian way—and in walking distance of The Shops at Wailea restaurants and stores.

Best beachfront condos Wailea Elua beachfront units have a prime spot between the Renaissance and Marriott.

Best condo value Grand Champions Golf and Tennis Villas—Wailea amenities on one side of you, Kihei amusements on the other, the beach a short walk downhill.

Best-kept secret Diamond Resort sits high on the hillside, with capacious units and large open-air onsen with sweeping views, plus authentic Japanese food and style.

Upcountry Maui and Hana

From Kahului, a highway runs up the base of Haleakala and becomes a country road as it winds through the cool, pastoral community of **Kula,** where, at 3,000 feet, exotic protea, roses, and carnations grow in the fields and the blue jacaranda trees bloom in late spring. Visitors can stay at **Kula Lodge** or in a variety of bed-and-breakfast accommodations up here on the shoulder of the mountain. Kula is a stop on the way up to **Haleakala National Park.** You can keep on going to reach the summit or remain closer to Kula. It's a place to escape from the tropical heat of the shoreline, featuring botanical gardens, flower farms, and a winery at Ulupalakua Ranch, **Tedeschi Vineyards.** Pineapple wine and other vintages, including sparkling wines, are available to sample and buy at the tasting room. A cool grassy setting under wild avocado trees is fine for picnics. But then you must turn around and retrace your route, since the road doesn't connect to the Wailea-Kihei shoreline below.

Upcountry roads do come down to the sea on the opposite, North Shore end. Descending Haleakala, you pass **Makawao,** a ranching and rodeo town with colorful Western-style storefronts; the working plantation village of **Haliimaile,** site of one of Maui's best Hawaii regional-cuisine restaurants, the **Haliimaile General Store; Haiku,** a rural area with bed-and-breakfast lodging mostly used by windsurfers; and **Paia,** a former plantation town now transformed into a busy, picturesque tourist shopping village.

If someone tries to tell you of Hana that getting there is half the fun, don't believe it. The arduous nature of the 52-mile switchback road to Hana along Maui's northeastern shore is somewhat overstated, now that it's been properly paved in many areas. However, being in Hana is more than worth the drive that serves to keep the world somewhat at bay, in terms of unabashed old Hawaii romance. The **Hotel Hana-Maui,** long neglected, has undergone a restoration to its former glory, with new amenities still under construction, including a planned spa. Besides the hotel, which is expensive, and its restaurant, lodging is limited to a few rooms and condos and state park camping cabins.

Our Choices in Upcountry Maui and Hana

Best on the beach at any price The Hotel Hana-Maui's ocean-facing Sea Ranch Cottage has a private hot tub on the deck.

Best value on the beach Four miles out of Hana, 120-acre Waianapanapa State Park offers 12 cabins plus tent-camping sites. Where else can you overnight at one of Hawaii's most picturesque black-sand beaches for free (in tents) or in cabins that sleep six, for a mere $45 a night? But bring insect repellent and book six months ahead in writing. For details see National and State Parks on page 245.

Best condo on the beach Hamoa Bay Bungalow has a Balinese-style cottage for two (and a house for up to four), walking distance from black-and-white-sand Hamoa Beach.

Best condo value on the beach Not exactly on the beach, but beside a lava rock stream that runs to the sea, Hana Kai Maui Resort, with 18 condos, is the closest and only beach condo in Hana. Clean, modern studios and one-bedroom units that sleep four range from $125 to $195 per night with daily maid service. Write 1433 Uakea Road, P.O. Box 38, Hana, HI 96713; call (800) 346-277 or (808) 248-8426; or visit **www. hanakaimaui.com.**

Best-kept secret No secret to seasoned visitors, Aloha Cottages, seldom seen in guidebooks and never advertised except by word of mouth, represent travelers' best bargain in Hana. Clean, comfortable, and close to the beach and stores, they start at $45 per night. Write to Box 205, Hana, HI 96713; or call (808) 248-8420.

Molokai

The least developed of Hawaii's main islands, Molokai can be described by what it doesn't have: traffic lights, shopping malls, action. The lifestyle is slow and unpretentious, and people pride themselves on being a more traditional Hawaiian community than most in the Islands today. Restaurants and bars and even rental cars are few and funky on Molokai, and the airport is as down-home and unassuming as the island itself.

Head east from the airport on Kamehameha V Highway and you'll find the lush, green, and tropical **East End,** with ancient fishponds along a palm-lined coast. Head in the other direction and you'll encounter the **West End,** arid and spiked with cactus. Condo resorts, bed-and-breakfasts, and vacation beach houses are available in either direction.

Most of the available rooms are aging, if well-kept, condos, except for a jewel of a small new upland lodge at **Maunaloa,** the West End headquarters of 54,000-acre Molokai Ranch. The ranch is the island's dominant lodging provider, but offers a range of accommodations. Molokai Ranch's distinctive and recently built tourism facilities include the stylish 22-room **Molokai Ranch,** done in what might be called upscale *paniolo* (cowboy) decor recalling ranch history. You can also opt to stay at **Kaupoa Beach Camp,** a fancy-camping compound. The ranch offers a full complement of outdoor activities, not the least of which are trail riding, dude rodeo riding, and other horseback activities that are available to off-ranch guests, too.

The ranch has rebuilt **Maunaloa,** a small plantation town complete with movies, shops, eateries (including the island's first genuine fast-food joint, a Kentucky Fried Chicken outlet), and new plantation-style homes. The ranch, with 6,000 head of cattle, encompasses one-third of Molokai, mostly wide-open spaces. You're sure to get a good night's sleep overlooking quiet pastures and the sea. Molokai Ranch is just what the island needs to attract ecotravelers seeking a different kind of Hawaii experience. Just don't expect much nightlife, although there are a couple of town bars.

Smaller operations offer condo and bed-and-breakfast stays. **Kaluakoi Resort,** Molokai's only resort area and once a favorite weekender for Honolulu residents, who like its seaside golf course and meticulously maintained grounds despite unappealing hotel rooms, has been closed for an extended shutdown, but efforts are under way to resurrect it.

Our Choices on Molokai

Best on the beach at any price The upland Lodge at Molokai Ranch recalls the island's ranching heyday with beautifully decorated rooms and lobby. The Beach Village at Molokai Ranch is an ecotourism village of cool canvas tents down by remote Kaupoa Beach and is special, too, particularly for a family. A full agenda of outdoor activities is included in the price.

Best value on the beach Two cottages, Puunana and Pauwalu, sit like sisters on a private gold-sand beach on Molokai's East End, just past mile marker 18 on Kamehameha V Highway. If you are lucky enough to reserve one of Kip and Leslie Dunbar's sweet little two-bedroom, plantation-style cottages, you'll be sitting pretty. If Pauwalu cottage were any closer to the beach, it would be in the water. Rates average $140 per night, with a three-night minimum. Call (800) 673-0520 or (808) 558-8153; or visit **www.molokai-beachfront-cottages.com.**

Best condo on the beach Paniolo Hale is on Molokai's west end next to defunct Kaluakoi Resort; when the golf course that surrounds the place reopens, these tastefully designed units will appeal to players. The beach is a short walk across a green.

Best condo value on the beach Hands down, Paniolo Hale offers Molokai's best condo value on the beach, too, although the three-mile gold-sand beach is a short walk away (which is okay since the surf's too rough to swim and you may just want to catch the rays on your lanai).

Best-kept secret On Molokai's far East End, a good hour's drive from Kaunakakai, at mile marker 25, on 14,000-acre Puu O Hoku Ranch, there's a lone cottage under the stars with a view of the Pacific that will stay in your mind long after you've returned to reality. This two-bedroom, two-bath cottage with a full kitchen goes for $750 a week—and now it's no longer a secret, but what good's a secret if it's kept secret? For more information, write to P.O. Box 1889, Molokai, HI 96748; call (808) 558-8109; or visit **www.puuohoku.com/cottage.**

Lanai

Lodging on Lanai is your choice of two fabulous luxury hotels, a charming old lodge and a few rentals. Up in the cool highlands surrounded by Norfolk Island pines, quaint plantation cottages are still clustered around the ambitiously named plantation village of **Lanai City,** along with the rustic ten-room **Hotel Lanai,** built in the 1920s for plantation guests. Nearby, the elegant 100-room **Lodge at Koele** commands a cool Upcountry view, while eight miles below on the coast, the lavish, Mediterranean-style 250-room **Manele Bay Hotel** nestles on a sunny coastal hillside, with a conference center for small high-spending groups. The Lodge sits on a high hill at the head of a pine-lined lane and looks so important that you think a royal retainer might greet you instead of a hostess with a flower lei. It is cool at night here, which makes it a favorite with weekending Honolulu residents, who love to dress up in sweaters and sit by a roaring fire. Downhill, beside the only safe swimming beach at **Hulopoe Bay,** Manele Bay Hotel simmers around its pool, a lobby full of European and Asian art, and tropical gardens lining a man-made stream.

At Lanai's resorts, amenities include stables, tennis courts, and croquet lawns, fine dining that features dishes made with fresh produce and venison from Lanai, and a special brand of hospitality. These are not snooty resorts but gracious places where the staff, from boss to busboy, actually seems to care whether everything is right for you.

Golfers can play either of the island's two magnificent 18-hole courses: the ocean-side **Challenge at Manele** or the upland **Experience at Koele,** possibly the most beautiful course anywhere. Yet while visitors are signing up for substantial fees, local golfers choose the little nine-hole upland course where fees are paid on the honor system, a few bucks in a tin can.

Visitors can explore at will the private wilderness prized by hunters and fishermen, divers and sailors. Four-wheel-drives and other rental vehicles are available through the hotels and village gas station. But if you don't want to drive at all, resort shuttles link the resorts, airport, village, and best beach. Honeymooners, this is your island, so long as you can forgo boogie bars. Nightlife is limited to whatever amusements the hotels have lined up in terms of local music and hula and lectures by visiting luminaries.

Our Choices on Lanai

Best on the beach at any price Simple. If you care about being next to the sea, pick Manele. If you are intrigued by the thought of cool Upcountry in tropical Hawaii, pick Koele. Or stay at both.

Best value The Hotel Lanai above Lanai City, historic and charming, with good food. You can take the resort shuttle to the beach.

Best condo on the beach Sorry, no condos on the beach on Lanai.

Best-kept secret Wedding? Reunion? Golf shoot-out? Lanai Hui's Captains Retreat, a contemporary 3,000-foot cedar house in the uplands near Lanai City, may fit the bill. The vacation rental that sleeps ten runs $450 per day for a two-day minimum, or $2,500 per week. Call (888) 565-6106 or visit **www.lanairental.com.**

Great Places to Stay That Suit Your Interests

The following are some other recommendations to consider, based on what you most want from a Maui vacation.

Hopelessly Romantic

Hotel Hana-Maui, Maui In misty green, tropical Hana, this idyllic inn by the sea offers private cottages with bubbly hot tubs on the deck, gardened outdoor baths, and thick towels to get dry again. Your tropical fantasies come to life in this 66-room, 67-acre, old-Hawaii setting. Explore the neighborhood on foot or horseback—this area is all part of a large ranch. Call (800) 321-HANA, or visit **www.hotelhanamaui.com.**

Manele Bay Hotel or Lodge at Koele, Lanai You don't have to indulge in a luxury blowout to prove your love, but then again, why not? This setting is dedicated to your privacy and enjoyment—as hassle-free as possible, classy but not intimidating. Your worst dilemma is choosing the mountains (Koele), where it's cool enough to snuggle, or the sea (Manele), where the warm sun bakes away inhibition. But you can go to both in the same trip. Call (800) 321-4666, or visit **www.lanairesorts.com.**

Ritz-Carlton Kapalua, Maui Hawaii's only Ritz commands the last outpost of resort life in West Maui, which ensures it unmatched views up the wild northwest coast and out to sea. Its caring management and celebrations of Hawaiian culture and art add to its romantic setting, on an old pineapple plantation at the foot of the West Maui Mountains. You can get married in the historic little church on the grounds. An oasis of calm with old-fashioned Hawaiian hospitality: At this Ritz, it's your pleasure. Call (800) 262-8448, or visit **www.ritzcarlton.com.**

Great for Families

Fairmont Kea Lani Maui, Wailea, South Maui With shockingly white towers and turrets, like something out of *Arabian Nights,* the luxury Fairmont Kea Lani Maui hotel delivers far more than fantasy. All the rooms are well-equipped suites with stereos and kitchens, except for the townhouse-style private villas with more bedrooms and private plunge pools. Kealani has a great beach and great restaurants. Kids are so welcome that they get their own pool; there's also one for adults only. Find the hotel at the south end of Wailea Resort, in walking distance on the coastal trail to neighboring shops and restaurants. Call (800) 659-4100, or visit **www.kealani.com.**

Great Onsen Spa, Diamond Resort, Wailea Resort, South Maui Diamond Resort, 15 acres on a hill above Wailea's Blue Golf Course, is an unexpected jewel: 72 terraced suites and a full-on Japanese onsen, with separate men's and women's large, open-air soaking pools that have extraordinary panoramic views of islands and ocean to contemplate while you soak, plus the most unusual spa treatments this side of Beppu. The resort began life as a private Japanese club, but now has gone public and welcomes Western trade. If you appreciate Japanese design, food, and onsen, you'll like this. The rooms are Western style, not tatami, but the sushi bar is authentic. Call (800) 800-0720 or (808) 874-0500, or visit **www.diamondresort.com.**

Westin Maui at Kaanapali Beach Resort, West Maui Th
airy beachfront hotel looks like a Disney fantasy—tropical jungle ......age,
waterfalls, and parrots everywhere inside the open atrium, and Kaanapali
Beach outside. Kids love the aquatic playground with 128-foot slide, the
easy-breezy feeling, and year-round summer camp–like fun. Big kids like
it, too. Call (800) 937-8461 or visit **www.westinmaui.com.**

Great Historic Traditions

Hotel Lanai, Lanai City Built in 1923 for the pleasure of James Dole's
guests, this little (ten rooms and a cottage) lodge was the only place to
stay on Lanai, the world's biggest pineapple plantation, until everything
changed in 1990. The plantation shut down, and two world-class hotels
started up, but the little lodge stayed pretty much intact. Run now by a
chef, Henry Clay Richardson, the inn is also famous for Henry Clay's
Rotisserie restaurant, which boasts a Cajun flair. It's cool up here under
the tall pines, so the country quilts come in handy. Call (808) 565-7211,
or visit **www.hotellanai.com.**

Pioneer Inn, Lahaina, Maui Overlooking Lahaina Harbor, the Pioneer
Inn turned 100 years old in 2001, holding on after a $5 million facelift.
This once-rowdy sailor's haunt is now a charming relic fit for all who
"collect" old hotels and prefer tradition over trend. Call (800) 457-5457.

The first time we checked into the Pioneer Inn in the 1970s, a second-
story room overlooking Lahaina Harbor went for $20 and included a can
of Raid. The screen door was rusty, the ceiling fan was broken, and the
bed sagged almost to the floor. The lone towel was threadbare, swarms
of termites took wing after dark, and downstairs in the smoky bar the
band played all night long, robbing guests of sleep. None of that mattered; what mattered is that the pile of old green wood still stood—and
still stands today, the oldest inn on Maui, a century-old sole survivor of
an era past.

Great Bargain

The Mauian Hotel at Napili Bay, Maui Owned and run by a Hawaiian family, this small 44-unit beachfront complex has to be the deal of
them all on Maui. It has a perfect position on Napili Bay, a scenic and
swimmable cove with Molokai on the horizon, and its studios cost $100
a night less than their neighbors and substantially less than nearby luxury
hotels that would have benefited from this prime location. The ambience
is low-key, with meticulously kept grounds and comfortable, not fancy,
interiors that include kitchenettes. Call (800) 367-5034 or (808) 669-
6205 or visit **www.mauian.com.**

Great Escape

Huelo Point Flower Farm   Perched on a spectacular, secluded, 300-foot seacliff near a waterfall stream, yet only about 20 minutes driving time beyond Paia on the Hana road, this vacation rental estate puts you in a Maui setting beyond your most romantic dreams. Four architecturally stunning contemporary homes are available in a lush tropical garden setting, accommodating up to 18 people altogether. Six people can share the artfully designed main house; there is also a studio cottage with three walls of glass so as not to miss a view, a carriage-house apartment with glass walls facing the sea that sleeps four, and a two-bedroom guest house with soaring (18-foot ceiling) interiors. A group can rent the whole two-acre estate. The ocean views are incredible. Amenities include a pool and three hot tubs, not to mention a garden where guests can help themselves to vegetables, fruit, and flowers. The homes are completely equipped. It's enough to make you want to thank the hosts for sharing such a splendid retreat. Call (808) 572-1850, or visit **www.maui flowerfarm.com.**

Getting a Good Deal on a Room

Now that you've had a preview of some of Hawaii's great places to stay, here's how to get the best deal.

- Book early.

- Go in spring and fall months (September through November, or April through early June).

- Educate yourself on what you want and where and when you want it, before you go to a travel agent. They may have suggestions that alter your plan, but they'll surely do a better job for you if you narrow the search for them. More agents are charging customers a fee for their services nowadays, as well as collecting a percentage of the booking as their commission. In Hawaii, hotel and condo commissions are usually 10 percent. Ask your agent's fee policies in advance.

- Ask a travel agent to research package rates and other specials that combine your lodging with sports and spa facilities, car rentals, and other features. They have access to information you won't find as a consumer.

- Call the hotel to see what rate you can negotiate. Ask for the best rate they can offer. Check the Internet, too—sometimes rates and fares are cheaper if you book online.

- Pursue discounts for corporate travel, seniors, kids staying in your room, military, travel club, and other special-status travel. And see what frequent flyer mileage you may gain from your hotel stay.

Several factors determine a hotel's room rate: demand, location, season, availability, view, grade of room, and proximity to beach, shopping centers, and entertainment. Hawaii room rates are highest from late December through late March, when everyone wants to escape winter. Average hotel room rate then is $146–$151. In the spring and fall, average room rates fall to $130–$144.

Hawaii's visitor industry provides a quarter of the state's gross state product, a quarter of the state's tax revenue, and one-third of the jobs. Hawaii's dependency on tourism is unlikely to improve. That means competitive rates and good deals for you.

Where the Deals Are

Newspaper travel sections   Check the travel sections of major U.S. newspapers for good room deals and airfare, hotel, or condo, and car combinations.

Surf the Internet   If the search is part of your journey, surf the Internet. You can preview islands, beaches, golf courses, and hotels, condos, and vacation rentals. The Internet and this guidebook, which highlights Web sites, will make your search easy.

Money-saving suggestions for booking a room   Many hotels and condos offer their own periodic package deals with value-added amenities like a free rental car, food-and-beverage credits, rounds of golf, spa treatments, extra-special treatment for honeymooners (chocolates and champagne) and for families, and free or cheaper second rooms when you book the first room. Some offer a free extra night if you book a room for a certain number of nights (usually four to seven). Off-beach properties are cheaper, so are mountain- or garden-view rooms. Ask if kids can stay in your room free.

Travel packages   Travel packages save money, provide value, and eliminate the search for separate deals for airlines, rooms, and car rentals. In recent years, they have become very flexible and include a wide range of rates and places to stay. Be a good shopper by knowing what your cost would be for each component of the package, and be sure the package total is cheaper and, hopefully, includes extras.

These packages have a single inclusive rate, but they differ from tour travel. On a tour, you are escorted by a guide who handles everything on the trip for you. Travel packages are for independent travelers.

If you make your own reservation   If you hunt your own bargains, call the hotel instead of the toll-free number. The toll-free clerk may be in Iowa, unaware of special local rates. The quoted, or "rack," room rates—the ones printed once a year for brochures in a lobby rack—are nothing if not flexible. Virtually no one pays the full rack rate, except perhaps at Christmas and other peak travel times. Don't be shy about inquiring about lower rates, especially during the low season when your bargaining position is improved. Ask for the lowest and best rates available to you. Hotels would rather fill rooms at discounted prices than leave them empty.

Corporate rates   Many hotels provide corporate rates (up to 20 percent off regular rack rates). Ask your hotel about them. Some hotels require a written request on company letterhead, while others will guarantee the rate regardless of your work status.

Travel clubs   Travel clubs offer discounts of up to half off participating hotels' rack rates, but with restrictions. They generally apply on a space-available basis and are not available in blackout periods. Some may apply only on certain days of the week. Not all hotels offer a true 50 percent discount. Some base their discount on an exaggerated base rate.

Most travel clubs or half-price programs charge an annual fee, up to $125. When you join, you receive a membership card and directory of participating hotels. These travel-club programs offer lodging in Hawaii:

Encore   (800) 638-0930

Entertainment Publications   (800) 285-5525

International Travel Card   (800) 342-0558

Quest   (800) 638-9819

Travel Advisory

- Be wary of deals that are too good to be true.

- Don't be pressured into accepting a deal on the spot. A good offer today should be a good offer tomorrow. Do not send money by messenger or overnight mail. Question any requests for you to send money immediately. Do not provide your credit card number or bank information over the phone unless you know the company.

- Ask questions. Find out what's covered in the total cost. Ask if there are additional charges. Ask about cancellation policies and refunds.

- Get all the information in writing before you agree to purchase a travel package, and read it .

Tour wholesalers   Tour wholesalers annually purchase blocks of hotel rooms at a low, negotiated rate. They resell rooms during the coming year to travel agents and the public. Wholesalers sometimes offer rooms at bargain prices to avoid returning unsold rooms to the hotel. They prefer that you reserve packages through your travel agent. More than 100 tour wholesalers offer Hawaii travel packages, including these:

All About Hawaii   (800) 274-8687

Classic Custom Vacations   (800) 221-3949

Creative Leisure International   (800) 426-6367

Globetrotters/MTI Vacations   (800) 635-1333

Pleasant Hawaiian Holidays   (800) 2-HAWAII

Internet wholesalers The dot-coms of travel—**travelocity.com, hoteldiscount.com, travel.yahoo.com, cheaphawaiitickets.com,** to name a few of the best-known—offer good rates for Hawaii trips. Travelocity puts travel packages together just like the tour wholesalers above, many of whom also have Web sites.

Other Ways to Stay: Condos and B&Bs

Condominiums

Condo units, the building blocks of Maui tourism, can be the perfect way to go for family trips, couples traveling together, or anyone seeking more space, privacy, and value than a hotel room can offer. Good condo resorts exist on all the islands except Lanai. Together, they form a pool of thousands of choices for you, at all budget levels.

Often located beachfront with many of the services offered by hotels, these condo resorts range from standard to first-rate, with all the comforts home may lack. They come in small clusters or large buildings, often with lobbies, front desks, and maid service. Frequently, they are located in major resort areas with the full menu of extras, including golf, tennis, pools, restaurants, and shuttles. The difference between some resort condos and hotels, particularly suite hotels, is hard to discern as a guest, other than the additional space and homelike facilities of condos. The units are individually owned, but the rentals are managed in a pool. Units in one complex may be managed by several different companies, some of them hotel firms (including locally owned Aston Hotels and Resorts and Outrigger Hotels and Resorts), just to confuse it further, and individual owners may rent their own units, too.

Units normally range from 600 to 800 square feet for a one-bedroom unit to 2,000 square feet or more for a two- or three-bedroom unit. With kitchens, you have the option of cooking or just putting together a quick breakfast or lunch, then having dinner in restaurants. A kitchen means you can sample fresh tropical fruit, Maui coffee, and other Island specialties, and it erases problems with fussy eaters or special diets. Most condo units also have laundry facilities.

Maui condo unit prices can range from under $100 per night to more than $300 per night, depending on the type of accommodation, its location, and your dates of stay.

You can book through one of the dozens of condo reservations agencies to find units that suit your needs. State your preferences on location, size, price, amenities, ambience, and the number in your party, and you'll receive a list of properties from which to choose. Some condo representatives offer extra services, like car rentals and lei greetings, and some handle private resort home rentals as well.

Kapalua Resort on Maui is one of several luxury resorts that has an on-site management operation handling some 200 luxury units and homes in several areas of the resort. Destination Resorts Hawaii at Wailea is another, handling a wide variety of condo units at Wailea.

If you go condo shopping on your own, you'll find plenty of condo travel packages are available in the same way that hotel packages are offered, with car, flights, activities, and special services or gifts included. Watch the ads, use the Internet, ask your friends, and keep on top of special offers. Also, individual owners may rent their units through the Internet and ads in magazines or newspapers.

Terms and policies differ. A deposit is usually required, payable by a major credit card. It's wise to book several weeks in advance, although late bookings are entirely possible. Holidays and other high-demand periods, like spring break, will bring more competition for the unit you want.

RECOMMENDED CONDO RESERVATIONS AGENTS

Aston Hotels and Resorts
(800) 92-ASTON
www.aston-hotels.com

Kapalua Villas
(800) 545-0018 or (808) 669-8088
www.kapaluavillas.com

Destination Resorts Hawaii
  (Wailea Resort)
(800) 367-5246 or (808) 879-1595
www.maui.net/~dhr

Kihei Maui Vacations
  (affordable homes too)
(800) 541-6284 or (808) 879-7581
www.maui.net/~kmv/

Hawaiian Condo Resorts
(800) 487-4505 or (808) 949-4505
www.hawaiicondo.com

Outrigger Hotels and Resorts
(800) 688-7444
www.outrigger.com

Recommended Condos

Below are some recommended condos to check out, chosen for their locations and special features. See page 121 for the "$" conversion chart.

South Maui

KAMAOLE SANDS $$$

2095 South Kihei Road, Kihei, HI 96753; (800) 822-4409 or (808) 874-8700

Across the street from Kihei's best beach park, Kamaole Sands is at the quiet Wailea end of this busy little beach town, near good restaurants and upscale Wailea shops and resorts. Its proximity to the beach and high-rent district of Wailea is appealing. The one- and two-bedroom units with open lanai overlook the lush, tropically landscaped courtyard with adult and child swimming pools, pool house with snack bar, hot tub, and outdoor barbecue grill. You may bump into someone famous at Kamaole Sands because Maui Arts and Cultural Center lodges its visiting entertainers here.

WAILEA ELUA VILLAGE $$$

3600 Wailea Alanui Drive, Kihei, HI 96753; (800) 367-5246 or (808) 891-6200; fax (808) 874-3554

Just a lawn away from irresistible Ulua Beach, these luxury units are situated on 24 acres that include two pools, an entertaining pavilion, a paddle-tennis court, a putting green, and a whirlpool tub. Designer furnishings grace one-, two-, and three-bedroom units with spacious lanai. Guests in the 152 units get special golf and tennis rates at Makena and Wailea Resorts.

WAILEA GRAND CHAMPIONS VILLAS $$$

3750 Wailea Alanui Drive, Kihei, HI 96753; (800) 367-5246 or (808) 891-6200; fax (808) 874-3554; www.drhmaui.com/grandchamp/index.asp

Off-beach but next to tennis courts and golf greens, this newer complex at the south end of Wailea is attractively decorated and well appointed but substantially less dear than the oceanfront Wailea condos. Two great Wailea beaches—Ulua and Keawakapu beaches—are a short downhill walk or drive away. Destination Resorts handles reservations for 188 one-, two-, and three-bedroom units. Another agency, Maui Condo and Home Realty, handles just 30 units, but often at lower rates (phone (800) 822-4409 or (808) 879-5445, or visit **www.resortquestmaui.com**).

West Maui

KAANAPALI ALII $$$$

50 Nohea Drive, Lahaina, HI 96761; (800) 642-6284 or (808) 661-3539; fax (808) 667-1145; www.kaanapali-alii.com or www.classicresorts.com

Beachfront, between the Maui Marriott and Westin Maui, this award-winning mid-rise luxury complex of 264 one- and two-bedroom units is just like a resort hotel, only nicer and with bigger units. Planning a blowout celebration? Get one of the palatial club suites with a wrap-around view and watch the whales, all of them, from your deck chairs. The $850-per-night rate includes a package of grocery goodies delivered every morning, a full-sized car and reserved parking, twice-a-day maids with nightly turndown service, robes, flowers, a bar, newspapers, and a concierge to arrange your activity trips, plus 2,000 square feet of ocean-front space for up to six of you to kick around in.

KAHANA SUNSET $$

4909 Lower Honoapiilani Road, Lahaina, HI 96761; (800) 669-1488 or (808) 669-8011; fax (808) 669-9170; www.kahanasunset.com

Terraced into a bowl-like cliff on a horseshoe curve in the shoreline road near its northern Napili end, this low-rise cluster of 79 one- and two-bedroom units enjoys a secluded beautiful beach. Units are roomy and handsomely appointed (ask for a renovated unit) with large decks or, at the lower edge, patios on the beach.

THE KAPALUA VILLAS $$$

500 Office Road, Kapalua, HI 96761; (800) 545-0018 or (808) 669-8088; www.kapaluavillas.com

These luxurious, spacious villas are set in low-rise clusters with good views in close proximity to the beach or on a hillside golf course. One, two, and three bedrooms available, with plenty of room and designer furnishings in all, including equipped kitchens and laundries. Bring the whole clan and celebrate.

MAUI ELDORADO RESORT $$$

2661 Kekaa Drive, Lahaina, HI 96761; (800) 688-7444 or (808) 661-0021; fax (303) 369-9403; www.outrigger.com

These 204 spacious studio and one-bedroom units with nice views are spread over a green hillside setting, wrapped by Kaanapali Golf Course, accessible by the middle of three resort entries. Lots of appeal for families, including daily maid service, pools, grassy play areas, shops, and barbecue areas. They offer the comforts you need for an extended stay at Kaanapali Resort that won't break the bank.

Central Maui

THE INN AT MAMA'S FISH HOUSE $$$

799 Poho Place, Paia, HI 96779; (800) 806-4852 or (808) 579-8594; www.mamasfishhouse.com

One- and two-bedroom duplex cottages snuggle next to the restaurant, just a lanai away from the sands of picturesque Kuau Cove on the North

Shore near Hookipa Beach. Coco palms à la central casting dot this beach; swimming and snorkeling are possible in the reef-protected waters before the famous winds come up in the afternoons. The six units are tastefully decorated with tropical styling, terra-cotta floors, and gas grills on the lanai. Guests get a discount off Mama's pricy lunches and dinners. Mama's also has two studios and a one-bedroom cottage six minutes up the road in an Edenlike private tropical garden. Guests are invited to sample the flowers and fruit in "Mama's Secret Garden," off the beach.

KANAI A NALU (AT MAALAEA BAY VILLAGE) $$$

280 Hauoli Street, Wailuku, HI 96793; (800) 367-6084 or (808) 244-5627; fax (808) 242-7476; www.maalaeabay.com

These 80 two-bedroom units, with a South Maui ocean view, framed by Haleakala in the backdrop, have direct beach access to a strand that goes for miles across the isthmus. Stay longer, and the daily rates are cheaper. This is one of eight buildings in the same cluster with reservations handled by Maalaea Bay Rentals. The units are done in tropical pastels with two baths and laundry facilities. A heated pool by the sea and barbecue facilities beckon outside your room.

Molokai

PANIOLO HALE $$

P.O. Box 190, Maunaloa, HI 96770; (800) 367-2984 or (808) 552-2731; www.paniolohaleresort.com

Wrapped by Kaluakoi Golf Course, beside golden Kepuhi Beach, this architecturally appealing ranch-style retreat is the most interesting of the low-rise condo complexes at Molokai's west end. The resort and golf course are currently closed, but not Paniolo Hale, which operates independently. It is close to the beach and probably the best moderately priced way to stay on Molokai. You can shop for food and find movies up the hill at Maunaloa town. The studio and one- and two-bedroom units have laundries, kitchens, and color TVs inside; a pool, paddle-tennis courts, barbecue grills, picnic tables, and free parking outside. Long walks along the seacliffs may scare up a few of the resident wild turkeys.

Bed-and-Breakfasts

A Hawaii-style bed-and-breakfast can offer a satisfying personal island experience, like staying at a friend's home. It can also be a disappointment with spare-room ambience and little privacy.

With more than 700 bed-and-breakfast operations in Hawaii, you should do some investigating before you book. You can often preview your choice on the Internet before you reserve it. Be sure to check whether units have private baths and entries.

On the mainland, a "bed-and-breakfast" usually means a refurbished mansion or historic house. In Hawaii, it's usually a studio cottage with some kitchen facilities or a guest room in a private home.

You probably won't get a home-cooked breakfast at most of the in-house bed-and-breakfasts, thanks to restrictive laws. But you can expect a basket of tropical fruit, breads, and Kona coffee.

Beach properties rent fast and are usually booked year-round, often by return guests. Plan to make reservations two or three months in advance, more for holiday periods.

Per-night prices range from $55 up to $300 and average $75–$100 per night for two people with a continental breakfast. Most operators require a minimum three-night stay.

Off the beach, a studio with private entrance, bath, and kitchenette runs $65–$125 per night. A cottage averages $75–$150 per night for two people.

To book, you can call the hosts directly or use a reservation service; we've provided a list of the largest, most reputable services. Rental terms and policies vary. At All Islands Bed & Breakfast, for example, a 20 percent deposit is required to hold a reservation. Personal checks and credit cards are generally accepted. A 3 percent fee is also charged on deposits. Deposits are refundable (minus a $25 service fee) if you cancel your reservation at least two weeks prior to your arrival date. Otherwise, you pay the balance to the host family when you arrive. You will receive a confirmation letter shortly after your deposit is received, followed by a welcome letter, a map, and a brochure.

BED-AND-BREAKFAST RESERVATIONS (STATEWIDE)

All Islands Bed-and-Breakfast
(800) 542-0344 or (808) 263-2342
www.home.hawaii.rr.com/allislands

Bed-and-Breakfast Hawaii
(800) 733-1632 or (808) 822-7771
www.bandb-hawaii.com

Bed and Breakfast Honolulu
(877) 866-5402 or (808) 595-7533
www.aloha-bnb.com

Hawaii's Best Bed-and-Breakfasts
(800) 262-9912 or (808) 885-4550
www.bestbnb.com

Recommended Bed-and-Breakfasts

Here are a few of our favorite bed-and-breakfasts, cottages, and similar vacation rentals:

Maui

Blue Horizons B&B
3894 Mahinahina Street
Lahaina, HI 96761
(808) 669-1965 or (800) 669-1948
www.maui.net/~chips

Dreams Come True
P.O. Box 525
Lanai City, HI 96763
(808) 565-6961 or (800) 566-6961
www.go-native.com/inns

Silver Cloud Ranch
RR II Box 201
Kula, HI 96790
(808) 878-6101 or (800) 532-1111
www.maui.net/~slvrcld

Molokai

Kamalo Plantation B&B
HC01 Box 300
Kaunakakai, HI 96748
(808) 558-8236
www.molokai.com/kamalo

Hotels Rated and Ranked

We've ranked more than 20 hotels on Maui, Molokai, and Lanai based on room quality (cleanliness, spaciousness, views, amenities, visual appeal), value, service, and location. These are our ratings, independent of any travel organization or club.

The first number of stars in a rating applies to a property's overall quality. The second applies to the quality of rooms only.

For details on a specific property, see hotel profiles in this chapter.

How to Make the Ratings Work for You

The chief factors we used to rate hotels are location (on the beach or nearby), views, service, amenities, character, price, and value. However, not every room at a given resort is the same; some are superlative, while others are lackluster. When you choose your lodging, ask whether construction or other noisy endeavors are going to be happening nearby, whether your room was recently renovated, whether it has one of the outdoor patios Hawaiians call *lanai,* what extras are included in the rate (in-room coffee maker, daily paper, movies, dataports, minibar, beach gear, continental breakfast), and whether airport transfers are available. Most deluxe hotel rooms and condo units come equipped with hair dryers, irons and boards, and safes; some have CD players. If these extras are important to you, ask.

Upscale travelers who appreciate value should inquire about the club floors. Rooms on these floors have keyed elevator access, a lounge with free drinks, free food including a continental breakfast, light buffet lunch, evening *pupu* (appetizers), and sinful fresh-baked cookies; plus club floors have a concierge to call their own. The rates are higher, but the buffets take care of breakfast, lunch, snacks, and cocktails, all costly at resorts. You can get your morning coffee and children's breakfasts fast and easy and take things back to your room on a tray if you want.

You don't have to go first class to get great service. Usually service at Hawaii hotels is friendly and courteous at every level, from maids to general managers, without regard to price levels. Staff members exhibit lots of aloha spirit and wear flowers and tropical uniforms. They may not all speak your language, but they are anxious to please you.

All lodging is subject to an 11.5 percent state tax.

What the Ratings Mean

★★★★★	Best of the Best
★★★★½	Excellent
★★★★	Very Good
★★★½	Good
★★★	Average
★★½	Below Average
★★	Poor

Each hotel is rated for room quality and overall quality, both expressed on the five-star scale. As the terms imply, the former rating is specific to accommodations while the latter takes into account all facets of the hotel. The overall quality rating considers the entirety of the property. A hotel with prime location, excellent restaurants, or a gorgeous lobby might rank highly despite mediocre rooms. Conversely, a property with elaborate rooms and little else may rank lower overall. A room's size, the quality of its furnishings, and the level of cleanliness are the prime factors in room quality. *Unofficial Guide* researchers and writers also take pride in scrutinizing aspects of a hotel room that most guests only notice when something goes awry: noise levels, lighting, temperature control, ventilation, and security.

The value ratings, also expressed using a five-star scale, are a combination of the overall and room quality ratings, divided by the cost of an average guest room. They indicated a general idea of value for money. If getting a good deal means the most to you, choose a property by looking at the value rating. Otherwise, quality ratings are better indicators of a satisfying experience. If a wonderful property is fairly priced, it may only get an average value rating, but you still might prefer the experience to an average property with a higher value rating.

Cost Indicators

$$$$$	Above $350
$$$$	$250–$350
$$$	$150–$250
$$	$100–$150
$	Below $100

Cost is expressed on a five-dollar symbol scale. The scale was devised with Maui's typical room rates in mind: Roughly, a hotel's cost indicator coincides with its star rating. In other words, expect to see as many of dollar signs as stars. The rates are based on the rack rate for a standard ocean-view room (or suitable equivalent) during high season, from December through March. Don't be intimidated by the cost indicators. Lower and higher prices (depending on the room category) are available at each hotel.

HOW THE HOTELS COMPARE

Hotel	Overall Rating	Room Rating	Value Rating	Cost
Maui				
Hotel Hana-Maui	★★★★★	★★★★★	★★★★½	$$$$$
Ritz-Carlton, Kapalua	★★★★★	★★★★★	★★★★	$$$$$
Fairmont Kea Lani Maui	★★★★½	★★★★★	★★★½	$$$$$
Grand Wailea Resort Hotel and Spa	★★★★½	★★★★★	★★★	$$$$$
Embassy Vacation Resort Kaanapali Beach	★★★★½	★★★★	★★	$$$$$
Kapalua Bay Hotel	★★★★	★★★★	★★★★	$$$$$
Sheraton Maui	★★★★	★★★★	★★★★	$$$$$

HOW THE HOTELS COMPARE *(continued)*

Hotel	Overall Rating	Room Rating	Value Rating	Cost
Maui (continued)				
Westin Maui	★★★★	★★★★	★★★★	$$$$$
Hyatt Regency Maui Resort and Spa	★★★★	★★★★	★★★½	$$$$$
Marriott Wailea Beach Resort	★★★★	★★★★	★★★½	$$$$
Renaissance Wailea Beach Resort	★★★★	★★★★	★★★	$$$$
Kaanapali Beach Hotel	★★★★	★★★½	★★★★	$$$
Maui Prince Hotel	★★★★	★★★½	★★½	$$$$
Plantation Inn	★★★★	★★★	★★★★	$$$
Maui Marriott Resort	★★★½	★★★★	★★	$$$$
Lahaina Inn	★★★½	★★★½	★★★	$$
Mauian Hotel on Napili Beach	★★★½	★★★½	★★★★	$$$
Maui Coast Hotel	★★★½	★★★	★★	$$$
Lahaina Shores Beach Resort	★★★	★★★½	★★★½	$$
Maui Beach Hotel	★★★	★★½	★★★½	$$
Molokai				
Lodge and Beach Village at Molokai Ranch	★★★★½	★★★★★	★★★★	$$$$$
Lanai				
The Lodge at Koele	★★★★½	★★★★	★★★½	$$$$$
The Manele Bay Hotel	★★★★½	★★★★	★★★½	$$$$$
Hotel Lanai	★★★½	★★★	★★★½	$

HOTELS BY LOCATION

West Maui

Embassy Vacation Resort Kaanapali Beach
Hyatt Regency Maui Resort and Spa
Kaanapali Beach Hotel
Kapalua Bay Hotel
Lahaina Inn
Lahaina Shores Beach Resort
Maui Marriott Resort
Mauian Hotel on Napili Beach
Plantation Inn

HOTELS BY LOCATION *(continued)*

West Maui *(continued)*

Ritz-Carlton, Kapalua
Sheraton Maui
Westin Maui

South Maui

Fairmont Kea Lani Maui
Four Seasons Resort Maui
Grand Wailea Resort Hotel and Spa
Maui Coast Hotel
Maui Prince Hotel
Marriott Wailea Beach Resort
Renaissance Wailea Beach Resort

Central Maui

Maui Beach Hotel

Hana

Hotel Hana-Maui

Molokai

Lodge and Beach Village at Molokai Ranch

Lanai

Hotel Lanai
The Lodge at Koele
The Manele Bay Hotel

Hotel Profiles

Maui

EMBASSY VACATION RESORT KAANAPALI BEACH $$$$$

OVERALL ★★★★½ | ROOM QUALITY ★★★★ | VALUE ★★ | WEST MAUI

104 Kaanapali Shores Place, Lahaina, HI 96761; (800) 669-3155 or (808) 661-2000; fax (808) 667-5821; www.mauiembassy.com

Opened in 1988, this was the first Hawaii property to offer all-suite accommodations. Ninety percent of the suites provide ocean views (you can also see the neighboring islands of Molokai and Lanai). A variety of Island-flavored art adorns the resort's lobby. A popular feature here is the 42-foot water slide, which plops you straight into a one-acre swimming pool. The young ones can participate in Beach Buddies, the resort's year-round children's program (ages 4–10), which includes lei making, beach combing, coconut weaving, and other activities.

SETTING AND FACILITIES

Location On Kaanapali Beach.

Dining The North Beach Grille serves steaks, seafood, chicken, and other American favorites.

Amenities and services Room service, laundry and housekeeping service, workout room, children's day care, parking ($10/day).

ACCOMMODATIONS

Rooms 413, all suites; 12 ADA-approved rooms. Most rooms are designated nonsmoking.

All rooms A/C, big-screen cable TV, VCR, phone, sleeper sofa, microwave, mini-refrigerator, in-room safe, hair dryer.

Comfort and decor Spacious (over 800 square feet), with separate living-room area. An oversized soaking tub, separate shower, walk-in closets, dual marble vanities, and 35-inch-screen TV are among the luxuries. Elegant and stylish, with a cool tropical appeal, cheerful and airy.

RATES, RESERVATIONS, AND RESTRICTIONS

Family plan Children ages 17 and under stay free with parents if using existing bedding.

Deposit 1-night deposit due within 10 days of booking. Cancellation notice must be given 72 hours prior to arrival for refund.

Credit cards All major credit cards accepted.

Check-in/out 4 p.m./11 a.m. Early check-in and late check-out available on request. Hospitality suite available for early arrivals and late departures.

FAIRMONT KEA LANI MAUI $$$$$

OVERALL ★★★★½ | ROOM QUALITY ★★★★★ | VALUE ★★★½ | SOUTH MAUI

4100 Wailea Alanui, on Polo Beach, Wailea, HI 96753; (800) 882-4100 or (808) 875-4100; fax (808) 875-1200; www.kealani.com

This all-suite hotel features an extensive menu of in-room amenities, including a complete home entertainment system. The hotel's open-air, Mediterranean-style architecture evokes a quaint village feel. Children ages 5–12 can participate in Keiki Lani, the hotel's year-round children's program, which features hula and lei-making lessons and swimming. The hotel has two marvelous swimming lagoons that are connected by a 140-foot water slide and swim-up beverage bar. One of the most interesting features on the property is the Organic Garden, which features more than 150 varieties of produce, including 18 varieties of rare exotic fruits. (These garden items are utilized in the hotel's restaurants; inquire about a guided garden tour.) Readers of *Condé Nast Traveler* have repeatedly voted the Kea Lani as one of the best resorts in the Pacific.

SETTING AND FACILITIES

Location On Wailea Beach.

Dining Nick's Fishmarket Maui is a popular seafood bistro. Caffe Ciao serves Italian cuisine in garden setting. Put together a picnic with goodies from Caffe Ciao Deli. Buffet and à la carte breakfasts are served at the Kea Lani Restaurant, while the Polo Beach Grille and Bar offers poolside lunch.

Amenities and services Spa and fitness center, 3 swimming pools, tennis, golf, children's program, indoor/outdoor meeting and conference space.

ACCOMMODATIONS

Rooms 450, all suites, including 37 oceanfront villas, 201 nonsmoking suites, and 11 suites for the disabled.

All rooms A/C, cable TV, stereo entertainment center (with CD player, VCR, and laserdisc player), sleeper sofa, private lanai, phone.

Some rooms Private pool, gourmet kitchen, sun deck, barbecue grill, extra bedroom.

Comfort and decor Very spacious, with separate bedroom and living room, exceptionally clean. Soft tropical colors provide cheerful ambience. Luxurious furnishings with Island-theme artworks. Large European marble bathroom and soaking tub and twin pedestal sinks.

RATES, RESERVATIONS, AND RESTRICTIONS

Family plan Four persons can stay in a suite with no extra charge. For a third child, a rollaway bed is available for $30.

Deposit 2-night deposit due within 14 days after booking. Cancellation notice must be given 72 hours prior to arrival for refund.

Credit cards All major credit cards accepted.

Check-in/out 4 p.m./noon. Early check-in and late check-out available on request.

FOUR SEASONS RESORT MAUI $$$$$

OVERALL ★★★★ | ROOM QUALITY ★★★★ | VALUE ★★★★ | SOUTH MAUI

3900 Wailea Alanui; Wailea, HI 96753; (800) 334-6284 or (808) 874-8000; fax (808) 874-6449; www.fourseasons.com

Condé Nast Traveler magazine named the Four Seasons the Top Tropical Resort in the World in 1993, shortly after it opened, and this luxurious resort continues to rate high among repeat travelers—including the Hollywood set, which frequents it. The resort first garnered the AAA Five Diamond Award in 1999 and has earned it ever since. A honeymoon favorite, this gracious place makes a fine art of pampering, from the Evian spritzes by the pool to room service at the lounge chairs on the beach below. The new Spa at Four Seasons offers indoor treatments and outdoor ocean-view massage huts. The breezy, open lobby is testament to the resort's Island-accented architectural design, which also includes commissioned reproductions of early Hawaiian furniture as well as paintings, sculptures, and other Hawaii-inspired artworks. On-site features include a children's program, health club, game room, and salon. The service is professional and courteous. To top everything off, the Four Seasons is located at Wailea Resort, which offers the swanky Shops at Wailea shopping and dining complex, three championship golf courses, and the 11-court Wailea Tennis Center (known as "Wimbledon West"). Overall, the Four Seasons has to rate as one of the best resorts (if not the best) on Maui. It doesn't hurt a bit that in winter you can lounge on your ocean-facing lanai and watch the humpback whales going by.

SETTING AND FACILITIES

Location On Wailea Beach.

Dining Ferraro's Bar e Ristorante offers Italian cuisine under the stars, while Spago presents Wolfgang Puck's contemporary California dishes. Pacific Grill serves breakfast and dinner (seafood and steaks).

Amenities and services Spa services, 24-hour room service, full laundry service, workout facilities, business center, children's program, game room.

ACCOMMODATIONS

Rooms 377 including 74 suites. ADA-approved and nonsmoking rooms available.

All rooms A/C, cable TV, VCR, lanai, in-room safe, minibar, hair dryer, dataport, robes.

Some rooms Fax machines, extra bedroom.

Comfort and decor Very spacious (Maui's largest hotel rooms), exceptionally clean and well maintained. Soft white and gentle sunset hues; deep-cushioned rattan and wicker furnishings. Large bathrooms include marble counters and dual vanities. Elegant island-themed artwork adds to the warm atmosphere.

RATES, RESERVATIONS, AND RESTRICTIONS

Family plan Children ages 17 and under stay free with parents if using existing bedding.

Deposit 1-night deposit due within 7 days of booking. Cancellation notice must be given 14 hours prior to arrival January 3–April 30; 7 days prior May 1–December 18.

Credit cards All major credit cards accepted.

Check-in/out 3 p.m./noon. Early check-in and late check-out available on request.

GRAND WAILEA RESORT HOTEL AND SPA $$$$$

OVERALL ★★★★½ | ROOM QUALITY ★★★★★ | VALUE ★★★ | SOUTH MAUI

3850 Wailea Alanui Drive, Wailea, HI 96753; (800) 888-6100 or (808) 875-1234; fax (808) 874-2411; www.grandwailea.com

Even if you don't stay here, this $600 million ultra-luxury resort is worth a visit. There are six major design themes—flowers, water, trees, sound, light, and art—and all are on full display throughout the 40-acre property. More than $30 million in artworks decorate the public areas. The resort has added an artists-in-residence program as well, featuring local artists' works. Among the features here are Camp Grande, a 20,000-square-foot children's facility; the 50,000-square-foot SpaGrande; a breathtaking wedding chapel complete with stained glass windows; and a 2,000-foot-long river pool that includes valleys, water slides, waterfalls, caves, grottos, whitewater rapids, a Jacuzzi, a sauna, and the world's only "water elevator," which lifts guests from the lower-level pool to the higher-level pool. Everything here is "grand"—perhaps too grand. But the food could be better to match the general surroundings. While many will love this place, others will find it over the top. It's worth a walk-through to admire the art, even if you stay elsewhere. If you want opulence, this is it.

SETTING AND FACILITIES

Location On Wailea Beach.

Dining Kincha serves Japanese cuisine in a traditional setting, embellished with 800 tons of rock from Mount Fuji. Bistro Molokini offers California and Hawaii cuisine for lunch and dinner. Cafe Kula presents lighter fare and Humuhumunukunukuapuaa specializes in fresh seafood (and has one of the longest names around).

Amenities and services Room service, full-service spa and fitness center, three championship golf courses, squash/racquetball courts, parking, children's program, swimming pools, and fantasy water complex (including a water-powered elevator and pool-linking "canyons" to speed up the ride) with swim-up bar and man-made beach beside the real one. Grand Wailea boasts Wailea's prime nightspot, Tsunami, with techy super-sound and laser light show.

ACCOMMODATIONS

Rooms 761, including 51 suites, 10 rooms for disabled. Nonsmoking rooms available.

All rooms A/C, cable TV, lanai, in-room safe, honor bar, coffee maker, hair dryer, robes, slippers.

Some rooms Larger accommodations, extra baths.

Comfort and decor Very spacious, ultraluxurious, with opulent furnishings and decor. Warm colors and high ceilings add to the elegant setting.

RATES, RESERVATIONS, AND RESTRICTIONS

Family plan Children ages 17 and under stay free with parents if using existing bedding. Maximum 4 people per room.

Deposit 2-night deposit required within 14 days of booking. Cancellation notice must be given 72 hours prior to arrival for refund (14 days notice for suites).

Credit cards All major credit cards accepted.

Check-in/out 3 p.m./noon. Early check-in and late check-out available on request.

HOTEL HANA-MAUI $$$$$

OVERALL ★★★★★ | ROOM QUALITY ★★★★★ | VALUE ★★★★½ | HANA

P.O. Box 9, Hana, HI 96713; (800) 321-4262 or (808) 248-8211; fax (808) 248-7202; www.hotelhanamaui.com

What this cozy small hotel lacks (television and air-conditioning, no need for either), it makes up for in charm, location, and friendly, attentive service. Hana sits on expansive landscaped gardens by the sea, and the ocean and mountain views are, like Hana, heavenly. Remote, quiet, romantic, this is the epitome of a honeymoon hotel. A weekly luau is held on the beach. Available outdoor activities include horseback riding, hiking, snorkeling, bike riding, and historical tours. Treatments at the new full-service spa involve Hawaiian traditional ways and materials— ginger, coconut, or red sea salt scrubs, kukui nut oil, slightly narcotic awa, and seaweeds. The Hana-Maui, built in 1946, is Maui's oldest hotel and one of its most expensive. The hotel has new owners (owner of The Post Ranch in California's Big Sur) who just refurbished it, and a new executive chef, Larry Quirit, a native of Hawaii who serves up his own brand of contemporary Hawaiian cuisine using local produce and seafood. Curing the dining room's prior shortcomings will be critical to the effort to bring the Hana-Maui back to its most recent glory days, the 1980s, when the Hunt family of Texas remade it.

SETTING AND FACILITIES

Location In Hana, on the east end of Maui. Shuttle available to Hamoa Beach.

Dining The hotel dining room serves contemporary Hawaiian cuisine.

Amenities and services Room service (breakfast only), laundry service, parking, spa.

ACCOMMODATIONS

Rooms 66 spacious suites and cottages.

All rooms Wet bar, lanai, coffee and tea maker.

Some rooms Jacuzzis.

Comfort and decor The Hana-Maui's luxurious brand of rustic decor features bleached hardwood floors, wicker and rattan furnishings, hand-made quilts, wet bars, sitting and dining areas, and large private lanai. The oversized tiled baths open onto private shower gardens.

RATES, RESERVATIONS, AND RESTRICTIONS

Family plan Children ages 12 and under stay free with parents if using existing bedding.

Deposit 1-night deposit required. Cancellation notice must be given 72 hours prior to arrival for refund.

Credit cards All major credit cards accepted.

Check-in/out 4 p.m./noon. Early check-in and late check-out available on request.

HYATT REGENCY MAUI RESORT AND SPA $$$$$

OVERALL ★★★★ | ROOM QUALITY ★★★★ | VALUE ★★★½ | WEST MAUI

200 Nohea Drive, Lahaina, HI 96761; (800) 233-1234 or (808) 661-1234; fax (808) 667-4497; www.hyatt.com

The Hyatt Maui was the first of Hawaii's celebrated, larger-than-life "fantasy hotels," complete with an elaborate water playground with waterfall cave, a suspended rope bridge, and other features designed to appeal to the kid in everyone. The atrium lobby is lush with tropical plants and exotic birds. Its nightly *Tour of the Stars* program gives guests a guided tour of the Hawaiian skies and allows them to peer through a state-of-the-art, computer-controlled 16-inch reflector telescope. A wildlife tour brings visitors face-to-face with penguins, swans, parrots, macaws, flamingos, and koi. You can also tour the tropical gardens (it's about a two-mile walk) or browse the $2 million art collection. This property offers something for travelers of all ages and interests.

SETTING AND FACILITIES

Location   On Kaanapali Beach.

Dining   Swan Court features Continental cuisine with a Pacific Rim flair, Spats Trattoria serves Italian food, and Cascades Grille and Sushi Bar offers fresh seafood and steak.

Amenities and services   Full-service spa and fitness center, tennis, golf, outdoor dinner theater, activities desk, children's program, shops, meeting and convention facilities, rooftop astronomy program.

ACCOMMODATIONS

Rooms   807

All rooms   A/C, cable TV, phone, honor bar, in-room safe, hair dryer, robes, coffee maker.

Some rooms   Living room, dining area, wet bar, refrigerator.

Comfort and decor   Spacious and clean, with warm earth and mauve Asian/Pacific tones reflecting stylish elegance. Furnishings are comfortable and wall hangings attractive.

RATES, RESERVATIONS, AND RESTRICTIONS

Family plan   Children ages 17 and under stay free with parents if using existing bedding. Maximum 4 per room.

Deposit   2-night deposit due within 14 days after booking. Cancellation notice must be provided 72 hours prior to arrival for refund.

Credit cards   All major credit cards accepted.

Check-in/out   3 p.m./noon. Early check-in and late check-out based on availability.

KAANAPALI BEACH HOTEL   **$$$**

OVERALL ★★★★ | ROOM QUALITY ★★★½ | VALUE ★★★★ | WEST MAUI

2525 Kaanapali Parkway, Lahaina, HI 96761; (800) 262-8450 or (808) 661-0011; fax (808) 667-5978; www.kaanapalibeachhotel.com

Located on one of the widest stretches of Kaanapali Beach, the Kaanapali Beach Hotel prides itself on being Maui's "most Hawaiian" hotel. The management and staff are dedicated to the aloha spirit, and their easygoing friendliness makes up for a lack of needed renovations. The spirit of this place is reminiscent of the romantic past, with its four wings like arms sheltering a ten-acre garden courtyard. A variety of Hawaiian activities—including hula lessons, lei making, lauhala weaving, and ti-leaf skirt making—are held daily, and employees provide Hawaiian entertainment three days a week. They've released two CDs, one a prize winner in the Hawaii Visitors and Convention Bureau's annual "Keep It Hawaii" awards.

For visitors seeking a hotel with a strong emphasis on Hawaiian hospitality, look no further.

SETTING AND FACILITIES

Location On Kaanapali Beach.

Dining The Tiki Terrace Restaurant serves continental and Island cuisine. The Kupanaha Dinner Show is held at 4:30 p.m., Tuesday–Saturday. The Polynesian show features magician Jody Baran and costs $69 for adults, $49 for ages 12–20, and $29 for ages 6–12.

Amenities and services Laundry service, parking, children's program.

ACCOMMODATIONS

Rooms 430, including 15 suites. Nonsmoking rooms and rooms for the disabled available.

All rooms A/C, cable TV, phone, in-room safe, refrigerator, coffee maker.

Some rooms More space, upgraded amenities.

Comfort and decor Rooms are spacious, clean, and well maintained. Tropical green and golden sand hues accentuate the Hawaiian setting, along with Hawaiian quilt–design bedspreads, light tropical furniture, and local artwork.

RATES, RESERVATIONS, AND RESTRICTIONS

Family plan Children ages 17 and under stay free with parents if using existing bedding.

Deposit 1- or 2-night deposit due 10 days after booking. Cancellation notice must be given 3–7 days prior to arrival.

Credit cards All major credit cards accepted.

Check-in/out 3 p.m./noon. Early check-in and late check-out available on request.

KAPALUA BAY HOTEL $$$$$

OVERALL ★★★★ | ROOM QUALITY ★★★★ | VALUE ★★★★ | WEST MAUI

One Bay Drive, Kapalua, HI 96761; (800) 367-8000 or (808) 669-5656; fax (808) 669-4694; www.kapaluabayhotel.com

The Kapalua Bay Hotel is older than its neighbor, the Ritz-Carlton, Kapalua, but it's every bit as elegant. This is a world-class facility fronting one of Maui's finest beaches. The hotel exudes an understated elegance that blends with its natural surroundings. Piano and Hawaiian music are provided nightly at the Lehua Lounge, located below the lobby area. The Kapalua Shops, a minimall of some 20 boutiques, is on the premises, and golf aficionados have a choice of three championship golf courses, one of which hosts the prestigious PGA Mercedes Open each January.

SETTING AND FACILITIES

Location On Kapalua Bay, a short walk from the beach.

Dining The Bay Club serves seafood specialties for dinner. Gardenia Court serves breakfast daily and dinner Tuesday through Saturday, including prime-rib specials Wednesday, seafood buffet Friday, and Sunday brunch. Plumeria Terrace serves lunch and snacks daily.

Amenities and services Room service, laundry service, daily maid service, tennis courts, children's program, shops.

ACCOMMODATIONS

Rooms 194, including 3 suites, 1 floor of designated nonsmoking rooms, 6 rooms for the hearing impaired, and 8 wheelchair-accessible rooms.

All rooms A/C, cable TV, in-room safe, mini-bar, lanai, 3 phones, hair dryer.

Some rooms Washer and dryer, Jacuzzi, second bedroom.

Comfort and decor Spacious, oversized rooms are decorated in natural colors and marble accents; each has a large private lanai.

RATES, RESERVATIONS, AND RESTRICTIONS

Family plan Children ages 17 and under stay free with parents if using existing bedding.

Deposit 1-night credit card guarantee (5-night deposit during the Christmas holidays). Cancellation notice must be given 72 hours prior to arrival for refund.

Credit cards All major credit cards accepted except Discover.

Check-in/out 3 p.m./noon. Early check-in and late check-out available on request.

LAHAINA INN $$

OVERALL ★★★★ | ROOM QUALITY ★★★½ | VALUE ★★★ | WEST MAUI

127 Lahainaluna Road, Lahaina, HI 96761; (800) 669-3444 or (808) 661-0577; fax (808) 667-9480; www.lahainainn.com

Lahaina Inn is proof that good things can come in small packages. Rick Ralston, founder and owner of the popular Crazy Shirts stores, is also a collector of fine antiques and other nostalgic things. It was Ralston who restored the dozen rooms of his historic inn; pieces from his personal collection furnish each individually decorated room. Because of the valued furnishings, children under the age of 15 are not allowed. A complimentary continental breakfast is served at the end of the hall every morning. The inn's close proximity to Front Street is a "good news, bad news" situation: It's good to be close to the action (Lahaina is Maui's most bustling town), but it also gets noisy. Also, there are no television sets at the inn, but who needs sitcoms when you have a view of Lahaina?

SETTING AND FACILITIES

Location In the heart of Lahaina, across from waterfront; no beach.

Dining David Paul's Lahaina Grill, one of Maui's best restaurants, serves New American cuisine.

Amenities and services Parking ($5 per day).

ACCOMMODATIONS

Rooms 12, including 3 suites. All are nonsmoking rooms (smoking permitted on lanai).

All rooms A/C, ceiling fans, daily continental breakfast, hair dryers, iron and board.

Some rooms Lanai, full bath and shower, king-size bed.

Comfort and decor Rooms are smallish, but well maintained and clean, if dimly lit. Antique furnishings include restored brass and wood beds, period wall decorations, and armoires.

RATES, RESERVATIONS, AND RESTRICTIONS

Deposit 1-night deposit required. Cancellation notice must be given 10 days prior to arrival for refund.

Credit cards All major credit cards accepted except Discover.

Check-in/out 3 p.m./11 a.m. Late check-out (until noon) on request.

LAHAINA SHORES BEACH RESORT $$

OVERALL ★★★ | ROOM QUALITY ★★★½ | VALUE ★★★½ | WEST MAUI

475 Front Street, Lahaina, HI 96761; (800) 642 6284 or (808) 661-4835; fax (808) 661-4696; www.lahaina-shores.com

If you want to stay beachfront in the heart of Lahaina, this is the place. Oceanfront rooms allow whale-watching in winter from your own lanai. The airy lobby, with arched colonnades on either side, opens onto a panoramic sea view. The style is rambling, old-style plantation comfort. Families like its spacious rooms and central location. Tennis courts are across the street; shopping, restaurants, and entertainment right at hand.

SETTING AND FACILITIES

Location Beachfront, in walking distance of downtown Lahaina.

Dining In-room kitchens, restaurants in walking distance.

Amenities and services Daily maid service, free parking, pool, whirlpool tub, on-property laundry facilities, baby-sitting referrals.

ACCOMMODATIONS

Rooms 199 studios, one-bedrooms, and one-bedroom penthouse suites, with magnificent ocean and mountain views.

All rooms A/C, TV, in-room movies, lanai, hair dryers.

Some rooms Extra space (penthouse sleeps up to 5), microwaves, coffee makers.

Comfort and decor Tropical pastel decor.

RATES, RESERVATIONS, AND RESTRICTIONS

Deposit $150 deposit required. Cancellation notice must be given 72 hours prior to arrival for refund.

Credit cards All major credit cards accepted.

Check-in/out 3 p.m./11 a.m.

MARRIOTT WAILEA BEACH RESORT $$$$

OVERALL ★★★★ | ROOM QUALITY ★★★★ | VALUE ★★★½ | SOUTH MAUI

3700 Alanui, Wailea, HI 96753; (800) 688-7444 or (808) 879-1922; fax (808) 874-8331; www.outrigger.com

This is the value property in an expensive, luxury resort area. Rack rates are similar to two other hotels here, but packaging brings them way down. It's the oldest hotel here (it opened in 1976 as the Maui Inter-Continental Resort), has a strong return-guest contingent, a central oceanfront position, and a comfortable, Hawaiian air about it. Outrigger, a chain owned by a Hawaii family, renovated everything in the past couple of years, then sold to Marriott. It's a kid-friendly place with one pool devoted to a water-slide playground. The resort's low-rise building design is a comfortable fit on 22 oceanfront acres. Lei-making classes and craft demonstrations are offered regularly, and Hawaiian entertainment is provided nightly. Arcade games, billiards, darts, and air hockey are among the diversions offered at Paani, a game bar. A shuttle provides transportation to the Maui Ocean Center, one of the island's newer visitor attractions. Overall, the Marriott Wailea Beach Resort is a pleasant gem suitable for families and couples alike.

SETTING AND FACILITIES

Location At Wailea Resort, on the beach.

Dining Lea's specializes in seafood, poolside Hula Moons features lighter fare and popular Island favorites.

Amenities and services Laundry service, children's program, parking, business facilities, game room.

ACCOMMODATIONS

Rooms 516, including 46 suites, 446 nonsmoking rooms, and 10 rooms for the disabled.

All rooms A/C, cable TV, phone, in-room safe, refrigerator, coffee maker, hair dryer, iron and board.

Some rooms Robes. Most rooms have private lanai.

Comfort and decor Very spacious, clean, well appointed, with sunny pastels, attractive tropical furnishings, artwork, and private lanai.

RATES, RESERVATIONS, AND RESTRICTIONS

Family plan Children ages 12 and under stay free if staying with parents and using existing bedding.

Deposit 1-night deposit required. Cancellation notice must be given 72 hours prior to arrival for refund.

Credit cards All major credit cards accepted.

Check-in/out 3 p.m./noon

MAUI BEACH HOTEL $$

OVERALL ★★★ | ROOM QUALITY ★★½ | VALUE ★★★½ | CENTRAL MAUI

170 Kaahumanu Avenue, Kahului, HI 96732; (800) 367-5004 or (808) 877-0051; fax (808) 871-5797; www.castleresorts.com/MBH

It's more motel-by-the-bay than Maui-of-your-dreams, but this 145-room waterfront hotel on the shores of Kahului Bay has something none of the dream resorts have—proximity to the Kahului Airport (two miles away, with a free shuttle service) and the attractions of Upcountry, Iao Valley, and the North Shore. If you need an airport connection in a hurry or want to get the jump on all those other people headed up to the top of Haleakala or out to Hana, consider staying here. It is conveniently located near shopping malls (Queen Kaahumanu Center), sports activities (golf at Dunes at Maui Lani or Pukalani), the harbor, dining (Manana Garage), entertainment (Maui Arts and Cultural Center), and attractions. The amenities include pool and sundeck, restaurants, cocktail lounge, and rooms with mountain or ocean views.

SETTING AND FACILITIES

Location Kahului, on Kahului Bay beach.

Dining Breakfast, lunch, and dinner buffets at Rainbow Terrace; or nearby restaurants.

Amenities and services Daily maid service, free parking.

ACCOMMODATIONS

Rooms 145, renovated recently with pleasant tropical furnishings. Non-smoking rooms available.

All rooms A/C, color TV, phone, refrigerator, in-room safe, hair dryers.

Some rooms Lanai.

Comfort and decor Beige and earth tones, with some floral accents.

RATES, RESERVATIONS, AND RESTRICTIONS

Deposit 1-night deposit required.

Credit cards All major credit cards accepted.

Check-in/out 3 p.m./noon.

MAUI COAST HOTEL $$$

OVERALL ★★★½ | ROOM QUALITY ★★★ | VALUE ★★ | SOUTH MAUI

2259 South Kihei Road, Kihei, HI 96753; (800) 895-MAUI (6284) or (808) 874-6284; fax (808) 875-4731; www.mauicoasthotel.com

Kihei's only full-service hotel and one of Maui's few moderately priced hotels is a block from a good swimming beach at Kamaole Beach Park I, and near Kihei restaurants, bars, and shopping, as well as a choice of golf courses, from pricy Wailea Golf Club to Ellair public course in Kihei. Your fifth night is free, and room-and-car and activity packages are available, the latter including golf at Dunes at Maui Lani.

SETTING AND FACILITIES

Location Off beach, Kihei near Wailea

Dining Spices Restaurant serves breakfast, lunch, and dinner; the hotel also has a cocktail lounge and poolside entertainment nightly until 10 p.m.

Amenities and services Room service, pool, two outdoor whirlpool tubs, children's wading pool, fitness facilities, lighted tennis court, gift shop, free laundry facilities and parking, meeting room.

ACCOMMODATIONS

Rooms 265, including one- and two-bedroom suites; ADA-compliant rooms available.

All rooms A/C, cable TV, Nintendo system, safe, voicemail, lanai, ceiling fans, coffee maker, mini-refrigerator, hair dryer, iron, and board.

Some rooms Whirlpool tubs and wet bars in suites.

Comfort and decor Recently renovated rooms feature tropical pastels and art.

RATES, RESERVATIONS, AND RESTRICTIONS

Deposit 1-night deposit required. Corporate rates available.

Family plan Children ages 17 and under stay free if staying with parents and using existing bedding.

Credit cards Major cards accepted.

Check-in/out 3 p.m./11 a.m.

MAUI MARRIOTT RESORT $$$$

OVERALL ★★★½ | ROOM QUALITY ★★★★ | VALUE ★★ | WEST MAUI

100 Nohea Kai Drive, Lahaina, HI 96761; (800) 763-1333 or (808) 667-1200; fax (808) 667-8300; www.marriott.com/marriott/HNMHI

This is a full-service resort with a casual, family-oriented atmosphere and friendly service. Waterfalls, koi ponds, and tall coconut palms adorn the attractive grounds. A year-round children's program is available, as are Hawaiian craft lessons and a full menu of recreational sports and activities. The Marriott also has one of the island's best luau, held on the beach. A minimall with 20 shops is on the premises. The Marriott is in the process of converting to timeshare use, but for now, hotel operations continue in part of the property.

SETTING AND FACILITIES

Location On Kaanapali Beach.

Dining VaBene serves Italian cuisine, three meals daily.

Amenities and services Room service (until 10 p.m.), valet and self-parking ($7 per day), nightly luau (except Monday), 2 swimming pools, 2 Jacuzzis, fitness center, coin-operated laundry service.

ACCOMMODATIONS

Rooms 720, including 19 suites, 14 rooms for the disabled. Nonsmoking rooms available.

All rooms A/C, cable TV, lanai, phone, refrigerator, in-room safe, coffee maker.

Some rooms Sofa sleeper, larger lanai, separate dressing area.

Comfort and decor Spacious rooms adorned with tasteful furnishings and Islands artwork. Soft pastel colors add to overall ambience.

RATES, RESERVATIONS, AND RESTRICTIONS

Family plan Children ages 17 and under stay free with parents if using existing bedding. Maximum of 2 adults and 2 children per room.

Deposit Credit card guarantee, required. Cancellation notice must be given 72 hours prior to arrival for refund.

Credit cards All major credit cards accepted.

Check-in/out 3 p.m./noon. Early check-in and late check-out available on request (no guarantees).

MAUI PRINCE HOTEL $$$$

OVERALL ★★★★ | ROOM QUALITY ★★★½ | VALUE ★★½ | SOUTH MAUI

5400 Makena Alanui, Kihei, HI 96753; (800) 321-6248 or (808) 874-1111; fax (808) 879-8763; www.princehawaii.com

Situated on the cool slopes of Mount Haleakala and fronting lovely Maluaka Beach, this 1,800-acre resort is an isolated haven on the edge of a wilderness. The picturesque grounds offer a courtyard with a colorful koi pond and waterfall, all of which adds to the resort's tranquil, understated atmosphere. All rooms have views of the ocean as well as the neighboring islands of Molokai, Lanai, and Kahoolawe. The service level here is impeccable. The rooms are sparsely decorated, reflecting the Japanese background of this chain. It's something we like but many Western travelers may find disconcerting. Snorkeling and scuba diving are among the outdoor activities available; there are six tennis courts at the nearby Makena Tennis Club, and two championship golf courses. A hula show is presented at the oceanfront Molokini Lounge.

SETTING AND FACILITIES

Location In Makena in south Maui, short walk to Makena Beach.

Dining The award-winning Prince Court features seasonal, contemporary Island cuisine with fresh seafood, steaks, and some game dishes. Hakona serves traditional Japanese cuisine as well as Hawaiian/Japanese fusion dishes and 100 kinds of sushi.

Amenities and services Room service, welcome baskets on arrival, laundry service, fitness center, parking, children's program.

ACCOMMODATIONS

Rooms 300, including 57 suites; up to 10 rooms for the disabled. Non-smoking rooms available.

All rooms A/C, cable TV, lanai, in-room safe, phone, hair dryer, iron and board, bottled water, coffee maker.

Some rooms Second bedroom.

Comfort and decor Spacious and clean rooms have simple decor with creamy pastel tones and Island-theme artworks that create a modern, casual setting.

RATES, RESERVATIONS, AND RESTRICTIONS

Family plan Children ages 12 and under stay free with parents if using existing bedding, $40 charge per extra person.

Deposit 1-night deposit required. Cancellation notice must be given 72 hours prior to arrival for refund.

Credit cards All major credit card accepted.

Check-in/out 3 p.m./noon. Early check-in and late check-out available on request.

MAUIAN HOTEL ON NAPILI BEACH $$$

OVERALL ★★★½ | ROOM QUALITY ★★★½ | VALUE ★★★★ | WEST MAUI

5441 Lower Honoapiilani Road, Napili, HI 96761; (800) 367-5034 or (808) 669-6205; fax (808) 669-0129; www.mauian.com

Plain and simple, with a 1950s style on the outside and tasteful and comfortable inside, the Mauian endures with lots of homey Hawaiian spirit—from the heart, since it is owned and managed by a local Hawaiian family. The two acres of well-tended grounds feature fascinating flora, like jade vine used for lei-making and Hawaiian medicinal plants, as well as bountiful bananas and other fruits, which are served to guests. But the star attraction is Napili Beach at the end of the low-rise buildings, with Molokai and Lanai framing the scene. The Mauian occupies a central position on this swimmable stretch of golden sand with a few palms thrown in for atmosphere. The units are studios, done in tropical style with bright Island art and accents, bamboo beds, and teak or rattan furniture. If you care more about enjoying the beach in a tranquil, nostalgic Islands atmosphere than fancy bells and whistles, this is a very satisfying choice. Casual and fine restaurants, golf, and tennis are a short walk or drive away. The Kapalua Airport and Napili Plaza supermarket are just up the hill. You skip all the fuss of a big hotel in exchange for carrying your own things, parking your own car, and making your own dinner if you choose. You'll also be making phone calls from the desk in the open-air *ohana* (family) lounge where the television and other amusements are located, but there's no charge for local calls. Fresh tropical fruit and juice, coffee, breads, and cereals are served buffet style for breakfast, and your room comes with a tray for your do-it-yourself room service. Being here is the next best thing to visiting a friend's comfy beach house.

SETTING AND FACILITIES

Location On Napili Beach.

Dining Continental breakfast buffet; units have kitchen facilities.

Amenities and services Laundry, daily maid service, free parking, lounge with books, games, VCR and TV, courtesy phone.

ACCOMMODATIONS

Rooms 44 studios that sleep three people.

All rooms Refrigerator, stove, coffee maker, kitchen.

Comfort and decor Spacious rooms have clean, tropical furnishings and artwork and a private lanai with beach or ocean/island view.

RATES, RESERVATIONS, AND RESTRICTIONS

Family plan Children ages 5 and under stay free. Rates are based on double occupancy; there is a nominal charge per extra person.

Deposit 1-night deposit required. Cancellation notice must be given more than 14 days before arrival for refund.

Credit cards All major credit cards accepted.

Check-in/out 3 p.m./11 a.m. Early check-in and late check-out available on request.

THE PLANTATION INN $$$

OVERALL ★★★★ | ROOM QUALITY ★★★ | VALUE ★★★★ | WEST MAUI

174 Lahainaluna Road, Lahaina, HI 96761; (800) 433-6815 or (808) 667-9225; fax (808) 667-9293; www.theplantationinn.com

Lahaina is fortunate to have two neighboring bed-and-breakfast inns, Lahaina Inn (described above) and Plantation Inn, which also features an excellent restaurant on the premises and boasts even more appeal as a surprising refuge of peaceful sanity in the busy town. Quiet is one advantage of several at this property. The style is Victorian; the construction and amenities are modern, with a pool and whirlpool tub. The inn is a sister property with the Kaanapali Beach Hotel (described above) and guests have beach and other privileges at the resort three miles up the road. Breakfast is served around the pool and at the guest pavilion.

SETTING AND FACILITIES

Location Off-beach in Lahaina.

Dining Gerard's is an excellent French dining spot, a longtime favorite serving what chef Gerard Reversade terms "contemporary Island French" cuisine. Guests get a discount on the price of dinner.

Amenities and services Free parking, pool and Jacuzzi, outdoor pavilion for guests.

ACCOMMODATIONS

Rooms 19, including 4 suites.

All rooms A/C, ceiling fans, deluxe continental breakfast, private baths, TV/VCR, telephones, iron and board, hair dyer, refrigerator, sound proofing.

Some rooms Suites have kitchenettes. Most rooms have private lanai

Comfort and decor Rooms are well maintained and clean. Wood floors, antiques, canopy four-posters or brass beds, armoires, wicker, and the like set the mood.

RATES, RESERVATIONS, AND RESTRICTIONS

Deposit 1-night deposit required. Cancellation notice must be given 10 days prior to arrival for refund; $10 per night surcharge and 7-night minimum during the peak holiday week, Christmas Eve through New Year's Eve. Available packages combine a stay with dinner, whale-watching, rental cars, a dolphin cruise, and additional nights.

Credit cards All major credit cards accepted.

Check-in/out 3 p.m./noon. Late check-out on request.

RENAISSANCE WAILEA BEACH RESORT $$$$

OVERALL ★★★★ | ROOM QUALITY ★★★★ | VALUE ★★★ | SOUTH MAUI

3550 Wailea Alanui, Wailea, HI 96753; (800) 992-4532 or (808) 879-4900; fax (808) 874-5370; www.renaissancehotels.com

Another jewel property in Wailea, the Renaissance opened in 1978 as the Stouffer Wailea Beach Resort. The 15-acre property received a makeover in 1990. The elegant main lobby is made of marble and limestone and features hand-blown Italian glass fixtures and a grand stairway. Outside, the landscape is dotted with waterfalls and tropical flora. Golfers choose from three championship courses in Wailea, and tennis action is available at the 11-court Wailea Tennis Center. The Renaissance also offers a recreational rarity among Hawaii resorts: half-court basketball. For ambience and scenery, enjoy late-afternoon cocktails at the Sunset Terrace.

SETTING AND FACILITIES

Location At Wailea Resort, on the beach.

Dining The Palm Court features Mediterranean cuisine and buffets for dinner. Hana Gion is an intimate Japanese eatery.

Amenities and services Room service, laundry service, parking, fitness center.

ACCOMMODATIONS

Rooms 347, including 12 suites. Rooms for the disabled and nonsmoking rooms available.

All rooms A/C, cable TV, VCR, private balcony, phone, hair dryer, mini-refrigerator, coffee maker.

Comfort and decor In spacious and clean rooms, light colors and subtle tropical touches add to the bright atmosphere. Decor features Island-theme furnishings and artworks.

RATES, RESERVATIONS, AND RESTRICTIONS

Family plan Children ages 17 and under stay free with parents if using existing bedding.

Deposit 1-night deposit due within 10 days of booking. 72-hour cancellation notice required for refund.

Credit cards All major credit cards accepted.

Check-in/out 3 p.m./noon. Early check-in and late check-out available on request.

RITZ-CARLTON, KAPALUA $$$$

OVERALL ★★★★★ | ROOM QUALITY ★★★★★ | VALUE ★★★★ | WEST MAUI

One Ritz-Carlton Drive, Kapalua, HI 96761; (800) 241-3333 or (808) 669-6200; fax (808) 669-2028; www.ritzcarlton.com

This Ritz is a perennial AAA Five Diamond Award recipient, and it's not hard to understand why. Everything here, from service to guest rooms to dining, is perfect. The atmosphere here is one of quiet, blissful elegance. Set on 50 acres, the Ritz features two six-story wings that contour to the area's rolling terrain. Public areas are enhanced by 18th- and 19th-century artworks as well as paintings and ceramics created by gifted local artists. Recently added to the property is a 19,200-square-foot pavilion, located adjacent to the hotel's entrance. The Ritz Kids program allows children to learn about Maui's culture, nature, art, and ecology. Evening entertainment is provided at the Terrace Restaurant and Lobby Lounge. Kapalua Resort has a trio of championship golf courses and ten tennis courts. The Ritz hosts several notable annual events, including the PGA Mercedes Championships (January), the Celebration of the Arts (April), the Kapalua Wine and Food Symposium (usually July), and the Earth Maui Nature Summit (September). The Ritz-Carlton, Kapalua, is currently the world's only Audubon Heritage Cooperative Sanctuary Resort Hotel.

The sand dunes of Kapalua nearby, where 1,200 Hawaiian bones were unearthed, are held in perpetual trust. There are signs that say, "Kapu"—no trespassing—where the hotel originally was to be built. Often, we have seen tourists pay no heed to the kapu signs; they walk across the old Hawaiian graveyard as if it were a golf course. Please, don't behave so carelessly, should you stay at the Ritz.

SETTING AND FACILITIES

Location At Kapalua Resort in West Maui, a short walk to beach.

Dining The breezy Banyan Tree is the signature restaurant, serving Four Diamond–rated cuisine that stretches Pacific Rim in a new direction—

Down Under, with Australian fusion dishes. The Terrace Restaurant serves a popular buffet for breakfast and fresh local seafood for dinner. The restaurant also serves a Friday night seafood buffet and Sunday night Italian buffet.

Amenities and services 24-hour room service, twice-daily maid service, laundry service, fitness center, spa treatments, multilevel swimming pool, hydrotherapy pools, business facilities, children's program, golf, tennis, ocean activities.

ACCOMMODATIONS

Rooms 548, including 58 suites. ADA-approved rooms and nonsmoking rooms available.

All rooms A/C, cable TV with pay movies, 3 phones, lanai, in-room safe, honor bar, hair dryer, dataport, bathrobes.

Some rooms Personal concierge service, complimentary food and beverages.

Comfort and decor Oversized rooms, clean and well maintained. Warm colors and tropical-inspired furnishings with Hawaiian artworks. Large private lanai (80 percent of rooms have ocean views).

RATES, RESERVATIONS, AND RESTRICTIONS

Deposit No policy given. Cancel reservations 7 days prior to scheduled arrival for refund.

Credit cards All major credit cards accepted.

Check-in/out 3 p.m./noon. Early check-in and late check-out available on request (no guarantees).

SHERATON MAUI $$$$$

OVERALL ★★★★ | ROOM QUALITY ★★★★ | VALUE ★★★★ | WEST MAUI

2605 Kaanapali Parkway, Lahaina, HI 96761; (800) 782-9488 or (808) 661-0031; fax (808) 661-0458; www.sheraton-maui.com

After an extensive remake, the Sheraton Maui was repositioned as an upscale beach destination on 23 prime acres on Kaanapali Beach. Its elevated ground lobby opens to a wide panoramic view of the Pacific Ocean and a spectacular 147-foot-long oceanfront swimming lagoon. The resort is built atop and beside Black Rock, a lava rock landmark. During the summer, children ages 5–12 can participate in the complimentary Keiki Aloha Club, which includes lei-making and hula lessons, beach activities, and field trips to historic sites. Locals regard Black Rock as one of the best snorkeling areas on Maui. At sunset, a cliff-diving ceremony says aloha to another sunny day. The Hawaiian art on display throughout the public rooms is worth a look; so is the poolside bar with a smoking volcano for atmosphere.

SETTING AND FACILITIES

Location On Kaanapali Beach.

Dining The Kekaa Terrace serves seafood specialties and roasted or grilled meats. Teppan Yaki Dan offers an intriguing and delicious blend of European and Pacific cuisines; chefs prepare meals while you watch.

Amenities and services Swimming pool, room service, laundry facilities, parking ($5 per day), fitness center, spa, children's program.

ACCOMMODATIONS

Rooms 510, including 46 suites, 15 rooms for the disabled. Nonsmoking rooms available.

All rooms A/C, cable TV, phone, in-room safe, mini-refrigerator, coffee maker, iron and board, hair dryer.

Some rooms Microwave, second TV, parlor.

Comfort and decor Spacious, clean, well-maintained rooms have custom bedspreads and tropical furnishings, as well as large lanai. Hawaiian artworks adorn the walls.

RATES, RESERVATIONS, AND RESTRICTIONS

Family plan Children ages 17 and under stay free with parents if using existing bedding.

Deposit 1-night deposit due 10 days after booking. Cancellation notice must be given 72 hours prior to arrival for refund.

Credit cards All major credit cards accepted.

Check-in/out 3 p.m./noon. Early check-in and late check-out available on request.

WESTIN MAUI $$$$$

OVERALL ★★★★ | ROOM QUALITY ★★★★ | VALUE ★★★★ | WEST MAUI

2365 Kaanapali Parkway, Lahaina, HI 96761; (800) 937-8461 or (808) 667-2525; fax (808) 661-5831; www.westinmaui.com

The Westin is an elegant resort with Asian influences and artwork throughout the property. The most notable physical feature here is the resort's 87,000-square-foot aquatic playground. There are five pools, three joined together by a pair of water slides, and two divided by a swim-through grotto with twin waterfalls and a hidden Jacuzzi. One of the pools is designated "adults only" and features a swim-up bar. The Westin Kids Club provides supervised fun and games for the *keiki* (kids).

Island-style entertainment is provided nightly. For night owls, a side benefit of staying in Kaanapali is that it's just a five-minute drive away from Lahaina, where most of West Maui's after-dark action takes place.

SETTING AND FACILITIES

Location On Kaanapali Beach.

Dining Tropica specializes in fresh seafood and steak as well as Pacific Rim flavors. For breakfast, the fastest, cheapest solution is the Colonnade Cafe, serving Starbucks, fruit, juice, and pastries or rolls.

Amenities and services Full-service spa, room service, laundry/valet service, parking, business center, health club, children's program.

ACCOMMODATIONS

Rooms 713, including 28 suites, 14 rooms for the disabled. Nonsmoking rooms available.

All rooms A/C, cable TV, phone, balcony, minibar, in-room safe, coffee maker, iron and board, hair dryer.

Some rooms Sofabed in living room, upgraded amenities.

Comfort and decor Spacious and clean rooms are decorated with light colors and comfortable furnishings to create a modern setting. The ambience is elegant without being stuffy.

RATES, RESERVATIONS, AND RESTRICTIONS

Family plan Children ages 17 and under stay free with parents if using existing bedding. Maximum of 4 guests per room.

Deposit 2-night deposit due within 15 days after booking. 72-hour cancellation notice required for refund.

Credit cards All major credit cards accepted.

Check-in/out 3 p.m./noon. Early check-in and late check-out on availability.

Molokai

LODGE AND BEACH VILLAGE AT MOLOKAI RANCH $$$$$

OVERALL ★★★★½ | ROOM QUALITY ★★★★★ | VALUE ★★★★ | MOLOKAI

100 Maunaloa Highway, Maunaloa, HI 96770; (888) 627-8982 or (808) 552-2741; fax (808) 552-2773; www.molokairanch.com

Molokai's only upscale lodge, a member of the prestigious Small Luxury Hotels of the World, sits on a 54,000-acre working cattle ranch with a long-distance view of the Pacific. The 22-room inn is decorated in a paniolo heritage theme and offers low-key, friendly service that isn't particularly *wikiwiki* (fast, swift, or hurry-hurry). This is, after all, Molokai, and where else does the waitstaff serve your dinner and then dance hula among the tables? You can go to the beach, but it's a long, bumpy ride; you might prefer to splash in the infinity pool and hot tub. Activities include horseback trail riding, mountain-bike riding, kayaking, beach-combing, dude rodeo, archery, beach adventures, clay shooting, cultural hikes, ocean expeditions (shoreline casting, throw netting, guided snorkeling, and spearfishing), a paniolo round-up, and spa treatments. Activity rates range from $25 to $500; a $15 per room daily fee covers on-ranch transportation, Internet access, and local calls. For a different look at Molokai Ranch, the Kaupoa Beach village is a cluster of 40 two-bedroom tentalows (canvas cabins on private decks) with ecologically correct appointments such as solar lighting and private outdoor rest rooms incorporating solar showers and compost toilets. Make no mistake; this is upscale camping with soft fleece blankets and in-room coolers full of drinks, but it's fun for kids of all ages and perfect for a ranch getaway. Campers eat communally at the open-air dining pavilion (kids under 12 eat free with adults) and have at their toetips a very scenic little double-crescent beach accessible only through the ranch.

SETTING AND FACILITIES

Location There's rare old-Hawaii ambience in this handsome new lodge overlooking horse pastures and the blue Pacific. Located at the entrance to the historic (and rebuilt) plantation town of Maunaloa, the lodge features wrap-around verandahs for the panoramic views.

Dining Breakfast, dinner, and theme buffet dinners (pasta on Wednesday, Asian buffets on Sunday) are served in the Maunaloa Room and its adjoining view deck. Lunch, cocktails, and lighter fare are served in the Paniolo Lounge. Guests can elect to hop on a bus and ride down to Kaupoa Beach pavilion for breakfast, lunch, or dinner cookout buffets.

Amenities and services Great Room with fireplace, meeting room, heated swimming pool, day spa and fitness center, in-room Internet access, room service, activities desk, children's program.

ACCOMMODATIONS

Rooms 22.

All rooms Private lanai, TV with in-room cable, refrigerator, in-room safe, high-speed dataports.

Comfort and decor Each room, with a big ocean-facing view and outdoor lanai, is furnished differently, in a tasteful, rustic ranch style, including claw-foot tubs, *hikiee* (large Hawaiian bedlike couches), and other spots to curl up and read.

RATES, RESERVATIONS, AND RESTRICTIONS

Family plan Children ages 12 and under stay free with a paying adult.

Deposit 1-night deposit, refundable on cancellation within 72 hours.

Credit cards All major credit cards accepted.

Check-in/out 3 p.m./11 a.m.

Lanai

HOTEL LANAI $

OVERALL ★★★½ | ROOM QUALITY ★★★ | VALUE ★★★½ | LANAI

P.O. Box 520, Lanai City, HI 96763; (800) 795-7211 or (808) 565-7211; fax (808) 565-6450; www.hotellanai.com

Opened in 1923 for visiting Dole Pineapple execs, the 11-room Hotel Lanai has always attracted a following, even more so since Henry Clay Richardson opened his Creole-inspired bistro in 1996. If you can't afford to stay at The Lodge at Koele or Manele Bay Hotel, this is your alternative. Rooms are clean and comfortable, service is friendly, and you'll likely meet some interesting local characters at *pau hana* ("work done") time.

SETTING AND FACILITIES

Location In Lanai City, no beach.

Dining Henry Clay's Rotisserie serves a hearty selection of spit-roasted meats, seafood, pasta, gourmet pizzas, and more.

Amenities and services Free parking. No room service or laundry service.

ACCOMMODATIONS

Rooms 11. All are nonsmoking.

All rooms Ceiling fans, phone.

Some rooms TV, bathtub.

Comfort and decor Medium-sized rooms have pine floors, ceiling fans, custom quilts, and original photographs depicting the island's plantation days.

RATES, RESERVATIONS, AND RESTRICTIONS

Family plan Children ages 8 and under stay free with parents if using existing bedding.

Deposit Half of total stay due in advance on booking. Cancellation notice must be given 14 days prior to arrival for refund, minus a $10 processing fee.

Credit cards　Visa, MasterCard, and American Express.

Check-in/out　1 p.m./11 a.m. Early check-in and late check-out available on request.

THE LODGE AT KOELE $$$$$

OVERALL ★★★★½ | ROOM QUALITY ★★★★ | VALUE ★★★½ | LANAI

P.O. Box 310, Lanai City, HI 96763; (800) 321-4666 or (808) 565-7300; fax (808) 565-4561; www.lanai-resorts.com

Nestled on the island's central highlands, the Lodge is reminiscent of an English hilltop manor, complete with manicured lawns, cozy fireplaces, and afternoon tea. Paintings, sculptures, and artifacts adorn the resort's interiors. Paths meander through flower gardens, past an English conservatory, to an inviting swimming pool. The atmosphere is calm and relaxed, providing a welcome escape. You'll want to get some exercise, of course, and the Lodge doesn't disappoint there either: Work out at the new fitness center, explore the countryside on a mountain bike, play tennis, or enjoy a round at one of Lanai's two award-winning championship courses. An unusual feature at the Lodge is the Visiting Artist Program, where guests meet and mingle with noted authors, chefs, and entertainers.

SETTING AND FACILITIES

Location　Upcountry, among the tall, cool Cook pines, no beach.

Dining　The award-winning Formal Dining Room showcases Pacific rim cuisine with local touches.

Amenities and services　Room service, concierge, laundry service, fitness center, swimming pool.

ACCOMMODATIONS

Rooms　102, including 14 suites, 2 rooms for the disabled. The Lodge is a nonsmoking facility.

All rooms　Ceiling fans, cable TV, VCR, phone, private lanai, minibar, in-room safe, robes, slippers.

Some rooms　Fireplaces, larger space, upgraded amenities.

Comfort and decor　Very spacious, luxurious, and exceptionally clean rooms feature hand-carved poster beds, quiet ceiling fans, and oil paintings by local artists.

RATES, RESERVATIONS, AND RESTRICTIONS

Family plan　Children ages 15 and under stay free with parents if using existing bedding. Maximum of 4 guests per room (2 adults and 2 children). $40 charge per extra guest.

Deposit 2-night deposit due within 14 days of booking. Cancellation notice must be given 14 days prior to arrival for refund.

Credit cards All major credit cards accepted except Discover.

Check-in/out 3 p.m./noon. Hospitality rooms available.

THE MANELE BAY HOTEL $$$$$

OVERALL ★★★★½ | ROOM QUALITY ★★★★ | VALUE ★★★½ | LANAI

P.O. Box 310, Lanai City, HI 96763; (800) 321-4666 or (808) 565-7700; fax (808) 565-2483; www.lanai-resorts.com

Perched atop windswept red-lava cliffs, the Manele overlooks Lanai's magnificent coastline and Hulopoe Bay. A blend of Mediterranean and Hawaiian design, the Manele Bay Hotel is full of Oriental artifacts and grand murals. Lush tropical gardens add color to landscapes, but nothing surpasses the ocean views. It's just a short stroll to Hulopoe Beach, one of the best beaches in Hawaii, with excellent water clarity for snorkeling and scuba diving. Great golf awaits you at The Challenge at Manele. Like the Lodge at Koele, the Manele delivers a memorable experience.

SETTING AND FACILITIES

Location At Hulopoe Bay, a short walk from the beach.

Dining The Hulopoe Court serves fine Hawaii regional cuisine. The Ihilani serves memorable Mediterranean-style cuisine.

Amenities and services Room service, valet and self-parking, spa, golf, tennis, concierge service, children's program.

ACCOMMODATIONS

Rooms 250, including 13 suites, 6 rooms for the disabled. Nonsmoking rooms available.

All rooms A/C, cable TV, VCR, phone, radio, in-room safe, lanai, minibar, hair dryer, sitting area, tub and shower.

Some rooms Butler service.

Comfort and decor Spacious, comfortable rooms have refined furnishings, floral-theme decor, and accessories collected from around the world.

RATES, RESERVATIONS, AND RESTRICTIONS

Family plan Children ages 15 and under stay free with parents if using existing bedding. Maximum of 4 guests per room (2 adults and 2 children).

Deposit 2-night deposit due within 14 days of booking. Cancellation notice must be given 14 days prior to arrival for refund.

Credit cards All major credit cards accepted except Discover.

Check-in/out 3 p.m./noon. Early check-in and late check-out available on request (no guarantees).

Part Four

Going Holoholo: Getting Around and Getting to Know Maui

When You Arrive

In Hawaiian, going holoholo means traveling around, a perfect way to get to know the islands of Maui County. But first you've got to get on the ground. It's likely you'll pass through Honolulu International Airport, one of the busiest in the United States, before flying on to your Maui County destination: Kahului Airport, Hana Airport, and Kapalua Airport on Maui; Hoolehua Airport on Molokai; and Lanai Airport on Lanai. The airports are simple to navigate, particularly the smaller local ones. Gates have numbers; just follow the signs. Baggage claims are designated by letters of the alphabet in the primary mainland arrival terminals, and by numbers in the interisland terminal. Note, however, that West Coast flights by the local carriers, Hawaiian Air Lines and Aloha Air Lines, use the interisland terminal for ticketing and baggage. Latest arrival and departure times appear on the usual video monitors. Baggage claim is on the street level. The wait only seems longer because you're anxious to hit the beach.

Arriving in Maui is a sensual experience. You smell flowers, hear ukulele and people singing Hawaiian music, and feel the tropical warmth and tradewinds. Outside baggage claim, you will find car-rental agencies and courtesy phones, taxis, buses, shuttles, car-rental shuttles, and private or hotel limousines. If you arrive in Honolulu on an international flight, the first to wish you "aloha" in their fashion are U.S. Customs and Immigration agents. Honolulu is today a far better staffed and more efficient port of entry than it was in the past.

We've noticed that interisland airlines and airports tend to be very efficient at handling the constant loads of passengers and bags—much more so than commuter connections on the mainland. For people who live on the islands, this process replaces public transit.

Of Maui's three airports, Kahului Airport, at the island's center, is the main terminal for interisland and mainland flights. Car-rental desks and taxi service are available outside baggage claim. Most people take a shuttle to the car compound a few minutes away. Kapalua/West Maui Airport serves only interisland flights on smaller aircrafts but is handy to area resorts and towns. Car rentals are available nearby, and resort shuttles serve the airport. Tiny Hana Airport serves small plane traffic. Molokai's airport is an older, Island-style, open-air facility located midisland near Kaunakakai. Lanai's airport is a new, modern facility below Lanai City. Arriving guests are met by resort staff and transported by resort bus.

Ground Transportation at Airports

For detailed information on car rentals, including contact numbers, see Part Two, "Planning Your Visit." Although you can generally rent a car on arrival, it's a good idea to book one in advance; you're guaranteed a car and sometimes a better rate. You don't have to rent a car to reach your hotel, as many offer shuttle service (ask when you book) and there are independent shuttle operators and taxis available at the airports. Nevertheless, a vehicle greatly expands your touring options, particularly on Maui. We recommend securing one at some point during your visit.

Maui: Kahului Airport

Rental Cars   Alamo, Avis, Budget, Dollar, Hertz, and National are just outside the main terminal (turn right as you leave the baggage area). Thrifty, Regency, and Word of Mouth have a courtesy phones at the airport's information board inside the baggage-claim area.

Taxis   Maui Airport Taxi has a dispatcher inside baggage claim. Or you can just walk directly across the street and hail a cab at the curb.

Shuttles   Use the courtesy phone mentioned above to contact the Airport Shuttle or Speedy Shuttle. The wait is usually less than 15 minutes; costs vary depending on the destination. The Airport Shuttle, for example, charges $22 for two passengers bound for Wailea and $32 to Kaanapali. To reserve a shuttle in advance, call the Airport Shuttle at (808) 661-6667 or Speedy Shuttle at (808) 875-8070.

Roberts Hawaii also provides transportation to the Kaanapali Beach Resort area from 9 a.m. to 4 p.m. daily, with an evening run between 6:30 and 7 p.m. Look for the customer-service desk marked Airport Hotel Shuttle in the baggage-claim area (directly across from carousel #4). Shuttles depart every half-hour. The cost is $13 per person.

Maui: Kapalua-West Maui Airport

Rental Cars   Use the courtesy phone at the baggage claim area for a free shuttle van to car-rental offices. Taxis are curbside outside baggage claim area.

Molokai: Molokai Airport

Rental Cars   Budget and Dollar are the only car-rental agencies at the Molokai Airport. Their customer-service desks are located by the baggage claim area.

Taxis   One company serves the airport on Molokai but offers no white courtesy phone (remember why you came to Molokai: to escape modern life). If you don't spot a taxi outside the open-air baggage-claim area, call Molokai Off-Road Tours and Taxi (see below for number).

MAUI COUNTY TAXI OPERATORS

Maui

AB Taxi (808) 667-7575	La Bella Taxi (808) 242-8011
Alii Cab (808) 661-3688	Royal Sedan and Taxi Service (808) 874-6900
Central Maui Taxi (808) 244-7278	
Classy Taxi (808) 665-0003	Wailea Taxi and Tours (808) 874-5000
Kihei Taxi (808) 879-3000	

Molokai

Molokai Off-Road Tours and Taxi
   (808) 553-3369

Lanai

No full-time taxi companies serve Lanai. Dollar Rent-A-Car provides taxi service on a driver-available basis. Call (808) 565-7227.

Lanai: Lanai Airport

Rental Cars   Dollar Rent-A-Car is the only car-rental agency on Lanai. On arrival, walk to the reception desk and use the red courtesy phone. A van will pick you up and transport you to Dollar's pickup location, about three miles away.

Shuttle   A convenient way to get around is Lanai Resort's shuttles. The $10-per-person charge includes round-trip airport transportation and all shuttles between the island's two resorts, The Lodge at Koele and the Manele Bay Hotel. The shuttle vans are located right outside the airport's baggage-claim area.

Maui Driving Tours

Rent a car or a guide and get out into exotic Maui. You'll see intriguing natural sights, glimpse a different way of life, and burn a few rolls of film—or if you're an active explorer, a lot of calories, and if you're a shopper, a dollar or two. You probably won't burn a lot of gas, because these islands are not very big and the roads are not very fast.

The following Maui driving tours highlight both the island's natural and man-made attractions, including the elaborate resorts, which we recommend touring. All are open to the public (especially those with shopping centers). And that goes for beaches, too. We provide basic driving directions, sticking to the main roads. Purchasing a detailed map of the island is a must if you plan to venture off the main arteries (see page 58). Depending on where you're staying, you may opt to augment these tour routes (especially if your hotel is in the middle of a route), and backtracking is sometimes a necessity, as roads do not circumnavigate the island.

MAUI DRIVE TIMES	
From Kahului Airport to:	**Time to Travel**
Haleakala National Park	1 hour, 45 minutes
Hana	2 hours, 30 minutes
Kaanapali	50 minutes
Kapalua	1 hour
Kihei	25 minutes
Lahaina	45 minutes
Makena	40 minutes
Wailea	35 minutes
Wailuku	10 minutes

West Maui

It's a pleasant drive from Central Maui to the island's western shore, where old **Lahaina** town and **Kaanapali** are the main attractions. Two-lane Highway 30 passes through a tunnel on the coastal route; there's a free whale-watch turnout at **McGregor Point,** little tree-shaded beach parks, old Japanese graveyards, and channel views of Lanai and Molokai.

Hot and dry Lahaina (it means "the heat"), with its historic district and harbor, is a popular hangout day or night. There is a great sense of history here—in fact, the entire town is designated a National Historic Landmark—and Lahaina's storied past lives on in its restored relic structures that cluster around a mammoth banyan tree in the town square.

Lahaina was the focal point of the Pacific whaling industry in the mid–nineteenth century; at the height of the whaling era, more than a hundred whaling ships rode at anchor offshore in Lahaina Roads, the naturally protected mooring. Along with the whaling ships came hundreds of pleasure-seeking sailors who turned Lahaina upside down with their wild cavorting. A town prison was built in 1852 to contain the worst offenders.

The sailors were frequent antagonists to the disapproving Christian missionaries who lived in Lahaina. It was a constant battle between the two factions. Once, in 1825, a mob of British sailors threatened to kill William Richards, one of the first missionaries to settle on Maui, and set his house on fire unless a law forbidding prostitution and the sale of alcohol was repealed. Two years later, a cannon struck Richards's home from a visiting whaler. One missionary wrote in 1837, "As a mass, the seamen are sunk in vice."

Today, a stroll through Lahaina includes many historical points of interest (see our walking tour map on page 243). At the **Baldwin Home Museum,** for example, take a guided tour of the fully restored home of the Reverend Dwight Baldwin, a prominent Protestant missionary in the nineteenth century, and gain insights into the triumphs and tribulations of Hawaii's missionaries. Nearby is **Hale Paahao,** the old prison itself (appropriately enough, on Prison Street), where hundreds of whaling-era sailors took "shelter" for the night, mostly for public drunkenness, still an all-too-common condition after sundown in Lahaina today.

Front Street is the site of **Friday Night Is Art Night,** a weekly celebration of Maui art featuring street entertainment and art demonstrations at participating galleries. Each Halloween night, Front Street hosts Maui's biggest costume parade, Hawaii's version of Mardi Gras.

A short drive up from Lahaina is **Kaanapali** ("cliffs of Kaana"), where sugar barons Samuel Alexander and Henry Baldwin converted cane fields into the island's first master-planned resort on a four-mile gold-sand beach. Today it includes two championship golf courses and an open-air mall with shops and restaurants.

The nearly half-century old resort is touristy but enduring, a popular family resort on a good beach. The shopping center, **Whalers Village,** is home to the **Whale Center of the Pacific**—dedicated to the life and history of the state mammal, the 40-ton Pacific humpback whale (*Megaptera novaeangliae*), which migrates to Maui waters from Alaska every year. Whale-watch boats depart daily from Lahaina Harbor when the whales are in the Islands.

You can ride from Kaanapali to Lahaina via the **Lahaina-Kaanapali & Pacific Railroad,** better known as the "Sugar Cane Train." In the heyday of Maui's sugar era, plantations used privately owned railroad lines to transport crops. The Sugar Cane Train represents the last of these railroads. It's a plodding but scenic half-hour round-trip, and the conductor provides narration and entertainment on the way.

In the late eighteenth century, King Kamehameha declared Lahaina capital of the kingdom. The city was favored for its weather, lush thickets of banana and breadfruit trees, and prime location, tucked comfortably

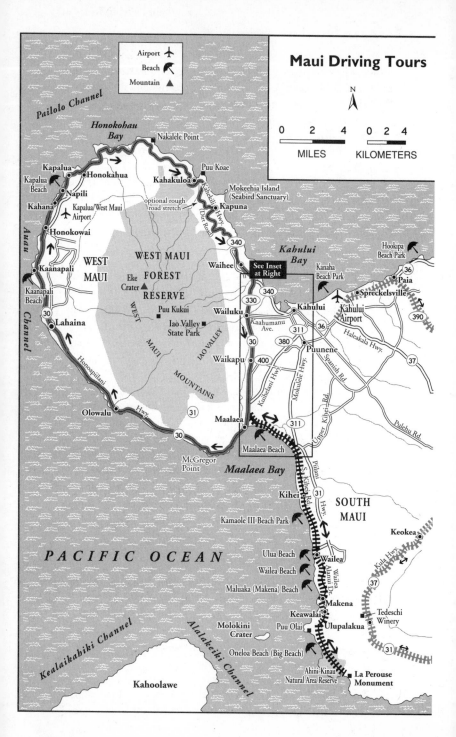

Maui Driving Tours

Airport ✈
Beach ⚓
Mountain ▲

N

0 2 4   0 2 4
MILES   KILOMETERS

Pailolo Channel

Honokohau Bay

Nakalele Point

Kapalua
Kapalua Beach
Honokahua
Napili
Kahana
Kapalua/West Maui Airport
Honokowai

Puu Koae

Kahakuloa

optional rough road stretch

Mokeehia Island (Seabird Sanctuary)

Kapuna

340

Kahului Bay

Hookipa Beach Park

36

Paia

Spreckelsville

390

WEST MAUI

WEST MAUI FOREST RESERVE

Eke Crater ▲

Puu Kukui ■

Iao Valley State Park

Waihee

See Inset at Right

340

330

Kanaha Beach Park

Kahului

Kahului Airport

Kaanapali
Kaanapali Beach

Auau Channel

30

Lahaina

Wailuku

Kaahumanu Ave.

311

36

Haleakala Hwy.

37

WEST MAUI MOUNTAINS

Waikapu

30

380

Puunene

Spanish Rd.

Honoapiilani Hwy.

Olowalu

31

30

Maalaea

400

311

Pulehu Rd.

McGregor Point

Maalaea Bay

Maalaea Beach

Kihei

31

SOUTH MAUI

Keokea

Kamaole III Beach Park

PACIFIC OCEAN

Ulua Beach

Wailea

Wailea Beach

Maluaka (Makena) Beach

Makena

37

Tedeschi Winery

Keawalai

Ulupalakua

Molokini Crater

Puu Olai

Oneloa Beach (Big Beach)

31

Kealaikahiki Channel

Alalakeiki Channel

Ahini-Kinau Natural Area Reserve

La Perouse Monument

Kahoolawe

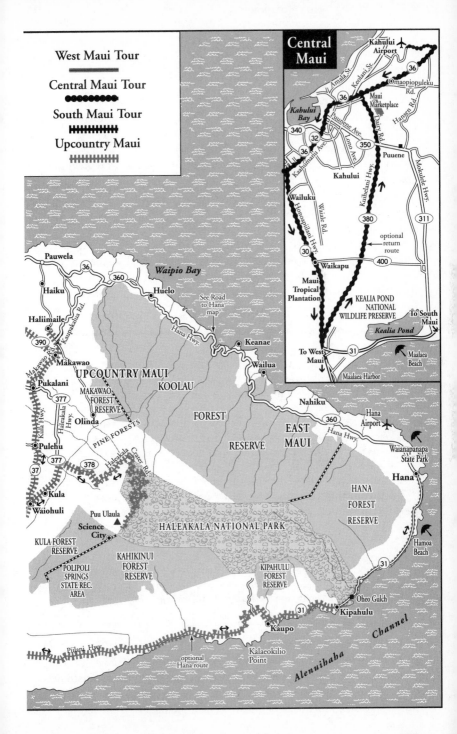

West Maui Tour

Central Maui Tour

South Maui Tour

Upcountry Maui

Central Maui

Kahului Airport

Amala St.
Keolani St.
maopiopuleku Rd.
36

Kahului Bay

Maui Marketplace

340
32
36
36
Puunene Ave.
Hansen Rd.
Lono Ave.
350
Puunene
Mokulele Hwy.

Kahaumanu Ave.
Waiale Rd.
Kahului
Kuihelani Hwy.

Wailuku

Honoapiilani Hwy.
380
311

30

optional return route

Waikapu
400

Maui Tropical Plantation

KEALIA POND NATIONAL WILDLIFE PRESERVE

To South Maui

To West Maui
31
Kealia Pond

Maalaea Beach

Maalaea Harbor

Pauwela
36
360
Waipio Bay

Haiku

Huelo

Haliimaile

See Road to Hana map

Kaupakalua Rd.

390
Hana Hwy.
Keanae

Makawao

UPCOUNTRY MAUI
KOOLAU
Wailua

Makawao Rd.
377
MAKAWAO FOREST RESERVE

Pukalani

Haleakala Hwy.
Olinda

FOREST

Nahiku

360
Hana Airport
Hana Hwy.

Kula Hwy.
PINE FORESTS
RESERVE
EAST MAUI

Pulehu

Haleakala
Crater Rd.

37
377
378

Waianapanapa State Park

Kula

Waiohuli

Puu Ulaula

HANA FOREST RESERVE

Science City

HALEAKALA NATIONAL PARK

Hana

KULA FOREST RESERVE

KAHIKINUI FOREST RESERVE

KIPAHULU FOREST RESERVE

Hamoa Beach

POLIPOLI SPRINGS STATE REC. AREA

31

Oheo Gulch
Kipahulu

Piilani Hwy.

optional Hana route

Kaupo

31

Kalacokilio Point

Alenuihaha Channel

157

between the West Maui Mountains and the Pacific Ocean. And so it remained for 50 years, until another king moved the political center of Hawaii to Honolulu.

Before establishing Lahaina as capital, Kamehameha secured Maui from the control of its most notorious high chief, the ferocious Kahekili, who built houses out of the skulls of defeated warriors. Kahekili gives his name to a nearby beach and Kahekili's Leap, where he made a daring dive off a cliff. The plunge is reenacted nightly at sundown at **Puu Kekaa (Black Rock)** on Kaanapali Beach. Despite a lifetime of war, Kahekili survived into his 80s; he died at Waikiki Beach.

Beyond Kaanapali, at Maui's northwest end, lies **Kapalua Resort,** a picturesque resort on former pineapple plantation land with a string of exquisite bays. (Although Kapalua literally translates to "two borders," the preferred interpretation is the more poetic "arms embracing the sea.") Two luxury hotels anchor the resort, which includes condominiums, three championship golf courses, two tennis complexes, and a cluster of shops, restaurants, and a grocery store.

THE OO BIRD

We love provenance—the lives objects have lived. Which is why we look to haunt small, out-of-the-way museums like the Bailey House in Wailuku on Maui. Every time we come, we see and learn about something new. Last time, it was a Maui Oo, an extinct bird last seen on Molokai in 1904, which we had somehow overlooked before. Yet here it was, in a glass case, a black bird with bright yellow wing feathers, its little feet crossed as if it had just dropped out of the sky, not endured a century of extinction. The Kauai Oo (*Moho braccatus*), a related species, was last seen in the Alakai Swamp in 1986. The Oo trophy is now so rare that the Bishop Museum in Honolulu keeps a solitary taxidermy specimen in a dark safe.

If you happen to be in England, you may see a cape once worn by Hawaiian kings made of 20,000 bright yellow Oo thigh feathers at the Pitt-Rivers Museum at the University of Oxford. It's not the same as seeing an Oo on the wing, but Simon Winchester of the *Manchester Guardian* called the Oo cape "certainly one of the most remarkably lovely things in any museum in England." Where, Hawaii folks believe, it has no business being.

For hiking enthusiasts, the **Kapalua Nature Society** (call (808) 669-0244) offers guests hikes in the West Maui Mountains, including one of the world's most expensive walks—a $500 trek into the Puu Kukui rainforest for 12 hikers who win the opportunity by an annual lottery. **Puu Kukui,** the 5,788-foot peak of the West Maui mountains, is the second wettest spot on Earth (after Mount Waialeale on Kauai). Its summit hides a boggy rainforest filled with rare native species of birds and stunted trees. The lucky hikers are flown by helicopter beyond Iao Needle to 4,751-foot Eke Crater, which early Hawaiians believed was heaven's gate.

Down on the shore below, beyond Kapalua, the **Northwest Coast** turns rugged and rocky as the highway winds past Honolua Bay, Nakalele Bay, and the fishing and farming village of **Kahakuloa,** where drivers stop for shaved ice and a break from the tightly curving, often one-lane road. Just beyond the village up at the top of a cliff, look for **Kaukini Gallery,** featuring 100 local artists' works. Drivers with off-road vehicles and others willing to brave a trip down the unpaved Kahekeli Highway can complete a loop by returning to Highway 330 via Highway 340. The cautious can backtrack around the West Maui Mountains.

KAHULUI, THE LEAST HAWAIIAN PLACE

On every island, we suppose, there's got to be a practical place where you can commit retail—you know, get gas, find film, eat pizza by the slice, sip lattes, shop for Nikes, get fast cash at the ATM, and otherwise hang out at the mall. Until recently, there was little of this mainland stuff on Maui. Perhaps it all surfaced overnight while everybody was snorkeling. Now, Kahului looks like the place you went to Maui to get away from. It's got a big new mall, streets lined with used car lots, fast food joints, pizza parlors, and blocks of traffic lights and traffic jams. What used to be a wide spot in the road is now an excellent example of bad urban planning—there's a Costco next to a wildlife preserve, with Maui's three main roads ending in a killer intersection that puts lost, deplaning tourists at direct odds with home-bound locals. Unless you're a serious mall rat on holiday, or need to fill up your rental car on the way out of town, you may opt to avoid this least Hawaiian place. But if you need to resupply, you might be grateful to patronize Kahului's shops along with the locals.

Central Maui

Starting in the north, from Kahalui Airport en route to Kahului, you pass **Kanaha Pond** on the right, a bird preserve in the middle of commercial district complete with Costco, K-Mart, and a Borders bookstore. Once a Hawaiian fishpond, the sanctuary is now Maui's prime waterfowl preserve and home of the endangered Hawaiian stilt, which (birders, please note) can often be seen pecking the mudflats—from your car or from a viewing area at the junction of Highway 36 and Highway 396.

Wailuku is the gateway to **Iao Valley** and a good stop for lunch or to stroll and shop. Maui's historic clapboard county seat, Wailuku is a shopper's haven with art galleries, antiques stores, jewelers, goldsmiths, gift shops, and a farmer's market, which is worth a visit if you've never seen such tropical fruits as durian, starfruit, and lychee.

The **Bailey House Museum,** run by the Maui Historical Society, is a relic missionary house full of artifacts dating to 1833, with gardens, early artwork, and a gift shop stuffed with made-on-Maui arts and crafts.

Most travelers pass through Wailuku on the way to **Iao Valley State Park,** the most photogenic valley easily visited in the West Maui Mountains. The centerpiece of the 6.2-acre park is **Iao Needle,** a 1,200-foot volcanic spire sculpted by eons of erosion. Also in Iao Valley is **Kepaniwai Park,** an outdoor museum highlighting Maui's cultural heritage, and the **Hawaii Nature Center** (see page 197) with guided hikes designed for children. The center also has 30 hands-on exhibits focusing on Hawaii's natural history.

Headed west, **Maui Tropical Plantation** is a roadside attraction and garden of tropical delights, where admission is free but a 40-minute narrated tram ride for two through remnant fields of pineapple, sugar, and other tropical crops will break a $20.

An architectural surprise appears at **Waikapu Golf and Country Club,** intended as a private Japanese golf club, on the way west from Wailuku. The clubhouse is based on plans designed—but never built—by Frank Lloyd Wright as a house for playwright Arthur Miller and his wife, Marilyn Monroe. You can gaze at the design, but the course is now closed. To return north, take Kuihelani Highway (Highway 380). Riding through the cane fields, you will pass the **Baldwin Sugar Museum** and the **Puunene Sugar Mill,** a short side trip down Puunene Avenue. Take Highway 30 to reach West Maui or Highway 31 to South Maui.

South Maui

At Maui's "chin" is **Maalaea Bay**, a cluster of commerce around a boat harbor (a key embarkation for Molokini-bound snorkel boats) and surfing area. There you'll find **Maui Ocean Center,** a 600,000-gallon aquarium with hundreds of ocean creatures, including rays, sea turtles, reef fish, and a tiger shark. A transparent walk-through tunnel at the center of the tank provides a 240° view as schools of fish glide overhead.

Driving south along Maalaea Bay, you pass **Kealia Pond National Wildlife Preserve,** home to the endangered green sea turtle. Notice the yellow-and-black Turtle Crossing signs and what look like snow fences along the beach; those are measures to keep the turtles from crossing the busy highway. Maalaea Beach is good for surfing, but not for sunning in the afternoon, when a hard wind kicks gritty sand in your face.

Beyond Maalaea is **Kihei,** a beach resort town with three roadside beach parks, **Kamaole I, II, and III** (III is most popular), some 50 condominium complexes, shops, restaurants, businesses, and a rarity: nightlife, including dancing spots, nightclubs, sports bars, and karaoke bars. If you need a mall to feel at home, the newest is **Piilani Village Shopping Center,** complete with Roy's Kihei Restaurant and Outback Steakhouse, out on Piilani Highway on the way to Wailea.

South of Kihei is the master-planned resort of **Wailea** ("water of Lea," goddess of canoes), a 1,500-acre oasis of luxury hotels and condos, set on five gold-sand crescent beaches. Wailea is fine dining, boutique shopping, and 54 holes of championship golf. It is the prime luxury resort destination on Maui.

In ancient lore, a mysterious birdman named Manupae arrived at Paeahu, where Wailea is today, in search of a mate. He met and fell in love with a lovely young woman named Kahaea o Kamaole. Kahaea's father, a wealthy and powerful man on the island, did not approve of Manupae and banished him and Kahaea from the area. The young lovers fled to the high slopes of Haleakala Volcano, near a cinder cone called Puu Makua, and had a daughter. They named her Lelehune ("fine rain" or "spray"), after the refreshing mountain mists that breathed life to Maui's dry, thirsty lowlands. Today, the lelehune mists still kiss the shores of Wailea, a gentle reminder of enduring love in the Islands.

If you go hotel hopping (and you should), start with the Disneyesque **Grand Wailea Resort Hotel and Spa,** the elegant **Four Seasons Maui Resort,** and the Arabian fantasy **Fairmont Kea Lani Hotel Maui.** The Hawaii-style **Marriott Wailea Beach Resort** is the best bargain on this luxury coast. It is exactly what you expect a Hawaii resort to be: open, airy, full of sea breezes, tropical flowers, and gracious staff, with the best location for shopping. Next door are **The Shops at Wailea,** Maui's version of Rodeo Drive, a two-story $70 million mall of boutiques, including Tiffany, Prada, Mont Blanc, Banana Republic, and Florida import Tommy Bahama's, complete with lifestyle emporium and ocean-view café restaurant. Lappert's Ice Cream, home of the $3.50 single scoop of ice cream, is another one of several food outlets, including Ruth's Chris Steakhouse, Longhi's, and Honolulu Coffee Co., where you can get an early-morning latte.

Three miles offshore is the islet of **Molokini,** a natural attraction for fish and folks alike. The 165-foot-high tip of a submerged tuff cone draws fish, and consequently divers, like a magic lure. Fish go to Molokini because it's there. Snorkelers follow the bright tropical fish, and scuba divers explore the sheer, convex side of the volcanic tuff cone to see big, pelagic fish, including sharks (see page 224). Molokini is a Marine Life Conservation District. All you can take away are pictures or memories of the fish. Feeding them is *kapu* ("taboo" or "forbidden"), too. Out to sea beyond Molokini, you can spot the red-dirt island of **Kahoolawe,** the "target" island used for a half century by the U.S. Navy for aerial bombing runs. When the bombs were stopped by presidential order, the island was returned to native Hawaiians for the creation of a cultural preserve. You can go there only by special invitation, unless you want to help clear the island of unexploded ordnance.

Up on the hill above Wailea is **The Diamond Resort,** a unique Japanese retreat with onsen spa bathhouses, sushi bar, and teppanyaki restaurant, created as a private retreat for Tokyo millionaires; it's now open to all and worth a visit, if only for the udon noodles.

Along the Wailea Coast are million-dollar condos and private estates of the rich and famous (Clint Eastwood bought a $7.5 million Wailea oceanfront lot for his wife's birthday present). After Wailea, the paved road dead-ends at the isolated resort of **Makena,** where the restrained, elegant Maui Prince Hotel sits in the lee of 360-foot Puu Olai cinder cone, amid 1,800 acres of mostly rugged, natural beauty graced by two championship golf courses. The hotel's beach is bordered by a big sandy dune that is such a favorite haul out for green sea turtles that snorkel tours dub it **Turtle Town.** Should you happen upon a turtle, remember, they are an endangered species and federally protected from harm.

Makena is a historic embarkation, or landing, where Ulupalakua Ranch cowboys once loaded cattle onto barges bound for market. Locals still say their prayers at the 1832 white coral rock **Keawalai Congregational Church,** where Sunday services are said in Hawaiian. A seaside graveyard with lei-draped tombstones crawls with feral cats.

On the other side of Puu Olai stands Oneloa, the Hawaiian word for aptly named **Big Beach;** it's a 3,000-foot-long strand, 100 feet wide, and good for swimming, snorkeling, or tanning. Ahead, the road grows narrow and the terrain looks terrible, with the sharp black lava of a 210-year-old flow masked only with sparse vegetation before the road ends. **Ahihi-Kinau Natural Reserve** and **La Perouse Bay** show off Maui's still primitive, natural side. That's it; time to turn around and go back.

Top Ten Free Things to Do on Maui, Molokai, and Lanai

1. Go to the beach, any beach
2. Look for whales or spinner dolphins
3. Sunrise at Haleakala
4. Take a hike at Iao Valley State Park
5. Look for fishnet floats on Lanai's Shipwreck Beach
6. Visit Iliiliopae Heiau on Molokai
7. Catch a wave at Kapalua
8. Snorkel marine-life preserve at Lanai's Hulopoe Bay
9. Swim in the waterfall pools at Oheo Gulch, Hana
10. Watch the coconuts fall in Kapuaiwa Grove, Molokai

Upcountry Maui

Heading in the northeast direction from Kahului Airport on Highway 36 takes you to **Paia,** a breezy former plantation town now famous for art and crafts shops, like Maui Crafts Guild, a collective of 25 local artists; Natural Impressions, a shop that makes Gyotaku impressions of fish on rice paper in the ancient Japanese style; Moana Bakery and Cafe, famed for Thai curries and upside-down pineapple muffins; and Jacque's Northshore Restaurant Bistro, where you can dine on fresh seafood under a giant monkeypod tree or at a sushi bar that's the local evening surfer hangout.

Strong year-round winds and ideal wave conditions at nearby **Hookipa Beach Park** draw the world's top windsurfers, dubbed the Maui air force for their aerial antics. It is a sight to see these daredevils hit waves head-on, to gain hang time up in the air, before splashing down in the sea. Nearby, Haiku has inexpensive lodging in B&Bs and vacation rentals.

From Paia, head inland and Upcountry to the cooler heights of Maui. The drive up the foothills of **Haleakala,** a dormant volcano and the island's top attraction, takes you to **Makawao.** This *paniolo* (cowboy) village has avoided becoming a ghost town by becoming a kind of art and boutique center, somewhat eclipsed these days by Paia down the road. A cappuccino at Casanova's, an open-air roadside bistro, is a good reason to stop. Then browse David Warren Gallery, Gallery Maui, and Kirstin Bunney for local art. Monsoon and Tropo are chic shops with jazz, books, and ubiquitous Tommy Bahama's togs.

On the way up or down to Makawao, browse the **Hui Noeau Visual Arts Center,** in a Charles Dickey–designed 1917 Mediterranean-style villa on a 10-acre estate that once belonged to Maui sugar baron Harry Baldwin. Hui Noeau is Hawaiian for "society of artists." And do, like all who love good food, stop for lunch or dinner (reservations required) at Bev Gannon's **Hailiimaile General Store.** A meal in this old plantation store is on the top-ten checklist for the perfect Maui visit.

Farther upcountry is **Kula,** a scenic community that clings to Haleakala's side at 3,000 feet. Kula is known for its cool climate, perfect for growing varieties of flowers and vegetables that don't always thrive at tropical temperatures. Among the strangest blooms are the South African imports called protea, a large family of bushes and plants painted from Mother Nature's other canvas, with flowers in black and pink or neon orange or yellow; weird, spiky edges; and stiff dark maroon leaves. You can see some of the 700 varieties of protea and other blooms at **Kula Botanical Gardens** on the way to **Ulupalakua Ranch,** where the road leads off into the hinterlands behind Haleakala. The 20,000-acre ranch, a nearly vertical spread where the volcano last erupted around 1790, raises cattle and elk and grows wine grapes. Drop by the tasting room at

Tedeschi Vineyards to sample their premium wine. Better yet, bring a picnic basket, pair it with a Maui vintage (forget the pineapple wine, created as a novelty) and enjoy the afternoon in the cool uplands.

Beyond Tedeschi, the road runs through eucalyptus groves at the 2,000-foot-elevation then drops down along a majestic sea coast few ever see. You can reach Hana via **Kaupo** (where there's a store) and **Kipahulu** on little, celebrated Piilani Highway (named for the first great chief of Maui), but plan on a trip of two hours or more to get there on roads that are slow and partly paved.

From Kula you can take a road leading up to **Haleakala National Park,** the island's greatest natural spectacle. Haleakala, the name of a dormant volcano rising more than 10,000 feet above sea level, translates to "House of the Sun."

Soon after noon we began to descend; and in a hollow of the mountain, not far from the ragged edge of the crater, then filled up with billows of cloud, we came upon what we were searching for; not, however, one or two, but thousands of Silverswords; their cold, frosted silver gleam making the hillside look like winter or moonlight. One thinks of them rather as . . . a prize at Ascot . . . than anything organic.

—Isabella L. Bird, *Six Weeks in the Sandwich Islands*

What really sets Maui apart from all the other islands in Hawaii and the rest of the Pacific is the sleepy volcano that last erupted more than 200 years ago. One of the world's great natural wonders, Haleakala is a red, orange, and black bowl so big and so deep that it makes its own weather, has its own mountain range, and can swallow the island of Manhattan whole. When people say they want to see the real Hawaii, we always steer them away from the coco palm beaches and plummy coastal resorts and send them up 38 steep miles to the hard edge of the cold summit to peer down into the very heart of the matter.

According to Hawaiian legend, the demi-god Maui captured the sun with his magic lasso on Haleakala. He convinced the sun to slow down in its travels, effectively lengthening the days and giving his mother Hina more time to dry her tapa cloths.

It's cold and windy up there, but blanket-wrapped sun worshipers who witness a Haleakala sunrise are seldom disappointed. Mark Twain called it "the sublimest spectacle" he'd ever seen.

Haleakala is one of only two places in the world (the Big Island is the other) where you may see the exotic Silversword, an odd-looking plant with silvery leaves and yellow and violet flowers. Once in its 15-year life it blooms, from June through October, then it dies. Park rangers offer free hiking excursions and informative lectures on topics ranging from Haleakala's geological history to Hawaiian culture.

You'll have to backtrack down Haleakala Crater Road to Kula Highway (Highway 37) to either return to West, Central, and South Maui via Paia the way you came or head on to Hana on Piilani Highway.

Hana

Taking a different route from Paia starts you on the long road to **Hana,** a three-hour drive that crosses 56 one-lane bridges and takes 617 twists and turns (about 12 curves a mile). The rental-car parade goes slow so everyone can ogle Maui's natural beauty: crashing surf, steep green hills, gushing waterfalls, and flowers.

Must stops along the way include: **Puohokamoa Stream** (mile marker 11), with two pools and picnic tables, and the palmy **Keanae Peninsula** (just past mile marker 16), a relic taro pond village with 1856 Congregational Missionary Church and a few homes. Those who get car sick or impatient with traffic usually turn back here, content to sample this segment of the Hana Highway, while the hardy press on to Halfway to Hana Fruit Stand for a fresh papaya or mango, and stop at **Puaa Kaa State Wayside Park** (mile marker 22) for a memorable tropical picnic beside waterfall pools.

Blink and you might miss **Hana;** it's a small community of about a thousand residents. Lifestyle here is slow and unpretentious, and the locals wouldn't want it any other way. Highlights include the Hana Cultural Center, which retells area history, Hana Coast Gallery, Hana Gardenland, and Hasegawa General Store, celebrated in a local pop tune.

A single resort hotel, Hotel Hana-Maui, now owned by the California folks who developed Big Sur's famed Post Ranch, plus a few condos, and bed-and-breakfasts like Aloha Cottages provide lodging.

Ten miles south of the town of Hana is **Kipahulu,** where Charles Lindbergh is buried in the back yard of a cliff-side church. The famed American aviator—the first person to fly solo across the Atlantic Ocean, in 1927—first visited Kipahulu in the 1950s. "I love Maui so much, I would rather live one day in Maui than one month in New York," a cancer-stricken Lindbergh told his doctor. The "Lone Eagle" spent the final eight days of his life in a guest cottage near Hana. He died on August 26, 1974, at 72. No signs point to the site, but Lindbergh's grave lies near **Palapala Hoomau Congregational Church.**

The grave, built according to Lindbergh's sketches, is 8 feet square, 12 feet deep, with walls of lava rock. A large piece of Vermont granite is covered with loose, smooth, round ilili stones, in the Hawaiian tradition. He

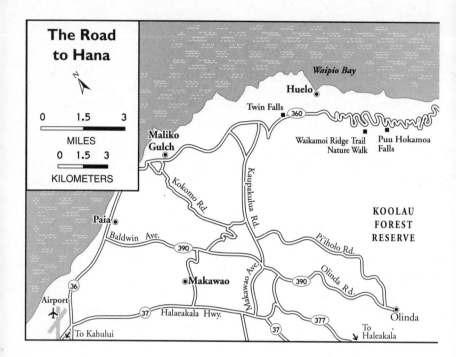

was placed unembalmed in a casket made of eucalyptus and lined with a Hudson's Bay blanket that Lindbergh received from his mother; a cushion from his plane, *The Spirit of St. Louis,* was placed under his body; and a Hawaiian tapa cloth covered his body. His wife, Anne, added three white flowers before the casket was nailed shut. He was buried barefoot in khakis. His grave notes that Charles Lindbergh died on Maui in 1974 and is inscribed with verse 9 of Psalms 139: "If I take the wings of the morning and dwell in the uttermost part of the sea." Thousands of curious visit his grave each year. Some bring him hibiscus and plumeria blossoms, others take ililil stones from Lindbergh's grave as souvenirs.

Beyond Kipahulu, the two-lane asphalt winnows down to an often rutty trail over the serrated, nearly vertical southeast side of Haleakala that in big storms sometimes washes out and slides into the sea. Off to the south, across the **Alenuihaha Channel,** you can see the more than 14,000-foot summits of Mauna Loa and Mauna Kea, two of the five volcanoes of the Big Island.

At **Kaupo** a country store sells cold drinks and century-old photos of the coast that, except for the old folks in vintage clothing, look like they were taken yesterday. Along the coast, the main road turns northwest across the **Kaupo Ranch** and 4WD dirt roads run down to the sea where

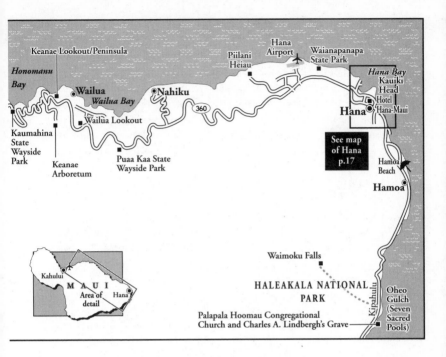

surfcasting, opihi hunting, and beachcombing are popular local pursuits. At **Pakowai Point,** look for the **Natural Arch,** a coastal landmark that means you soon will leave the splendid isolation of this seldom-seen part of Maui.

Always check weather and road conditions before you set off around the back side of Maui, and don't go there when flash-flood warnings or days of rainy storms might turn the unpaved portions of road into a threat. Wherever the road crosses a stream, federal bridge funds have dictated a few hundred feet of standard road with pavement, yellow line, and all, but it soon reverts to slow-going over gravel and dirt. Further on toward **Ulupalakua,** the road begins to rise, paved, into big views of open land and sea, with rolling terrain and curves you can handle. It's a driver's pleasure against the ever-present majestic backdrop of the huge volcano. Few vehicles use this road except to go between ranches and fishing spots and on backroads tours. The flora, climate, and general countryside change dramatically moment to moment, a trick of Haleakala's weather control, and it's as open and sweeping a panorama as the first part of the drive past Kipahulu was cloistered by vegetation and sharp bends in the road. It's a fitting conclusion to a tour of East Maui, and here you are at Tedeschi Vineyards waiting for the tasting room to open.

OLD BONES

We sat at Orchids at Halekulani one golden Waikiki afternoon, talking about old Hawaiian bones that surfaced in sand dunes of Kapalua, Maui, when the Ritz-Carlton Hotel was built a decade ago. It was an odd encounter—two militant Hawaiian men, Clifford Naeole and Lopaka, and Yvonne Landavazzo Biegel, the public relations woman for the Ritz-Carlton. It was her idea to get us together. "Every day more and more bones surfaced," Lopaka said. "It got to the point where it was too much. Enough was enough."

"How many burials?"

"About 1,200. Nobody knew it was that extensive. They just had a few when they started taking them out." The unearthing of ancestral Hawaiian bones happened in 1990, but Lopaka was still angry, a sullen Hawaiian not yet at peace. "All over the state," he continued, "it's been done, but this time we protested, we stopped the construction, we forced the hotel to move away from the graveyard."

"I did the reburial work personally," Lopaka said. "It was spiritual, real spooky, handling the bones of my ancestors." We shivered a little in the tropical sun. "It was hard for me to go to the hotel, even be there," he said. "They didn't move out of the kindness of their hearts; they were forced to, I mean it was like they fought it all the way, they were forced, but they had no choice. If they had their way, they would have put the hotel on the coast."

The public relations woman from the Ritz-Carlton Hotel at Kapalua

---

In Hasegawa's General Store, "You'll find a baseball bat and a piano hat, sunburn creams and the latest magazines, muumuu and mangoes and ukuleles, too." A least according to Paul Weston who wrote the 1961 local hit song, "The Hasegawa General Store," Best of all, you can buy the sheet music and, if you're lucky, a cassette recording of "Hasegawa General Store" by Arthur Godfrey, Hilo Hattie, and local residents Jim Nabors and Carol Burnett. The other noted local musician, the late George Harrison of Beatles fame, frequently shopped Hasegawa's but never got around to recording the song.

Molokai Driving Tour

Molokai, least-developed of Hawaii's main islands, is a visual reminder of old Hawaii. Some of it is lush, fern-forested wilderness valley, and some,

looked nervous, but also saddened. "Don't you think anyone was sensitive to the issue?"

"Well, personally, no," Lopaka said, and Clifford Naeole agreed. Everyone laughed nervously. "It was an outrageous act, but something good came out in the end, though," Naeole said.

"It was really hard to deal with the hotel," he said. "I never wanted to go there, never wanted to be associated with them until I saw some of the programs that they sponsored, and I felt they really cared about the place.

"You know," he said, "it took a while, but finally I decided these people are good people and should be forgiven." The public relations woman for the Ritz-Carlton Hotel gave a faint smile that flashed bright as the glare off the waves at Waikiki. The sensitive subject was breached, but proved surmountable.

Today, the sand dune area at Kapalua, where 1,200 Hawaiian bones were unearthed, is now held in perpetual trust. There are signs that say "Kapu"—no trespassing—where the hotel was originally to be built. Occasionally, tourists pay no heed to the kapu signs; they walk across the old Hawaiian graveyard as if it were a golf course.

Strange things, restless things, happen at the Ritz-Carlton at Kapalua. Doors open and close, there are odd shadows in the halls on moonlit nights, and sometimes the elevators seem to have a mind all their own. It's enough to make you wonder if everyone, living or dead, is at peace.

hot, dry, and dusty, so unappealing that Captain James Cook sailed by on his "discovery" voyage in the late 1700s, choosing not to drop anchor.

Although much improved, Molokai even today appeals only to a few visitors who prefer the peace and quiet of a simple, rural island virtually untouched by the veneer of commercial tourism. Of the 6.3 million people who visited the Hawaiian Islands last year, according to state data, only about 66,000, a little over 1 percent, made it to Molokai.

Centuries ago, Molokai was a more vibrant place. It is, after all, where hula was born and where, at one of the largest *heiau* in the Pacific, a four-tier stack of sacred rocks, longer than a football field, ancient wizards called kahunas taught the dark art of human sacrifice and set taboos that still send shivers down the spines of those who believe in ways of the old. But today with no industry save farming and tourism, Molokai is peaceful and quiet, the ideal place to do nothing but take in fresh air, listen to the silence, and stare out to sea in what Robert Louis Stevenson called "a fine state of haze." Here, each day passes under the tropic sun much like the one before . . .

MOLOKAI DRIVE TIMES	
From Molokai Airport to:	**Time to Travel**
Halawa Valley	2 hours
Kaunakakai	15 minutes
Kepuhi Beach	25 minutes
Mapulehu	35 minutes
Maunaloa	15 minutes
Papohaku Beach	30 minutes

In Cook's time, Molokai was known as Molokai Pule Oo, or "Molokai of the Potent Prayers." The island was home to priests known as kahuna, who were revered for their *mana,* or spiritual power. Since they could "pray" someone to death, and others knew it, their presence spared Molokai from bloody battles waged by chiefs on other islands.

Inhabitants of Molokai today appear to use other powers to thwart change on this island, which is best described by what it doesn't have: stoplights, shopping malls, a single nightclub, or a building taller than a palm tree. For better or worse, Molokai has been spared "progress," and the island's 7,000 residents lead a near-subsistence lifestyle enhanced by a little tourism and a welfare check.

Formed by two volcanoes—1,381-foot-high **Mauna Loa** on the west and 4,961-foot-high **Kamakou** on the east—the long, slender island appears like a big wedge in the sea, rising from rock-rimmed fishponds on the south shore to 3,000-foot-high cliffs on the north.

You arrive at **Hoolehua Airport,** the small, open-air lava rock terminal in the middle of cornfields after a short hop from busy Honolulu. The first thing you notice is the silence, then the soft patois of others, then smiling, friendly faces. "Welcome to Molokai," a sign says. "Go Slow. You're on Molokai now."

After Honolulu International and Kahului Airport on Maui, Hoolehua Airport looks abandoned, and it often is, between flights—although there are rental-car windows and a lunch counter serving the local favorites of chili rice and Spam musubi (a sandwich of molded rice with a piece of Spam on top, wrapped together with a piece of nori, or papery dried seaweed, served room temp) and cold drinks.

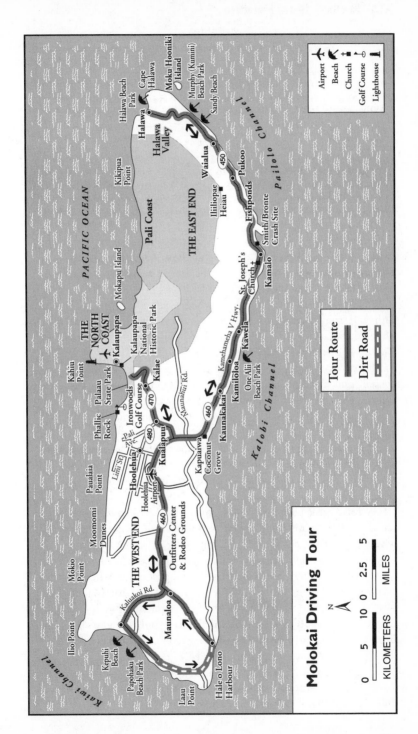

Molokai Driving Tour

MOLOKAI'S MUSICAL CLAIM TO FAME

In 1934, the late R. Alex Anderson, one of Hawaii's most prolific song composers, wrote "The Cockeyed Mayor of Kaunakakai," which Hilo Hattie made famous in the 1940s. Anderson used the term *cockeyed* "mainly because it combined nicely with the last two syllables of the word Kaunakakai," according to *Hawaiian Music and Musicians*. Anderson, who composed nearly 200 songs, including "Lovely Hula Hands," "I Will Remember You," and "I Had to Lova and Leva on the Lava," died in 1995. He was 101 years old. Since Molokai is part of Maui County, there is no mayor in Kaunakakai.

On Molokai, there are two main directions, east and west, and two main regions, the **West End** and the **East End.** Those who live in **Kalu-apapa,** on the peninsula 3,000 feet below the sea cliffs of the North Shore, call the rest of the island **Topside.**

Which way you head depends on whether you like it hot and dry, or lush and tropical, because the 38-mile long island divides at **Kau-nakakai,** the funky island capital, into two different climate zones. The West End looks like Mexico, the East End, like Tahiti. The West End has a defunct resort and golf course; the East End has a collection of small, coastal condos and bed-and-breakfasts. We'll start by heading west from the island's center, then loop back and head east.

A sun-faded, three-block town with harbor and pier, **Kaunakakai** looks more like an old Western movie set than a tropical village. It is the island's center of commerce, politics, and social affairs. **Maunaloa High-way,** the main approach into town, is lined with spires of churches and the spiky palm trees of **Kapuaiwa Coconut Grove,** planted in 1860 for King Kamehameha V, who was known as Kapuaiwa.

The royal garden originally was planted with 1,000 trees; today only a remnant grove stands. Venture here to collect an authentic souvenir only when there is no wind; a falling coconut can brain you. At the shore, you may spot the spring of fresh water that pours into the sea.

Molokai's chief settlement includes a bank, post office (where you can mail a coconut home), drug store, and grocery, all on **Ala Malama,** the town's main street. Nearby are the medical center and family-run busi-nesses: the **Friendly Market, Molokai Drive-Inn, Oviedo's Filipino Restaurant, Outpost Natural Foods,** and **Kanemitsu Bakery,** where 19 different types of bread are baked fresh daily.

At night, you may find a few open shops, but the brightest lights in town shine on **Mitchell Pauole Center,** site of softball games, "huli-huli" chicken roasts, carnivals, and community events.

Unless you brought your own food and drink, you will, like everyone else on Molokai, make the obligatory stop at **Misaki's Market,** a third-generation store where antlered deer-head trophies guard aisles of canned goods. Once a week when Sause Bros. sends its life-line barges from Honolulu across the **Kaiwi Channel,** the market is replenished with fresh food and milk. When seas are high, the island's food supply dries up and you will be eating at **Molokai Pizza Cafe,** the only pizza parlor on the island. The only other vital establishment is **Rawlins Chevron Station,** one of two gas stations on the island.

Above Kaunakakai looms defunct **Kamakou Volcano,** the island's tallest mountain and home to a virgin forest of native trees, including rare sandalwood, which was harvested for the China trade.

A MOLOKAI POSTCARD

Margaret (Peggy) Keahi-Leary, the postmaster at Hoolehua post office on the Island of Molokai, has a lovely bunch of coconuts. She gives them away to tourists. "I provide coconuts free of charge at the post office," Keahi-Leary said. "All the tourists have to do is write or draw or do anything they want on the coconut and then I ship them by priority mail anywhere in the U.S.A." She calls her service Post-a-Nut. The Hawaiian coconut, according to the U.S. Postal Service, is a perfectly acceptable shipping container. "It can go right out in the mail," Keahi-Leary said. "No wrapper, no nothing, just $3 in postage for up to two pounds. As the weight goes up, the postage cost rises accordingly. The coconut is like the spirit of Hawaii. It's a good positive image for Molokai, too," said Keahi-Leary, born and raised on the island, and proud of her small role in Hawaii tourism. "When I came up with the idea I was asking myself, 'if I were a tourist, what would I like?' I'd want something that was authentic and genuine Hawaii. And so the coconut idea came about." She began the Post-a-Nut program in 1992, but lost track of how many coconuts she's shipped. "Some days it's three bags full, other days only two or three coconuts," she said. "The thing is, not every place has access to coconuts. On Molokai, over here, we got a whole coconut grove."

Up here, 2,774-acre **Kamakou Preserve** is home to native Hawaiian birds and 219 plants that exist nowhere else; you can see them with **Nature Conservancy** permission. Another protected wilderness is **Moomomi Dunes** where Smithsonian Institute scientists unearthed skeletons of flightless birds like the long extinct dodo.

Leaving Kaunakakai, most visitors head to the **West End,** where the **Molokai Ranch** dominates red-dirt rolling hills covered by kiawe, brush, and cactus. But there is a lot to see en route, and Molokai's **North Coast** merits a side trip, too. At midisland, you can see, crack, and taste a macadamia nut at **Purdy's Macadamia Nut Farm** in **Hoolehua** before heading up to **Coffees of Hawaii Plantation Store** in **Kualapuu,** where the island's best fresh coffee is served from field to roaster to your cup in espressos and lattes. Much better than hanging out at Starbucks, even if there was one.

Highway 470 leads from Kualapuu to the **North Shore Lookout** in **Palaau State Park,** a cool upland forest with the island's best campsite and **Phallic Rock,** a famous fertility stone that many claim works too well. You can stand on the edge of the lookout and take in the majesty of Molokai's North Shore, but the best way to experience the seacliffs is the **Molokai Mule Ride,** which takes you on a heart-pounding traverse down the 26-switchback trail to **Kalaupapa,** the former leper colony, now a national historical park. You can also hike down the trail or fly in from Hoolehua Airport via **Damien Tours.** The ground tour includes a visit to **Saint Philomena Church,** built in 1872, and the graveyard where Father Damien de Veuster was buried (after nomination for sainthood, his body was reinterred in his native Belgium).

Hawaiians stricken with leprosy were banished to **Kalaupapa** beginning in 1860. (They were literally pushed from a boat into the waters off the peninsula and had to swim to shore.) Father Damien de Veuster, a Belgian priest, arrived in 1873 and embraced the outcasts. "The sick are arriving by the boatloads," he wrote to his superiors. "They die in droves." Father Damien spent 16 years caring for his congregation. It was an exhausting labor of love, and he was mostly alone in his efforts. Any contributions by visiting doctors were left on a fence post to avoid physical contact with patients. By the end of the 1870s, approximately 1,000 people were exiled to Kalaupapa. On April 15, 1889, Father Damien himself succumbed to the disease at age 49.

He did what we have never dreamed of daring . . .

—Robert Louis Stevenson on Father
Damien, the leper priest of Molokai

On the way to or from the edge, you pass coffee plantations, the nine-hole **Ironwood Golf Course,** which was built in 1920 by sugar planters, and **Molokai Museum and Cultural Center,** housed in the restored **Meyer Sugar Mill.** The mill's namesake, German professor Rudolph W. Meyer, came to Molokai in 1849, married a Hawaiian chieftess, and started a steam-engine sugar mill in 1878.

Returning via Kualupuu to Highway 460, you can head east to the 54,000-acre spread of Molokai Ranch (covering a third of the island), headquartered at **Maunaloa**, a plantation town torn down and rebuilt a few years ago, where retro sugar shacks (made of steel to discourage termites) cost $250,000 or more and the island's sole concession to the twenty-first century is a Kentucky Fried Chicken. There's a movie theater, art gallery, and Jonathan and Daphne Socher's **Kite Factory,** featuring handmade tropical kites. The favorite is a red and green hula girl with a green skirt that swishes in the wind.

A big brown barn painted with murals of cowboys adorns the **Outfitters Center.** Sign up here for adventures on horseback on **Molokai Ranch.** You can learn traditional rodeo events like barrel racing or join in a roundup of calves. The annual **Molokai Rodeo** is the big event here.

For many years, most Molokai visitors stayed at **Kaluakoi Resort**— long the island's only resort area—but it is closed pending new ownership and renovation. The 103-room **Kaluakoi Hotel and Golf Club,** an airy structure of lava rock and ohia logs, overlooks Kupuhi Beach and adjoins three-mile-long **Papohaku Beach,** Molokai's biggest. The island's only 18-hole golf course also is closed.

On a nearby plateau is **Kaana,** where tradition holds that Laka, the goddess of the hula, created the native Hawaiian dance. Molokai celebrates the birth of the hula at the annual **Molokai Ka Hula Piko,** held each May at **Papohaku Beach Park,** in a shady seaside grove. The daylong festival features performances, Hawaiian music, food, and local arts and crafts.

From this point, circle south past Laau point to the hamlet of Hale o Lono before returning to Maunaloa and then Kaunakakai via Highway 460. From there, it's on to the East End. The trip from Kaunakakai to Puu o Hoku Ranch is only 25 miles, but it seems farther on two-lane King Kamehameha V Highway, because the coast is lush, green, and tropical and there is much to enjoy.

As you head to the East End, you will see some of the most distinguishing man-made features of Molokai—**ancient fish ponds.** Built of stone and big as lakes, they were built by early Hawaiians who caught fish on the incoming tide and blocked their escape with gates. The first and best of 25 restored fishponds, **Kalokoeli,** appears on the outskirts of Kaunakakai just beyond the **Kaunakakai Harbor.** Many fishponds are still in use today.

Just past **Saint Joseph Church,** about 10 miles out of town, on the makai side of the highway, look for a hand-painted sign in kiawe brush that says **Smith and Bronte Crash Site.** This is not a memorial to an auto fatality. The sign marks the historic end to the first civilian trans-pacific flight by Ernie Smith and Emory Bronte in 1927. Bound for Maui, they flew 25 hours and 2 minutes at 6,000 feet from Oakland in a single-engine Travelaire monoplane but ran out of gas and crashed on Molokai.

Our Lady of Sorrows Church, one of five built by Father Damien on the island, stands by tombstones draped with lei. The cemetery often crawls with orange tabby feral cats, which you should avoid petting; they are wild and may bite.

On **King Kamehameha V Highway** you discover affordable seaside condos, like **Wavecrest Resort,** and perfectly sited vacation rentals like **Dunbar Beachfront Cottages** and the **Country Cottage** at **Puu O Hoku Ranch.** The only major retail outlet along the way is **Pukoo Neighbor Store n' Counter,** which sells cold drinks, ice, and plate lunches. It's just beyond **Mapulehu Mango Grove,** a botanical wonder where 2,000 mango trees of various species flourish in a verdant grove perfumed by their blossoms.

At Mapulehu, you can hitch a ride on the **Molokai Horse and Wagon Ride,** to one of the spookiest places in Hawaii: **Iliiliopae Heiau,** a school of sacrifice where more than 700 years ago, kahuna (priests) taught final rites in a massive temple of doom, three stories high and bigger than a football field. The heiau, legend has it, was built in one night of car-sized boulders passed hand-to-hand by a human chain of 10,000 men, over the spine of the nearly mile-high island from **Wailau Valley,** ten miles away. Each man received one shrimp (*opae*) in exchange for the stone (*iliili*).

If you're ready for a swim, now's the best time, because you're at one of Molokai's best beaches—**Waialua Beach** at mile marker 19. If it's too crowded, head down to **Sandy Beach,** a small pocket roadside beach at mile marker 20.

Now King Kamehahema V Highway begins to climb toward **Puu O Hoku Ranch,** where a few lucky folks can bunk for the night in a cabin. The highway turns to hairpins on the very East End and, after scenic vistas of pocket beaches, offshore islets, and dense jungles, dead-ends at **Halawa Valley,** once a major taro growing valley that rivaled the Big Island's Waipio Valley for production.

Inundated by a 30-foot tsunami in 1946, and by a second in 1957, **Halawa Valley,** a Hawaiian settlement since the seventh century, was abandoned. Now privately owned, the 9,000-acre valley is closed, and the trailhead to 250-foot **Moaula Falls,** once the most accessible waterfall on the island, is posted with "no trespassing" signs. Private treks into the valley are periodically possible. Contact the Molokai Visitors Association for details at (800) 800-6367 or (808) 553-3876.

King Kamehameha V Highway winds and narrows and doubles back on itself. Off shore you will see the islet of **Hooniki,** a World War II bombing target of the U.S. Navy (bombing practice was halted in 1958 just before Hawaii became a state), now a seabird sanctuary. At several scenic turnouts you can see, across the **Pailolo Channel,** the north shore of **Maui** and **Kapalua Resort** and the ridges of the **West Maui Mountains,** which rise like green peaks above the cobalt sea. King Kamehameha V Highway comes to a dead-end at **Halawa Beach,** a black-sand beach with two bays and the island's only decent surf break. **Halawa Beach County Park** includes a restroom, barbecue grills, and a parking area, but no lifeguard or other facilities. The water can be murky at Halawa due to runoff from the waterfalls at the head of the valley— which means it's not safe for swimming, since murky water is the favored haunt of reef sharks, especially at sundown. Halawa is as far as you can go by car, but those of you with a kayak may press on around **Cape Halawa** (only in summer when the sea is calm) to discover the raw North Coast, one of Hawaii's natural wonders.

PEARLY SHELLS

Islands were once home to thousands of colorful tree snails, known as Pupu kanioe, according to Hawaiian conchologists. How they reached the islands can only be imagined, but they did and they flourished. Jewels of the forest, the pearly shells came in many colors—yellow, red, orange, green, and white—and thrived in such abundance that in 1912 Hawaiian poet George Kane described "the songs of the land shells that have a sound as sweet as that of a dove on a clear night." When a single shell sold in Europe for $10, it sparked a shell rush. Hundreds of thousands were collected. Today, of the 41 species in this genus, 22 are extinct and 19 are endangered. They cling to survival in Molokai rain forests. A few specimens may be seen in glass cases at Oahu's Bishop Museum.

Lanai Driving Tour

Long ago early Hawaiians believed Lanai (the Hawaiian word for "hump" or "swelling") was haunted by spirits so wily and vicious that no human who went there could survive. Today, nearly everyone who goes there not only gets a good night's sleep but always leaves refreshed, if reluctantly. Spirits still haunt the island—it is said that the legendary Madame Pele often visits—but mostly Lanai is a high-end retreat for urban souls.

Once home to the world's largest pineapple plantation, Lanai survives now by cultivating well-heeled visitors seeking peaceful surroundings, luxurious resorts, outstanding golf, and one of the best dive spots in the Pacific.

The sweet and juicy fruit that once covered more than 19,000 acres of the island's red-dirt Palawai Basin is gone (cheaper labor in the developing world hastened the end of Hawaii's plantation era); all that remains is a relic field at the gateway to Lanai Airport, growing the gray-green, spiky-leafed plant with football-sized golden fruit.

LANAI DRIVE TIMES	
From Lanai Airport to:	Time to Travel
Garden of the Gods	45 minutes
Hulopoe and Manele Bays	25 minutes
Lanai City	5 minutes
Munro Trail	15 minutes
Shipwreck Beach	35 minutes

In 1987, a California tycoon named David Murdock acquired a controlling interest in Castle & Cooke, one of the Islands' oldest companies, and found in his new portfolio the deed to the Island of Lanai, a place he'd never seen. Since Hawaii's plantation era was ending and plans were already forming to welcome tourists to Lanai, he envisioned an island resort like no other. His vision became reality in the early 1990s when the first of two luxury hotels, the **Lodge at Koele,** opened its doors. A year later, the **Manele Bay Hotel** made its debut. The resorts are as distinct in appearance as in location: The Lodge at Koele, reminiscent of an English manor, stands miles from the beach on a hill in the center of the island on an old ranch site amid tall Norfolk Island pine trees, while the Manele Bay Hotel overlooks **Hulopoe Bay** and was designed with Mediterranean influences amid elaborate gardens. Snorkelers take the plunge at Hulopoe Bay, a marine-life preserve with a postcard beach. The two palatial properties are a stark contrast to the venerable 1920s-era **Hotel Lanai,** a ten-room inn above Lanai City that's a kind of crossroads with locals and guests chatting and sipping as they wait for a table at **Henry Clay's Rotisserie,** a New Orleans–inspired bistro.

Lanai City is the old plantation town, a collection of small, brightly painted tin-roof houses in a hillside grove of pine trees. The town includes the island's post office, high school, small hospital, even smaller library, one-prisoner jail, and shops, like **Akamai Trading** and **Local Gentry,** and cafés, like **Blue Ginger** for plate lunch and **Tanigawa's** for cheeseburgers, set around piney **Dole Park** at the center of town. The **Lanai Arts and Culture Center** displays art by local residents.

Golf is the sport of choice on Lanai. Two 18-hole championship courses are available here: **The Experience at Koele,** designed by golf superstar Greg Norman and architect Ted Robinson, and the **Challenge**

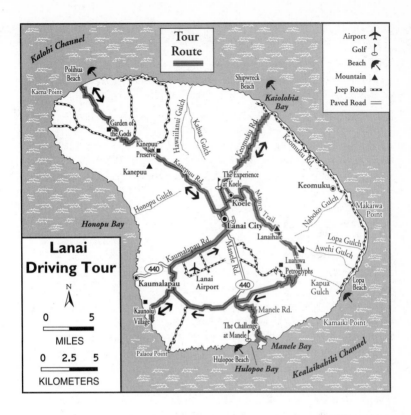

Airport ✈
Golf ⛳
Beach 🏖
Mountain ▲
Jeep Road ≡≡≡
Paved Road =

Kalohi Channel
Polihua
Beach
Kaena Point
Garden of
the Gods
Kanepuu
Preserve
Kanepuu
Hawaiilanui Gulch
Kahua Gulch
Honopu Gulch
Kanepuu Rd.
Honopu Bay
The Experience
at Koele
Koele
Lanai City
Lanaihale
Kaumalapau Rd.
Manele Rd.
Lanai
Airport
Kaumalapau
Palaoa Point
Kaunolu
Village
The Challenge
at Manele
Hulopoe Beach
Hulopoe Bay
Manele Rd.
Manele Bay
Luahiwa
Petroglyphs
Kapua
Gulch
Kamaiki Point
Kealaikahiki Channel
Lopa
Beach
Lopa Gulch
Awehi Gulch
Naboko Gulch
Keomuku Rd.
Keomuku Rd.
Keomuku
Makaiwa
Point
Kaiolohia
Bay
Shipwreck
Beach
Munro Trail
440
440

**Lanai
Driving Tour**

N
↑

0   5
MILES

0   2.5   5
KILOMETERS

at Manele, designed by Jack Nicklaus. Other popular activities on Lanai
include swimming, snorkeling, horseback riding, whale-watching, fishing, archery, lawn bowling, croquet, clay shooting, and deer, sheep, and
wild turkey hunting (in season). It's easy to get around Lanai on foot or
using the island's shuttle van, a golf cart, or a four-wheel-drive vehicle.
The sights may be few, but they are naturally appealing, not man-made.
The chief landmark is 3,366-foot **Lanaihale,** the highest point on the
island. A hike or drive up **Munro Trail** to the summit on a clear day will
afford a sweeping view of most of the major islands. Historians believe
Lanaihale served as vantage point for high-ranking chiefs who could keep
an eye on canoe traffic in the kingdom's sea lanes. Offshore, along the
southwest the sea channel is known as **Kealaikahiki,** or "the way to
Tahiti," because that's where it goes, sweeping nearly 2,000 miles like a
river to the ancestral islands where archeologists believe the first voyagers
departed for Hawaii in A.D. 650. The first settlers on this island called it
"Nanai" and lived around the coast in small clusters of thatch and stone.

SUPERNATURAL HAWAII

The supernatural world so easily embraced by Polynesians affects visitors in different ways. Hawaiians do not concern themselves with solving riddles. They accept the insoluble. While most tourists want supernatural things to make sense, locals are content not to understand. They know if you solve a puzzle, it is broken.

Consider our recent trip to see Iliiliypae, the great Molokai heiau, where Hawaiian kahuna practiced rites of human sacrifice only 150 years ago. We hired a car at Hoolehua Airport and drove to Kaunakakai, once the summer place of King Kamehameha V, now only a sun-bleached cluster of clapboard stores covered by fine red dust. It was around Christmas, so icicle lights twinkled in 82°F heat, and shops displayed cheery Santa masks.

At Misaki's Market, where antlered deer-head trophies guard aisles of rusty canned goods, we found shelves stripped bare by a run on fresh goods. A clerk said seas in Kaiwi Channel were so high, boats couldn't reach Molokai.

We grabbed the last six-pack of Hinano and local venison jerky and headed down two-lane King Kamehameha V Highway past tranquil fishponds, big as lakes and protected from the sea by coral-stone walls.

We passed a white clapboard church bathed in a bold ray of light. In its graveyard cats prowled among tombstones draped with dead flower lei. We then drove by a roadside sign commemorating a 1927 plane crash. We added the church and crash site to our list of unusual attractions on Molokai, which already included the flirty mahus at Pau Hana Inn, a huge penis-shaped boulder known as the Phallic Stone, and the mule ride down the world's steepest sea cliffs to see the old leper colony at Kalaupapa.

Where the island became lush, green, and tropical, we turned makai, down an unmarked red dirt road, and entered the cool, shady oasis of Mapulehu, one of Hawaii's botanical wonders.

Someone long ago had planted a specimen grove of mango trees by the sea, and the many varieties—Atkins, Haden, Ataulfo, Keitts, and Cebu, to name but a few—flourished to create a dreamy Green Mansions–like orchard steeped in perfume so strong it stung our eyes.

Under the sheltering mango trees, we stood in half-light, blinking, just as two galloping horses rounded a corner pulling a wagonful of screaming children, who at first looked terrified, then delighted. The wagonful of children disappeared in a cloud of fine red dust that settled on the green mango trees, and all over us, as a smiling woman appeared to welcome us with a warm aloha.

We've forgotten her name, but not what she told us: Mapulehu, where we stood, once was a *puuhonua,* or place of refuge. In ancient days, an errant subject could avoid death by seeking sanctuary here. The location was appropriate; a short hike up the hill Iliiliypae, the biggest, oldest, most famous heiau on Molokai, served as a school of sorcery.

We had missed the wagon to the heiau, the Hawaiian woman said, but we could go on foot if we liked. She pointed mauka toward cloud-spiked Mount Kaunolu, the 4,970-foot island summit, and issued a caveat: "If you see a rainbow over the valley, look out for the *waikoloa,*" she said.

"What's the *waikoloa*?"

"A hard, wet wind that comes suddenly down the valley," she said, and disappeared, like that, into the mango grove.

We set out on the upland trail through a hale koa thicket spiked by Java plum trees and, after passing an abandoned house, arrived hot, sweaty, and light-headed at the heiau just as the children were hiking back to the wagon. The heiau would be ours alone to explore.

Having read *Molokai: A Site Survey,* by Catherine C. Summers, the definitive work on the island's archeology, we knew the stone altar was 22 feet high, but no words can prepare visitors for its bulky reality.

Long as a football field, nearly three stories high, Iliiliypae looks more like an early Roman fortification than a Hawaiian temple of doom. It rises in four tiers on the hill overlooking the green mango grove and four fishponds on the south shore of the island. What we found most amazing is that boulders big as Volkswagens had been fitted together so tightly that the temple had been held together for centuries not by mortar, but by its own mass.

Originally, the heiau was three times larger, according to Ohulenui, who grew up in the shadow of the temple and was 96 years old in 1909, when he was interviewed by archeologist John F. G. Stokes, then director of the Bishop Museum. The heiau once stretched 920 feet across both east and west arms of Mapulehu Stream.

Temple rocks were swept away in legendary storms, or were taken to bolster fishpond walls and build the coast highway, which may account for roadside sightings of the legendary squid woman.

Legend says Iliiliypae was built in one night by a human chain of 10,000 men who passed rocks hand over hand up and over the spine of the long narrow island from Wailau Valley, ten miles away via a precipitous mile-high trail. Each received one shrimp (*opae*) in exchange for the rock (iliili), hence the name.

SUPERNATURAL HAWAII *(continued)*

Even under the glaring tropical sun in full daylight, the heiau is a very eerie place. Heat waves shimmer off the flat surface rocks. The walls vibrate with *mana* (spiritual energy) strong enough to lean on. We felt like someone was watching us.

Having read accounts of what transpired here centuries before no doubt intensified the mystic aura of the heiau. People were summoned by the beating of drums and loud shouting on the 24th to the 27th days of the moon, when the sacrificial victim was carried into the temple tied to a scaffold. Victims were always men, not young virgins, and they were strangled while priests sat on lauhala mats watching silently. Victims never were buried, always burned; there was no boneyard, only ashes.

Against all advice, we stepped out on the heiau, walked right out on the flat table-sized rocks to gain a sense of the whole, meaning no disrespect, only wanting to get closer. To what? The primal past, the secrets of the heiau. It's hard to say what compelled us to commit this minor trespass. We knew better, and yet kept walking out farther on the heiau, drawn by something larger than curiosity.

Midway across the heiau, we grew dizzy in the hot sun. It beat down and radiated up from the rocks. Deciding to turn back, we stumbled, slipped ankle-deep between the rocks and fell to the stone. It was as though the altar, having drawn us in, now refused our departure.

For a moment, we both felt as if the heiau had reached out to grab us. We panicked and scrambled along the rocks. Clambering from the heiau,

Early artifacts—knives, awls, scrapers, files, fish sinkers, and pounders and pestles collected by archeologist Kenneth Emory of Honolulu's **Bishop Museum**—are displayed at **Lanai Conference Center** next to Manele Bay Hotel. Emory's 1920 field survey of Lanai found scores of burial sites, 11 large temples or heiau, the largest at **Kaunolu** on the island's west bank, and more than 300 petroglyphs, an early Hawaiian art form. The pecked or incised stone etchings on 20 boulders in **Luahiwa Petroglyph Field** above **Pulawai Basin** depict a running dog, a turtle, a bird, lizards, and human figures. Kaunolu is the most significant historic site, and was the island's first resort of sorts, built by ancient Hawaiians on 1,025-foot-high sea cliffs. A national historic landmark, the fishing village overlooking **Kaunolu Bay** once included 86 house sites, 35 stone

we touched down on terra firma to catch our breath. Looking back, there were no spirits, no ghosts; only a misstep on a wobbly rock.

We cautiously continued up the steep mauka ridge, attempting to get a picture, but the heiau proved too big for our simple lenses. Only an aerial shot would capture the full image in proper context.

I looked up toward the mountain and saw a rainbow beginning to appear and remembered what the Hawaiian woman said. "It's the waikoloa," I nearly shouted, as the rainbow grew bigger and brighter. We decided to hurry back down the dry streambed and reached the sheltering mango grove just as hard rain came pelting down.

That afternoon on Molokai a flash flood sent water coursing once again through Mapulehu's dry streambed, and rain pounded the hot rocks of the ancient sacrificial heiau, sending up clouds of steam, and the fresh water seeped around old smooth stones and trickled down to the soul of the temple, where relic ashes repose.

Water ran through the rocks and across the highway, into the mango grove and over the beach, turning the fishponds and the sea blood-red with the island's soil. We saw that the entire south coast of Molokai was stained red the next morning from our flight back to Honolulu.

Did one thing have to do with the other? Surely it was all coincidence. We never understood what happened that day and probably never will. But, like the Islanders, we are content not to understand.

shelters, 30 garden patches, and 9 piles of stones marking graves. King Kamehameha I, who visited Lanai between 1778 and 1810, worshiped in a massive pyramid-shaped temple, **Halulu Heiau,** now a jumbled ruins of uncut stone and boulders. His majesty also tried his hand at fishing with the blessing of **Kunihi,** a three-foot stone fish god, filled with *mana* (power). The idol is believed to still exist somewhere on Lanai. If you see it, do not touch it. The last person to touch the idol died.

At the cliff edge is **Kahekili's Leap** where Hawaiians practiced the sport of *lelekawa,* or cliff jumping. The king punished his soldiers, according to Emory, by forcing them to "jump 62 feet into 12 feet of water, clearing a 15-foot shelf at the base of the cliff."

IOWA OF THE PACIFIC

The anxious faces of first-time Lanai visitors make us smile—chic, overdressed women in white linen, boldly jacketed men in tasseled loafers—as they look about the Magritte-like landscape for palm trees, tropical flowers, or any of the usual island icons. Instead they see pine trees, mud-spattered pickup trucks, and cute Filipino girls in blue jeans, sweatshirts, and cowboy boots. We once arrived in hunting season to see a trophy deer, its red tongue hanging, splayed over a rusty Jeep hood. Gradually, tourists notice the soft, almost code-like speech of local people (their pidgin patois sounds like an exotic foreign language), catch the scent of tangy salt air mingled with pine trees, and even shiver a little in the cool tropical air. All the incongruities only add to the mysterious attraction of this odd little island.

Lanai sits in the middle of the inhabited Hawaiian chain, in plain sight of every island except Kauai, yet feels removed in time and place. Like the Heartland: Iowa of the Pacific. Sometimes, we think it feels like the late 1930s on Lanai, or what we imagine the '30s were like in America: agrarian and uncertain, with a great gap between rich and poor. In the back of your mind, it is easy to hear distant echoes of Benny Goodman tunes. When people leave Lanai after spending only a few days, they say it seems like they have been gone for weeks. The time-expanding nature of Lanai may be its most compelling virtue, the reason it is such a great island escape. You don't just go there, you return to a place almost lost in memory.

To learn more about Lanai's early days, ask for the free interpretive guide to Kaunolu at the hotels or check out *Lanai: A Survey of Native Culture* by Kenneth P. Emory (Bishop Museum Press) at the Lodge library.

Other sites worth exploring include Lanai's version of Stonehenge, set on **Kanepuu,** a mountain ridge near the center of the island. This mysterious collection of strewn boulders and red lava cliffs is the **Garden of the Gods,** which some claim is the dwelling place for spirits of ancient Hawaiian warriors. Go during sunrise or sunset, when the low light casts eerie shadows in the area, and judge for yourself.

Slightly further inland (east) you can take a self-guided tour of a rare dryland native forest at **Kanepuu Preserve.** You'll see 48 plants found only on Lanai, including native olive trees, ebony, and rare sandalwood. The forest, about five miles from the Lodge at Koele, is operated by the Nature Conservancy of Hawaii.

Nature lovers should also consider **Polihua Beach,** on the northwest shore. A favorite green sea turtle nesting site, the remote, nearly two-mile-long golden beach, the island's largest, is accessible only by boat or four-wheel-drive vehicle. The beach is blasted by wind and the water is too roiled for swimming, so few go to Polihua except to see the turtles, or to comb the wide beach for Japanese glass fishing-float balls, paper nautilus shells, and other flotsam that washes ashore.

A PARADE OF PETROGLYPHS

We sat in full sun on the steep hillside overlooking the broad caldera known as Palawai Basin, studying petroglyphs one afternoon on Lanai. That's the best time of day to see the Stone Age art, because the sun lights up the indented stick figures.

It's an amazing cast of characters unlike any on Lanai, or any other island for that matter. The first time we visited Luahiwa Petroglyphs it was raining so hard we couldn't even see the 20 boulders bearing the artwork. So we returned the following year on a hot August day, climbed up the hillside through bone dry brush, and, a little out of breath, sat down amid the petroglyph boulders. Maybe it was the heat, or just imagination, but the figures came alive and seemed to move as if in an ancient cartoon. A sailing canoe cruised across the face of a gigantic red boulder, a curly tailed dog barked at a centipede, and a horseman with a hat rode a thin horse while two V-chested men walked down a trail. A pair of turtles even seemed to inch across the rock. That's when we felt an icy wind, despite the hot afternoon, and decided to go. Back at the lodge, when the young Hawaiian woman who serves as concierge asked about our visit with the petroglyphs, we smiled and said it was wonderful. We even suggested that she should go see them herself someday, but she winced and shivered and said, "Too spooky, yeh?"

So many ships have run aground the shallow reef off northeastern Lanai since 1820 that this eight-mile stretch is known as **Shipwreck Beach.** Two early groundings were the British ship *Alderman Wood* and the American *London,* followed by interisland steamers, pineapple barges, U.S. Navy landing craft, World War II vessels, and pleasure boats. The reef holds a World War II Liberty Ship, and the beach is strewn with debris from the breakup a half century ago of four-masted schooner *Helene Port Townsend,* out of Seattle's Puget Sound.

Kahoolawe: The Target Island

From Maui or Lanai, the island of Kahoolawe appears forbidding and bleak, lost in time. Although the island is only 15 miles across the sea channel from Lanai, its huge red scars were the work of U.S. Navy pilots who for nearly a half century dropped tons of bombs during practice air raids.

LIVING LARGE ON LITTLE LANAI

If we have but one night to spend like royalty, please, please let it be in a butlered suite at the Manele Bay Hotel on secluded, exclusive Lanai. We did it once and would sure like to do it again.

The Lanai experience begins at the state's newest small island airport when your Aloha Airlines jet lands after a short hop from Honolulu, a form of time travel back to simpler days.

Green-uniformed staff, who seem to know who to expect on this real-life Fantasy Island, call you by name on arrival, whisk away your bag, and point toward a big cushy bus, already running and air-conditioned.

It ferries new arrivals on the short ride down to the sea and the Manele Bay Hotel or up to the pine-forested Lodge at Koele, the island's other upscale jewel. The route, one of three paved roads, leads through miles of neglected former pineapple fields, red dirt still littered with fluttering bits of black plastic, once used to keep down the weeds that now thrust up defiantly. It's been a decade since Lanai gave up the battle to maintain its status as the world's biggest pineapple plantation. The new crop is well-heeled tourists.

En route, passengers chatter with anticipation. One family of five—parents, teens, and grade-schoolers—has been several times before for a week or two at one hotel or the other, sometimes both. No one is sulking, no whining about what's to be done for amusement on this remote islet. Instead, they debate the relative merits of the two golf courses, where all plan to play daily. They recall four-wheeling over dusty, rutty dirt tracks to remote beaches and horseback rides in the shady, cool uplands near the Lodge. They talk about old croquet games on the Lodge lawns. Discussion ensues about kayaking and snorkeling. There's a lot to do on Lanai.

But then the chariot pulls into a grand porte cochère entry with a wall-to-wall view of the surrounding sea beyond, and guests are swept away to registration and glasses of pineapple cider.

A tall, dark, and mysterious fellow in a suit approaches. "I am Enrique, your butler. If you'll follow me upstairs, we can complete registration in your suite." A lady's gentleman, he is charming, not at all intimidating, newly arrived from Italy and willing to unpack your suitcase.

He shows you around Suite No. 2, larger than some apartments and centered thoughtfully over the pool and lobby with a smashing view. The room, with walls of light peach and rugs of green, boasts light-spirited antiques and tasteful art, and a sumptuous bath.

Your butler points out the fresh pineapple and flowers. He brings ice and tea. He leads you on a tour of the gardens and grounds.

Want something special? A wake-up double tall latte with 2 percent milk and raw sugar, fixed Italian style. He beams. You'll have another butler tomorrow, but he can make sure you get the latte from her.

It can be hard to tear yourself away from the lavish surroundings and head for the pool, to splash around with a familiar-faced couple and infant. You might recognize Mom as a television star. She carries the baby off to a sunchair to apply a diaper; nanny must be on break.

Then it's time for dinner up at the Lodge, a half-hour shuttle ride away, with a stop first at "Downtown Lanai City," a tiny village of time-worn old plantation stores around a square filled with towering Island pines. For guests sated with hotel haute cuisine, Lanai City offers something else to explore for dinner: a pizza place and the popular bar and grill at quaint Hotel Lanai, a historic 12-room lodge on a hill.

But if you're living it up, Koele's Formal Dining Room is more than able to provide five-star fare. Well fed, you may be too languid to get off the return bus for a nightcap at the Hotel Lanai. Besides, your palace awaits, with turndown pillow treats and cool evening breezes billowing through lanai doors.

Most hotel turndown maids are taught steadfastly to shut and lock the doors, even if guests leave them open in lieu of air conditioning, and to turn on all the lights and perhaps some awful radio station so that bright blare will greet you when you return to go to sleep. Ah, but not on Lanai. Peace reigns, and guests dream of spinner dolphins in a sparkly sea.

The next sunny morning goes far too quickly—that precious latte, breakfast on the open air terrace, personal greeting from the attentive hotel general manager, messages from your new butler, more disappearing luggage, and the inevitable airport shuttle, coda on your Lanai sojourn.

Visitors scan the horizon anxiously for storms, fog—anything to delay the departure. Although it's rare, sometimes Lanai guests do get lucky and find themselves weathered in for an unexpected addendum to their vacation plan. No worries: Most of them can afford it, and there's always plenty more to do on Lanai.

SHOOTING AXIS DEER

Out on the western plains of Lanai, bumping along in a GeoTracker with the wife of the local butcher (who can fill a freezer with a few well-placed rounds), we watch, fascinated, as a herd of Axis deer leaps together in a grand ballet. It's as if the whole Earth moves at once, a phenomenon we've seen often underwater while snorkeling, when thousands of fish move as one. The herds on Lanai, many of them imported species, are so great that deer—and pheasants, wild turkeys, quail, and francolins—outnumber people, some say 100 to 1. Press on to the interior and you'll also see biblical-looking Mouflon rams posing stoically in deep ravines that crease the island.

Hunting season is weeks away, and the deer know it; we see them readily and plentiful. They appear at sundown, stepping out of the forest in the open savannas and sometimes may be seen grazing on the lawn at the Lodge, like the statues people put on country estates. Come season—nine weekends from April to June—the deer vanish in canyons to dodge birch arrows and silver bullets.

Deer hunting is a survival skill on an island like Lanai; it keeps the deer from gnawing the island clean to the surf. On certain weekends you often hear distant gunfire and see critters draped over truck fenders. We never fail to notice on Lanai City houses deer antlers and ram horns, small, important triumphs of man over nature.

The bombing was halted in 1990, by President George H. W. Bush, who was shocked to learn the U.S. Navy was still bombing a Pacific island—one of the Hawaiian islands, at that—nearly 50 years after the end of World War II. The 45-square-mile island, about the size of San Francisco, was returned to native Hawaiians in 1993, and the navy was ordered to spend $400 million over the next ten years to sweep the island of unexploded bombs.

Now undergoing a slow, costly cleanup, the uninhabited island served as a penal colony in the monarchy period, a cattle ranch during territory days, and, during World War II, the staging zone for U.S. forces preparing for the invasion of Okinawa. In 1965, the navy dropped a 500-ton bomb on Kahoolawe to simulate an atomic explosion; the impact cracked a submarine's water lens and turned the island's fresh water brackish.

Permission is needed to visit Kahoolawe. For information on three- or five-day visits to the island, call Protect Kahoolawe Ohana at (808) 956-7068, or visit **www.kahoolawe.org.**

REMEMBERING BOMBS . . .

We remember bombs falling on Kahoolawe in the summer of 1976. We could see them every night from Ben Keau's green plantation-style house on the slope of Haleakala. The air raids lit up the night like the Fourth of July. Keau was the first person to tell us that the U.S. Navy—our navy—was bombing one of the Hawaiian Islands. We didn't believe him at first. "It's true," he said. "Look tonight." And we did, and there it was—a time warp rerun of a World War II air battle. Only 12 miles away from where we sat, drinking cold beer on the lanai of his house in Kula, navy planes dive-bombed the neighboring island. You could feel the vibrations across the sea channel. Other U.S. bombs were falling that summer on Vietnam and Cambodia, and what fell on Hawaii was of little concern. Nobody voiced frustration about the bombing practice air raids, even after an errant, unexploded 500-pound navy bomb was discovered in a West Maui sugarcane field. The island had been in navy hands since World War II, but local discontent was swelling.

In the summer of 1976, nine native Hawaiians, led by Dr. Emmit Aluli, a Molokai physician, made the first of many risky and unauthorized landings on Kahoolawe to protest the navy's use of the island. They filed a federal lawsuit charging violations of laws pertaining to the environment, historic preservation, and religious freedom. The bombing was finally halted in 1990. Three years later, it was returned to Hawaiians "to be used solely and exclusively for the preservation and practice of all rights customarily and traditionally exercised by native Hawaiians for cultural, spiritual, and subsistence purposes."

Part Five

Attractions

Choosing which attractions to visit during your Maui vacation can be daunting. So much to see and do and so little time! Many of Maui's top visitor attractions, from museums and gardens to historic sites, have a nominal fee, but others are free. Reference the maps in the introduction to locate the attractions.

In Hawaii, a man neither rises to heights nor sinks to real depths. He develops acute Polynesia which is related to the Mexican manana . . . a realization that tomorrow will be very like today, that nothing is of colossal importance beyond the moment. The days slip away uncounted, a month, a year, a life- time passes with nothing to mark its passing except a blur of happiness, tainted only by a vague feeling that he "should do something about some- thing."

—Don Blanding, *Hula Moons*, 1930

The following profiles provide basic information on the attractions, such as location, hours of operation, and cost. Each also features a rating for five age groups and a brief description. Given on a five-star scale, the ratings don't guarantee that a certain segment of visitors will love or hate the attraction, but they do provide a reliable evaluation of each group's typical reaction. For example, some teenagers want to visit historical sights, but more want to go to the beach. Together, the information, rat- ings, and descriptions will help you plan an itinerary pleasing to all mem- bers of your family or group.

MAUI COUNTY ATTRACTIONS

Attraction Name	Type of Attraction	Authors' Rating	Region
Alexander and Baldwin Sugar Museum	Museum	★★★	Central Maui
Bailey House Museum	Museum	★★★	Central Maui
Baldwin Home Museum	Museum	★★★	West Maui
Haleakala National Park	National Park	★★★★	Upcountry Maui
Hana Cultural Center	Museum	★★★	Hana
Hawaii Experience Theater	Theater	★★★½	West Maui
Hawaii Nature Center	Museum	★★★★	Central Maui
Hui Noeau Visual Arts Center	Gallery	★★★	Upcountry Maui
Kepaniwai Cultural Park	Gardens	★★★	Central Maui
Kula Botanical Garden	Gardens	★★★	Upcountry Maui
Lahaina-Kaanapali and Pacific Railroad	Hawaiian Railway	★★★	West Maui
Maui Ocean Center	Aquarium	★★★★	South Maui
Maui Tropical Plantation and Gardens	Historic Home and Country Store	★★★	Central Maui
Molokai Museum and Cultural Center	Museum	★★★	Molokai
Tedeschi Winery	Winery	★★★	South Maui
Whalers Village Museum	Museum	★★½	West Maui
Wo Hing Temple Museum	Museum	★★½	West Maui

MAUI COUNTY ATTRACTIONS BY TYPE

Attraction Name	Authors' Rating	Region
Aquarium		
Maui Ocean Center	★★★★	South Maui
Gallery		
Hui Noeau Visual Arts Center	★★★	Upcountry Maui
Gardens		
Kepaniwai Cultural Park	★★★	Central Maui
Kula Botanical Garden	★★★	Upcountry Maui

MAUI COUNTY ATTRACTIONS BY TYPE *(continued)*		
Attraction Name	**Authors' Rating**	**Region**
Historic Home		
Maui Tropical Plantation and Country Store	★★★	Central Maui
Museum		
Alexander and Baldwin Sugar Museum	★★★	Central Maui
Bailey House Museum	★★★	Central Maui
Baldwin Home Museum	★★★	West Maui
Hana Cultural Center	★★★	Hana
Hawaii Nature Center	★★★★	Central Maui
Whalers Village Museum	★★½	West Maui
Wo Hing Temple Museum	★★½	West Maui
National Parks		
Haleakala National Park	★★★★	Upcountry Maui
Theater		
Hawaii Experience Theater	★★★½	West Maui
Train Ride		
Lahaina-Kaanapali and Pacific Railroad	★★★	West Maui
Winery		
Tedeschi Winery	★★★	South Maui

Maui's Attractions Rated and Ranked

Alexander and Baldwin Sugar Museum

Location 3957 Hansen Road, Puunene, Central Maui

Phone (808) 871-8058

Web site www.sugarmuseum.com

Hours Monday–Saturday, 9:30 a.m.–4:30 p.m.

Admission $5 adults, $2 children ages 6–18

When to go Anytime

How much time to allow 45 minutes

Authors' rating ★★★; A look at Maui's sugar plantation history.

Overall appeal by age group

Preschool ★½		Teens ★★½		Over 30 ★★★½
Grade School ★★		Young Adults ★★★		Seniors ★★★½

Description and comments In a converted 1902 superintendent's six-room home, visitors gain a sense of plantation life from the viewpoint of a sugar planter who controlled the Island economy. The museum features artifacts, photographs, tools (including a red Cleveland Model 336 trench digger), and other relics of an era gone by.

Bailey House Museum

Location 2375-A Main Street, Wailuku, Central Maui

Phone (808) 244-3326

Web site www.mauimuseum.org

Hours Monday–Saturday, 10 a.m.– 4 p.m.

Admission $4 adults, $1 children ages 7–12

When to go Anytime

How much time to allow 1 hour

Authors' rating ★★★; Worth a stop for history buffs.

Overall appeal by age group

Preschool ★½		Teens ★★½		Over 30 ★★★½
Grade School ★★		Young Adults ★★★		Seniors ★★★½

Description and comments The missionary-era Bailey House, built in 1833 of lava rock and native woods, sits on land given to the missionaries by Hawaiian chiefs. Hawaiians attended reading and writing classes here, using Hawaiian-language books printed on Maui. Today, the Bailey House displays Hawaiian artifacts, including tapa, weaving, featherwork, and tools made out of stones, shells, and bones. A gallery of paintings—all from the late 1800s—portrays the beauty of the Valley Isle, and a stroll through the outside gardens reveals rare native plants, a koa wood canoe, and a surfboard once used by legendary surfer/swimming champion Duke Kahanamoku. A gift shop offers crafts, apparel, Hawaiian music, and books.

Other things to do nearby The Hawaii Nature Center and Kepaniwai Park are a short drive away.

Baldwin Home Museum

Location 120 Dickenson Street, Lahaina, West Maui

Phone (808) 661-3362 or (808) 661-3262

Hours Daily, 10 a.m.–4 p.m.

Admission $5 for families, $3 for individuals, $2 for senior citizens

When to go Anytime

How much time to allow 1 hour

Authors' rating ★★★; A peek into Hawaii's missionary era.

Overall appeal by age group

Preschool ★½	Teens ★★★	Over 30 ★★★½
Grade School ★★	Young Adults ★★★	Seniors ★★★½

Description and comments This two-story structure was the home of Reverend Dwight Baldwin, a Protestant medical missionary from 1838 to 1871. Today, the home and its grounds, lovingly restored by the Lahaina Restoration Foundation, give visitors a glimpse of what life was like for 19th-century missionary families in Lahaina. On display are various household items and furniture, photographs, and other historic artifacts. Ask for a free self-guided tour map of Lahaina's other restored treasures.

Other things to do nearby Located at Dickenson and Front Streets, the Baldwin Home is one of several historic sights in Lahaina.

Haleakala National Park

Location The park extends from the 10,023-foot summit of Haleakala down the southeast flank of the mountain to the Kipahulu coastline near Hana. The summit area is accessible from Kahului via Routes 37, 377, and 378. The park's Kipahulu area, at the east end of the island between Hana and Kaupo, can be reached via Highway 36. Driving time is about 3–4 hours each way.

Phone (808) 572-4400

Web site www.nps.gov/hale

Hours Park Ranger Headquarters is open daily, 7:30 a.m.–4 p.m. The visitor center is open daily, sunrise–3 p.m. (Overnight camping is permissible. The Hosmer Grove Campground in the summit area, located just inside the park's entrance, can be used without a permit; all other camping areas require permits.)

Admission $10 per vehicle. The entrance fee is good for 7 days.

When to go Anytime. Haleakala is renowned as a setting for dramatic sunrises and sunsets, although most people come for the sunrise. Be sure to arrive at least 30 minutes before either event.

How much time to allow Half a day or more, depending on whether you plan to spend time hiking or taking part in one of the park's programs.

Authors' rating ★★★★; One of the great natural wonders of the world.

Overall appeal by age group

Preschool ★★	Teens ★★★½	Over 30 ★★★★
Grade School ★★★	Young Adults ★★★★	Seniors ★★★★

Description and comments Haleakala ("House of the Sun"), a dormant volcano that last spilled lava a bit more than 200 years ago, was designated as a national park in 1961. The park consists of nearly 29,000 acres, most of it wilderness. In the summit area, see the park headquarters and Haleakala Visitor Center, which houses a variety of cultural and natural history exhibits. Rangers are on duty and can be a tremendous help in making the most out of your visit. In the Kipahulu area, see the Kipahulu Ranger Station/Visitor Center. Each facility has a selection of books, maps, postcards, and other souvenirs for sale.

Touring tips Check the park's bulletin board for a schedule of daily programs and guided hikes. Obey all posted warning signs. It can be cold at the summit, so be prepared. Due to the high elevation (nearly 2 miles high) and reduced oxygen at the park, anyone with a heart or respiratory condition is advised to check with a doctor before visiting.

Hana Cultural Center

Location 4974 Uakea Road, Hana

Phone (808) 248-8622

Web site www.planet-hawaii.com/hana

Hours Daily, 10 a.m.–4 p.m.

Admission Donations accepted

When to go Anytime

How much time to allow 1 hour

Authors' rating ★★★; A reward after the long journey to Hana.

Overall appeal by age group

Preschool ★★	Teens ★★½	Over 30 ★★★
Grade School ★★½	Young Adults ★★★	Seniors ★★★

Description and comments This cultural center is home to more than 500 artifacts, 600 books, 680 Hawaiian bottles, and 5,000 historic photographs of the Hana district. Opened in 1983, the nonprofit museum houses Hawaiian quilts, poi boards, stones, kapa, ancient tools, fish hooks, gourd bowls, stone lamps, and a century-old fishing net. Also featured are tributes to some of Hana's most notable citizens. The cultural center also includes a series of old Hawaiian *hale* (houses), the historic Hana courthouse, and a jailhouse.

Hawaii Experience Domed Theater

Location 824 Front Street, Lahaina, West Maui

Phone None available

Hours Daily, 9 a.m.–11 p.m.

Admission $7 adults, $4 children ages 4–12. If you purchase $25 worth of merchandise at the gift shop, you receive a free ticket to the show.

When to go Anytime

How much time to allow 50 minutes

Authors' rating ★★★½; a pleasant diversion in the heart of Lahaina.

Overall appeal by age group

Preschool ★★★	Teens ★★★½	Over 30 ★★★½
Grade School ★★★½	Young Adults ★★★½	Seniors ★★★½

Description and comments A planetarium-like theater with a domed screen more than three stories high, this attraction features a spectacular 40-minute film shown every hour.

Other things to do nearby Historical attractions in downtown Lahaina, including the Wo Hing Temple and Baldwin Home Museum, are within easy walking distance.

Hawaii Nature Center

Location 875 Iao Valley Road, Wailuku, Central Maui

Phone (808) 244-6500

Web site www.hawaiinaturecenter.org

Hours Daily, 10 a.m.–4 p.m.

Admission $6 adults, $4 children ages 4–12

When to go Anytime

How much time to allow 1 hour

Authors' rating ★★★★; Good hands-on learning experience.

Overall appeal by age group

Preschool ★★★	Teens ★★★★	Over 30 ★★★★
Grade School ★★★★	Young Adults ★★★★	Seniors ★★★★

Description and comments The Nature Center's Interactive Science Arcade features more than 30 interactive exhibits celebrating Maui's natural environment. The main exhibit hall features an amazing 10-foot-high, 30-foot-long, three-dimensional replication of four streams that feed into the Iao Stream. Aquariums, rain-forest explorations, arcade games, telescopes, and live insect and animal exhibits are among the other highlights. The gift shop features an extensive selection of nature-themed merchandise. All proceeds go to environmental education programs for Maui elementary-school children.

Touring tips The best is Rainforest Walk, a guided tour into the wet, wonderful world of Maui where you meet carnivorous creatures and exotic plants under the rainbow. Tickets include price of admission; $30 adults, and $20 children ages 5 and older.

Other things to do nearby Kepaniwai Cultural Park and the Bailey House Museum.

Hui Noeau Visual Arts Center

Location 2841 Baldwin Avenue, Makawao; 1 mile below Makawao town, Upcountry Maui

Phone (808) 572-6560

Web site www.maui.net/~hui

Hours Monday–Friday, 8:30 a.m.–5 p.m. Gallery hours are Saturday, 10 a.m.–4 p.m.

Admission Donations accepted

When to go Anytime

How much time to allow 1 hour

Authors' rating ★★★; A haven for art lovers

Overall appeal by age group

Preschool ★★	Teens ★★★	Over 30 ★★★½
Grade School ★★½	Young Adults ★★★	Seniors ★★★½

Description and comments Occupying a beautiful nine-acre estate in Makawao, this nonprofit art center features works by both local and international artists. The estate itself is a historic landmark (built in 1917 for Harry and Ethel Baldwin) dotted with pine and camphor trees and adorned with an immaculate formal garden and reflecting pool. The arts center features classes and workshops for aspiring artisans, and exhibits are open to the public on Saturdays. The gift shop offers a selection of original artworks, note cards, books, and other gift items.

Kepaniwai Cultural Park

Location Iao Valley Road, Central Maui

Phone No phone

Hours Daily, 7 a.m.–7 p.m.

Admission Free, self-guided tour

When to go Anytime

How much time to allow 1 hour

Authors' rating ★★★; A pleasant stop if you're in the area.

Overall appeal by age group

Preschool ★★	Teens ★★★	Over 30 ★★★½
Grade School ★★½	Young Adults ★★★	Seniors ★★★½

Description and comments Picturesque gardens and architectural pavilions representing Hawaii's ethnic groups.

Other things to do nearby The Hawaii Nature Center and Bailey House Museum are nearby.

Kula Botanical Garden

Location 0.7 miles from Kula Highway, on Kekaulike Avenue (Highway 377) in Kula, Upcountry Maui

Phone (808) 878-1715

Hours Daily, 9 a.m.–4 p.m.

Admission $5 adults, $1 children ages 6–12

When to go Anytime

How much time to allow 90 minutes

Authors' rating ★★★; A botanist's dream come true.

Overall appeal by age group

Preschool ★★	Teens ★★½	Over 30 ★★★
Grade School ★★½	Young Adults ★★½	Seniors ★★★½

Description and comments Kula, blessed with a mild, cool climate and fertile soil, is the home of this five-acre wonderland originally owned by Princess Kekaulike. Opened in 1969, the garden today features more than 1,700 tropical plants, including exotic flora such as proteas, heliconias, orchids, anthurium, and gingers.

Lahaina-Kaanapali and Pacific Railroad

Location 975 Limahana Place, Suite 203, Lahaina, West Maui

Phone (808) 667-6851 or (808) 499-2307

Hours 12 rides scheduled daily, beginning at 10 a.m.

Admission $16 adults, $10 children ages 3–12 (round-trip)

When to go Anytime

How much time to allow 90 minutes

Authors' rating ★★★; A short train ride offering views of the West Maui coastline.

Overall appeal by age group

Preschool ★★½		Teens ★★		Over 30 ★★
Grade School ★★★		Young Adults ★★		Seniors ★★½

Description and comments The "Sugar Cane Train," with its 1890s locomotive and distinctive whistle, was used by the Pioneer Mill to transport sugar crops until the early 1950s. Today, the train shuttles visitors between Lahaina and the resort area of Kaanapali. The six-mile route through a cane field lasts about 40 minutes each way. A friendly conductor shares the history of Maui's sugar industry.

Maui Ocean Center

Location Maalaea Harbor Village, 192 Maalaea Road, South Maui

Phone (808) 270-7000

Web site www.mauioceancenter.com

Hours Daily, 9 a.m.–5 p.m.

Admission $20 adults, $13 children ages 3–12, children under age 3 are free. Senior citizens and military personnel, 10 percent discount.

When to go Anytime

How much time to allow 2 hours

Authors' rating ★★★★; A must-see for anyone interested in understanding Island marine life.

Overall appeal by age group

Preschool ★★★★½		Teens ★★★★★		Over 30 ★★★★★
Grade School ★★★★		Young Adults ★★★★★		Seniors ★★★★½

Description and comments The star attraction is a 600,000-gallon ocean aquarium tank with a walk-through acrylic tunnel that lets you get a good view of the more than 2,000 inhabitants, including a six-foot tiger shark and other sharks, spotted eagle rays, mahimahi, triggerfish, sea turtles, eels, and a dazzling array of colorful reef fish. Other exhibits include a supervised touch pool for kids, allowing them to hold sea critters; interactive displays about the humpback whale; and smaller aquariums affording a close look at eels, shrimp, coral, and other sea life. The Reef Cafe and Seascape Cafe and Bar provide food and drinks, and the large gift shop carries logo and ocean-themed goods.

Other things to do nearby The Ocean Center overlooks busy Maalaea Harbor, where cruise boats come and go. Try combining a trip to the aquarium with a snorkeling tour to look at the sea creatures in the wilds.

Maui Tropical Plantation and Country Store

Location 1670 Honoapiilani Highway, Central Maui

Phone (808) 244-7643

Hours Daily, 9 a.m.–5 p.m.

Admission Free. Tram tours cost $10 adults and $4 children ages 5–12 (plus tax).

When to go Anytime

How much time to allow 75 minutes

Authors' rating ★★★; When you want to know more about tropical crops, this is the place. Pick up fresh fruits at the country store.

Overall appeal by age group

Preschool ★★	Teens ★★★	Over 30 ★★★★
Grade School ★★½	Young Adults ★★★½	Seniors ★★★★

Description and comments From the visitor center, head out to the plantation's 50-acre garden, which is filled with tropical plants, including pineapple, sugarcane, papaya, guava, star fruit, anthuriums, and protea. A restaurant and plant nursery are also available.

Touring tips Narrated 45-minute tram tours of the garden are available. The first train leaves at 10 a.m.; the last train leaves at 3:15 p.m.

Other things to do nearby The Bailey House Museum is a mile or so to the north.

Molokai Museum and Cultural Center

Location On Kalae Highway, just west of Kaunakakai, Molokai

Phone (808) 567-6436

Hours Monday–Saturday, 10 a.m.–2 p.m.

Admission $3 adults, $1 students ages 5–18

When to go Any time

How much time to allow 1 hour

Authors' rating ★★★; Not terribly exciting, but filled with history.

Overall appeal by age group

Preschool ★½	Teens ★★½	Over 30 ★★★
Grade School ★★	Young Adults ★★★	Seniors ★★★½

Description and comments The museum is located in a converted sugar mill that was established in 1878 by Rudolph Wilhelm Meyer, an engineer and surveyor who arrived on Molokai in 1851 and married a Hawaiian princess. Now listed on the National Register of Historic Places, the mill houses original machinery and other artifacts from the island's sugar plantation days. Guided tours and Hawaiian cultural programs are offered.

Tedeschi Winery

Location Ulupalakua Ranch, about 10 miles past the junction of Highways 377 and 37 in Kula, Upcountry Maui

Phone (808) 878-6058

Web site www.mauiwine.com

Hours Daily, 9 a.m.–5 p.m. Guided tours are held daily, 9:30 a.m.–2:30 p.m.

Admission Free

When to go Anytime

How much time to allow 1 hour

Authors' rating ★★★; Worth a taste for wine lovers.

Overall appeal by age group

Preschool ★½	Teens ★★½	Over 30 ★★★
Grade School ★★	Young Adults ★★★	Seniors ★★★

Description and comments Tedeschi Vineyards is known for its Island-style wine, including Maui Blanc Pineapple Wine, a popular fruit-forward novelty souvenir. Wines are available for tasting and purchase at the tasting room in the King's Cottage, once used as a retreat by King Kalakaua. Hawaii-made specialty goods, books, and gifts are also on sale.

Touring tips The tour explains how the wines are processed and bottled. But it's not necessary to take a tour to enjoy sampling the wines and walking through the shady lawns and gardens.

Whalers Village Museum

Location Whalers Village (3rd floor), 2435 Kaanapali Parkway, Kaanapali Beach Resort, West Maui

Phone (808) 661-5992

Web site www.whalersvillage.com

Hours Daily, 9:30 a.m.–10 p.m.

Admission Free

When to go Anytime

How much time to allow 1 hour

Authors' rating ★★½; Displays and historic artifacts about whaling, to entertain the family if they get restless shopping.

Overall appeal by age group

Preschool ★★	Teens ★★½	Over 30 ★★½
Grade School ★★½	Young Adults ★★½	Seniors ★★½

Description and comments This museum traces the history of Lahaina's colorful whaling era, roughly from 1825 to 1860. Among more than 100 items on exhibit are a six-foot model of a whaling ship, harpoons, maps, logbooks, and an extensive collection of scrimshaw.

Wo Hing Temple Museum

Location Front Street, Lahaina (between Papalaua and Lahainaluna Streets), West Maui

Phone (808) 661-3262

Hours Daily, 10 a.m.–4 p.m.

Admission Donations accepted

When to go Anytime

How much time to allow 30 minutes

Authors' rating ★★½; Good for historians; young kids will be bored.

Overall appeal by age group

Preschool ★	Teens ★★	Over 30 ★★½
Grade School ★★	Young Adults ★★½	Seniors ★★★

Description and comments A Buddhist shrine is the centerpiece of this restored 1912 Chinese temple, which provides a revealing look at how early Chinese settlers lived in Lahaina. Old photographs and artifacts are also on exhibit. A cookhouse (built separately from the main building to reduce the risk of a house fire) sits just to the right of the building. Two Hawaii films shot in 1898 and 1906 by Thomas Edison are among the highlights. The temple is affiliated with Chee Kung Tong, a Chinese fraternal society with branches throughout the world.

Other things to do nearby The Baldwin Home Museum is nearby.

Part Six

Outdoor Adventures

The True Nature of Maui

If you think Maui is only for honeymooners, game show prize-winners, or the rich and famous, take another look. If you never heard of Molokai or Lanai, better keep reading.

These islands are more than just a collection of fancy resorts and shops. Maui is the land of adventures, and you have so many choices. It's the nature of the place: reliable tradewinds, beaches, lagoons, waterfalls, the biggest dormant volcano in the world, the second wettest spot on Earth, and neighboring islands that beg to be explored. Each element provides an entry to adventure unlike what you know back home.

TWAIN IN HAWAII

During his 19th-century Hawaiian sojourn, a young Mark Twain dropped his pen for six weeks. "In explanation and excuse, I offer the fact that I spent that time on the Island of Maui," wrote Twain. "I never spent so pleasant a month before, or bade any place goodbye so regretfully." When he got back home, Twain went on to become one of America's best loved and most successful writers.

You can snorkel in the clear waters of the crescent islet of Molokini Crater (between South Maui and the Island of Kahoolawe), splash in waterfall pools all the way to Hana, soar through challenging waves on high-tech windsurfing boards on the North Shore, four-wheel or mountain-bike through the red-dirt Lanai backcountry, kayak the Molokai wilderness coast, or lounge on a booze-cruise sailing deck and watch the sun set over your mai tai. Don't forget hiking the moonscape inside Haleakala Crater or coasting down the volcano, 38 miles from summit to sea, on a specially equipped bicycle. Of course, you could do nothing more than commute from your vacation digs to the nearest beach cabana. Then again, if fabulous golf courses are your dream, you're going to be busy. Maui's storied links, crafted by world-class designers in world-famous settings, are too numerous to play on one trip. Watch for unusual natural hazards, such as the sight of a whale leaping from the sea just when you've planned your shot.

Wildlife Watching

Wildlife, too, is different on Maui's islands. No snakes or alligators, only curious critters that resemble escapees of Alice's Wonderland. In fact, the allure of exotic fauna is as much a reason to explore Maui's outdoors as extreme sports or the promise of a great tan. For example, Maui is home to the mongoose, the low-slung creature of Rudyard Kipling's *Rikki Tikki Tavi,* thanks to a failed sugar baron's rat-control experiment; the diurnal mongoose was introduced to thwart nocturnal rats in the cane fields, but the twain never met. Then there are the endangered Nene geese, birds whose ancestors blew in from Canada on a tailwind and stayed, but over time transformed their tender webbed feet into claws to walk on lava; the little Happy Face spiders (*Theridion grallator*), so called because a pattern resembling a smiling clown face appears on the thorax; and migrating giants who prefer Maui's waters to any others for the world's largest annual meeting of Pacific humpback whales, who quit Alaska's chilly waters each winter in favor of Maui's tepid Maalaea Bay.

Out There, In the Water

If you go to Maui in winter and don't see a whale, you've missed the really big show. Actually, it's difficult to go to Maui in winter and not see a whale. They're everywhere offshore: Look for the telltale spouts and belly-flop splashes. Whale-watching in winter is the Islands' major spectator sport. Boat tours will take you close enough to get a good look, but not too close, for the whale's sake. The best free spot on Maui to whale-watch is **McGregor Point,** a scenic turnout on the road to Lahaina. Bring your binoculars to see leviathans at play.

Spinner dolphins frolic year-round on Maui's southwest and northwest shores and often flash across **Lanai's Hulopoe Bay;** they are an unforgettable sight, from the shore and from the sea, where they sometimes perform elaborate ballets for boat passengers. Manta rays "fly" through these tropical waters. Huge turtles play in the surf, then clamber ashore to make nests and lay eggs. Maui's effort to keep them safe is evident in the beach fence that now lines the shore by the busy highway between Maalaea and Kihei.

Other, more menacing denizens of the deep include moray eels and sharks, particularly tiger sharks that patrol the coast in search of food and sometimes mistake board surfers or swimmers for tasty turtles or seals. A surfer's silhouette—squat body, little flippers—is the same to a shark, who is always looking for something to eat. Sharks may be considered friendly by local custom—they are venerated as sacred *aumakua,* or family guardians—but nonetheless, they bite, so beware. Two attacks have occurred in recent years at **Olowalu Reef,** a popular snorkeling spot along the West Maui highway outside Lahaina, prompting the placement of seven permanent shark warning signs (written by lawyers to avoid civil liability) along the shore. If you see such a sign, don't go in the water there. There are other commonsense ways to avoid sharks: Never swim at sunset, when sharks like to eat. Avoid murky water; what you can't see can hurt you. Always swim with a buddy. If a shark attacks you, punch it on its sensitive nose or eye, then swim for shore. Fortunately, most folks only see sharks close-up at Maui Ocean Center.

BLACKBIRD, BYE-BYE

Everywhere else the crow is a pest. In Hawaii, *Corvus hawaiiensess* is nearly extinct. Hunters shot them; developers spoiled their habitat; the birds were plagued by disease and reproductive disorder.

Hawaiians, who considered the crow an aumakua, or family guardian, denied Captain James Cook a specimen. After the last flock began to go extinct on Maui in the 1980s, the captive birds were taken to the Big Island's Endangered Species Facility, where at last count, 11 Hawaiian crows cling to existence.

Up There, on the Land

On land, Maui is home to some distinctive flora as well as fauna. The rare Silversword plant clings to the lava cinders of Haleakala and blooms but once before it dies, spouting a hundred purplish daisy-like buds at once on a tall, slim stalk above feathery silver leaves, like some kind of mutant delphinium. Lanai's most common tree isn't the ubiquitous palm, but the towering Cook and Norfolk pines of its uplands, planted years ago by a wise rancher. The thick ridgetop groves snag rain clouds and milk their moisture onto the dry land. The island teems with Axis deer (imported from China as a gift to an ancient king), Mouflon rams with curved biblical horns, wild turkeys, and game birds called chukkars that call out like lost souls. Molokai is famous for its mules that daily traverse the world's steepest sea cliffs, but cows and horses outnumber people. Molokai also has herds of diminutive deer.

Seven Natural Wonders of Maui

Some people come to Maui only to sit on the beach, and there's nothing wrong with that. But if you like active sports, the great outdoors is just too good to miss, from climbing Puu Olai on the southern end of Maui, to plunging in Kipahulu's waterfall pools, to trailriding on Molokai Ranch, to snorkeling and diving off Lanai, in pursuit of the sunshine-yellow long-nosed butterfly fish, the most common in a rainbow collection of tropical fish. Many adventures and guided tours can be arranged by a concierge or hotel activity desk. You can do many on your own. Below, we highlight some favorites for your must-see list.

Haleakala Crater

Known as the "House of the Sun," this crater is reputed to be the biggest hole on Earth, big enough to hold the Big Apple. It is 10,023 feet above sea level, 33 miles wide, and 2,000 feet deep. With its own weird weather, a nine-peaked mountain range, and strange inhabitants like a bird that barks like a dog, it is like no place on Earth. This primal Hawaii has virgin fern forests, scorched badlands, cinder cones, bubble caves, lava tubes, boiling pots, and here and there, the burial sites of ancient Hawaiians, best left untouched. For more information, see the profile of Haleakala National Park that follows in the "State and National Parks" section.

Molokini Crater

Hawaii's most popular dive site, Molokini, is a sunken crater with one edge above water off the coast of South Maui. It is a natural habitat for fish large and small. Bright little tropical reef fish thrive inside the crescent's concave embrace while big, pelagic fish roam the outer depths. Snorkelers and divers can choose one of the fast charter boats that leave Maalaea Harbor, choose a side, and spend the day with Maui's tropical schools.

Puu Kukui Forest

Puu Kukui, the summit of the West Maui Mountains, is a great green place best seen by helicopter. The second wettest spot on Earth (with 340 inches of rain a year), Puu Kukui includes the Wall of Tears, a weepy vertical massif; a dwarf forest of native plants; and Eke Crater, which early Hawaiians considered to be Heaven's gate, the doorway from this world to the next. Each year 12 lucky hikers who win the Kapalua Nature Society's lottery and buy their $500 tickets can enter the otherwise *kapu* (forbidden) native forest with a guide to see rare native plants and birds. For information, contact the Kapalua Nature Society at (808) 669-0244. To arrange a fly-over, call Sunshine Helicopters at (808) 871-0722 or (800) 469-3000 or visit **www.sunshinehelicopters.com.**

Seven Pools of Kipahulu

Nearly an hour's drive beyond Hana, 24 pools cascade down Oheo Gulch to the blue Pacific—but only seven get all the attention. Sometimes called "sacred," the seven pools inspire legend and bravado. Some folks try to swim in each pool; others are content to gaze at the watery spectacle from the bridge over Pipiwai Stream. The pools naturally attract a crowd, so go early or stay late, and remember, get out of the steep waterway canyon immediately if it starts to rain. You could get washed out to sea. Rangers are posted in the area, which is part of Haleakala National Park.

Ahihi-Kinau Natural Area Reserve

Where Haleakala lava last ran into the sea in about 1790, the stark black coast at Maui's southern tip ends in one of Maui's best snorkel sites: Ahihi-Kinau Natural Area Reserve. The 2,000-acre preserve includes the barren shoreline and its black lava pools filled with turquoise water and tropical fish. All sea life is protected here, so leave your speargun at the bar. Only looking is permitted. Call Snorkel Bob's for more information on diving safely here. (808) 879-7449.

Sea Cliffs of Molokai

The highest sea cliffs in the world (according to *The Guinness Book of Records*) form the north shore of Molokai, a sheer precipice that stretches 14 miles and drops 3,500 feet to the crashing surf. One misstep and you're *limu* (seaweed). You can see the cliffs from above by small plane or from below by kayak in the summer when the Pacific is calm. Some hike or ride a mule down to Kalaupapa National Historic Park to look back at the monumental cliffs. Contact the Molokai Ranch Outfitters Center at (808) 552-2791 for details. Or, you can stand in awe at the edge of Palaau State Park and soak up the grandeur. It's the best scenic outlook in Hawaii. For more information, see the park's profile in the "State and National Parks" section that follows.

Garden of the Gods, Lanai

On this island that once was the world's largest pineapple patch, you will find what appears to be a vestige of Arizona, a geologic badlands so ethereal that it's dubbed the Garden of the Gods. This boulder-strewn gulch looks so eerie that some believe it to be the work of aliens. Geologists say Lanai's rock garden is just an "ongoing posterosional event" not unlike the Painted Desert of the American Southwest. This badlands, accessible from the roadside, is worth exploring, especially at sunset when sun rays turn the stones into red, yellow, orange, and ochre gems.

The Beach Experience

With approximately 33 miles of sandy shoreline, Maui has more than 80 beaches—too many to explore in a single visit. Maui's best beaches are mostly pocket beaches tucked between sheltering reefs, safe for swimming,

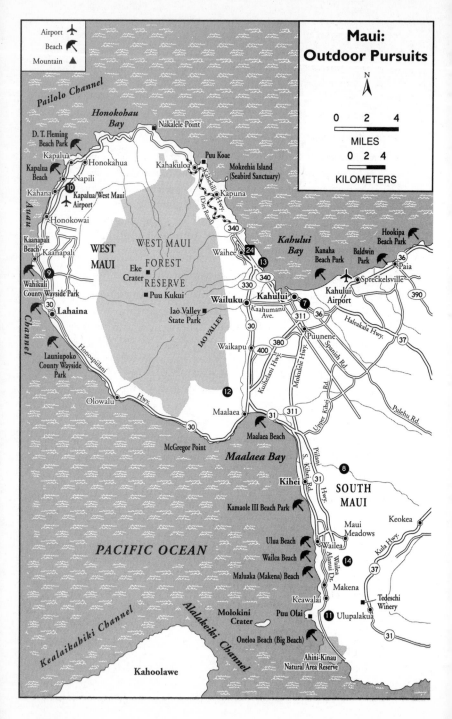

**Maui:
Outdoor Pursuits**

N

0   2   4
MILES

0   2   4
KILOMETERS

Pailolo Channel

Honokohau Bay

Nakalele Point

D. T. Fleming Beach Park

Kapalua

Honokahua

Puu Koae

Kahakuloa

Mokeehia Island (Seabird Sanctuary)

Kapalua Beach

Napili

Kahana

Kapalua/West Maui Airport

Kapuna

Auau

Honokowai

340

Kahului Bay

Hookipa Beach Park

Kaanapali Beach

Kaanapali

WEST MAUI

WEST MAUI FOREST RESERVE

Waihee

Kanaha Beach Park

Baldwin Park

36

Paia

9

Wahikuli County Wayside Park

Eke Crater

340

13

30

Puu Kukui

330

Kahului

Spreckelsville

390

Wailuku

7

Kahului Airport

30

Lahaina

Iao Valley State Park

Kaahumanu Ave.

311

36

Haleakala Hwy.

37

IAO VALLEY

30

Waikapu

380

400

Puunene

Launiupoko County Wayside Park

Honoapiilani Hwy.

12

Kuihelani Hwy.

Mokulele Hwy.

Spanish Rd.

Olowalu

30

Maalaea

31

311

Pulehu Rd.

Maalaea Beach

McGregor Point

Maalaea Bay

S. Kihei Rd.

Piilani Hwy.

8

PACIFIC OCEAN

Kihei

31

SOUTH MAUI

Kamaole III Beach Park

Maui Meadows

Keokea

Ulua Beach

Wailea

Kula Hwy.

Wailea Beach

Wailea Alanui Dr.

14

37

Maluaka (Makena) Beach

Makena

Tedeschi Winery

Keawalai

Kealaikahiki Channel

Molokini Crater

Puu Olai

11

Ulupalakua

31

Alalakeiki Channel

Oneloa Beach (Big Beach)

Ahini-Kinau Natural Area Reserve

Kahoolawe

Airport ✈

Beach

Mountain ▲

Kahekili Hwy. (Dirt Road)

24

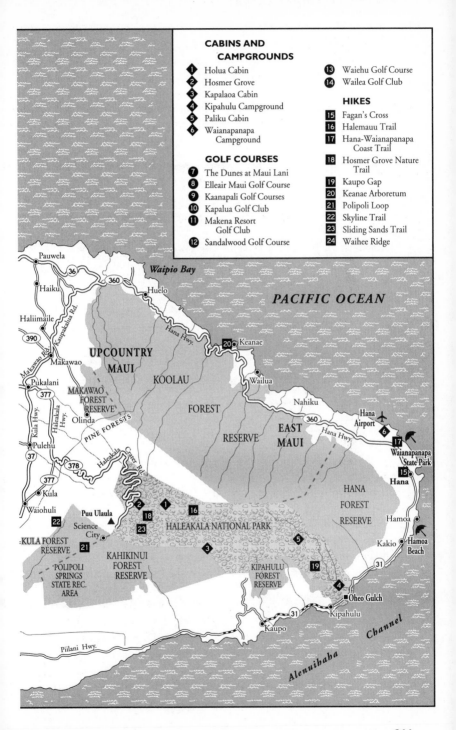

CABINS AND CAMPGROUNDS

1. Holua Cabin
2. Hosmer Grove
3. Kapalaoa Cabin
4. Kipahulu Campground
5. Paliku Cabin
6. Waianapanapa Campground

GOLF COURSES

7. The Dunes at Maui Lani
8. Elleair Maui Golf Course
9. Kaanapali Golf Courses
10. Kapalua Golf Club
11. Makena Resort Golf Club
12. Sandalwood Golf Course
13. Waiehu Golf Course
14. Wailea Golf Club

HIKES

15. Fagan's Cross
16. Halemauu Trail
17. Hana-Waianapanapa Coast Trail
18. Hosmer Grove Nature Trail
19. Kaupo Gap
20. Keanae Arboretum
21. Polipoli Loop
22. Skyline Trail
23. Sliding Sands Trail
24. Waihee Ridge

snorkeling, body-surfing, and splashing in the waves. So that you won't waste a minute, we selected our favorites, based on safety, access, scenic qualities, and swimmability. State law provides that all beaches in the Islands are open to the public, and public accessways, parking, and facilities such as restrooms and outdoor showers are provided free even within private resorts and residential areas. In return, the public is expected to respect neighbors and their property.

TAKE THE PLUNGE

Hawaii's waterfall pools are idyllic, but freshwater lakes, ponds or marshes are rare, curious delights if you can find them. And we have—in a Maui cloud forest.

Lake Violet is a deep blue puddle dotted by red dragonflies in a jade green cloud forest. Anywhere else this dollop of a pond wouldn't rate a second look, but up on the boggy slopes of 5,871-foot high Puu Kukui in the West Maui Mountains, it's a rare find. Only a few hikers can visit Lake Violet on this still forbidden mountain, which, according to legend, marked the intersection of heaven and earth. Now part of Kapalua Nature Preserve (see page 208) Puu Kukui is one of the last unspoiled upland forests and the second wettest spot on the planet. It rained 654.83 inches in 1982—that's 54½ feet! You would think Lake Violet would be bigger.

Lanai and Molokai

Each of these islands has plenty of beaches, but only one one each island is nearly perfect—a relative paucity compared to Maui, but it's one more perfect beach than most places. Lanai has 18 miles of sandy shoreline, including long empty beaches like Shipwreck Beach, an ideal spot for beachcombing with a real ship wrecked just offshore, and Polihua, where green sea turtles cavort. But Lanai's jewel is the accessible, golden crescent beach called Hulopoe, best all around for swimming, snorkeling, and watching spinner dolphins play. This is the beach just below the Manele Bay Hotel.

With 23 miles of shoreline, Molokai has long, lonesome gold beaches on its West End and a nearly beachless collection of fishponds on its East End. The most outstanding beach is Papohaku, a three-mile stretch of sand so golden that it has been used for export to replenish Waikiki Beach. The water is usually too rough for safe swimming, but this beach is good for sunning, picnics, sunset barbecues (bonfires are allowed), and long walks under a full moon.

West Maui

Kaanapali Beach

Location Honoapiilani Highway, fronting Kaanapali Beach Resort.

Activities Body-surfing, bodyboarding, snorkeling, scuba diving, windsurfing, kayaking, sailing, fishing.

Special appeal Places to hang for students and other young people, coastal walkway, boats that cruise from beach landings.

Comments Swimming conditions are good when the surf is flat; this is subject, however, to strong currents and surf. The base of Black Rock, a volcanic cinder cone jutting up at the center of the four-mile beach, is excellent for snorkeling and diving. A lifeguard is on duty at the Lahaina end. Beach concessions and outdoor showers are available all along the walkway that links Kaanapali's neighboring hotels and condos.

Every afternoon a spanking breeze comes up and sends sailboats streaking out in the channel. If you're too comfortable to go over to Lahaina harbor to catch a cruise, some launch from the beach to enjoy a sunset sail or snorkel tour.

Kapalua Beach

Location Lower Honoapiilani Highway, Kapalua Resort.

Activities Swimming, snorkeling, scuba diving, sailing, kayaking.

Special appeal Quiet atmosphere, good swimming and snorkeling, safe for kids, vivid scenery.

Comments This secluded strand in front of Kapalua Bay Hotel, the best of several spectacular strands in the area, is one of Maui's most beautiful and most swimmable beaches. The water is so clear that it's easy to see where the gold of the sand turns to green and then blue as the water gets deeper. Lava promontories protect both sides of the beach from rough seas. Public facilities are available, and a resort service desk rents equipment and makes reservations for adventure activities, but no lifeguards are posted. The sunset is often spectacular, spotlighting Molokai across the channel. This gold-sand beach and its see-through water lures swimmers, snorkelers, and kayakers, who can test their skill here before paddling down the coast to Honolua Bay to snorkel. Go in the morning when the wind is light and the sea calm.

Fish hang out by the rocks, as if they know this is a marine preserve. The beach is not so wide that you burn your feet getting in or out of the water. It's bordered inland by a shady path and cool lawns with outdoor showers at both ends. Public access and parking are located behind the oceanfront Kapalua Bay Club restaurant.

South Maui

Big Beach, Makena State Park

Location Makena Alanui, Makena.

Activities Swimming, surfing, snorkeling, body-surfing, bodyboarding, fishing.

Special appeal Scenic beauty, undeveloped nature, good for walking.

Comments Makena State Park at Maui's southern end has two scenic golden-sand beaches, known as Big Beach and Little Beach. Big Beach, 3,300 feet long, is Maui's longest and a favorite spot for experienced bodyboarders and body-surfers. Little Beach, meanwhile, is a small cove with gentler ocean conditions, a good prospect for novice wave riders. No lifeguards are on duty, nor are there public restrooms or showers. Secluded Little Beach is a popular "unofficial" nude beach, although public nudity is prohibited by law.

On the southern end of the Maui resort coast, development dwindles and succumbs to a wild, dry countryside covered with thorny green kiawe trees. The Maui Prince Hotel sits grandly by itself, the only hotel on 1,800 acres of Makena Resort, shared with some condos and homes, a couple of first-rate golf courses, and a necklace of perfect beaches. The strand nearest the hotel is Maluaka Beach, noted for its beauty, good swimming conditions, frequent turtle sightings, and view of Molokini crater and Kahoolawe.

Under the sea, at the 80-foot depth, sits a World War II–vintage U.S. Army tank that serves as a fish magnet. Every sea denizen seeking shade goes to the tank, and so should you. The South Maui coast offers Maui's best scuba diving for easy viewing and diversity of underwater life.

Kamaole Beach III

Location On South Kihei Road in Kihei town.

Activities Swimming, body-surfing, picnicking.

Special appeal Easy access, wide, sandy beach, grassy knoll.

Comments Sunbathers like Kamaole Beach Parks I, II, and III, the top draw of Kihei town. If every small town in America had a beach like Kihei's, nobody would ever leave home. This long, wide golden strand in the heart of town has a shaded grassy knoll with picnic facilities for families, a lifeguard, views of the West Maui Mountains and the islands of Lanai and Kahoolawe, and plenty of inexpensive beachfront condos nearby that make Kihei Maui's best beach bargain. Bars, restaurants, and shopping plazas line the busy main drag for lots of accessible action. Popular with early Hawaiians, who lived in thatched huts along the shore, this beach area was "discovered" in the 1970s by Canadian snowbirds looking for an affordable warm place to dodge winter.

Wailea Beach

Location Wailea Alanui, Wailea Resort.

Activities Swimming, body-surfing, bodyboarding, snorkeling, scuba diving, windsurfing, kayaking, fishing.

Special appeal Scenic beauty, gentle waves, luxury resort surroundings.

Comments Wailea Resort has five golden-sand beaches: Polo, Wailea, Ulua, Mokapu, and Keawakapu. Of all the beaches on Maui's sun-baked Gold Coast, none is finer for swimming than Wailea, the mile-long, gold-sand beach named for Lea, the Hawaiian goddess of canoe makers. Beach-goers can enjoy the gorgeous view of Molokini crater and the island of Kahoolawe on one side of an ocean channel and Lanai and West Maui on the other. The clear waters tumble to shore in waves just the right size for riding, with or without a boogie board. Wailea Beach is protected on both sides by lava reef points. It's the front yard of the Four Seasons Wailea and Grand Wailea Resort Hotel and Spa, two of Maui's most elegant and spectacular beach hotels. The Four Seasons beach boys run a dripper hose down the sandy slope so that beachgoers can get across the hot sand between the water and a paved coastal path without scalding their feet.

Ulua is the centermost beach, 1,000 feet long and 200 feet wide, between the Renaissance Wailea and Marriott Wailea Beach. Locals regard the offshore reef here as one of Maui's best snorkeling spots. A deeper reef, excellent for scuba diving, is about 100 yards out from shore.

A 1.5-mile coastal trail throughout Wailea Resort links several public accessways to all beaches and hotel and condo properties. The popular trail features native plants (each with a name tag), an old village site, and various architectural styles from ancient heiau to Kea Lani's Arabian fantasy. Panoramic views take in neighbor islands, unreal sunsets, and Pacific humpback whales in season.

Public facilities include parking, restrooms, and showers. Resort beach concessions offer board rentals and instruction. No lifeguards are posted.

Central Maui

Hookipa Beach

Location Paia town, off Hana Highway.

Activities Windsurfing and watching windsurfing.

Special appeal Constant strong wind, big waves.

Comments Skilled windsurfers head directly for world-famous Hookipa Beach on the north shore, to join the "Maui air force," daredevils who sail into waves and go airborne. They now attach kites to their rigs to increase hang time and allow them to hop over the waves. Home of the annual Aloha Classic windsurfing meet, Hookipa is the proving ground for gutsy experts who challenge each other to fly higher, farther, faster; it's the sailboarders' Bonneville and, for the rest of us, a must-see photo-op stop just past Paia, on the way to Hana.

Hana

Hamoa Beach

Location Adjacent to the Hana Pier.

Activities Swimming, bodyboarding, surfing.

Special appeal Little visited, scenic beach with good body-surf waves.

Comments Half moon–shaped Hamoa Beach is a gray-sand beach (a salt-and-pepper mix of coral and lava sands) in a truly tropical setting. It's a favorite of VIP sunbathers who seek rest and refuge at the Hotel Hana-Maui, side by side with neighborhood kids who demonstrate by example how best to enjoy the water conditions of the day—boogie-boarding, for instance, or riding waves in a plastic kayak, or windsurfing. The 100-foot-wide beach, 300 yards long, is bordered by 30-foot sea cliffs, traversed by stone steps. Surf breaks offshore and rolls up on the beach. Its stunning beauty inspired author James Michener to remark, "Paradoxically, the only beach I have ever seen that looks like the South Pacific was in the North Pacific—Hamoa Beach, on Maui Island in Hawaii, a beach so perfectly formed that I wonder at its comparative obscurity."

Kaihalulu Beach (Red-Sand Beach)

Location On the ocean side of Kauiki Head crater.

Activities Hiking, swimming.

Special appeal Rare red sand beach, semiprotected in-shore pool, scenic beauty.

Comments Hana sightseers visit Hasegawa's General Store but often miss the most unusual natural attraction nearby—a red-sand beach. It's officially known as Kaihalulu Beach, which means "roaring sea," but everyone here calls it "Red-Sand Beach." It's easy to see why. The beach is a strand of dark-red cinnabar sands, lining an exotic cove reached by a sometimes daunting and precipitous dirt path along the steep hillside.

Kauiki, a 390-foot-high volcanic cinder cone, lost its seaward wall to erosion and spilled red cinders everywhere to create the building blocks of the red-sand beach. The redness is the result of volcanic iron deposits; the only other known red-sand beach in the world is in Iceland. Maui's is warmer.

Waianapanapa Beach

Location Waianapanapa State Park, off Hana Highway, north of the city of Hana.

Activities Tent and cabin camping.

Special appeal Dreamlike tropical pocket beach with black sand edged by palms, clouds of sea mist.

Comments Shiny black-sand Waianapanapa Beach features bright-green jungle foliage on three sides and cobalt blue water lapping at its feet. *Waianapanapa* is Hawaiian for "glistening water," which you can see for yourself on a day trip to this unusual beach park near Hana. Surf is rough at times, with a rugged shore break and dangerous rip currents offshore.

The park features tent sites and a dozen rustic beach cabins with ocean views, the cheapest beachfront retreat on Maui at a mere $14 a night for two. The cabins sleep six and are equipped with kitchens, utensils, and linens. It's such a deal that reservations are booked a year in advance. Call (808) 984-8109 to try to secure yours.

Molokai

Papohaku Beach

Location Kaluakoi Road, just beyond Kaluakoi Resort.

Activities Surfing, bodyboarding, body-surfing, snorkeling.

Special appeal Broad strand, wild beauty, shady picnics, excellent sunset views of Oahu.

Comments Three miles long and 400 feet wide, Papohaku Beach is the biggest beach on Molokai and one of the only sandy Molokai beaches that is easily accessible for families. This isn't a swimming beach, but board riders like it. It has a wilderness atmosphere thanks to a shoreline kiawe forest, but with good paved road access and public beach park facilities—restrooms, showers, parking, and sheltered camping sites under the trees. Dangerous swimming conditions exist because no reefs offer protection from the full force of sea and surf, which pounds the sands impressively. High-surf conditions can occur any time of year. No lifeguards are on duty.

MAUI BEACH FACTS

- Beaches on Maui, Molokai, and Lanai are composed of coral, lava rock, erosional runoff, and shell sands, which cause them to be golden, black, red, gray, and black and white.
- Beaches change. They may be big in winter and small in summer, or vice versa. Strong Pacific surf can rearrange a flat, hard beach into one with a steep slope of loose sand. Strong storms also rearrange beaches.
- Lucky beachcombers can find treasures like shells and glass fishing floats on certain beaches, including those on Maui's north and east shores. We have also found shells on Kihei beaches. People-watchers are endlessly entertained at more crowded beaches, such as Kaanapali. Seekers of solitude can easily find remote strands where the only footprints are their own, right along the highway in West Maui.
- Wailea and Kaanapali resorts have inviting coastal paths to walk or jog that lead by all the hotels and public accessways. The resorts also maintain historic sites for public view, such as those at Kapalua fronting the Ritz-Carlton and on the Wailea trail between Four Seasons and Kea Lani. The public is welcome in hotel restaurants, spas, stores, and bars, although the hotels restrict use of their pools to guests.

Sandy Beach

Location Kamehameha V Highway, seven miles past Wave Crest Resort, near Kaunakakai and mile marker 21 on the East End.

Activities Swimming, body-surfing.

Special appeal Good swimming, views of Maui.

Comments It's not easy to find a swimming beach on Molokai, with its rough open seas, sheer cliffs, and muddy fish ponds. This small, reef-sheltered pocket beach is the rare exception. Soft, golden sands and gentle waters make it safe for kids. Don't stub your toes on the rocky bottom while admiring the West Maui Mountains across the channel. Restrooms are available, but not lifeguards. Good swimming conditions also prevail at nearby Waialua Beach, just before mile marker 19.

Lanai

Hulopoe Beach Park

Location Manele Road, near Manele Bay Hotel.

Activities Swimming, surfing, bodyboarding, body-surfing, snorkeling, fishing, picnicking, camping.

Special appeal Kids' tidepool, shade, scenery.

Comments This is the only beach park on Lanai. But it's a fine one, much prized by island residents who play and camp there, along with the Manele Bay patrons who walk down a trail shaded by a kiawe grove to reach it.

Hulopoe features a large tidepool carved into a lava cliff with all-season swimming for children. Palms dot the golden beach, which is 1,500 feet long and 200 feet wide. Beach swimming is subject to wave action, but it's usually calm enough inshore. Snorkeling is rewarding along the sheltering lava headland, a place to hike and explore on shore, too. Public restrooms, showers, picnic areas, and campsites are provided by the private owner.

Maui Waters: What You Should Know

Though the beaches are grand, the water is even better. The sea water is clear, ideal in temperature, and salty enough to keep you afloat. To swim easily in the ocean or play in the waves is one of the most special aspects of a trip to Maui.

The same mid-Pacific location that keeps Island waters clean and warm demands attentive respect for the seas and their hazards. The biggest dangers are seasonal surf and currents, posted on most park beaches. Heed warning signs and never turn your back on the ocean. Many beaches are sheltered by reefs, but those that are not get pounded by relentless waves that slap the shore with such force that they can knock the unwary off their feet and send them out to sea.

You can see and hear rising surf; it's an awesome phenomenon, best observed safely from shore. When the surf comes up, surfers head out to meet the challenge. But novices and swimmers are wise to head out of the water and stay ashore to watch.

Currents are insidious, because you can't always tell when and where they are. The Hawaiian Islands are sunken mountains with steep sides that result in strong, swirling ocean currents. Kealaikahiki Channel, off the south coast of Lanai, is famous for a powerful current that leads to Tahiti, 1,500 miles away. Should you get carried out by a rip current, don't panic. Conserve your strength, determine which direction is perpendicular to the current and also leads toward shore, and swim across the current toward safety.

You might meet the mild Hawaiian version of Portuguese man-o-war jellyfish, known as blue bottles, which float in from time to time. On the water's surface, this jellyfish appears as an innocent floating bubble, but a nearly invisible blue tendril trailing behind it leaves a searing burn and may take a while to go away. Our hint for a quick antidote is the blue-colored aloe vera gel widely sold in Hawaii as a sunburn soother. A dab on a blue bottle sting will usually extinguish the fire, but more extreme allergic reactions may need medical care.

Swimmers and snorkelers sometimes run into sharp pieces of coral and get cut or scraped. Coral cuts tend to infect quickly, so keep a bottle of inexpensive hydrogen peroxide handy to flush and treat them.

Obviously, a foremost protective item is sunscreen. No paleskin wants to return home from the islands without a golden tan. But this close to the equator, the tropical sun is especially strong, the air is clear, and burns happen very quickly, particularly on children's tender skin. Sunscreen is essential. Apply it before you go outside; reapply it after swimming, snorkeling, or sweating a lot; and try to avoid midday exposure. You can still get a head-turning tan at 9 a.m. or after 3 p.m., even with SPF 15 sunscreen.

One other precaution: Leave your most valuable belongings in your room safe when you head for the beach. If you carry a good camera or money, don't leave it unattended. You wouldn't tempt fate at home; don't do it in the Islands.

The authoritative beach book is *The Best Beaches of Maui County* (revised and updated), by John R. K. Clark. The 156-page book published by the University of Hawaii Press includes details on Molokai, Lanai, Kahoolawe, and Molokini. Or try Dr. Stephen Leatherman's "Dr. Beach" Web site, **www.topbeaches.com.**

Different Strokes: Paddling Maui

To see Maui the way early Hawaiians did, go down to the sea and paddle. Since the first voyagers landed from the South Pacific, paddling boats in the seas has been a way of life. Outrigger canoe paddling is a fiercely competitive local sport. You'll often see teams of paddlers practicing in the waters off Kihei.

Kayaking is the way to go if your interest in paddling is strictly recreational, although it can be competitive as well. The biggest kayak contest, the annual World Championship Kayak Race, takes off from Kepuhi Beach on Molokai each May, when solo paddlers run across the dunes and beach carrying their kayaks, jump in the sea, and paddle to Oahu 32 miles away. Expert kayakers take on wilderness trips, such as a summertime paddle around Molokai's back side, where wild valleys pierce the wall of tall sea cliffs that plunge down to the coast. Just for the fun of it, you can rent a kayak or, better yet, go on a guided kayak trek with a local paddler.

Maui Eco-Tours guides kayak snorkel trips at La Perouse Bay in South Maui and guarantees you'll at least see spinner dolphins, if not swim with them. Tours depart daily at 7, 8, and 9 a.m., since playful dolphins are most likely to be there in the mornings. Call (808) 891-2223 or visit **www.mauiecotours.com** for details.

Kayaks are available for rent at Kaanapali, Kapalua, and Wailea Resorts and cost about $25–$32 for a single-person kayak for a full day and $35–$40 per day for a tandem kayaks. A short lesson is usually included in the price. Two of the best kayak adventures are found at opposite ends of Maui.

Kayak to Ahihi-Kinau

Take a kayak down Maui's rugged Makena coast with local waterman Dino Ventura to see a natural shoreline—jagged black lava fingers, emerald lagoons, and gold-sand beaches often tracked by green sea turtles. You may meet dolphins out there, or even a whale.

Embark from historic Makena Landing, where cowboys once herded cattle into the sea so the herd could be hoisted onto ships bound for market. It's a brisk five-mile paddle south past Turtle Town (so dubbed because turtles haul out of the sea there) and around Puu Olai, the distinctive cinder cone overlooking Makena Beach that punctuates the southwest end of the island.

Paddlers anchor at Ahihi-Kinau Natural Area Reserve, a 2,000-acre marine-life sanctuary that offers Maui's finest snorkeling. Then it's just you and about a million fish who thrive in black lava tide pools. Call **Makena Kayak** at (808) 879-8426.

Kayak to Honolua Bay

From Kapalua Bay, head out toward Molokai and turn starboard—that's right for you landlubbers. You are bound for Honolua Bay. High surf in winter turns this picturesque bay into a surfer's paradise (it's regarded as the best break on Maui) but summer belongs to the kayakers. The bay's calm, clear water is full of tropical fish—it's a marine conservation district—and sometimes boils with schools of akule, a big-eyed small fish, which like glassy water. Honolua (Hawaiian for "two harbors") won a footnote in nautical history on May 1, 1976, when Hokulea, the first modern-day replica of a twin-hulled Polynesian voyaging canoe, set sail here on the first twentieth-century Pacific crossing from Hawaii to Tahiti. The 34-day sea voyage revived interest in Pacific voyaging and helped spark a renaissance in Hawaiian culture.

Call **Kapalua Bay Hotel Activities Center** at (808) 669-5656 or (800) 367-8000, or visit **www.kapaluabayhotel.com**.

RECOMMENDED KAYAK TOUR OUTFITTERS

Hana Maui Sea Sports Snorkel and Kayak Tours: (808) 248-7711
Hana Ranch Ocean Adventures: (808) 248-7711 or (808) 264-9566
Maui Ocean Activities, Kaanapali Beach: (808) 667-2066
South Pacific Kayaks, Kihei: (808) 875-4848

Dive, Dive, Dive

Maui's underwater treasures—lava caverns, reefs filled with tropical fish, and marine preserves filled with wintering humpback whales, corals, and other sea life—lure divers to Maui, Molokai, and Lanai. *Skin Diver* magazine rates Lanai one of the top ten snorkel and scuba sites in the world. Its waters, exceptionally clear since little runoff clouds the edges of this dry island, include some 20 different dive sites with intriguing submarine lava formations and large schools of brightly colored fish among the attractions. Spinner dolphins live along its coast year-round.

Most divers arrive for dive tours already certified, but certification courses are offered at local dive shops. Rates range from $60 for a beach-side lesson to $300 or more for full open-water instruction and certification. You pay an additional $14 for a scuba certification card. Equipment is provided.

Most dive tours require participants to be certified by a scuba training organization, such as the Professional Association of Diving Instructors (PADI), National Association of Underwater Instructors (NAUI), National Association of Scuba Diving Schools (NASDS), or World Association of Scuba Instructors (WASI). Specialized dives—including explorations of wrecks or caves and night diving—require more advanced training.

Introductory dives, often conducted in a swimming pool, give would-be divers a chance to experience diving. Participants receive basic instruction, get fitted for scuba gear, and dive with the instructors. The entire experience lasts two to four hours, with rates ranging from $100 to $150.

Snuba is another option for uncertified divers who want to explore the Islands underwater. It's a hybrid of snorkel and diving that takes place at dive sites, but anyone can do it. Just breathe through a 20-foot hose linked to a floating oxygen tank. Jump in the water and take a deep breath, towing your tank behind you. Several snorkel cruises offer snuba.

Rates for certified dive tours range from $75 to $175, depending on the size of the boat, equipment, and number of dives included on the trip. Booking deposits are usually required, refundable if you cancel in advance. Expect to spend at least half a day on a guided scuba adventure. The actual time you spend in the water will vary—the deeper the water, the faster you use your air supply—but usually it's 90 minutes to 2 hours. The diver-to-guide ratio has a legal maximum of six to one.

A Few Tips for Divers

- In choosing a dive operator, ask about their dive experience, their safety expertise, the type of boat, the dive destination, and other details to make sure the guides meet your expectations.
- Be careful where you put your hands and feet underwater. Some marine life—such as eels, jellyfish, and scorpionfish—can bite or sting. Do not touch any animal you don't recognize. Try to avoid touching or crushing coral, which leaves a permanent dent in the underwater environment and puts you at risk for coral cuts.
- Never dive alone.
- If you're attempting underwater photography for the first time, shoot from within four feet. For best results, use an underwater camera with a 15 mm or 20 mm lens.

Maui's Top Dive Sites

The most popular and one of the best Maui dive sites is **Molokini,** the sunken cinder cone about three miles off the coast of South Maui, near Kahoolawe. Molokini, a Marine Life Conservation District, has high visibility and thriving ocean life, including reef fish, sea turtles, and manta rays. But it gets congested with snorkelers and tour boats as the day goes on, so it's best to book an early boat.

A favorite South Maui dive site is **La Perouse Pinnacle,** in the middle of picturesque La Perouse Bay beyond Makena. The pinnacle rises 60 feet from the sea floor to about 10 feet below the ocean's surface and is exceptional for snorkeling as well as shallow dives. Look for brilliant damsel fish, triggerfish, puffers, and wrasses.

Divers of all skill levels probe **Five Caves** in Makena, South Maui. Lava ridges and small pinnacles provide food and shelter for angler fish, sea turtles, eels, and white-tipped sharks. The depth here is 30–40 feet, and the waters can be accessed from shore as well as boat.

At **Cathedrals,** off the south shore of Lanai, a stained-glass effect occurs when sunlight pours through the holes in twin underwater caves. This dive site is for experienced divers.

If diving with giant wintering whales is your dream, sign up with Captain Ed Robinson on Maui, a veteran dive captain who knows how to find them (contact information below).

RECOMMENDED DIVE COMPANIES

Ed Robinson's Diving Adventures: (808) 879-3584,
 www.maui-scuba.com
Lahaina Divers: (808) 667-7496 or (800) 998-3483,
 www.lahainadivers.com
Maui Dive Shop: (800) 542-3483, www.mauidiveshop.com
Mike Severns Diving, Kihei: (808) 879-6596,
 www.mikeseyernsdiving.com

Snorkeling: Discover the Undersea World

Snorkeling adds an undersea dimension to your Island adventures, even if you don't dive as deep as scuba tanks allow. You can go to many of the same sites and see the fish and sealife below you from near the surface of the water. It's not difficult or scary. Just jump off the boat stern, paddle your flippers, look through your face mask, and breathe through your tube.

Snorkeling Tips

- Know how to swim, to ensure your own safety in the water, even if you're snorkeling close to shore or a boat.
- Novices should practice in shallow water.
- Always snorkel with a buddy or in groups.
- Don't stray too far from shore or the boat.
- Check your snorkel gear carefully before entering the water. Popular wisdom suggests you spit on your mask's eyepiece and rub the lens before dunking it in salt water and then putting it on. Make sure it fits, airtight, to your face.

Maui's Top Snorkeling Beaches

Ahihi-Kinau Preserve, South Maui

Location On the remote south shore of Maui, beyond Makena, at the end of a dirt road.

Activities Snorkeling.

Comments Black, barren lava reefs reach into aquamarine pools full of tropical fish. The best snorkeling on Maui is in this scenic 2,000-acre nature preserve on the rugged south coast, where Haleakala last spilled red-hot lava into the sea in 1790. It's difficult to reach but easy to enjoy. No facilities.

Five Needles, Lanai

Location Off the remote south shore of Lanai.

Activities Snorkeling, swimming.

Comments Spiky sea stacks dominate an almost secret snorkel spot on Lanai's rugged south side. Go there only by kayak, sailboat, or launch, mostly by tours departing from Maui. Take Trilogy for this unforgettable outing (see information on guided tours below). Water clarity and abundant sea life make this an outstanding snorkel site. No facilities.

Kaupoa Beach, Molokai

Location West End, on Molokai Ranch property (access is limited to ranch guests, unless you can navigate a boat there).

Activities Summer snorkeling, swimming, beachcombing, sunbathing.

Comments Head for Kaupoa Beach by ranch bus or on horseback, swap boots for flippers, and take a plunge in the warm salt water, soothing after a morning in the saddle on Molokai Ranch. Horses graze under coco palms while you snorkel with triggerfish. The trail boss grills rib-eye steaks. Way out west on Molokai, this is what surf and turf is all about. Facilities include a beachside bar and dining pavilion, a restaurant, showers, and bathrooms.

Guided Snorkel Tours

Guided snorkeling adventures are available from an abundance of tour boats for rates mostly $50 and up for adults. In addition, many shops rent snorkeling fins, masks, snorkels, and gear bags. Guided snorkel tours take half a day or more. Instruction for beginners is available. Snorkel outings are weather dependent. The following are our favorite guided snorkel tours.

Maui

Trilogy Excursions, oldest and best snorkel and scuba operator on Maui, sails a fleet of sailing catamarans on snorkel and scuba dives to Molokini, an area off Kaanapali Beach and its best-known tour, Lanai, combined with a land tour of the island. Its six-hour excursions include barbecue lunch and continental breakfast. Trilogy Excursions, owned and operated by brothers Jim and Rand Coon and their families, has a well deserved reputation for delivering a superior experience. Call (888) MAUI-800, or visit **www.sailtrilogy.com.**

Navatek II is a special high-tech boat, an 82-foot, 149-passenger SWATH vessel, designed to ease queasy stomachs, which sails from Maalaea Harbor to Lanai's south shore on a "Voyage of Discovery," as well as sunset dinner cruises and whale-watching trips in season. The vessel, also available for weddings and private functions, is fast and fully equipped, and the tours include gear, hamburgers to order for lunch, and cold drinks. The boat is easy to get on and off in deep water. *Navatek II* and several other snorkel sail cruises are operated by **Royal Hawaiian Cruises.** Call (800) 852-4183 or visit **www.royalhawaiiancruises.com.**

Molokai

Walter Naki of **Molokai Action Adventures** takes four snorkelers on four- or six-hour dives in seldom-explored territory aboard his 21-foot Boston whaler. Call (808) 558-8184.

Lanai

Trilogy Ocean Sports operates a concierge desk at Manele Bay Hotel to book Lanai guests on tours and as an arrival point for day-trippers from Maui. Snorkel adventures, introductory dives on Hulopoe Beach, sunrise scuba tours to the Cathedrals, marine-mammal watches for adventurers ages three and up, guided kayak rides, and private charters are available. Trilogy cautions scuba divers that because of the upland elevation of the Lodge at Koele, divers must spend 24 hours at sea level before returning to that hotel. Fortunately, because of shared ownership, they can easily arrange a stay at the Manele Bay Hotel during that time.

On Sundays, local Lanai captain **Dustin Kaopuiki** and crew operate a snorkel run on a new high-speed jet drive ocean-going raft, complete with lunch prepared by the hotel chefs. Call the hotel concierge for details. Private charters are also available on the 53-foot *Kila Kila* through the hotel concierge desks. Call (808) 565-2387.

Catch a Wave

Hawaii's own kings perfected *hee nalu*—that's wave sliding in Hawaiian— and the rest of the world soon discovered the joy of surfing. No place does it better or offers more consistent surf, bigger waves, or deeper tubes.

On Maui, the best surf spots are Honolua Bay in winter, Lahaina Harbor in summer, Maalaea (beyond the breakwater), and Hookipa Beach in the morning, before the wind comes up and the windsurfers take over the waves.

No one knows exactly when surfing originated, but many historians believe Polynesians were already well versed in the sport when they migrated to the Hawaiian Islands nearly 2,000 years ago. Only the high chiefs enjoyed access to the best surf spots. King Kamehameha I was said to be an avid surfer.

RECOMMENDED SURFING RESOURCES

Schools

Andrea Thompson's Maui Surfing School, Lahaina: (800) 851-0543, www.mauisurf.com

Buzzy Kerbox: (808) 573-5728, www.buzzykerboxsurf.com

Goofy Foot Surf School, Lahaina: (808) 244-9283, www.goofyfootsurfschool.com

Nancy Emerson School of Surfing, Lahaina: (808) 244-7873, www.surfclinics.com

Rentals

Local Motion, Kihei: (808) 879-7873

Local Motion, Lahaina: (808) 661-7873

Today, waves are shared according to skill. Beginning surfers can get quick lessons on Maui by signing up for formal training with an expert instructor, like Nancy Emerson, a champion surfer and stuntwoman since 1961, who claims she can get you up and surfing with one lesson. Surfing instruction is available year-round. Equipment is provided. Buzzy Kerbox, one of Maui's top surfers, also gives personal and group instructions and specializes in teaching beginners.

I saw it coming, turned my back on it, and paddled for dear life. Faster and faster my board went, till it seemed my arms would drop off. What was happening behind me I could not tell. One cannot look behind and paddle the windmill stroke. I heard the crest of the wave hissing and churning, and then my board was lifted and flung forward. I scarcely knew what happened the first half-minute. Though I kept my eyes open, I could not see anything, for I was buried in the rushing white of the crest. But I did not mind. I was chiefly conscious of ecstatic bliss at having caught the wave. At the end of the half-minute, however, I began to see things, and to breathe. I saw that three feet of the nose of my board was clear out of water and riding in the air. I shifted my weight forward and made the nose come down. Then I lay, quite at rest in the midst of the wild movement, and watched the shore and the bathers on the beach grow distinct

—Jack London, "A Royal Sport: Surfing at Waikiki,"
from A. Grove Day's *Hawaii and Points South, True Island Tales*

Activities desks and concierges at hotels know where to get good rental surfboards.

Lessons for one or two students or groups of up to five per instructor are conducted in areas where waves are small and the beach uncrowded. Students learn the basics on the beach, including ocean safety, how to paddle a surfboard, how to get up and stand on the board, proper foot placement, and where to shift body weight. Then they get in the water to do it again, and then catch a real wave and ride it. Once you get the hang of it, you'll learn other basic maneuvers, such as turning your board to move in a certain direction.

Surfers come in all shapes, sizes, and ages. You should know how to swim and expect to do a lot of paddling and kicking in the water. Most schools have a minimum age of five to seven years for surfing lessons.

Group rates are generally $50–$60 for one-hour lessons to $225–$250 for all-day lessons. Private lessons are about $85–$125 for one-hour lessons and $425–$450 for all-day lessons. Multiday and week-long rates are also available. Book at least a day in advance, although most surf schools will try to accommodate last-minute students.

Surfing Safety and Etiquette Tips

- Check with lifeguards first. They can point out the hazardous rip currents, jagged reefs, and tricky waves to avoid. Obey posted warnings.

- Never surf alone, and make sure someone on shore knows where you are.

- Be considerate of other surfers. Don't drop in on someone else's wave.

- Don't surf after dark.

- Use leg ropes to control your board, for your safety and the safety of fellow surfers.

- If you get in trouble, don't panic. Signal for help by raising one arm vertically.

The Surfers Guide to Hawaii by Greg Ambrose (published by Bess Press, **www.besspress.com**) is the best local surf book with tips, descriptions, and maps.

Ride the Wind

A whole different sport seeks to challenge the wind as well as the waves—windsurfing or board sailing, the combination of sailing and surfing. A day of brisk tradewinds prompts a hatch-out of colorful, butterfly-like sails as windsurfers zip here and there across the water, enjoying the pure sensation of natural speed. In the Islands, where water sports are a way of life, ocean devotees surf when the waves are right, windsurf when the winds are right, and kayak when it's calm.

But Maui's North Shore is famous for its superb combination of tricky strong winds and robust waves. Expert windsurfers will want to try their hand or just watch the pros at Kanaha Beach and Hookipa Beach on this stretch of coast, known as the Aspen of windsurfing, where the world's top wave riders gather.

All the action is centered around Kahului and Paia, the best places to find gear, rentals, and lessons. Some windsurfers travel to Maui to buy state-of-the-art gear as well as rent it.

RECOMMENDED WINDSURF OUTFITTERS AND SCHOOLS

Hawaiian Island Surf and Sport, Kahului: (808) 871-4981 or (800) 231-6958, www.hawaiianisland.com

Hawaiian Sailboarding Techniques (champion windsurfer Alan Cadiz shares his world-class techniques with beginners), Kahului: (800) YOU-JIBE or (808) 871-5423, www.hstwindsurfing.com

Maui Windsurf Company, Kahului: (808) 877-4816 or (800) 872-0999, www.maui-windsurf.com

---

Go Fish

With all that ocean, it's no surprise that saltwater fishing, by shorecasting and trolling, is a popular pastime and also a major commercial activity, which provides local tables with a rich bounty. Saltwater fishing in Hawaii does not require a permit, and many species are not subject to seasons or catch limits, except in waters protected by state or federal law.

Shorefishing from the beach or low reefs is popular on all islands, primarily in pursuit of feisty bonefish and tasty papio, the juvenile stage of jack trevally, known as ulua when it grows up. But the rough seas, four to eight feet on normal good-weather days, and dangerous channels rule out barebones (no crew) boat rentals and instead require a power boat and experienced captain, so charter sportfishing is the way to pursue your dream fish. The boats are expensive but can be shared or chartered for less than a full day.

Marine research suggests the major game fish tend to hang out 2 to 30 miles offshore along two undersea ledges that surround the Islands, one at 240 feet and another at 600, vestiges of past ice ages, when the sea level was lower. Some species choose the warm surface waters, such as marlin, ahi, and mahimahi, while others go for the cold bottom environment, notably prized snappers like onaga and opakapaka.

If you've dreamed of hooking a 1,000-pound "grander" Pacific blue marlin, your dreams may come true off Maui. The Big Island's Kona Coast is considered the big-game fishing capital of the world because of its history of record catches, but you never know what you may hook off Maui, Molokai, or Lanai, which are, after all, just up the channel from Kona. World-record fish—marlin, ono, ahi, and mahimahi—have been hooked off Maui. The best local fishing occurs around Lanai and Kahoolawe, islands easily reached aboard a charter boat out of Lahaina or Maalaea harbors on Maui, as well as Molokai and Lanai harbors. Below are some charter options; note that Lanai hotel concierges will arrange fishing charters on request.

RECOMMENDED FISHING CHARTERS

Maui

Aerial Sportfishing Charters: (808) 667-9089, www.aerialsport fishingcharters.com

Fish Maui: (808) 879-3789, www.fishmaui.com

Lahaina Charter Boats: (866) 888-6784

Luckey Strike Charters: (808) 661-4606, www.luckeystrike.com

Ocean Activities Center: (808) 879-4485, www.maui.net/~oac

Molokai

Alyce C Sportfishing: (808) 558-8377, www.worldwidefishing.com

Fun Hogs Hawaii: (808) 567-6789, www.molokaifishing.com

Lanai

Spinning Dolphin Charters: (808) 565-6613

Off-Road Shorefishing Expeditions

Serious fisherman, here's the best bet in the Islands. For eight years, David Bloch has led hard-core anglers in pursuit of giant ulua on his private, shorefishing expeditions. You take a four-wheel-drive to a secluded off-road site, then camp overnight to be in the right place at the right time and tide to nail Hawaii's fabled fish from the shore. Around the campfire, you likely will hear true fish tales, like how a 563-pound *hapuu* (sea bass) caught from shore on Maui still holds the shore-fishing record.

Call **Off-Road Shorefishing Expeditions** at (808) 878-8582 for overnight camping/fishing treks and shore at four-wheel-drive only sites.

Watch the Whales

Most of the Pacific humpback whale population migrates to warm Hawaiian waters each winter to breed, give birth, and nurse their young. Right behind them come the whale-watchers, in pursuit of the spectacle of a whale leaping out of the sea and crashing back with a huge splash, obviously having a great time. You can see such whale behavior from your hotel lanai or from the roads of any of the islands in winter. But it is off Maui's shores that the giants seem to congregate, and you'll get the best view from a boat in the whale season, between mid-December and mid-April. Whale-watching excursions are concentrated off the south and west coasts of Maui, the heart of the whale migration and, coincidentally, of the visiting humans as well.

WHALE-WATCHING: HAWAIIAN PASTIME

You must be careful driving on Maui in whale season. Especially along Olowalu, the flat coastal plain between McGregor Point and Lahaina. Motorists often jam on the brakes and leap out of their cars, abandon them right on Honoapialani Highway, at the sight of a distant spout.

The most whales we've ever seen in one place at one time in Hawaiian waters wasn't anywhere near Maui. It was late April one year on the forbidden island of Niihau. We spent the day snorkeling the crystal clear lagoons of Keamanu Bay in search of lobster with chopper pilot Tom Mishler. Suddenly, the blue water began to boil. Scores of whales began spy-hopping, chin-slapping, tail-slapping and fluking, and jumping straight out of the water. To our delight this great performance lasted more than an hour. We applauded when it ended. It was a whale of a party.

Luck plays a big role in observing interesting actions by large, live creatures on the move, but some tours are staffed by naturalists who offer substantial expertise and are equipped with state-of-the-art gear, such as hydrophones that let you hear whale songs. Some tours support nonprofit marine conservation and research groups like Pacific Whale Foundation and Whales Alive. The boat captains are required by federal law to keep a distance of at least 100 yards between their vessels and the whales. Some cruises guarantee sightings by giving you a rain check if you don't actually see a whale, and some do tours year-round, watching for other marine mammals when the humpbacks go north for the summer. Five other whale species can be viewed throughout the year—sperm whales, pilot whales, melon-headed whales, false killer whales, and beaked whales. Spinner dolphins live year-round in the waters around Maui, Molokai, and Lanai.

Watching for whales is much like watching for a lover. There is much expectation, and there is much time spent where there are no whales to see. I have always seen whales when I was not looking for them but was looking out, my eyes open for an instant.

—Joana McIntyre Varawa, *The Delicate Art of Whale Watching*

Whale-watching boats come in all sizes, from rigid-hulled rubber rafts that bounce through the surf to large, motorized catamarans and sleek sailing sloops, and offer a wide range of comforts, such as shaded decks and bathrooms on board.

The cost of daily whale-watching cruises ranges $20–$60 for adults and $10–$30 for children ages 11 and under. Book your tour several days in advance during holiday periods. Most tours last two to three hours and provide snacks and juice. Some tours offer hotel transportation. Wear swimsuits or casual attire, and bring binoculars and cameras. Here is a list of some good whale-watching tour operators.

WHALE-WATCHING CRUISES

Maui

Hawaii Ocean Rafting (rafts departing Lahaina): (808) 661-RAFT, www.hawaiioceanrafting.com

Maui Princess (yacht departs Lahaina): (808) 667-6165, www.mauiprincess.com

Pacific Whale Foundation (from Lahaina and Maalaea): (808) 879-8860, www.pacificwhale.org

Trilogy Expeditions (sails from Kaanapali Beach twice daily in season): (888) 225-MAUI, www.sailtrilogy.com

Molokai

Molokai Charters: (808) 553-5852

Lanai

Trilogy Expeditions: (888) 225-MAUI, www.sailtrilogy.com

Spinning Dolphin Charters: (808) 565-6613

Tip: To see whales best from shore, get to an elevated viewing post that gives you a better perspective. Look for spouts, geysers of sea spray that shine in the sun and seem to disappear into thin air, to alert you that whales are cruising by. Look for large black bodies poking their noses above water as they "spy-hop," possibly to get a better look at you. There's no best time of day for whale-watching, but we've noticed that when the sea is glassy and there is no wind, we always see more. A Scripps Institute marine biologist told us that's because whales are the only mammals without hair and they don't like wind on their body when they leap out of the water.

If you're in the resort area of Wailea, Maui, check the telescope in front of the Marriott Wailea Beach Resort. The first person to report a whale sighting to the café each day gets free breakfast.

Informative Web sites on humpback whales include **www.pacific whale.org** and **www.ilovewhales.com.** Every cruise and sailboat that runs tours goes whale-watching in winter, and you can charter private whale-watching excursions on most.

SEEING SPINNERS

If you want to see spinner dolphins from land, drive Maui's northwest coast to Nakalele Bay overlook. One early morning, bound for Kahaku-loa, several of us talked about Hawaii's wonderfully elusive sights—the green flash, moonlight rainbows, and spinners in motion. We confessed that after 15 years in Hawaii, we had never seen dolphins spinning. We rounded a curve and stopped to look at Nakalele Bay. Suddenly they came, hundreds of shiny gray chorus girls in a follies revue, twirling and dancing on wave tops, splashing and spinning clockwise and counter-clockwise and end to end, flipping for sheer joy. We screamed with delight. They danced all the more.

Yachting: Over the Ocean Blue

Looking at all that ocean, one would think Maui, Molokai, and Lanai would be overrun with yachts and sailboats. Plenty of watercraft fill the infrequent harbors, but not as many tourists as you would think actually go sailing—most of the cruise boats are motorized. Actually, there's too much ocean for all but expert blue-water sailors, and the seas are filled with deep-running channels and tricky currents, tossed about by strong winds and big waves and edged by boat-eating reefs. However, the intrepid seafarer thirsting for world-class sailing in the middle of the ocean will find several yachting options in Maui.

America II is a genuine America's Cup 12-meter racing yacht that makes three two-hour trips a day from Slip 5, Lahaina Harbor, between late morning and late afternoon, plus morning whale-watching in winter. Private charters are available. Call (808) 667-2195 to confirm sail times, or visit **www.galaxymall.com/stores/americaii** for details. *Paragon* offers sailing tours from Lahaina and Maalaea aboard high-performance sailing catamarans that also use America's Cup technology to fly like the wind in comfort. Call (800) 441-2087 or (808) 244-2087, or email paragon@maui.net for details.

Island Star, a 57-foot charter yacht that comfortably sleeps ten, will take you wherever you want to go around the Islands with a crew that includes a chef, a naturalist, and a scuba instructor. Call (888) 677-7238 or (808) 669-STAR or go to **www.islandstarsailing.com** for information.

Kapalua Kai, a 53-foot catamaran, sails from Kaanapali Beach to Honolua Bay north of Kapalua for snorkeling and sunset sails. Call (888) 667-5980 or (808) 665-0344, or visit **www.sailingmaui.com** for details. The sister ship, *Shangri La,* is available for luxury charters. For information, try the Web site or phone (888) 855-9977 or (808) 665-0077.

Take to the Trails

If you've finally exhausted the myriad watersports Maui offers, or if you're just a landlubber by nature, there's plenty of adventure inland. Why not start out on foot? Maui is laced by trails leading along the coastal cliffs, up into woods and along ridges, down among the cinders inside Haleakala crater, and on the ancient lava-stone path known as the King's Trail. You can hike to waterfalls, through bamboo forests, into valleys, to scenic points with views you'll never forget. You can go with a guide or just follow your feet along a marked trail. Conditions are generally fine for meeting the natural environment face to face, and the natural environment is extraordinary, presenting few dangers to detract from the rewards. You won't be risking a rash or a snake attack—there are no snakes and no wild plant leaves that are noxious to the touch (except, for some people, mango, which is a relative of poison ivy). Mosquitoes may find you irresistible in the damp green jungles, but generally the hiking climate is benign. These are some of the reasons why hiking is one of the most popular off-beach outdoor activities in the Islands.

Some trails are historic, smoothed by generations of ancient feet long before other means of overland travel were available. Some are fantasies-come-true, forested paths edged with leaves bigger than your head and tropical fruit like mountain apple, guava, wild mango, and avocado waiting to be plucked; waterfall streams with pools make ideal spots to cool off after a tropical trek. Maui, of course, boasts trails in Haleakala National Park and adjacent Polipoli Springs State Recreation Area. Plus, there are six forest reserves in Upcountry Maui: Makawao, Koolau, Hana, Kipahulu, Kahikinui, and Kula. The West Maui Forest Reserve and Iao Valley State Park await to the west. Molokai has a choice of wilderness trails, guided hikes, and one memorable tilt down a vertical cliff. The Nature Conservancy offers guided treks through its preserves in the high-country—boggy home of rare, native species—at Kamakou and on the shore at Moomomi sand dunes, where skeltons of extinct birds have been found (call the Conservancy at (808) 553-5236, or email, hike_molokai@tnc.org). Lanai has guided hikes in the Uplands' cool forest and on the sunbaked cliffs near Hulopoe Beach by the sea, but one you can find yourself leads to a spectacular viewpoint.

Guided Hikes

Guided hiking tours bring the countryside to life as only touching and walking through it can, in the company of expertise. This is the best way to get out into otherwise private and inaccessible country, discover shy indigenous creatures you might otherwise never see, and understand more about Maui. The best hiking guide on Maui is Ken Schmitt of **Hike Maui,** an Island naturalist since 1983 who has hiked every trail on the island during his time in Hawaii. He and his crew weave together bits of geology, botany, culture, history, myth, and legend out there on the trail. Hike Maui, the oldest, largest hiking company, brings water, lunch, and insect repellent on hikes that range from a few hours to all day.

Contact Hike Maui at P.O. Box 330969, Kahului; (808) 879-5270; or **www.hikemaui.com.**

Molokai Outdoor Adventures guides hikers with snacks and a day-pack to the heights of the island to find waterfalls and rainforest. They also rent equipment and offer a range of tours to the heart of the most natural island. Call (808) 553-4477, or visit **www.molokai-outdoors. com** for details.

Maui Hiking Tips

- Rainforest means slippery, muddy trails and mosquitoes.

- Waterfall valleys are steep and narrow and are sometimes inundated by flash floods after cloudburst deluges upstream, with frightening and even fatal results.

- Dry hikes on lumpy lava and steep, crumbly dirt trails require close attention to your footing and drinking lots of water. No matter what the locals do, avoid hiking in rubber slippers (beach thongs) in favor of supportive footwear, but not your favorite snowy white sneakers, which won't fare well after a Hawaiian red-dirt trek, muddy forest jaunt, or a rough lava trail.

- Don't let the views keep you from watching where you put your feet. Yes, it is *Green Mansions* and *Blue Lagoon* and *Castaway* all rolled into one, but stand still while you admire the scenery.

- Stick to the trails. Rainforested mountains swallow up injured or missing hikers from sight almost instantly. If possible, carry a charged cell phone on remote ventures.

- Inviting and wild though the streams may be, don't drink the water or swim with open cuts, as you risk getting leptospirosis, a wild pig–related bacterial fever that can turn into meningitis.

Three Short Maui Hikes, Two Longer Ones

Most folks don't like to trek very far, especially in the tropics, where the hot and humid climate slows down even the most avid hiker. So you don't miss a thing, here are a few short hikes with really big payoffs. They take you into Haleakala crater, to a waterfall on the Hana coast, and into a valley once inhabited by ancient people. One of these treks, to Kahakuloa Valley, requires a guide. The last two hikes are more difficult but arguably more rewarding: the switchback trail taken by the Molokai Mule Ride and the trek up Lanai's Mount Lanaihale. If you're looking for a more relaxing route, see "A Good Walk" below.

Each hike definitely will give you a memorable look at Maui's great outdoors.

Inside Haleakala

Sliding Sands Trail takes you down into the biggest hole on Earth for a glimpse into a surreal landscape. And the trail lives up to its name. Your feet slip and slide on lava cinders, making crunchy noises as you go. The two-hour, two-mile hike sounds easy until you step off the edge of the crater rim, elevation 9,800 feet, and onto a switchback trail. (Did you remember to check in first at the Summit Visitors Center?)

Your toes begin to squinch and complain as you descend a few thousand feet down to the crater floor, 6,600 feet above sea level. If you start to tire, turn back; remember, it's all uphill on the way back. Expect to be breathless at this altitude, and dizzy. The scenery, too, will leave you a little light-headed; it's like a backdrop from an alien planet.

Hikers with stamina to press on will find 27 miles of trails inside the crater that can occupy you for few hours or several days. (Did you bring the map?)

To the Falls

The best short hike on the Hana coast ends with a splash in a waterfall pool. Start at Pipiwai Stream from Oheo Gulch through a bamboo forest to 400-foot Waimoku Falls. The two-mile hike over a boardwalk leads through a noisy, rattling forest of green and yellow bamboo, a treat in itself. What makes this hike worthwhile is the waterfall pool at the end. Other hikes and a tour of the Hana Cultural Center are available free by contacting Haleakala National Park. Call (808) 248-7375 for a schedule or visit Kipahulu Visitors Center.

HIKING KAHAKULOA

Standing barefoot in a taro patch, wiggling our toes in the silky mud—it was an odd beginning for a most unusual hike into Kahakuloa Valley, a cleft on Maui's northwest coast where old Hawaii exists as if in a dream.

"Feel how smooth it is," said Oliver Dukelo, the Hawaiian caretaker who tends this taro patch in the valley, just as the first settlers did centuries ago.

The valley, long off-limits to visitors, lies beyond a locked gate like a Polynesian version of Camelot. It's an almost mythic place lost in the mists of time. You may go there now, but only with a guide like Dukelow, who will take you deep into the valley, carved by a stream that's the tag of a silvery waterfall.

Simple, tidy little houses with bright colorful Polynesian pareau in the windows stand amid banana and papaya trees and flowers galore on the wide western banks of Kahakuloa stream, which runs big enough at times to be called a river.

The stream is diverted here and there into loi, or taro patches, the cornerstone of Hawaii's early agriculture.

Here, ankle deep in primal mud, Hawaiians share their cultural roots, let you touch hard evidence of early inhabitants—remnants of shrines, platforms, terraces, and heiau. Here, you can see a house that stands in the path of the ghosts called night marchers and hear skin-crawling stories about spirits of ancient alii who stroll with alacrity through the valley, revisiting lifetime haunts.

There in Kahakuloa Valley, by the babbling stream that irrigates the taro, we sat in the sun, talking story, savoring the moment, wishing all Hawaii could be like this. When we had to go it was hard to leave this place, and we suddenly understood the dilemma of the departed and why they return.

Into the Valley of Ancients

Get a glimpse of Island life as it used to be, or as close as modern-day Hawaiians can get to it, in a remote stream valley on Maui's little-known northwest coast. Kahakuloa Valley was once off limits to outsiders, but now visitors can experience it with a guide. In our opinion, this tour is the

A PUEO TALE

People in Hawaii say owls are sacred. They are considered guardian angels. Hawaiians call them *aumaku*; it means family spirit.

We know people who claim owls have kept them from harm, warned them of danger, shown them the way home. Until one day in early September on Lanai, that sort of superstition struck us merely as quaint, if silly.

Overnight, a tropical rainstorm had battered the tin roof houses, disturbing the peace of Lanai City. It was a restless night, and we rose before dawn, leaving the empty Lodge in search of coffee.

As the sun rose, we could see it would be a good day to seek the 3,379-foot summit of Mount Lanaihale, the island's peak. Up there on a clear day, so longtime Island residents say, you can see six islands in a single glance: Maui, Molokai, the Big Island of Hawaii, Oahu, Kahoolawe, and Molokini. It's one of the eight natural wonders of Hawaii. The spectacle is possible because Lanai sits smack dab in the middle of the inhabited island chain. Only Kauai and Niihau are too far to the northwest to be seen.

In 20 years in the Islands, we had tried often but never managed to top the summit on a clear day. Clouds always obscured the view. Now, the morning after a storm, the clear blue sky held promise and we had a gassed-up Jeep.

A lone owl swooped low over abandoned pineapple fields of Puuwai Basin, as we turned left off the two-lane blacktop and followed a red dirt deer trail toward Lanaihale. Having never seen the Hawaiian pueo on the

best we've taken on Maui, because it puts tourists in touch with Hawaiians and their efforts to resurrect some nearly lost cultural skills. Any tour that starts with fording a stream rock to rock and then taking off your shoes to sink over your ankles in the silky mud of a taro patch has to be different.

What you will experience in this Valley of Ancients is a Maui seldom seen: tales and trails of night marchers; relics like early C-shaped rock shelters, native plants, and sometimes endangered birds; a well-tended taro patch fed by waterfalls; and caretakers eager to talk story about their experiences of trying to live Hawaiian in modern times and about the days of old, when Chief Piilani ruled and Maui thrived on fish and poi.

To arrange a trip, contact **Ekahi Tours,** in Kahului. Call (808) 877-9775, or (888) 292-2422, or visit **www.ekahi.com.**

Or, in Lahaina, contact **Maui Eco-Adventures** at (808) 661-7720 or (877) 661-7720, or visit **www.ecomaui.com.**

wing, we braked to watch the endangered bird glide across the fields, swooping low in search of prey, finding only little black, flapping scraps of plastic. The owl was the first rare sight that day.

In golden sunlight, we headed up the old shield volcano on the Munro Trail, the narrow, winding razorback ridge road that runs to Lanai's peak.

No road sign shows the way to the summit. No sign tells that you've arrived. A local man in Lanai City had instructed us, "Just go down the road, turn left, go up the hill. No need sign."

The Hawaiian pueo appeared now and again just ahead of the Jeep, obviously pointing the way. It disappeared behind bushes and trees but always reappeared ahead, leading us on.

At the summit, the owl landed on a wind-bent ohia tree and shut its eyes. Our eyes opened to see Maui, Hawaii, Kahoolawe, and Molokini, all laid out on a blue sea chart like a real-life topographic map. We looked for Molokai and Oahu but trees stood in the way, something of a disappointment.

The owl took wing again. It flew beyond the trees around a bend in the road. We followed to find a clear view of Molokai, more than 30 miles away, and in the distance on the horizon, the thin outline of Oahu.

A rare bird of prey and six Hawaiian islands visible from one peak. Some things must be seen to be believed.

Two Legs on a Mule Trail

You can ride a mule down Molokai's steep sea cliffs, or you can take a hike. Many do walk the thin trail, sidestepping mules, and claim it is the most challenging and rewarding hike in all the Islands. The trail is only 2 miles long, but it's got 26 hairpin turns within a drop of 1,600 feet and a panoramic view that will leave you breathless. At the bottom, you can join the bused tour of the Kalaupapa National Historic Park to see the settlement where victims of leprosy were once banished and also the haunting view of Molokai's wilderness coast. Call ahead to get a tour or at least a permit to enter the restricted peninsula park, where some former leprosy victims still live. When it's time to go back, you'll discover that while the downhill trip tested your balance, the uphill hike will test your legs. Somebody should hand out medals to all who accomplish this hike, one of the most unusual in all the tropical Pacific.

For guide information, contact **Damien Tours** at (808) 567-6171.

Lanai Lookout

Get up early on a clear, dry morning on Lanai and set off in pursuit of a very special phenomenon: the chance to see five major Hawaiian islands from one perch. To get there, hike the eight-mile Munro Trail, the red-dirt jeep road that runs over the razorback ridge of Mount Lanaihale, the 3,366-foot peak of Lanai. Lanai sits in the middle of the major islands, a geographic fact not lost on ancient Hawaiians chiefs, who could observe interisland canoe traffic from its strategic peak and tell who was coming for dinner or to violate the peace.

A RARE HIKE BETWEEN HEAVEN AND EARTH

The helicopter drops us on a wilderness ridge, the start of a rare adventure high in the West Maui Mountains. There are a dozen of us, winners of an annual lottery; the prize is a once-in-a-lifetime guided 6-mile hike through a virgin cloud forest on 5,871-foot-high Puu Kukui.

Off-limits except to scientists, Hawaii's largest private nature preserve is an 8,661-acre, 10-million-year-old enclave of rare native plants, birds, and snails.

Spiky Silverswords and unassuming sedges, rare daisies, wild orchids, and giant ferns flourish in a soggy sanctuary traversed by a narrow boardwalk. We stand in total silence amid a hundred shades of green. Nearly everything in the bog is only ankle high, stunted by Nature's own high-altitude pruning. It is as if we've suddenly grown 20 feet tall. Venturing out on the boardwalk, one cautious step at a time, guide Randy Bartlett warns that each foot of bog depth represents 10,000 years. A hiker's foot slips off the boardwalk and sinks an inch or so, back to about A.D. 650. Having gently pried the shoe from the viscous muck, the phrase "bogged down" takes on new meaning.

As we hike on, the almost surreal beauty of the setting emerges in tiny details. Little damsel flies dart across Lake Violet, so small and hopelessly blue it looks like a broken mirror that fell from the sky. Miniature Hawaiian land snails ease across the moss. Puffy clouds scud over Eke Crater, a lofty plateau amid spiky peaks. Survivors of "the great flood at the beginning of time" landed their canoe on Eke, according to Hawaiian legend. New Age disciples claim Eke is the landing zone of extraterrestrials. Neither canoe nor spacecraft is in evidence this day; we are the only strangers here.

Take your chances with Kapalua Nature Center, Kapalua Resort's ecotourism arm, which holds the Puu Kukui lottery and also conducts guided hiking tours in Kapalua's 17,000 acres of Upcountry watershed and pineapple plantation lands. Call Kapalua Nature Society at (808) 669-0244.

Up at the summit on a clear day, Maui, Molokai, Kahoolawe, Oahu, and the Big Island are all visible at spots along this trail. That's all the major islands except northernmost Kauai and Niihau. And you see most of Lanai getting there.

The abundant Cook pine trees are the legacy of George Campbell Munro, a rancher who planted them in the 1920s in a natural rain-making scheme. The trees snag clouds in their branches to water dry Lanai, situated in the rain-shadow of Haleakala. When it rains, get a good book or find another adventure, because the Munro Trail becomes slick and boggy.

Clubs such as Hawaiian Trail and Mountain and student groups from local colleges post helpful information and maps for Maui hiking on the Web (try **www.traildatabase.org** for links).

For free trail maps, call the State Department of Forestry and Wildlife at (808) 587-0166, or go to **www.hawaiitrails.org.**

More Information

Island bookstores and the Internet offer a wealth of information about island hikes. Here are a few books for those hoping to discover more of Maui, Molokai, and Lanai on foot:

Hawaiian Hiking Trails, by Craig Chisolm, published by Fernglen Press, 1999. A detailed look at 50 of the best hiking trails on the six major islands.

Great Outdoor Adventures of Hawaii, by Rick Carroll, published by Foghorn Press, San Francisco, 1991. The first ecoguide to Hawaii's best outdoor activities.

Hawaiian Heritage Plants, by Angela Kay Kepler, published by Fernglen Press, 1998. A thorough presentation of native plants, with color photos.

Trees of Hawaii, by Angela Kay Kepler, published by University of Hawaii Press 1990. A colorful and informative look at native and intro-duced trees.

Hawaii's Birds, published by the Hawaii Audubon Society, 1993. A full-color guide to native and introduced birds in the Islands.

A Good Walk

Maui has several good walks to enjoy, including the following favorites. One goes to an ethereal state park, one strolls through a nearby turn-of-the-century plantation town, and yet another takes a look at Lahaina's rich past.

Find the Needle

For a quick and cooling jungle fix, leave the toasty beaches behind, bring a picnic, and head up beyond Wailuku to Iao Valley, a misty state park filled with tropical plants, rainbows, waterfalls, swimming holes, and hiking trails, all rimmed by green mountains. It was the scene of a fierce battle in 1790, when King Kamehameha fought to gain control of Maui. When the fighting ended, so many bodies blocked Iao Stream that the battle site was named Kepaniwai, "damming of the waters."

Now the area has been transformed into a plantation heritage architectural park, with examples of cottages in Hawaiian, Japanese, Chinese, Filipino, and New England styles. Nearby is the Maui Nature Center, offering guided hikes, rainforest displays, and nature interpretive programs for children and others who like to learn.

Iao Valley Road ends at a parking lot for people stopping to view the landmark Iao Needle, a finger of basalt pointing skyward. The natural stone monument is a requisite photo-op stop that draws bus tours, but its singular beauty cannot be denied.

A Walk Through Wailuku

Wailuku, the 19th-century hillside plantation town overlooking Maui's north shore and central valley, was made for walking. The county seat of Maui since 1905, Wailuku is not all government business. It's slowly becoming a charming collection of funky shops, antiques stores, art galleries, and bistros. A federally funded Main Street restoration program helped put a spit shine on the old brown shoe, but Wailuku and its tin roof clapboard structures still have the flavor of early Maui and the days of sugar rule.

Several interesting shops are clustered along Market Street. After sipping what may be Maui's best lattes at Cafe Marc Aurel, check out the art galleries, antiques stores, goldsmiths, and jewelry shops, where black pearls gleam in the windows. Handsome Chinese and Japanese antiques dominate the collection at Gottling Ltd., oldest of the Antique Row shops of Wailuku. Worth a look: Sig Zane's original bold and graphic aloha shirts and muumuu at 53 Market Street, and next door, Gallerie Ha, where local artist Pat Matsumoto paints papayas, pineapples, and various close-ups of female body parts. Browse through the Farmer's Market next door, where apple bananas, fresh pineapple, and exotic Asian veggies can be bought at bargain prices. Don't leave town without visiting Bailey House Museum, an 1833 missionary home that houses the Maui Historical Society and a good selection of made-in-Hawaii arts and crafts in the gift shop. The Bailey House Museum is at 2375-A Main Street; call (808) 244-3920 for details.

Hungry for lunch? Do what Wailukuans do: Go to Sam Sato's at 1750 Wili Pa Loop (phone (808) 244-7124) for the town's best Japanese/Hawaiian saimin noodle soup laced with your choice of chicken, fish, or pork. Or, try A Saigon Cafe at 1792 Main Street (phone (808) 243-9560).

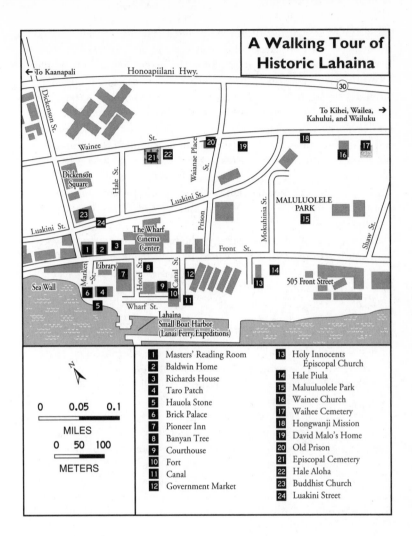

A Walking Tour of Historic Lahaina

← To Kaanapali   Honoapiilani Hwy.

To Kihei, Wailea, →
Kahului, and Wailuku

Dickenson St.

Wainee

St.

Dickenson Square

Hale St.

Waianae Place

St.

Prison

Luakini St.

Mokuhinia St.

MALULUOLELE PARK

15

Luakini St.

The Wharf Cinema Center

Front St.

505 Front Street

Shaw St.

Library

Market St.

Hotel St.

Canal St.

Sea Wall

Wharf St.

Lahaina Small Boat Harbor
(Lanai Ferry Expeditions)

1 Masters' Reading Room	13 Holy Innocents Episcopal Church
2 Baldwin Home	14 Hale Piula
3 Richards House	15 Maluuluolele Park
4 Taro Patch	16 Wainee Church
5 Hauola Stone	17 Waihee Cemetery
6 Brick Palace	18 Hongwanji Mission
7 Pioneer Inn	19 David Malo's Home
8 Banyan Tree	20 Old Prison
9 Courthouse	21 Episcopal Cemetery
10 Fort	22 Hale Aloha
11 Canal	23 Buddhist Church
12 Government Market	24 Luakini Street

N

0   0.05   0.1
MILES

0   50   100
METERS

Historic Lahaina

Lahaina's reputation as a party town goes way back. Blessed with a sheltered harbor, Lahaina was once the hub of the Hawaiian kingdom and also a rowdy winter R&R stop for the whalers and sailors who roamed the Pacific more than a century ago.

When New England whalers hit Lahaina in the 1800s, they found strong drink, sweet-smelling girls, and the tattoo parlor. You may still find them all in Lahaina, including Skin Deep, the Front Street tattoo parlor. The last time we stopped by, a Kona boat captain was having a shark etched on his ankle and an ex–fighter pilot from the Netherlands was getting a sea chart of the seven inhabited Hawaiian islands tattooed in four colors on his left shoulder. Good thing he liked Hawaii better than the Philippines—it's got 7,108 islands. Best-selling tattoos at Skin Deep seem to be Japanese and Chinese ideograms, and those wrap-around Polynesian bands of black-and-white triangles for biceps and ankles. Sailors don't get "Mom" or "Remember Pearl Harbor" tattooed on their forearms anymore.

The missionaries left their tempering influence, too. Grab your walk-ing shoes and check it out. There's so much to see in the relatively com-pact town of Lahaina that we've included a walking-tour map, to help make sure you don't miss the sights. Free maps and Lahaina information are available from the Maui Visitors Bureau and at key locations in Lahaina town.

History is found on every corner in the bustling town, now crowded with tourists from around the world. You can thank members of the Lahaina Restoration Foundation, who work tirelessly to keep Lahaina's history alive in its original buildings. Arrange a special group guided tour or take the self-guided walk back in time past Government House, Lahaina Prison, U.S. Seamen's Hospital and Seamen's Cemetery, the Hale Pai print shop, Wo Hing Temple, and the Pioneer Inn, circa 1901, at the corner of Hotel and Wharf Streets. Teachers, take note: One of the first things the missionaries established was Lahaina Luna High School, the oldest operating public school in the West, still housing students up the hill from the town center.

Begin at a former Master's Reading Room for sea captains, the mariners' haunt for a time after the missionaries shut down Lahaina's grog shops and banned prostitution. The oldest building on Maui, it is now the coral-block headquarters of Lahaina Restoration Foundation. Next door is the Baldwin Home at Dickenson and Front Street, which once housed the family of the Reverend Dwight Baldwin, a missionary doctor who built it in 1834. After nearly 20 years' service, he was granted 2,600 acres of land at Kapalua and began experimenting with the golden fruit Hawaiians called *hala kahiki*—pineapple. The Baldwins remain one of Maui's most prominent families, and pineapple is still a significant cash crop, now spreading over thousands of acres at Kapalua.

Don't miss the ancient giant banyan tree whose wandering aerial roots take up a whole block. For a historic brew, stop at the Pioneer Inn.

Someday Lahaina's treasures will expand with a truly important addition—Mokuula, the first native Hawaiian historic jewel to join the ranks of Lahaina's restored heritage sites. Across the street from the 505 Front Street complex, underneath tons of sand and dirt in a softball park, is the sacred site of the royal home of Prince Kauikeaolui, who became

King Kamehameha III in 1825 at the age of ten. The palace, built on an island in a small lake, was also the setting for a very sad love story. The king lived there with his sister, Princess Nahienaena. The relationship was viewed by Hawaiian nobility as appropriate royal behavior in order to protect royal bloodlines, but the just-arrived missionaries saw this incestuous marriage as the horrifying work of the devil. The young princess, torn between her love for her brother and the newly imposed Western morality, grew despondent and died at the age of 21. Kamehameha III lived on to preside over 29 eventful years in the Islands, a time when the kingdom became a constitutional monarchy and power and land began shifting into the hands of the opportunistic Westerners—missionaries, sugar planters, and merchants. The palace was plowed under in 1918, but a fundraising campaign is under way to bring it back to life. Check the progress at **www.mokuula.com.**

National and State Parks

Besides numerous forest reserves, private land sanctuaries, and county and city parks, Maui County is home to a major national park, three state parks, and a state recreation area. The crown jewel of Maui's public lands is Haleakala National Park, the celebrated House of the Sun, which encompasses the dormant volcano from its 10,023-foot alpine summit to the sea on its southeastern, tropical-wilderness side, at Kipahulu near Hana. Of its 28,655 acres, 19,270 are wilderness. Haleakala National Park was designated an International Biosphere Reserve in 1980. Its heights, above the vast caldera, house an Air Force Super Computer telescope that peers into near-space, searching out satellites that might be spying on the United States. Its depths are a world away, a rainforest where waterfall pools plunge into the sea. In between are a dizzying array of microclimates, from high lava desert to cloud forest and fertile uplands to coastal tropics, with rare plants and endangered birds.

Altogether, Haleakala is a singular ecological wonder that should not be missed, especially since it's easy to see. So set aside at least a day for Haleakala, if not a sunrise. Sunrise over the crater is a mystical experience that few viewers find disappointing, even though they arose in the middle of the night to drive up to see it. Maui's most famous ride is the guided bike tour on specially equipped cycles down the entire mountain (see the section "Bicycling: Pedal Power").

Haleakala National Park, Upcountry Maui

Location The summit area is accessible by way of Roads 37, 377, and 378 up the mountain through Kula, a community at the 3,000-foot level. The park entrance is above Kula. The drive to the top takes at least three hours round-trip from the Kahului area below. Add more time to get to and from resort areas. Kipahulu, at the island's East End, between Hana and Kaupo, can be reached via Hana Highway. Driving time is about three hours between Kahului and Kipahulu.

Phone (808) 572-4400

Web site www.nps.gov/hale

Hours Park Ranger headquarters open daily, 7:30 a.m.– 4 p.m.; Visitor Center open daily, sunrise–3 p.m.

Admission $10 per vehicle, good for a week; $5 per person without a vehicle.

When to go Anytime. Haleakala is renowned for dramatic sunsets and sunrises. Be sure to arrive at least 30 minutes early. It's also well worth the drive at other times of day—including evenings after dark, when it is a fabulous place for stargazing.

How much time to allow Up to half a day, depending on whether you take part in park programs. Rangers offer guided hikes on all Haleakala's trails, at the cindery summit, in the cloud forest, or down below in the lush tropical forests of Kipahulu. These are a good option for exploring the park. Take your pick of environments.

Comments At the summit, the park headquarters and visitor center house cultural and natural history exhibits. Haleakala, originally part of Hawaii Volcanoes National Park, was designated as an individual park in July 1961.

In the Kipahulu area, all trails begin at the ranger station/visitor center. The Kuloa Point Trail is an easy half-mile loop toward the ocean that affords a look at the pools and waterfalls, as well as the sea and the Big Island, but go early or late if you want to avoid crowds. Enjoy a picnic on the grass next to the remnants of an ancient fishing shrine and house site.

Check the park bulletin board for a schedule of daily programs and guided hikes. Obey posted warnings. Because the weather at the summit is unpredictable—temperatures range from 40°F to 65°F, but with wind chill factored in, can dip below freezing—wear lightweight, layered clothing and comfortable, sturdy shoes. No restaurants or gas stations are available in the park. People with heart or breathing problems should use caution because of the high elevation and thin air.

Limited drive-in and wilderness overnight camping is permitted in the crater and below at Kipahulu. The Hosmer Grove Campground in the summit area is located just inside the park entrance (see the "Camping in the Wilds" section for details).

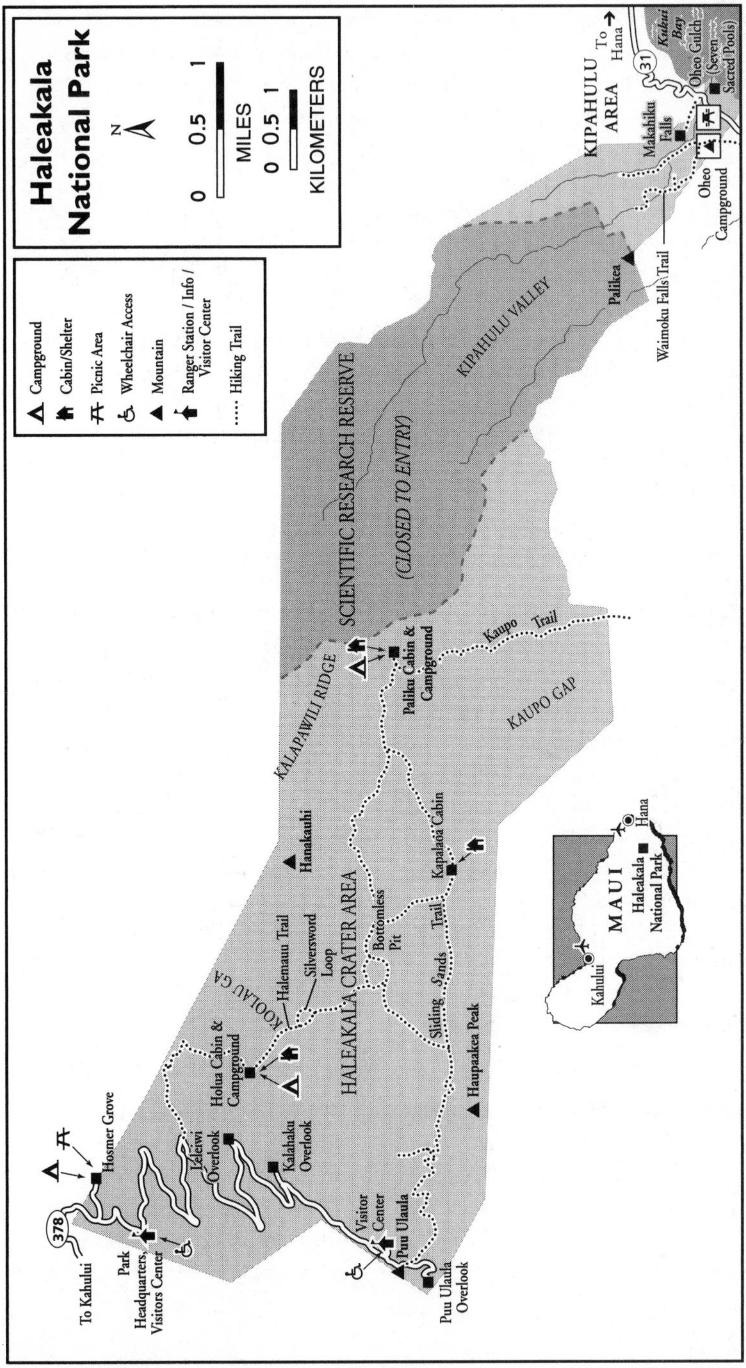
Haleakala National Park
N
0 0.5 1
MILES
0 0.5 1
KILOMETERS
Campground
Cabin/Shelter
Picnic Area
Wheelchair Access
Mountain
Ranger Station / Info / Visitor Center
Hiking Trail
To Kahului
378
Park Headquarters, Visitors Center
Hosmer Grove
Leleiwi Overlook
Kalahaku Overlook
Holua Cabin & Campground
Visitor Center
Puu Ulaula
Puu Ulaula Overlook
Haupaakea Peak
HALEAKALA CRATER AREA
KOOLAU GA
Halemauu Trail
Silversword Loop
Sliding Sands Trail
Bottomless Pit
Hanakauhi
Kapalaoa Cabin
KALAPAWILI RIDGE
Paliku Cabin & Campground
Kaupo Trail
KAUPO GAP
SCIENTIFIC RESEARCH RESERVE
(CLOSED TO ENTRY)
KIPAHULU VALLEY
Palikea
Waimoku Falls Trail
KIPAHULU AREA
Makahiku Falls
Oheo Campground
Oheo Gulch (Seven Sacred Pools)
Kukui Bay
31
To Hana
MAUI
Kahului
Haleakala National Park
Hana

State Parks

For information on Hawaii's extensive system of state parks, recreation areas, beach parks, historic sites, and other points of interest, write to the Division of State Parks, 1151 Punchbowl Street, Room 310, Honolulu, HI 96813, or call (808) 587-0300. The State Parks Office on Maui is located in Wailuku (phone (808) 984-8109).

For a free Maui recreation map detailing hiking trails and other points of interest, contact the State Department of Land and Natural Resources office on Maui, 54 South High Street, Room 101, Wailuku, HI 96793, or call (808) 873-3506.

In addition to Waianapanapa State Park near Hana (described under Beaches) and Iao Valley State Park (described under Hiking), another standout is found in the cloud forest high country, for dedicated hikers and drivers willing to take on a challenging mountain road off Highway 377 above Kula.

Polipoli Spring State Recreation Area, Central Maui

Location Waipoli Road, 10.5 miles above Highway 377.

Comments Way off the beaten path at the 6,000-foot level of Haleakala in the Kula Rainforest Reserve, surprises await the intrepid few who make it past the narrow, bumpy, switchback road that climbs 3,000 feet in the first six miles. This is a "good weather" expedition, more treacherous than fun in wet weather. Once in the ten-acre park, hikers will find themselves surrounded by towering redwoods. Hardy trekkers can climb another thousand feet to the top of a cinder cone with an amazing view of neighboring islands in the blue sea. Below Polipoli, connecting trails (Redwood, Plum, Haleakala Ridge, and Polipoli) form a satisfying 3.5-mile loop. Other trails of varying difficulty offer great views. One cabin is available through reservation with the State Parks Office in Wailuku, (808) 984-8109.

Palaau State Park, Molokai

Location End of Kalae Highway in Palaau.

Comments This leafy 230-acre park overlooks historic Kalaupapa, the peninsula where people stricken with Hansen's disease (leprosy) were once banished. Picnicking and camping areas are available. A short trail leads to a monolithic stone aptly named Phallic Rock, reputed to enhance fertility in women who sleep beside it overnight. Take a short walk to the very edge for an awesome view of the Island's north shore.

- Guard against tropical sunburn in high, thin air.
- Never leave your valuables unattended in a car at a scenic lookout.
- Drinking or possession of alcoholic beverages is prohibited in parks.
- Build fires only in fireplaces and grills. Portable stoves and other warming devices may be used in designated picnicking and camping areas.
- Do not disturb any plants or geological, historical, or archeological features.

Camping in the Wilds

Campsites on Maui, Molokai, and Lanai come in a royal choice of setting—beachside, hunkered under sheltering groves of trees, or out in a meadow beside waterfall pools, and upland, surrounded by open mountain terrain or lush (wet) rainforests—but are limited in number and sometimes tough to reserve. Nearly all require camping permits. Book as far ahead as possible, and be prepared to compete with residents in a lottery to get the permits. Camping is the affordable way to vacation in the Islands.

For gear, you'll need a tent with a rain flap or tarp to ward off overnight showers, a ground pad, and lightweight sleeping bags (to sleep on more often than in, unless you're headed for cool higher altitudes). You'll need bug repellent and drinking water , a water purifier, or a container to boil water until it's safe. Don't drink wild, untreated water.

The Islands have some bugs of tropical proportions, capable of nasty stings—giant centipedes, five inches or longer; small, delicate scorpions in rocky areas; and Black Widow and Brown Recluse spiders under damp wood. Shake out your shoes and bed gear before using them, and wear shoes or use a flashlight to watch your step, even in soft grass at night. Other than tropical creepy crawlies, the only animals there to encounter in the wild are escaped pets, chickens or turkeys, and the occasional feral pig or goat. You can scare them away by making lots of noise or sudden movements. Otherwise, leave them alone and they'll extend the same courtesy. Some plants are poisonous to eat, so consume nothing you're not entirely familiar with.

If you want to camp without lugging all the gear from home, rent equipment from suppliers such as those listed below, most of which also rent kayaks, mountain bikes, and other outdoor equipment.

CAMPING EQUIPMENT RENTALS
Maui
West Maui Sports & Fishing Supply, 1287 Front Street, Lahaina, HI 96761; (808) 661-6252 or (888) 498-7726
Molokai
Molokai Outdoor Adventures, P.O. Box 1236, Kaunakakai, HI 96748; (808) 553-4477 or (877) 553-4477; www.molokai-outdoors.com

Where to Camp

Here are our suggested campsites. You may also wish to contact the state parks mentioned above to inquire about sites and availability. Not all campgrounds require or grant reservations, but we strongly recommend making them whenever possible. Remember to get groceries and gas before you head to Haleakala National Park, home to our three Maui Island picks. A good resource to learn more is *Camping Hawaii,* resident camping expert Richard McMahon, published by the University of Hawaii Press.

Holua Wilderness Campground, Upcountry Maui

Location Inside Haleakala Crater, 4 miles down the Halemauu Trail.

Type of camping Tent and cabin camping.

Permit Tent permits are issued at the park headquarters on a first-come, first-served basis on the day of use. The campground is limited to 25 people, with no more than 12 in a single group. Reservations for wilderness cabins at Holua (and those at Paliku and Kapalaoa) must be made 3 months in advance. Be sure to include alternate dates. Write to Haleakala National Park, P.O. Box 369, Makawao, HI 96768, call (808) 572-4400 or go to **www.nps.gov/hale.**

Stay limit 3 nights.

Cost Free for tent campers. The 3 cabins are $40 (accommodates 1–6 people) and $80 (7–12 people) per night.

Comments Awe-inspiring views of Haleakala Crater, big enough to contain Manhattan with room to spare, are among the highlights here at the near-7,000-foot elevation. You are likely to meet the endangered Nene goose, the state bird, and see the rare native Silversword plants that bloom only once in 15 years, then die. Facilities for tent camping are sparse, and the campground is rocky. Cabins contain bunks with mattresses (but no bed linens), table, chairs, cooking utensils, and a wood-burning stove with firewood.

Hosmer Grove, Upcountry Maui

Location At the 6,800-foot level, just off Haleakala Crater Road. Watch for the sign for Hosmer Grove, which is almost 10 miles from the Crater Road turnoff.

Type of camping Tent and vehicle camping. Vehicles must stay in the parking lot.

Permits None required; first come, first served. The campground is limited to 25 people, with no more than 12 in a single group.

Stay limit 3 nights.

Cost Free.

Comments The campground, a grassy clearing surrounded by trees, has a covered pavilion with 2 picnic tables and 2 grills, restrooms, and drinkable water. Hiking is the activity of choice. A half-mile loop nature trail begins at one end of the parking lot. Pick up hiking trail information at the park headquarters. Bring extra blankets—it can get cold at night.

... and why are we the only ones enjoying this incomparable grandeur? Why aren't there thousands of people climbing over one another to hang all around the rim of 'the greatest extinct crater in the world?' Such reputation ought to be irresistible. Why, there's nothing on earth so wonderful as this!"

—Jack London, quoted in *Our Hawaii Islands and Islanders* by Charmian K. London

---

Kipahulu Campground, Upcountry Maui

Location Hana Highway, about 10 miles past Hana.

Type of camping Tent and vehicle camping.

Permits None required. Space is limited to 100 people, on first-come, first-served basis. On busy holiday weekends, arrive early to get your space.

Stay limit 3 nights.

Cost Free.

Comments Camping in this extraordinary spot, a grassy area overlooking the sea and the Oheo Gulch pools and waterfalls, is so memorable that even noncampers ought to get a tent and give it a try. Facilities include restrooms, picnic tables, and grills, plus the showers and pools provided by nature. Bring drinking water. No food or gas is available. Swimming and jungle hiking are right at hand.

Exploring the infamous curvy road to Hana and its old-time villages, swimmable waterfall pools, and botanical gardens can be one of Maui's finest experiences, when you combine the long drive with an overnight stay in the Hana area. Lodging is limited in Hana, and camping at Kipahulu is a fun alternative. Also nearby is Waianapanapa State Park (at the end of Waianapanapa Road off the Hana Highway; phone (808) 984-8109).

Papohaku Beach Park, Molokai

Location Just off Kaluakoi Road, western shore. Head west on Highway 460 to the turnoff to the Kaluakoi Resort; continue past the hotel along Kaluakoi Road.

Type of camping Tent and vehicle camping.

Permits Available at the Pauole Center Multipurpose Building in Kaunakakai. For advance reservations and more information, write to the Maui County Parks Department at P.O. Box 526, Kaunakakai, HI 96748; or call (808) 553-3204.

Stay limit 3 nights.

Cost $3 per person per night.

Comments This site is both easily accessible and fairly isolated. Facilities include restrooms, showers, picnic tables, grills, and drinking water. One drawback is that the water is too rough for swimming.

Hulopoe Beach Park, Lanai

Location At the end of the road in Manele Harbor.

Type of camping Tent camping at 3 sites, limited to 6 people each.

Permits Camping on this privately owned island requires a permit. Write to Lanai Company, Attn: Camping Permits, P.O. Box 310, Lanai City, HI 96763; or call (808) 565-8206.

Stay limit 1 week.

Cost $5 per person per night.

Comments Right up the hill, high-rollers are paying the price of your plane ticket per night to stay at the elegant Manele Bay Hotel. The next morning, you're already at the beach. You can thank island residents who fought to save their right to use this picturesque beach when the island owner considered making it off-limits to all but his guests. Park facilities include restrooms, showers, picnic tables, grills, and drinking water.

Bicycling: Pedal Power

Exploring the Islands by bike puts you in touch with your surroundings at your own speed. The Islands have mountains in the middle, which adds a challenging element. The most popular cycle adventure on Maui is cruising down the steep and scenic slopes of Haleakala Crater. Several tour companies will put you on special downhill-cruising bikes with heavy-duty brakes to keep you under control on the 38-mile descent down a serpentine road. From the summit to the seashore, you streak past pasturelands, farms, and forests. Some companies also provide hotel transportation and a snack; others offer unguided tours, letting you set your own pace. Be forewarned: Some deceptive grades and curves coming down the mountain have launched even experienced bikers over the side. Take the curves more slowly than you normally would. Dress in layers; the top third of the ride is alpine, while the bottom is tropical.

It's not even close to dawn, but here you are, rubbing your eyes awake, on the top of Maui's sleeping volcano. It's colder than you ever thought possible for a tropical island. The air is thin. Your shoes grind in the clinkers, crunch crunch, as you stomp your chilly feet while you wait, sipping some hot brew. Then comes the sun, exploding over the yawning Haleakala Crater. A mystic moment you won't soon forget, imprinted on a palette of dawn colors. Now you know why Hawaiians named it the House of the Sun. But there's no time to linger. Decked out in your screaming yellow parka, you mount your special steed and test its most important feature—the brakes. You are awake enough now to hear the instructions, the safety cautions, the itinerary. And off you go through the colorful early morning, a line of downhill cruisers, wobbly at first until you get the knack. You're about to see Maui top to bottom, a 38-mile coast down a 10,000-foot volcano. In a few hours. On a bike!

In the past millennia, Haleakala erupted every 200 years or so. It last erupted in 1790, which means it could be overdue right now. Hold that thought as you scan the black-and-brown cindery landscape for a glimpse of Hawaii's endangered bird, the Nene goose, which has adapted claw feet for walking on sharp lava. Or a spiky Silversword plant, growing determinedly in the scorched earth. This is quite a landscape, but it's just the beginning. You've got a lot more to see. Besides, if it erupted, you could probably outrun the flow on your cruiser bike.

Maui's single greatest physical feature is Haleakala, a mountain so big many people don't see it. By midday, the summit and the white knobs of observatories are often lost above a wreath of clouds. But your morning ride is sunny and crystal clear, as grass and trees begin to cover the lumpy volcanic terrain. By the time you get to Kula, it's an over-the-rainbow experience. Tall, fragrant eucalyptus forests. Blooming blue jacaranda. Flower farms and emerald pastures. Pleasantly cool temperatures, sweet country smells, a horsey idyll from a romance novel. There should be a yellow brick road for your bikes.

Down below, past the cane fields and commuter communities, you cruise to your objective—the sea-level floor of Maui and a return to the tropical breezes and warm seas, just the way you left them. This swim will be the best ever.

Multiple biking tours are available. **Backroads,** the well-known bike vacation agency in Berkeley (call (800) 462-2848 or visit **www.back roads.com**) has multisport adventures on Maui and Lanai.

Maui has bike-friendly lanes on some roads, with stunning views of neighboring Molokai, Lanai, and Kahoolawe. One road-biking candidate is the one-lane road around Maui's northwest end between Kahului and Kapalua. The scenery and the winding road slows everyone down. Stop and get a refreshing shaved ice at Kahakuloa. Or drive up to Kula, on the 3,000-foot shoulder of Haleakala, park the car and cruise by bike along the hilly country road to Ulupalakua Ranch and back, through flower farms, blue jacaranda trees, botanical gardens, and pastures. If you want to do it with special equipment and a tour with an expert, **Aloha Bicycle Tours,** run by a former state bicycling champion, cruises Upcountry Maui, starting after breakfast from a point just inside the Haleakala National Park entrance rather than the top of the summit. Bikers go at their own pace down 21 switchback turns through Haleakala Ranch and stop when they like, en route to the Tedeschi Winery at Ulupalakua Ranch for picnic lunch and wine-tasting. For information, call (800) 749-1564 or (808) 249-0911, or visit **www.maui.net/~bikemaui.**

Biking Safety Tips

- Wear a helmet and comfortable shoes.
- If possible, carry a first-aid kit and cell phone in case of emergency.
- Familiarize yourself with your rental bike and the tropic heat and humidity before riding off.
- Ride with a partner or a group.
- Bring drinking water, sunscreen, and sunglasses.
- If traveling in a group, keep at least five lengths between riders.
- Don't use headphones while riding or get distracted by views.
- Novice mountain bikers should avoid narrow, single-track trails, which sometimes skirt the edge of dangerous cliffs. Instead, ride on the dirt roads.

Maui, Lanai, and Molokai are terrific places for mountain biking, with a wide range of terrain, scenic sites, and trails. The favorite Maui venue for mountain bikers is Polipoli Spring State Park, where you'll find more than ten miles of single-track that winds through thick forests of eucalyptus and redwood trees. Molokai, with 125 miles of trails, is a favorite playground for mountain bikers. For off-road bike adventures on Molokai, go to Molokai Ranch, where you can stay in a plush tent cabin, eat communally in camp pavilions, and do your pedaling thing on the 52,000-acre ranch's superb single-track. Mountain biking is one of several activities included in the price of your stay. Here and elsewhere, the rugged trails provide optimal riding conditions, from dusty coastlines to lush forests. Plenty of dirt roads on Lanai call to mountain bikers, as well as the challenging climb to the 3,370-foot summit of Lanaihale, the island's highest point. Several of Lanai's destinations make appealing day trips by bike. You can ride the Expeditions ferry from Lahaina to Lanai for $25 per person plus $10 for the bike. Get ready for a workout.

Hawaii Bicycling League (call (808) 735-5756 or go to **www.hbl. org**) offers bike route maps and rides to remote places like sacred Kaaawa Valley on Oahu's Windward side. They also issue a newsletter for local biking enthusiasts. John Alford's *Mountain Biking the Hawaiian Islands* features maps and photos as well as detailed descriptions of best biking trails. You can order it through **www.bikehawaii.com.**

Daily rentals run $20–$35 for a mountain bike and $15 for a road bike.

BIKE RENTAL SHOPS

Maui

Haleakala Bike Co.: Haiku Marketplace, Haiku; (808) 575-9575; www.bikemaui.com

Island Bikes: 415 Dairy Road, Kahului; (808) 877-7744

South Maui Bicycles: 1993 South Kihei Road # 5, Kihei; (808) 874-0068

West Maui Bicycles: 840 Walnee Street, C-5, Lahaina; (808) 661-9005; www.westmauicycles.com

Molokai

Molokai Bicycle: 80 Mohala Street, Kaunakakai; (808) 553-3931; www.bikehawaii.com/molokaibicycle

---

Horseback Riding: Back in the Saddle

You may not often think of Maui as part of the Wild West, but it's really way out there.

RIDE TO THE SOURCE

The horses' forelocks are wrapped in cowhide to guard against the razor's edge of lava. Slowly, our train of riders picks its way around jagged shards of lava. A fall in this terra terrabilis could slash a person to shreds.

Riders lean far forward in the saddle as we head from Makena up the south side of Haleakala on Maui's Ulupalakua Ranch, a vertical spread on a nearly two-mile-high volcano that's not done yet. This old volcano is officially classified as dormant, meaning it could go off at any moment. Not today, we hope.

We are riding to Puu Mahoe, origin of lava that spilled from Haleakala crater around 1790, the last time Maui experienced a volcanic eruption.

In the deep time of geology that's only yesterday. Perouse, the first white man to set foot on Maui on May 29, 1786, described "a shore made hideous by an ancient lava flow," and sailed on, never to be seen again, yet another mystery of the Pacific.

The old, black lava reflects the sun's heat deep into your bones. A wide-brimmed hat and water in your saddlebag are must-haves.

The thought of eruption is very much on our mind as we ride to Maui's youngest crater. We ride by kiawe with stiletto thorns that can

Horses were brought to the Islands more than a century ago, and a grateful populace, who had either walked or sailed everywhere before that, eagerly took to riding when they got the chance. Big ranch spreads blossomed across the open volcanic slopes. Horseback riding is the best way to get off the roads and into the countryside of those vast ranches that invite visitors to come for tropical trail rides. In the islands, the wide open spaces lead between volcanoes, along beaches and sea cliffs, and into jungled valleys with waterfalls. The horses are well trained and know their trails, leaving you free to enjoy the views. Riding adventures abound on Maui, Molokai, and Lanai, with colorful and personable guides to share local lore. Rates range from $35 per person for a one-hour ride to $60–$100 for a two-hour trek. A three-hour ride, with lunch, runs $130.

Call for age, height, and weight restrictions if you're concerned: The minimum age for riders is usually eight years old but may be higher, and the maximum weight ranges up to 275 pounds. Book your reservation at least a day in advance, or a week ahead if you have a group. Most rides are limited to 12 people. You can secure a reservation with a credit card, and most operators also accept traveler's checks or cash. Call on the morning of your ride (or leave a phone number where you can be reached) to check weather conditions. All riders must sign liability waivers.

pierce a leather boot, past old, sun-bleached bones (whose? no one knows), across wide stretches of nothing but lava—lava that once was molten hot and dribbling down to the shore.

Nothing stirs in this dead zone except fine clouds of suffocating red dust kicked up by our horses. Riders wipe their sweating faces—another must-have is a bandana—as we ride on deeper into the land of Pele, Hawaii's fire goddess.

We rein in at the source: a classic cone crater with a telltale tongue of pahoehoe sticking out its down hill lip.

Walk to the edge, look down the throat of this old crater's hellhole, and you see only dead ashes. Way down there somewhere the pot still boils.

From there to the sea, Maui looks like an 18th-century engraving of itself, an island frozen in time, smothered by miles of lava in every direction as far as the eye can see, a black and silent place—Pele's world.

Out of the sun-struck sea a whale leaps. In that moment, on the dormant crater, Maui seems to have returned to a primeval state. We saddle up, glad to head down Haleakala and return to the present.

Prior riding experience is not a requirement; first-time riders are common. Operators will ask your experience level and match you to an appropriate horse. The group goes at the pace of the least experienced rider. A short orientation on horsemanship and safety precautions for the island's conditions precedes the tour. Certain ranches offer intermediate- and advanced-level rides. Most stables use thoroughbreds and quarterhorses. Rides often include stops for a picnic lunch or barbecue, a sampling of local fruit, or a cooling-off swim. Full-cover shoes or boots are mandatory, long pants are suggested, and sun protection such as a hat and long-sleeved shirt recommended.

Maui's Best Horseback Riding Adventures

Just Say Giddyup

If you wonder how to talk to a horse and make sense, or make a horse do what you want without a struggle, sign up for an **Adventure on Horseback** with wrangler Frank Levinson, also known as "the horse whisperer," on his 55-acre ranch in Haiku, on the way to Hana. He teaches you how to use the techniques made famous in Robert Redford's 1997 film, *The Horse Whisperer*, to train horses with respect and understanding instead of fear and punishment. If you learn improved motivational skills or something else pertinent to your personal life as well as equine psychology, so much the better. In Levinson's The Maui Horse Whisperer Experience program, you don't even have to ride but can elect simply to learn more about horses and spend a day or half a day in the tropical ranch country. Naturally, participants can elect to ride and put their skills to use. He offers a range of trail rides and a special program for families with teenagers, Horse Sense for Humans. You can talk, walk, whisper, and ride with horses, and private guided trail rides can be arranged. After you learn how to talk to your horse, go on a trail ride along the coast or through rainforest to a tropical waterfall pool for lunch. Something to whisper about, back home.

For details, contact **Adventures on Horseback** at P.O. Box 1419, Makawao; (808) 572-6211, or visit **www.mauihorses.com.**

Riding Ulupalakua Ranch

Trail riding on historic Ulupalakua Ranch affords a view of Maui you never suspected and can't get any other way. On Maui's largest ranch, a 20,000-acre spread that extends across the southwestern flanks of Haleakala, horses nimbly pick their way through razor-sharp lava on a trail to the last volcanic eruption site on Maui. Sometime around 1790, at about 2,000 feet, a crater belched fire and smoke and sent red-hot lava spilling into the sea five miles away.

The ribbons of black lava fanned out to create hundreds of acres of badlands in this dry territory, dotted by native ohia trees and thorny kiawe brush.

The black lunar-like landscape is a stark contrast to the sights below—the green waters of Ahihi-Kinau, a marine sanctuary of tropical fish; the deep blue Pacific; and in the distance across the ocean channel, the Island of Kahoolawe, former military bombing practice target now being rescued by Hawaiians. If you go at sunset, look for the fabled green flash. The green flash is a fleeting spot of intense stoplight green that occurs on the horizon for a split second just after the sun sets, or as it is rising. It's best seen when the horizon is cloud-free, especially in winter.

Contact **Makena Stables** in South Maui, (808) 879-0244 or go to **www.makenastables.com,** for information about guided two- and three-hour rides up the moody mountain.

Inside the Crater

When the **Pony Express** trailboss saddles up his tour on the south rim of Haleakala Crater, it's all downhill at first. He takes you down, down, down inside Haleakala on a unique trail ride only possible on Maui. The trail begins at Sliding Sands Trailhead (elevation 9,800 feet) and ends 2,500 feet below the rim, 3.8 miles later at Ka Moa O Pele Junction, where you dismount, often bow-legged, for a picnic lunch in a lunar setting. You may ride in and out of fog, brilliant sunshine, sometimes rain, and even snow; weather in the crater is unpredictable and changes fast. You may spot wild Nene geese, Hawaii's endangered state bird, and the rare Silversword plant Hawaiians call ahinahina. Experienced riders take the 12-mile round-trip to the Bottomless Pit, where volcano goddess Pele once lived. Then it's up, up, up all the way back.

Contact **Pony Express Tours** at P.O. Box 535, Kula; (808) 667-2200, or visit **www.ponyexpresstours.com.**

Mauka to Makai

The Mendes Ranch is a 300-acre working cattle ranch with all the essential elements of earthly paradise—rainbows, waterfalls, palm trees, coral sand beaches, lagoons, tidepools, and a mountain rainforest. You see it all on horseback on a ride that runs mauka to makai (mountain to the sea). Allan Mendes, a colorful third-generation rancher, leads the ride on his painted pony. He takes you past longhorn steers, Brahma bulls, and wild horses (often being broken by his father, Ernest, a champion steer roper). If you know how to ride, Allan will match you to a great steed and let you go for a gallop, rare for any trail ride. The $130, three-hour morning ride on Maui's wild northeast coast ends at the corral with a Maui-style cowboy barbecue with steak and beans.

Contact **Mendes Ranch and Trail Rides** at 3530 Kahekili Highway (four miles beyond Wailuku); (808) 244-7320, or visit **www.mendes ranch.com.**

Molokai Trail Ride

Ride a golden palomino to a secluded gold-sand beach for a Molokai-style beach party. It's the most popular trail ride on Molokai Ranch, a 54,000-acre spread that stretches over most of the West End, from mountains to the sea, and takes in an idyllic little beach on the sun-washed western shore. The Adventure Trail Ride, as it's known in these parts, begins at Molokai Ranch Outfitters Center in Maunaloa town, for six lucky riders, who head down across miles of pastures to the blue Pacific and a secluded beach. Water toys like kayaks, snorkels, fins, and masks are at your disposal. While you take a plunge and your horse grazes under coco palms, the grill is fired up for chicken and steak with all the trimmings. There's no better paniolo beach party.

For more information, contact **Molokai Ranch Outfitters Center** at (808) 552-2791, or visit **www.molokai-ranch.com.**

Molokai Mule Ride

The sea cliffs are a gasp. Almost vertical, they rise 3,000 feet out of the Pacific. You descend on a zigzag trail of 26 hairpin turns carved out of the rock in 1887. You can hike down and back (and save $150), but most prefer to ride a nimble mule. "We've never lost a rider yet," says trail boss Buzzy Sproat, who daily traverses the breathtaking three-mile trail with his trusted mule train. A surefooted mule is the steed you want on this trail ride down the world's steepest sea cliffs. The ride's a thriller, but the destination's chilling—Kalaupapa Peninsula, a place of haunting beauty and sad history. Here, 11,000 banished victims of leprosy lived in exile in the late 19th century, below the cliffs, which separated them from the rest of the island. Today, the peninsula is a national historic place where the few remaining residents are former patients, now cured, who choose to continue a life of near seclusion rather than coping with the rest of the world.

On the ground, visitors board a yellow school bus bound for the grave of Father Damien de Veuster, the Belgian priest who cared for the ill until 1889, when he too fell victim to the awful disease Hawaiians call the "separating sickness." Father Damien's tomb next to Molokai's St. Philomena Church, is empty; his body was disinterred and reburied in his native Belgium. Only his hand, a relic of his martyrdom, remains in Kalaupapa.

In the 1940s, sulfa drugs were found to cure leprosy. You try to count tombstones of hundreds who died of the disease now readily controlled. The slow, plodding climb back up Molokai's steep cliffs delivers sobered riders back to the twentieth century as Kalaupapa, never lost in memory, recedes in the sea mist.

For details, contact **Molokai Mule Ride** at (808) 567-6088 or (800) 567-7550, or visit **www.muleride.com.**

Lanai

To see this nearly roadless island the way its earlier residents did, take a horse. You can ride the upland wilderness trails with a wrangler from the **Lodge at Koele Stables,** to awesome view points notable for a plentitude of open land and sea and the absence of buildings. Call (808) 565-4424 or visit **www.lanai-resorts.com** for more information.

Hang-Gliding: The Bird's Eye View

Those of you who want to spread your kite and fly high can do it above Maui's most famous landmark: Haleakala Crater. You can sign up for an instruction course followed by a memorable tandem flight with your instructor, using a traditional glider or a motor-powered glider. Veteran pilot Armin Engert of **Hang Gliding Maui** offers a four-hour adventure from the top of Haleakala for $250, with shorter excursions using a motorized glider ($90 for a half-hour and $150 for a full hour). Call (808) 572-6557 or visit **www.hangglidingmaui.com** for more information.

ISLANDS ECOTOURISM

Ecotourism promotes community-based sustainable economic development that benefits local residents instead of foreign, corporate-owned tourism enterprises. Megatourism has flourished in Hawaii, sometimes degrading the environment and culture.

Today, noting the advantages of ecotourism, Hawaii has retooled itself in that direction. Ecotourism is reputed to bring $700 million a year to the Islands, or about 8 percent of total visitor expenditures. Some groups work hard to present Hawaii in a new, natural way and manage to eke out a living in the ecotourism business.

Naturalist Rob Pacheco of Hawaii Forest and Trails leads treks into Big Island rainforests. Chino and Micco Godinez lead guided kayak tours on the island of Kauai, up the Hanalei River and down Na Pali Coast. Dominic Kealoha Aki hosts visitors at Oahu's almost secret, sacred places. But there is ecotourism on Maui, too. Ken Schmitt takes hikers into the island's upland trails. Other Maui ecotourism opportunities (many outlined in this chapter) include whaling, sea kayaking, and camping.

"Most people have no idea how awesome Hawaii really is," says Pacheco. "They think it's only a place to sit on the beach."

His version of the real Hawaii doesn't include the beach. Pacheco leads folks into the rainforest on the slopes of a dormant volcano to see native birds. His patrons always leave "stoked"—meaning thrilled in the local surfer dialect.

Only a few years ago, when fantasy resorts were spreading across the Hawaiian islands faster than Starbucks, you could spend two weeks and a small fortune and never meet a real Hawaiian, learn anything about the culture, or experience the true meaning of aloha.

Hawaii slowly is regaining its sense of authenticity. It began when the fantasy resort bubble burst as ecotourism sprouted and Hawaii's sovereignty movement surfaced. Islanders began to realize just what makes Hawaii so special to the rest of the world.

"Ultimately, the only thing unique about Hawaii is its Hawaiian-ness," the late Hawaii educator and author George S. Kanahele told the Hawaii Hotel Association. "People come to a special place like Hawaii for the intrinsic cultural values and not for plasticized, fantasized mega-resorts. People who spend money know better than that."

Sure, you can still shell out $50 a person at a faux luau, drink sticky-sweet mai tais with nice folks from Indiana, and watch captive dolphins perform at Sea Life Park, but you can do the real thing, too.

The Spa Is Hot

Suddenly, spas are undergoing a healthy growth trend in the Islands—not only the de rigeur hot tub but the full-on massage/mud/seaweed bath/facial/herbal wrap routine of the full-service spa, and not just for women. This is especially true at the luxury hotels, which find their guests look forward to a soothing, indulgent, therapeutic spa timeout as an essential aspect of their tropical dreams. While not necessarily an outdoor activity, spa treatments in Hawaii often take advantage of the Islands' natural beauty and incorporate the age-old remedy of fresh air. Plus, if you've spent hours on a surfboard, on a mountain bike, or in the saddle, a massage might be the perfect ending to your active Maui vacation.

Just as East meets West on the Island table, the methods and traditions of Pacific Rim spas meet on the massage table and in the imaginative treatments and aromatic ingredients that make up the modern spa treatment. Ancient Hawaiians, who knew how to take good care of themselves, had a word for the process of safeguarding and restoring good health: *hooponopono,* or making things right. Our word for sinking into a tub filled with exotic scents, submitting to the heritage massage called lomilomi in a tent by the sea, feeling the water in a many-jetted shower zing your stress away, zoning out under the influence of hot lava rocks? Fantastic.

Hawaii is a healthy place by nature and tradition. If nothing else, get a lomilomi massage, a cultural experience. The therapist uses forearms as well as hands in a smoothing, stretching technique that is relaxing to the point of being hypnotic. So splurge: You owe it to yourself to do this. Don't hold back if you are uneasy about exposing that imperfect body to a stranger. It's their job. Don't use your sunburn for an excuse. They have stuff to fix that, like a cool aloe wrap. If you're a new mother, undergoing chemo, fighting off love handles, suffering from arthritic joints, sore-armed from too much golf, or nagged by a muscle ache, get into that spa. They'll make you feel better. You can request a male or a female massage therapist, as you prefer. Be sure to tell your therapist about any particular sensitivities, medical conditions, injuries, or allergies, and your preference for gentle or rigorous treatment. The Maui Marriott spa in West Maui publishes a card titled "How to Receive a Massage" that encourages new massage patrons to shut their eyes and relax, focus on deep breathing, go limp like a rag doll, and let the therapist move their arms or legs, avoid unnecessary talk, and even doze off if they want during the soothing treatment. It's normal.

One note of warning: Don't skip out on your spa appointment. All the spas have cancellation policies that include forfeiting part of the prepaid fee.

Spas devoted to rejuvenation and pampering care are now operating at moderately priced resorts as well as the luxury spreads. In the community, you can find Hawaiian practitioners devoted to the study of ancient healing arts such as massage and relaxation, as well as Hawaiian medicinal plant use, called Laau Lapaau. Look for spas that use Hawaiian medicinal plants and seaweeds, ocean water, peaceful surroundings, and methods like lomilomi and hot lava-rock massage to promote good health. All spas offer European, Asian, New Age, and other modern therapies.

Spa treatments have also become a guy thing, luring men beyond the workout room to the relaxing massages, facials, pedicures, and manicures that women have long enjoyed. Several spas, however, impose minimum age limits for treatments. Gratuities and taxes are added to the total bill. Spa treatments are not cheap, but it is easy to treat yourself to some first-class therapeutic pampering, in programs that take advantage of the beneficent Hawaiian outdoors—you'll find private outdoor massage cabanas near the sea and open-air pools, massage areas, and other facilities within spa buildings. You don't have to be a resort guest to sign up for spa treatments, but it may cost more if you're not. Put a little money aside to take home some spa lotions.

The following are some of Maui's top spa choices.

The Diamond Resort, South Maui

Location Wailea Resort
Phone (800) 800-0720 or (808) 874-0500
Hours Daily, 10 a.m.–10 p.m.; masseuse on call
Comments What's truly different about the Diamond Resort Spa is the authentic *onsen,* or Japanese-style bathing pools (one for men, one for women), in soaring open-air rooms with a riveting view of islands and sea far below to contemplate while you soak.

This spa is something akin to Beppu, the storied steam-bath city of Japan, only better, and nothing like anything else in Hawaii. The treatment approach is a blend of Japanese style and German "Kurhaus" hydrotherapy techniques intended to ease problems with neuralgia, bruises, jet lag, stiff muscles or back, and poor circulation.

In the condo rooms and in the onsen, Japanese bath stools stand like little sentinels to remind Westerners that scrubs and showers preceed a dip in the furo, Japanese hot tub, or onsen. The water-oriented therapies include foam baths, special hot-waterfall showers, wraparound showers, and a reclining bath in hot water with a cool stone pillow. Massage attendants stand at the ready, and the spa offers the most unusual treatments this side of Nippon.

The house favorite is a facial that involves nightingale droppings, transformed into a precious white powder and hand-carried to Maui from Japan. Songbird droppings have been used for many years by Kabuki dancers to rejuvenate their pale skin and remove make-up stains from their kimono. Nightingales eat caterpillars that feed on plum trees, then add their own power-packed enzymes and pass the results along quickly. The end product is regarded by Japanese cosmetologists as a highly efficient astringent cleanser when applied to human skin. The two-hour procedure begins with the application of nightingale droppings (odor-free and sanitized), followed by an Azuki bean scrub and a seaweed mask. The cost is about $100, far less than you would pay in Tokyo. For details, visit **www.diamondresort.com.**

Grand Wailea Resort Hotel and Spa, South Maui

Location Wailea Resort

Phone (808) 875-1234

Hours Daily, treatments 10 a.m.– 8 p.m.; fitness/workout rooms 6 a.m.– 8 p.m.; beauty salon 9 a.m.– 7 p.m.

Comments The Grand Wailea's Spa Grande is the island's largest, at 50,000 square feet and a favorite with the spa-going world. The Spa Grande mixes traditional Hawaiian healing techniques and ingredients with European, American, Indian, and Asian therapies. You can purchase massage treatments, aromatherapy, body treatments, facials, hair care, manicures, pedicures, and waxings; participate in yoga and meditation instruction; and play racquetball or basketball. Prices range from $15 for a nail polish change up to $220 for a one-hour "massage-in-stereo" (two therapists at once). Most soothing is the spa's Termé Wailea Hydrotherapy Circuit, a refreshing hour-long treatment that begins with a quick shower and includes some quality time in a Roman bath, the steam room, and sauna before a personalized loofah scrub, a cleansing treatment that exfoliates surface skin cells and produces healthier-looking skin. The treatment continues with a soak in specialty baths—Moor mud, limu/seaweed, aromatherapy, tropical enzyme, and mineral salt— followed by a Swiss jet shower. Sounds invigorating? The cost is $50 for hotel guests and $100 for nonguests.

Nonhotel guests pay a $30 surcharge added to the first spa treatment (salon and wellness services not included). The surcharge is waived if you book two or more spa treatments on the same day. Nonhotel guests need a major credit card to reserve an appointment. All spa and salon services are subject to an additional 15 percent service charge plus tax. Use of the cardiovascular gym, weight-training gym, and all fitness classes is free for hotel guests, or $15 a day for nonguests. Call the resort for more information, or visit **www.grandwailea.com.**

The Health Centre, Four Seasons Resort Maui, South Maui

Location Wailea Resort

Phone (808) 874-8000

Hours Daily, 6 a.m.–9 p.m.

Comments Here's the best headache relief prescription anyone has yet invented: Go down to the sea in front of your hotel early in the day and float in the womblike waters while a masseuse smooths the crimps and pains from your head, shoulders and neck. It's one of the new treatments at Four Seasons' Health Centre, the hotel's expanding fitness and spa facilities, which have undergone a $3 million update. The unique aqua cranial treatment, a type of cranial-sacral massage developed by Rebecca Goff, is administered in the clear, warm sea off Wailea Beach. Therapist and client don wet suits and head into the water. The guest lolls easily on the surface as the sun is coming up over Haleakala, while the therapist massages head, neck, and shoulders. Oh, what a beautiful morning. The spa also offers a variety of other massages, including a Thai technique that involves stretching and movement, without oil, performed in a tent outdoors or in your room. Couples can relax together with massage for two in a private outdoor cabana. Deep-tissue massages with neuromuscular and acupressure techniques get at the heart of sports injuries. Tennis and fitness services are also operated from the Health Centre. Visit **www.fourseasons.com/maui** for more details.

Hyatt Regency Maui Resort and Spa, West Maui

Location Kaanapali Beach Resort

Phone (808) 661-1234

Hours Daily, 7 a.m.–8 p.m.

Comments Besides a full range of massages and facials, the Hyatt Regency Maui Moana Spa offers workout classes so you can balance exertion and relaxation. The spa's newest fitness class, Beach Boot Camp, offers a workout with Mother Nature. No indoor weight bench, no treadmill, and no step machine here. Instead, you tackle the real thing—a three-mile stretch of beach, coconut weights, and the sparkling blue ocean, with a regimen of high-impact aerobics. The resistance provided by soft sand and ocean currents helps build muscle strength and endurance. Classes begin with beach stretches and go on to sprints along the sand, lunges through the water, and abdominal crunches along a hilly incline. The one-hour class is offered at 8 a.m. every Wednesday, Friday, and Sunday. Cost for the class is $5 per person for hotel guests and $7 per person for the general public.

Spa Kea Lani, Fairmont Kea Lani Maui, South Maui

Location Wailea Resort

Phone (808) 875-4100

Hours Daily, 7:30 a.m.–8 p.m. for treatments, 24 hours for fitness facilities

Comments Here's a way to deal with that pesky cellulite: a dose of natural black Moor mud and thermal mineral water. It rejuvenates tired muscles and dull skin as well. Cellulite activating gel is applied to tone and firm your skin while you get an acupressure facial massage. The cost is $85 for a 50-minute treatment.

Kea Lani also offers a glygolic facial peel aimed at removing fine lines, wrinkles, and age spots, and an anti–free radical face mask containing concentrated vitamins, a treatment that begins with a skin analysis and cleanings and concludes with a facial massage.

The Spa offers body wraps and polishes, a range of massage techniques, personal fitness training sessions, and spa lunches. For more information, visit **www.kealani.com.**

The Spa at Manele Bay Hotel, Lanai

Location Manele Bay, south Lanai

Phone (808) 565-2088

Hours Daily, 8:30 a.m.–7 p.m.

Comments Pineapple polishes and banana-coconut scrubs are among the luscious-sounding treatments available at the Manele Bay spa, just redesigned in a $1 million redo. If you're rarely kind to your feet, make up for it with the "hehi lani," or "step into heaven," foot treatment, which consists of a foot-wrap in hot eucalyptus-scented towels followed by an aromatic scrub, a foot massage with rich lotion, and a finishing spritz of cooling oils, 50 minutes of pedal bliss for $105. New treatments include hot-rock massages and hot-rock facials. Massage facilities come in indoor or outdoor environments, and massages in all varieties of technique, some intended to ease sports-aches and golf-aches. Separate rooms are set aside for hair, nail, and facial work. Guests can choose fitness activities such as aquatics and coastal trail hikes to tone those muscles. For more information, visit **www.manele bayhotel.com.**

ISLANDS OUTDOOR EXCURSIONS

Lying in a white caravan tent on the black lava coast of the Big Island of Hawaii, women we just met introduced us to lomilomi, the classic Hawaii massage. Tradewinds ruffled the palm trees. Waves lapped the shore. Now and then from a distance whale-watchers cried in delight as the aquatic behemoths leapt out of the blue Pacific.

Another blissful outdoor Hawaiian experience added to our list. After more than two decades in the islands, only a few goals still elude us—such as Mauna Loa's 13,679-foot summit on the Big Island and the 80-foot dive at Cathedrals off the south coast of Lanai. Although some such excursions border on the extreme, almost anyone can enjoy the real Hawaii. The choices are staggering.

You can kayak out for a sea-level encounter with humpback whales or dive among white-tipped sharks; visit the Puu Oo rainforest with a naturalist; explore coral reefs with marine experts, or volunteer to tag Hawaiian Monk seals on Kure Atoll in the seldom-seen northwest Hawaiian Islands; or hunt wild pigs with dogs on the slopes of Haleakala (and do Hawaii an eco-favor by eliminating descendants of the European boar introduced by Captain James Cook).

Many resorts now offer ecological tours. Some of the best are found at Maui's Kapalua Bay Resort, which sits between a marine preserve and the West Maui rainforest. Guests can explore Kahakuloa Valley, in the almost always off-limits Puu Kukui rainforest, and snorkel Honokohau Bay, which teems with tropical fish and occasionally spinner dolphins.

Or, take a Nature Conservancy hike through Molokai's eerie Moomomi Dunes where shifting sand yields skeletons of flightless dodo-like birds found nowhere else on the planet. You can ride from mauka to makai (mountain to sea) out in West Maui on the 300-acre Mendes Ranch owned for three generations by a proud Portuguese-Hawaiian family.

Stargazing is an old Island pastime. You can search for the Southern Cross, low on the horizon; or find Hokulea, Hawaii's own star that long ago led Polynesian voyagers in sea-going canoes to discover these islands between A.D. 300 and 500. For wilder nightlife, some visitors, no longer content with trying hula as a joke, now learn from real *kumu hula* (hula teacher).

Many of these adventures—and many more—are described in this chapter. If you want to arrange an authentic Hawaiian experience, your hotel concierge is likely in the know. The truth about Hawaii is this: Despite more than a century of American veneer, the Hawaiian Islands continue to offer travelers an authentic, natural, almost foreign experience. All you have to do is look beyond the big hotels.

Third Heaven Spa and Massage, West Maui

Location Napili Plaza Shopping Center, Suite 112-B

Phone (808) 665-0087 or (808) 665-1112

Hours On call daily, 9 a.m.–6 p.m.

Comments This is a storefront day spa near the Napili-Kapalua area of West Maui, one of dozens of independent spas and therapists operating on Maui. Third Heaven's therapist will travel to you in Lahaina, Kihei, or Napili to perform a variety of massage therapy techniques, facials, hand, foot, and scalp treatments with local ingredients—kukui-nut face therapy and seaweed hand mask, for instance, or a sea kelp facial, Maui sugar scrub, sea salt body scrub, an eye-lift treatment with collagen mask, and others. Make a double booking and save $20. Other services include acupuncture, yoga, and hot-stone therapy.

Molokai Ranch Spa, Molokai

Location West End

Phone (808) 552-2741

Hours Generally, 9 a.m.–7 p.m. daily, but flexible to accommodate guests' requests.

Comments "Spaventure" is designed to ease sore or stiff muscles after a hard day on the range, on the back of a horse or a mountain bike, hiking, kayaking, or doing myriad other activities offered as part of a stay at the Lodge and Beach Village at Molokai Ranch. Reflexology, lymph drainage, deep-tissue and Swedish massages, and aromatherapy are among the techniques to relax and refresh guests. Both spa and fitness center facilities are available.

MAUI HEALTH AND FITNESS ALTERNATIVES

Aloha Spa: Islandwide, on-call licensed massage therapists will come to your room or unit for lomilomi, sports, dual massages for two, or Swedish massage therapies. Call (808) 573-2323, or visit **www.alohaspamaui.com.**

Gold's Gym: (808) 874-2844 in Kihei; (808) 242-6851 in Wailuku

---

Other Health and Fitness Services on Maui

Most Maui resort hotels offer extensive fitness facilities so you can keep up your workout regimens. If you want to make certain you have access to a particular piece of workout equipment, ask your hotel before you book. If you're staying in a condo or B&B, on-site exercise facilities may not be an option, to say nothing of an on-site spa. However, it's easy to take advantage of local gyms at a day-use rate or local spas (like Third Heaven profiled above). And yet another option is to have a fitness trainer or massage therapist come to you. Contact the experts for details.

Spectator Sports

Maui hosts several major sporting events throughout the year. If you're looking to augment your beach time, here's a game plan.

Football

College football All-Stars gather on Maui in late January or early February for the annual Hula Bowl. After being held on Oahu for years, this contest has found new life on the Valley Isle, with the 20,000-seat War Memorial Stadium in Wailuku filled to capacity with rabid fans and, not coincidentally, talent scouts from every NFL team. Call (808) 244-3530 for information.

Although the National Football League's Pro Bowl, the All-Star end game, is held in Oahu's Aloha Stadium (a week after the Super Bowl, usually late January), most players head for Maui's high-end resorts to kick back after the final whistle. You are most likely to bump into your favorite NFL player in Wailea or Kapalua on the beach or golf course.

Golf

Three major professional golf events bring Maui into the homes of golf fans via television. If your vacation coincides with one of them, you may be lucky enough to see it in person. In early January, the Mercedes Championships at Kapalua, Maui, features top players competing for more than $4 million in prize money. Call (808) 669-2440 for details.

One of the final stops on the Senior PGA Tour is the EMC Kaanapali Classic on Maui. Held in October, this event annually draws some of the game's greatest legends and old-time favorites. Call (808) 661-3691.

Ocean Sports

Windsurf competitions are held on Maui's north shore at Kanaha and Hookipa beaches, at various times throughout the spring. The Professional Windsurfing Association's World Tour stops at Hookipa in April. Call (808) 244-3530 for information.

A surf meet provides a different kind of experience for sports fans. It's a good chance to see Hawaii's most prized individual sport at its finest while hanging out at the beach. Admission is always free. Competitors take to the water in four-man heats, each lasting 20–30 minutes. The surfers ride as many waves as they can. A panel of five judges uses a point system to name the winners. Criteria include the size of the waves, length of the rides, board control, and creative maneuvers. On Maui, check Kahului and Paia surf shops in winter (when surf's up) for details on local surf meets.

You won't be able to follow all the action of the annual Bankoh Na Wahine O Ke Kai and the Bankoh Mokokai Hoe, two 41-mile outrigger canoe races from Mokoki to Waikiki. Although the races are videotaped for local television specials, usually aired a week later from Honolulu. (The women's wahine race is held in late September, while the men's race takes place in early October.) But you can watch the exciting start on Molokai at Hale o Lono Beach as the paddlers go down to the sea and launch in the surf. Most spectators line Waikiki Beach (near Duke Kahanamoku Beach) to cheer on the six-member canoe teams paddling to a colorful finale. Both events draw international outrigger canoe teams from Australia, Canada, and Tahiti, as well as Hawaii and other states. For details, contact the Maui Visitors Bureau at (808) 989-4808.

Part Seven

Golf: Tee Time

Getting Linked on the Golf Coast

Maui, Molokai, and Lanai: the golfer's dream trio. That's why we've devoted an entire chapter to Maui County's favorite sport. Sixteen courses on three islands, with exotic names like Kapalua, Pukalani, Wailea, and The Challenge at Manele, are set like jewels by the sea, on turquoise lagoons, up on the slopes of old volcanoes, and in lush rainforests. Best of all: You can play under sunny skies virtually 365 days a year. No season, no downtime.

Nowhere else on Earth can you tee off to the sight of whale spouts out there in the largest water hazard, putt under rainbows, or play around a dormant volcano or an ancient heiau. But be forewarned: These courses are trickier than they look. They feature different grasses (from Bermuda to Kukuya, a thick-bladed African species) and hellish natural hazards, such as razor-sharp lava, gusty tradewinds, distracting views, an occasional wild pig, and tropical heat. There's only one big disadvantage: That blue ocean between you and the islands poses a time and distance problem. It's impossible to play all of Maui's courses unless you move here and take up golf full-time (which some do). The only alternative is to choose your preferred courses and catch the next plane to Maui.

Here are helpful resources for planning your Maui golf vacation:

- *Discover Hawaii's Best Golf,* an 86-page book by golf writer George Fuller. This volume provides vivid descriptions and photos of the state's top courses. Check your local bookstore, or call **(808) 487-7299**.

- *Island Golf,* a free monthly golf guide with reliable and well researched information. Visit **www.islandgolfreview.net,** or call **(808) 874-8300**.

When you choose where to stay and play, keep it in mind that many resort hotels offer package rates for room, car, and golf. Fees are lower and tee times more readily available to guests of the resorts where courses are located. Tee times are usually easy to reserve; the busiest times are weekends and winter tourist season. Most courses let you request a tee time a few days in advance. For a last-minute tee time, try **Stand-By Golf,** which gives visitors a discount. The company makes a small margin on each booking, you get discounted rates, and the course managers are happy to fill in empty time slots (call (888) 645-BOOK for details). **Maui Golf Company** also can help you arrange tee times and obtain discounts; phone (808) 874-8300. Or, ask your hotel front-desk clerk or concierge to help you. Shorts are acceptable golf attire on Hawaiian courses. Denim is kapu on some courses; that means no blue jeans. Collared shirts, a necessity to avoid sunburn on the back of your neck, are often required (no tees or tank tops). Soft-spiked shoes are common.

The Golf Courses of Maui, Molokai, and Lanai

Greens Fees

Below are Maui's typical greens fees, based on one 18-hole round, with or without cart. Rates are subject to change.

- Resort courses: $110–$180
- Semiprivate: $20–$135
- Private: $50–$100
- Public: $14–$135
- Municipal courses: $40–$54
- Military: $30–$50

Maui

The Dunes at Maui Lani, Central Maui

Established 1999; designed by Robin Nelson.

Location 1333 Mauilani Parkway, Kahului (From the Kahului Airport, head toward Lahaina on Dairy Road until you turn right on Kuihelani Highway [380]. The course is 1.5 miles off to the right. The entrance is marked by green flags.)

Phone (808) 873-0422

Web site www.mauilani.com

Status Public; 18 holes, par 72.

Tees
 Championship: 6,840 yards.
 Blue: 6,413 yards.

White: 5,833 yards.

Red: 4,768 yards.

Fees $98, includes cart. Twilight rate, $60 after 2 p.m. Club rentals, $30. Tee times accepted up to 3 months in advance (with possible cancellation fees). Accepts most major credit cards.

Facilities Driving range, 15-acre practice facility, putting greens, clubhouse, pro shop, and restaurant.

Comments Maui's newest and most surprising course is an Irish linksland–style course incorporating natural sand dunes not on the coast, where Maui has none, but inland, where the sea left them a million or so years ago in a valley. Architect Robin Nelson took advantage of ancient dunes up to 80 feet high to provide drama on several holes. His layout requires thought when playing. There is a peek of the sea now and then, but it's mostly rolling terrain with a forest of thorny kiawe trees. Instead of the beach, the killer views are of towering Haleakala. The short par 3 third hole is a classic dune hole fashioned after the sixth at Lahinch in Ireland. The course anchors a residential development.

Elleair Maui Golf Course (formerly Silversword), South Maui

Established 1987; designed by Bill Newis of Canada.

Location 1345 Piilani Highway, Kihei (on the mauka, or uphill, side of Highway 31).

Phone (808) 874-0777

Web site www.elleairgolf.com

Status Public; 18 holes, par 71.

Tees

Championship: 6,801 yards.

Men's: 6,404 yards.

Ladies': 6,003 yards.

Fees $100. $80 after 1 p.m. Carts included. Club rentals, $35. Tee times accepted 30 days in advance. Accepts Visa, MC.

Facilities Driving range, nighttime lighting, pro shop, and restaurant.

Comments Morning and late-afternoon tradewinds usually hit the course, and many holes bring the winds into play. Views of the sea are afforded from most of the greens on this public course. The signature ninth hole is a long par 4 with a pond on the right side.

Kaanapali Golf Course, West Maui

Established 1962 (North), 1997 (South); designed by Robert Trent Jones Jr.

Location Kaanapali Resort, Lahaina (Take Highway 30 past Lahaina to Kaanapali Beach Resort. Turn left at the first entrance, then right to the golf course.)

Phone (808) 661-3691 or (866) 454-GOLF

Web site www.kaanapaligolf.com

Status Resort; 8 holes, par 71 (both courses).

Tees

    Men's: North, 6,994 yards; South, 6,555 yards.

    Ladies': North, 5,417 yards; South, 5,485 yards.

Fees $130. $105 for resort guests. Includes cart. Special $75 twilight rate (South course only), noon–2:30 p.m. Twilight rate on both courses after 2:30 p.m., $77. Repeat rounds, $42. Club rentals, $45; $25 at twilight. Tee times accepted 2 days in advance. Accepts major credit cards except Discover.

Facilities Driving range, putting green, pro shop, restaurant, and locker room with showers.

Comments Two excellent 18-hole courses. The 18th on the North course is one of Hawaii's toughest finishing holes, with water hazards lined up on the right side and the kidney-shaped green bordered by two treacherous bunkers on the left. The shorter South course, with more forgiving greens and wider fairways, is the likely preference for less experienced golfers. The North hosts the annual Kaanapali Classic, a Senior PGA Tour event.

Kapalua Golf Club, West Maui

Established 1975 (Bay Course), 1980 (Village Course), and 1991 (Plantation Course); designed by Bill Crenshaw and Bill Coore.

Location 300 Kapalua Drive, Kapalua (Take Highway 30 past Lahaina and Kaanapali to Kapalua Resort, turn left at Kapalua Drive, then right to clubhouse.)

Phone Bay, (808) 669-8820; Village, (808) 669-8835; Plantation, (808) 669-8877

Web site www.kapaluamaui.com/golf

Status Resort. Bay, 18 holes, par 72; Village, 18 holes, par 71; Plantation, 18 holes, par 73.

Tees

    Men's: Bay, 6,600 yards; Village, 6,282 yards; Plantation, 7,263 yards.

    Ladies': Bay, 5,124 yards; Village, 4,876 yards; Plantation, 5,627 yards.

Fees Bay Course: $190, twilight $85. Village Course: $180, twilight $80. Plantation Course: $225, twilight $90. Club rentals, $45. Cart rentals, $20. Tee times accepted 4 days in advance. Accepts all major credit cards.

Facilities Driving range, putting green, pro shop, clubhouse, and restaurants.

Comments Surrounded by a pineapple plantation on Maui's northwest coast, Kapalua Resort's 1,500 tidy acres include three of the world's most beautiful and challenging 18-hole courses: the Village, Bay, and Plantation courses. These three courses provide drop-dead views at every turn.

The Village course features elevated tee shots on many holes, and the 367-yard, par 4 Hole 6 is one of the most scenic in Hawaii, with stately pines lined up toward the ocean. The Bay course's par 3 Hole 5 is one of the world's most dramatic signature holes, requiring a 205-yard-long tee shot over Oneloa Bay. The links-style Plantation course, highly regarded by many pros, is the home of the PGA Tour's Mercedes Championships. No tank tops or cut-offs allowed.

Makena Resort Golf Club, South Maui

Established 1983 (split into two separate courses in 1994); designed by Robert Trent Jones Jr.

Location 5415 Makena Alanui, Makena (From Kahului Airport, take Dairy Road to Piilani Highway, turn right at the end, then left at the stop sign on Wailua Alanui and go south past Wailea. The entrance is on the left.)

Phone (808) 879-3344

Web site www.makenagolf.com

Status Resort; 18 holes, par 72 (for both courses).

Tees
> *Championship:* North, 6,500 yards; South, 6,600 yards.
> *Men's:* North, 6,100 yards; South, 6,200 yards.
> *Ladies':* North, 5,300 yards; South, 5,500 yards.

Fees South Course: $140; twilight, $95. North Course: $130, twilight, $85. Club rentals, $45. Includes cart. Tee times accepted 3 days in advance. Accepts major credit cards except Discover.

Facilities Practice range, putting green, pro shop, and locker room with showers.

Comments Located by the Maui Prince Hotel. Both courses are among the state's best, with views of the ocean, Haleakala, and Molokai, Lanai, and Kahoolawe. This course was designed by noted golf architect Robert Trent Jones Jr. Severe slopes and fast greens make for very challenging play. The lack of strong winds at Makena is a big plus. The South

Course's 15th and 16th holes are among Hawaii's most picturesque oceanfront holes. The North Course is generally considered the more difficult of the two.

Sandalwood Golf Course, South Maui

Established 1991; designed by Robin Nelson and Rodney Wright.

Location 2500 Honoapiilani Highway, Wailuku (Turn uphill off Highway 30, just south of Wailuku.)

Phone (808) 242-4653

Web site www.sandalwoodgolf.com

Status Resort; 18 holes, par 72.

Tees
> *Championship:* 6,433 yards
> *Men's:* 5,918 yards
> *Ladies':* 5,162 yards

Fees $80. Golf program participants, $60. Includes cart. Twilight rate, $50 after 2 p.m. Club rentals, $35. Tee times may be reserved in advance over the phone or online. Accepts major credit cards except Discover.

Facilities Driving range, pro shop, banquet facility, locker rooms, clubhouse, putting and chipping greens, and restaurant.

Comments Robin Nelson and Rodney Wright designed this layout among sandalwood trees at Waikapu, nestled into the side of the West Maui Mountains overlooking Maui's isthmus of green cane fields. Sloping fairways and hefty tradewinds can make for a challenging day, along with a lot of elevated greens and par 4s that are long, straight, and into the wind.

Waiehu Golf Course, Central Maui

Established 9-hole course opened in 1933; back 9 added in 1966; designed by local civil engineers.

Location Wailuku (From Highway 340, make a right just past Waihee Park. The entrance is on the right.)

Phone (808) 244-5934

Web site www.mauigolf.org/waiehu

Status Municipal; 18 holes, par 72 (par 73 for women)

Tees
> *Men's:* 6,330 yards.
> *Ladies':* 5,555 yards.

Fees $26 weekdays, $30 weekends and holidays. Cart, $8 per person.

Club rentals, $16. Tee times accepted 2 days in advance. Accepts Visa, MC.

Facilities Driving range, putting green, pro shop, clubhouse, and restaurant.

Comments Maui's only municipal course is off the tourist trail. The front nine are relatively flat, the back nine are hilly in spots. This course features one lake and more than 40 sand bunkers. Three view holes front the ocean. The signature, par 5 Hole 7 plays along the beach.

Wailea Golf Club, South Maui

Established 1972 (Blue), 1993 (Gold), 1995 (Emerald); designed by Arthur Jack Snyder, converted by Robert Trent Jones Jr.

Location 100 Wailea Golf Club Drive, Wailea (From Kahului Airport, take Dairy Road to Piilani Highway, drive to southern end of the road and turn right. At the stop sign, turn left on Wailea Alanui. Turn left again into the entrances for Blue and then for Gold and Emerald.)

Phone Gold and Emerald courses, (808) 875-7450; Blue course, (808) 875-5155

Web site www.waileagolf.com

Status Resort; 18 holes, par 72 (all 3 courses).

Tees
> *Championship:* Gold, 7,078 yards; Emerald, 6,825 yards; Blue, 6,758 yards.
> *Men's:* Gold, 6,653 yards; Emerald, 6,407 yards; Blue, 6,152 yards.
> *Ladies':* Gold, 5,442 yards; Emerald, 5,268 yards; Blue, 5,291 yards.

Fees Blue Course: $95; twilight, $70 after 1 p.m. Gold Course: $185. Emerald Course: $125. Club rentals, $50. Tee times accepted 5 days in advance. Accepts all major credit cards.

Facilities Driving range, putting greens, pro shop, and restaurant.

Comments Three championship courses distinguish Wailea Resort in South Maui: the newer Gold and Emerald Courses, as well as the par 72, 18-hole Blue Course, considered the Grand Lady of Wailea. *Golf for Women Magazine* recently named the Wailea Golf Club one of the three most women-friendly golf facilities in the country. The Gold Course at Wailea gilds the lily on this island already noted for great courses. This Robert Trent Jones Jr. course is a rugged, natural-style 7,070-yard par 72 layout that plays over the foothills of Haleakala.

All three courses have breathtaking ocean and mountain views. The Blue Course, with wide, open fairways, is the easiest, but it does have 74 bunkers and 4 water hazards. The Gold Course has traditionally been host to the nationally televised Senior PGA Tour's Senior Skins game in January.

The Emerald Course offers stunning views of Haleakala and the Pacific. Considered a friendlier course for high-handicap players, the course's signature hole is the 18th, a 553-yard par 5 challenge with a downhill slope. Collared shirts are required.

Lanai

Lanai may have more deer than people, but it boasts two stunning resort golf courses: The Experience at Koele and The Challenge at Manele. The Challenge is a target-style course carved from lava cliffs by the sea. The water hazard on the par 3, signature 12th hole at Manele is a wave-lashed coast of jagged lava. This course on the south coast of Lanai will test your patience and increase your impolite vocabulary.

If you're still game, face The Experience's signature hole, which plays into a ravine from a knoll 250 feet above the fairway of this upland course. The layout begins high on the slopes of 3,366-foot Mount Lanaihale, complete with Norfolk pine forest and a gallery of deer, pheasant, and wild turkey. This course features the only bentgrass greens in Hawaii.

The Challenge at Manele

Established 1993; designed by Jack Nicklaus.

Location Manele Bay (Transportation via Lanai Resorts shuttle.)

Phone (808) 565-2222

Web site www.manelebayhotel.com

Status Resort; 18 holes, par 72.

Tees
  Championship: 7,039 yards.
  Men's: 6,684 yards.
  Ladies': 5,024 yards.

Fees $225. $185 for guests staying at The Lodge at Koele, Manele Bay Hotel, or Hotel Lanai. Club rentals, $50 for full round or $35 for 9 holes. Tee times accepted 30 days in advance. Accepts major credit cards except Discover.

Facilities Driving range, putting and chipping greens, locker rooms, pro shop, and restaurant.

Comments This links-style course offers great ocean views from every hole. Fairways are open; greens are small and fast. Built on the side of a hill, the course features several changes of elevation and requires several blind tee and approach shots. Winds often come into play. Bring extra balls for Hole 12, a 202-yard par 3 that includes a tee shot across 200 yards of Pacific Ocean. The tee area on a cliff 150 feet above the crashing surf is the picturesque spot where Bill and Melinda Gates were married in 1994. Archeological sites are among the course's features. Collared shirts are required; no denim allowed.

The Experience at Koele

Established 1991; designed by Greg Norman and Ted Robinson.

Location Lanai City (Transportation via Lanai Resorts shuttle.)

Phone (808) 565-4653

Web site www.lodgeatkoele.com

Status Resort; 18 holes, par 72.

Tees
  Championship: 7,014 yards.
  Men's: 6,217 yards.
  Ladies': 5,424 yards.

Fees $225; $185 ($100 for 9 holes) for guests staying at The Lodge at Koele, Manele Bay Hotel, or Hotel Lanai. Club rentals, $50 for full round or $20 for 9 holes. Tee times accepted 30 days in advance. Accepts major credit cards except Discover.

Facilities Driving range, putting and chipping greens, executive putting course, clubhouse, and snack bar.

Comments A magnificent course designed by Greg Norman and Ted Robinson, the front nine were carved from the side of a mountain, while the back nine are more open and flat. Water features are prominent, with seven lakes, streams, and waterfalls. The par 4, 444-yard Hole 8 is the signature, featuring a 250-foot drop from tee to fairway, with a lake bordering one side and thick shrubs and trees lining the other. Even Jack Nicklaus needed seven attempts to get the ball in play here. Hole 17 is surrounded by a lake. Collared shirts are required; no denim allowed.

Molokai

Nobody expects much of Molokai, so it is a big surprise when you discover one of the oldest golf courses in Hawaii and realize it's still one of the best. That's Ironwood Hills, an island-style course that is a real delight to play. Once there were two golf courses on Molokai, and there may be again when Kaluakoi Resorts reopens on the island's West End. With six holes along the sea, Kaluakoi Golf Course is another little-known and underplayed 18-hole, par 71 resort layout that will leave you gasping. While you wait, don't miss Ironwood.

DANGEROUS DEVELOPMENT

If you go to Hawaii, you must be careful. They are out there. Watching. You almost always can feel their presence. Sometime, you may even see them. Night marchers still walk ancient paths to conduct rituals and ceremonies. *Kahunas* (priests) talk to rocks and the rocks talk back.

More than a century and a half after the demise of idolatry and human sacrifice and despite the work of zealous Christian missionaries, Hawaii is alive with mystery. Some may call it devil's work, but in Hawaii where people live in both past and present, it's the old Hawaiian way.

The ancient ways are there just beneath the surface of modern island life. Hawaii is alive with ancestral spirits, animism, primal fears, and both old and new *kapu* (taboos); around the edges like myth and legend, plus religions introduced from Japan, China, and America.

Some places are still *kapu,* off-limits. Secret caves contain old canoes and feathered capes of long dead *alii* (chiefs, nobles). There are signs to heed, rules to obey. Or else . . .

Or else inexplicable things happen. Houses shake. Freeways collapse, And bulldozers fly. It happened on the Big Island where developers are carving multimillion-dollar beach estates on sacred land, suggesting that angry ancestral Hawaiians haunt the project.

It's enough to give you chicken skin. That's the local pidgin expression for goosebumps. In Hawaii, chicken skin is common as palm trees.

Ghosts of angry ancestral Hawaiians, it seems, regularly halt construc-

Ironwood Hills

Established　1939; designed by Del Monte plantation executives.

Location　Kualapuu, Kalae Highway, just before the Mule Ride Barn on the road to the lookout.

Phone　(808) 567-6000

Status　Private; 9 holes, par 35.

Tee　3,088 yards.

Fees　$18; cart, $6 per person. Accepts most major credit cards.

Facilities　Pro shop.

Comments　This historic plantation course at 1,200 feet in Molokai's cool uplands is one of the oldest golf courses in Hawaii and is still popular. Named for the two prominent natural elements—ironwood trees and

tion projects, especially golf courses where developers turn Hawaiian temples into hazards.

On Maui, the Ritz-Carlton Kapalua had to move its multimillion-dollar beachfront hotel off the beach when bulldozers uncovered a mass grave in coastal sand dunes. The Ritz avoided the wrath of displaced spirits by dedicating the graveyard as a memorial.

Not so lucky are Kieweit Pacific Co. crews who completed Honolulu's so-called H-3 interstate freeway, a ribbon of concrete snaking through the Halawa Valley in the majestic 3,000-foot high Koolau mountain range on Oahu. Strange mishaps kept stalling construction of what now is the world's most expensive freeway—a 16.1-mile stretch of road begun in the 1960s with a $1.6 billion price tag.

Hawaiians consider the valley to be sacred; the home of Papahanumoku, a female god of the native religion. In 1993, a curse was placed on the project when construction violated a rare, ancient heiau (altar or temple) where Hawaiian women once observed rites.

On July 27, 1996, the freeway's elevated ramp collapsed for no apparent reason. The incident, in which four 120-foot, 40-ton concrete girders fell, was the latest in a serious of mysterious accidents. Two workers died, eight were injured, and many walked off the job.

"Troubles on H-3 Strengthen Beliefs in Power of Supernatural Wrath," said a page one headline in the *Honolulu Advertiser*.

rolling hills—the course has open fairways, thick foliage, and excellent island views. One of the best, little-known courses in the Pacific, this course is just plain fun.

Part Eight

Dining and Restaurants

Everyone has to eat, especially on vacation, and dining island-style is one of the great joys of a trip to Maui County's islands. If yours is a timid palate, you'll be comforted to know that a wide assortment of familiar mainland fast-food restaurants and other chains can be found on Maui, and there is even a KFC on Molokai. But if your sense of adventure extends to dining, you have endless choices. You can enjoy the dishes of many cultures, served fast or leisurely, at great or small cost. You'll have to leave the resort environs to find a lot of the good, affordable restaurants, but hotels and resort shopping centers do offer excellent prospects as well. If you're cooking in a condo or vacation rental, the markets and fruit stands are full of intriguing ingredients. If your culinary talents include only cutting a ripe papaya in half and scooping it out with a spoon, you've got a promising start on the day.

Hawaii Regional Cuisine and Multicultural Cuisine

As luxury hotels proliferated during the late 1980s, they brought talented young chefs out to the Islands to tackle the food problem: Most of what had been served in Hawaii hotel dining rooms for decades was frozen, or at least made of ingredients from elsewhere, and predictable, if not boring. The Islands, despite their terrific growing weather, imported almost everything in the stores and restaurants. Tropical bugs were a problem for mass-grown produce, and there was little call for gourmet foods in a plantation-based local economy. But things changed. New farmers immigrated, including the Vietnamese, who grow the fresh herbs required for their own dishes. Many of the sugar and pineapple plantations of Maui, Molokai, and Lanai turned to tourism as a cash crop, changing the way local people live, shop, eat, and use the land. The chefs went out to coax farmers and fishermen to provide what was needed in the way of fresh ingredients: prime fish and seafood, flavorful vegetables, exotic fruits. The chefs also talked to local cooks and sampled homecooking and favorite local dishes. Inspired, they began to meld their classic European training and fresh local ingredients with Asian methods and flavors as well as the traditions of local tables, and a new cuisine was born. Hawaii Regional Cuisine, or HRC, was early to the fusion movement that subsequently swept the country, and it is still unmatched, in our opinion, since it is based on Island foods and geared to Island tastes.

HRC also raised "hotel food" in the Islands to a whole new standard. The chefs who developed it in hotels have moved on to start their own restaurants, but they left a strong legacy at the hotel kitchens. The Maui resorts continue to attract bright stars, including the Wolfgang Puck restaurant Spago at Four Seasons Maui at Wailea. Today, the HRC celebrity chef restaurants are often located in unlikely places—an old plantation general store, neighborhood and resort shopping centers— and count on local residents for a great share of their clientele. Their fare is definitely worth seeking out. Universally, hotel food today is at least pretty good in the Islands—but it's also, almost universally, outrageously expensive. If that matters to you, stay in a place where you can easily seek alternatives nearby, or in a unit or suite with a kitchen.

Although HRC is popular and pervasive, plenty of other Maui restaurants feature different cuisines entirely. If you're not a foodie, you can still eat very well, especially if you like Chinese food, Japanese food, Korean food, French food, Mexican food, American food, Southeast Asian food, Italian food, vegetarian food, seafood, and oh yes, Hawaiian food.

All kinds of cuisine are available in the Islands, because people of many ethnic and cultural backgrounds live there and love to eat the foods of their own heritage—and everyone else's, too. It's a Hawaiian passion. Island hospitality is based on an ancient tradition, the invitation to share food first with strangers or travelers who appear at the door and then find out why they stopped by. When it comes to fast food, it's hard to catch up with the Island pace. Plantation people were usally in a hurry to eat, because their lunchtime was short and their appetites sharpened by hard work, and the tradition lives on. In many local and Asian restaurants, patrons order from a to-go deli board or are barely seated with menus before a server appears. An enduring plantation legacy called the Plate Lunch remains a mainstay of local food to take out or eat in—two or three hearty entrees of various ethnic origins (fish tempura, beef stew, and pork adobo, for example), plus the obligatory two scoops rice and one of macaroni salad. However, for food on the go, none can beat the manapua truck, a mobile wagon whose driver sells food from a makeshift stand in the vehicle. Hot food is already cooked and waiting in steamers for patrons, who line up outside to get *manapua*, the Hawaiian name for the steamed Chinese dim sum called char siu bao (fresh rolls filled with barbecued pork), other hand-held snacks, and takeout plate-lunch meals. The lunch wagons, born of plantation days, still pull up in front of office buildings and beach parks. If you prefer a more leisurely meal, restaurants on Maui, Molokai, and Lanai range from old-fashioned 1950s eateries with unremarkable atmosphere and modestly priced favorite local dishes to very sophisticated world-class dining rooms with oceanfront views and prices to match. You can take advantage of the Islands' fine weather to eat in open-air restaurants or outdoors just about anytime, anywhere, and at any price.

Go Fish

Hawaii's bounty of ocean fishes is truly exceptional. Most coastal areas have at least a few prized regional fishes and shellfishes, but Hawaii has a whole bucketful of noteworthy species that move through or are native to the mid-Pacific, and more that are imported from around the Pacific Rim. A few basics you should know about fish in Hawaii: The catch of the day on Maui means just that. The fish on your plate was likely in the ocean that morning. When you order fresh seafood from Lahaina to Maunaloa to Hana, it's really fresh. That's in no small part because it is eaten raw in local dishes like Hawaiian poke—marinated cubes of fish, mixed with ingredients such as crunchy seaweed, onion, finely ground kukui nuts, hot pepper flakes, sesame seeds and sesame oil, soy sauce or ginger—and sashimi, slices of fresh raw fish served with wasabi (hot green Japanese horseradish) and soy sauce, garnished with pink slices of pickled ginger. Sushi, generally a molded tidbit of seasoned rice topped or rolled with a slice of raw fish or other seafood and seaweed, can be made with a host of fishes, or no fish, or even Spam (try musubi—rice and Spam wrapped in nori—for breakfast). Sometimes it's made vegetarian style with cucumber or Japanese vegetable pickles.

A land with many fishponds was called a "fat" land (aina momona).

—Samuel Kamakau, *The Works of the People of Old*

Fish in Hawaii is seldom frozen or battered and fried, the standard method of delivering seafood on the East Coast and elsewhere, and as a result, it's seldom cheap. Be aware that crabmeat in the Islands is often the imitation variety that features a bit of crab juice flavoring some innocuous white fish. There are a few local crabs, Kona crab and rock crabs, but there is no continental shelf for other crabs to prowl here. The rock crabs are eaten raw and seasoned as a kind of poke. Always with fish, if you have doubts, ask whether it is fresh or frozen. On Maui, there's no sense eating fish that is not fresh, since a new supply of one species or another comes in to the market every morning. Trouble is most visitors don't know their opakapaka from a rainbow trout.

The fish in Hawaii are known by a confusing but colorful jumble of Hawaiian and Japanese words. Since the State of Hawaii began marketing Hawaiian fish to the mainland some years ago, you may be familiar with fishes that fly well: Ahi, or yellowfin tuna, and mahimahi, or dolphinfish, are both so well known that local tuna and dolphin fish on the mainland coasts are sometimes identified by their exotic Hawaiian names. You more likely know a fish that formerly was only exported but now shows up on Island menus and in markets: shutome, or Pacific swordfish. But when opah, ono, moi, and monchong appear on the menu, you get caught in a fish trap. Don't let it happen. You can learn to talk fish like a local. Here's a quick guide to the fish of Hawaii most likely to land on your dinner table.

- **Ahi,** or yellowfin tuna, has red, translucent flesh that turns to a firm light gray when cooked. It's best when only seared on the outsides and still rare in the middle, or at least undercooked and still juicy. And by all means, buy ahi steaks at any Maui grocery store and grill them fast on hot coals with a soy and fresh ginger marinade for an excellent home dinner.

- **Mahimahi,** also called dolphinfish or dorado, has firm, light flesh that cooks to white. This is the fish that tastes so good they named it twice. Not to be confused with Flipper, the dolphinfish is a bullheaded fighter with gold colors that flash like neon rainbows when hooked. A good fish to catch, an even better fish to eat, it's the most common fish in Hawaii's restaurants. It's excellent solo when fresh, but it also goes well with trimmings, especially macadamia nuts and lemon-butter sauce.

- **Moi,** also called threadfish, was popular with early Hawaiians who raised it in captivity. Moi is a traditional favorite of Islanders today. Everyone likes the moist, mild white flesh of this fish steamed and served over rice with bok choi.

- **Monchong,** or big-scale pomfret, is an Asia-Pacific favorite. A smooth-textured, delicate-flavored fish, moonchong cooks to a moist white finish; it's excellent with Chinese vegetables.

- **Onaga,** the most prized snapper, is also known as ruby or long-tailed snapper. Its thick, pale-pink flesh cooks to white with a delicate flavor and silky texture when baked slightly underdone.

- **Ono,** or wahoo, is a firm-textured, mild-flavored flaky white fish often served in thick steaks. Once you're hooked on wahoo you may never eat mahimahi again. *Ono,* by the way, is Hawaiian for "delicious" and the ono lives up to its name. Most fishermen would rather hook and eat an ono than mahi.

- **Opah,** or moonfish, is a popular dinner entree around the Pacific. This big round fish is a rich delicate fish that cooks to light pink.

- **Opakapaka,** or crimson snapper, is a favorite Island fish (partly because people like to say its name). This pink-fleshed, delicate fish is often served steamed Chinese-style, or crusted and sautéed.

- **Shutome,** or broadbill swordfish, is a firm, well-textured, mild-flavored pinkish fish that cooks to white. Cook it fast, like ahi, and Hawaiian swordfish will be moist and flavorful, not dry and dull.

Going Shopping

If you don't know how to bait a hook and land a fish, don't worry. You can catch a good tasting fish at the local market. On Maui you can find many of the fish listed above in the supermarkets (24 hours a day at the Kahului Safeway) or occasionally, at the weekly produce markets where fish vendors may sell their fresh catch from coolers. You will also find sweet, juicy Maui pineapple, strawberry papaya, chermoya, small, lemony apple bananas, starfruit, sweet Maui onions, Asian greens, and long Japanese cucumbers and eggplants in the cornucopia of Maui farmers' markets. Fish vendors sell fresh line-caught Pacific ono, mahi, opakapaka, moonfish, and sometimes live, farmed shrimp.

Look for fresh green or purple *limu* (seaweed) at ethnic groceries or ask at the supermarket fish counters. As you shop, check out the Asian deli sections complete with a wide choice of chilled specialties like kim chee, fish cake, lomilomi salmon, and vegetables as well as a bewildering choice of condiments and Asian sauces.

In Lahaina, Nagasako, the large Japanese supermarket, sells wasabi, jasmine rice, glass noodles, and red Hawaiian sea salt, known as alae, best for seasoning poke. Look for fresh green or purple limu seaweed at ethnic markets, though even supermarkets carry pickled condiments, pickled ginger, and Asian sauces.

For a treat at home or in your condo or hotel room, slice sashimi and serve it with shredded daikon, soy sauce and wasabi, and pink pickled ginger. It's excellent with ice-cold beer.

The Restaurants

Our Favorite Island Restaurants

Explaining the Ratings

We have developed detailed profiles for the best restaurants and for those that offer some special reason to visit, be it decor, ethnic appeal, or bargain prices. Each profile features an easily scanned heading that allows you, in just a second, to check out the restaurant's name, cuisine, overall rating, cost, quality rating, and value rating.

Cuisine   In a locale where Hawaii Regional Cuisine has been seeking to define itself only since 1992, categorizing cuisine becomes a challenging endeavor. Hawaii Regional Cuisine itself is a blend of ethnic foods and cooking styles, so we've ended up with dishes that incorporate Asian flavors, Hawaiian flavors, Cajun flavors, Pacific Rim flavors, Mediterranean flavors, and more. Many chefs prefer not to be categorized at all, as they are afraid this will limit others' perception of their creativity. In most cases, we let restaurant owners or chefs name their own categories. In many cases, fusion cuisines are called simply "contemporary cuisine." Even restaurants that once served classic French cuisine now prepare sauces with a lighter hand and are innovative with island ingredients, one of the prerequisites of Hawaii Regional Cuisine. You can get an idea of the type of food served from the heading, then glean a better understanding by reading the detailed descriptions of specialty items and other recommendations.

Overall rating   The overall rating encompasses the entire dining experience, including style, service, and ambience, in addition to the taste, presentation, and quality of the food. Five stars is the highest rating possible and connotes the best of everything. Four-star restaurants are exceptional, three-star restaurants are well above average, and two-star restaurants are good. One star indicates an average restaurant that demonstrates an unusual capability in some area of specialization—for example, an otherwise unmemorable place that has great saimin (noodle soup).

Cost   To the right of the cuisine is an expense description that provides a comparative sense of how much dinner entrees will cost. Dinner entrees in Hawaii usually include salad or soup and vegetables. Appetizers, desserts, drinks, and tips are excluded. Categories and related prices are listed below:

Inexpensive	$14 and less per person
Moderate	$15–$30
Expensive	More than $30 per person

Quality rating   To the right of the cost appear stars that rate food quality on a scale of five stars, where five is the best rating attainable. It is based expressly on the taste, freshness of ingredients, preparation, presentation, and creativity of the food served. There is no consideration of price. If you want the best food available, and cost is not an issue, you need look no further than the quality ratings.

Value rating   If, on the other hand, you are looking for both quality and value, then you should check the value rating. Remember, the perception of value can vary from state to state and country to country.

Hawaii is a tourist destination, so restaurant prices in the state probably compare favorably with prices in New York, San Francisco, and other major tourist destinations, but not so favorably with smaller, residential towns. Because it is a common perception that hotel restaurants are universally overpriced (where else would you pay $4–$6 for a glass of orange juice?), we have indicated restaurants of this sort with a two-star rating rather than a discouraging one star. The two-star rating is meant to convey that yes, the restaurant charges perhaps more than you would pay for a similar entree somewhere else, but because the setting, service, and preparation are exceptional, it's still worth the splurge. We wouldn't want to rate the restaurant one star, causing a reader to automatically forgo a special dining experience. The value ratings are defined as follows:

★★★★★   Exceptional value; a real bargain

★★★★   Good value

★★★   Fair value; you get exactly what you pay for

★★   Somewhat overpriced

★   Significantly overpriced

Locating the restaurant   On the far right is a designation for the restaurants region: West, Central, South, or Upcountry Maui, Lanai, or Molokai. This will give you a general idea of where the restaurant described is located. The restaurants are plotted on the maps in the introduction, and their addresses are included to further assist you.

Payment   We've listed the type of payment accepted at each restaurant using the following codes:

AE   American Express
CB   Carte Blanche
JCB   Japan Credit Bank
D   Discover
DC   Diners Club
MC   MasterCard
V   Visa

Who's included   Restaurants open and close frequently in Hawaii, so most of those we've included have a proven track record. However, some of the newest upscale restaurants owned and operated by chefs who have become local celebrities have been included to keep the guide as complete and up-to-date as possible. The list is highly selective. Our leaving out a particular place does not necessarily indicate that the restaurant is not good, only that it was not ranked among the best in its genre. Detailed profiles of individual restaurants follow in alphabetical order at the end of this chapter. Below you will find our personal favorites for various cuisines. Under "More Recommendations" you'll find a few restaurants that aren't profiled, but for one reason or another have unique appeal to special appetites.

Our personal list of bests (profiles follow):

Best Asian Fusion Sansei Seafood Restaurant and Sushi Bar, Kapalua or Kihei

Best Celebrity Chef Wolfgang Puck, Spago at Four Seasons Resort

Best Fish on the Beach Mama's Fish House, Paia

Best French Chez Paul, Olowalu, West Maui

Best Hawaii Regional Fare Haliimaile General Store, Upcountry Maui

Best Let's-Go-Someplace-Spicy Manana Garage, Kahului

Best Pizza BJ's Chicago Pizzeria, Lahaina

Best Vegetarian Stella Blues Café, Kihei

MAUI'S BEST RESTAURANTS RANKED BY CUISINE					
Restaurant	Overall Rating	Cost	Quality Rating	Value Rating	Region
American					
Stella Blues Café	★★★★½	Mod	★★★½	★★★½	South Maui
David Paul's Lahaina Grill	★★★★	Exp	★★★★½	★★★	West Maui
Henry Clay's Rotisserie	★★★	Mod	★★★½	★★★★	Lanai
Contemporary					
The Formal Dining Room, The Lodge at Koele	★★★★★	Exp	★★★★½	★★★	Lanai
Spago at Four Seasons Resort Maui	★★★★½	Exp	★★★★½	★★★	South Maui
Gerard's	★★★★	Exp	★★★★	★★★★	West Maui
Plantation House Restaurant	★★★	Mod	★★★★	★★★	West Maui
Continental					
The Bay Club	★★★★	Exp	★★★★	★★★	West Maui
French					
Chez Paul	★★★★½	Exp	★★★★★	★★★★	West Maui
Hawaii Regional					
Haliimaile General Store	★★★★★	Mod/Exp	★★★★★	★★★★½	Upcountry Maui
IO	★★★★½	Mod	★★★★½	★★★	West Maui

MAUI'S BEST RESTAURANTS RANKED BY CUISINE *(continued)*

Restaurant	Overall Rating	Cost	Quality Rating	Value Rating	Region
Hawaii Regional *(continued)*					
PacificO	★★★★½	Exp	★★★★½	★★★	West Maui
Hula Grill	★★★★	Mod	★★★★	★★★★½	West Maui
Roy's Kahana Bar and Grill	★★★★	Mod/Exp	★★★★	★★★	West and South Maui
Kai Ku Ono	★★★½	Mod	★★★	★★★★	South Maui
Maunaloa Room	★★★	Mod	★★★	★★★	Molokai
Island (traditional)					
Aloha Mixed Plate	★★★	Inexp	★★★	★★★	West Maui
The Village Grill	★★	Mod	★★★½	★★★	Molokai
Blue Ginger Café	★	Inexp	★★★	★★	Lanai
Italian and Pizza					
Molokai Pizza Café	★★★	Inexp	★★★½	★★★★	Molokai
BJ's Chicago Pizzeria	★★★	Inexp	★★★	★★★	West Maui
Japanese Fusion					
Sansei Seafood Restaurant and Sushi Bar	★★★★★	Mod/Exp	★★★★½	★★★★	West and South Maui
Mediterranean					
Ihilani	★★★★½	Exp	★★★★½	★★★	Lanai
Longhi's	★★★	Mod	★★★	★★★	West and South Maui
Nuevo Latino					
Manana Garage	★★★★	Mod	★★★★	★★★	Central Maui
Seafood					
Maalaea Waterfront Restaurant	★★★½	Exp	★★★★½	★★★	Central Maui
Mama's Fish House	★★★½	Exp	★★★★½	★★★	Central Maui
Steak and Seafood					
Kimo's	★★★	Inexp/Mod	★★	★★★	West Maui
Vietnamese					
A Saigon Café	★★★	Inexp	★★★★	★★★★★	Central Maui

MAUI'S BEST RESTAURANTS BY REGION

Restaurant	Overall Rating	Cost	Cuisine
West Maui			
Aloha Mixed Plate	★★★	Inexp	Island
The Bay Club	★★★★	Exp	Continental
BJ's Chicago Pizzeria	★★★	Inexp	Italian and Pizza
Chez Paul	★★★★½	Mod/Exp	French
David Paul's Lahaina Grill	★★★★	Exp	American
Gerard's	★★★★	Exp	Contemporary
Hula Grill	★★★★	Mod	Hawaii Regional
IO	★★★★½	Mod	Hawaii Regional
Kimo's	★★★	Inexp/Mod	Steak and Seafood
Longhi's	★★★	Mod	Mediterranean
PacificO	★★★★½	Exp	Hawaii Regional
Plantation House Restaurant	★★★	Mod	Contemporary
Roy's Kahana Bar and Grill	★★★★	Mod/Exp	Hawaiian Fusion
Sansei Seafood Restaurant and Sushi Bar	★★★★★	Mod/Exp	Japanese Fusion
South Maui			
Kai Ku Ono	★★★½	Mod	Hawaii Regional
Longhi's	★★★	Mod	Mediterranean
Roy's Kihei Bar and Grill	★★★★	Mod/Exp	Hawaiian Fusion
Sansei Seafood Restaurant and Sushi Bar	★★★★★	Mod/Exp	Japanese Fusion
Spago at Four Seasons Resort Maui	★★★★½	Exp	Contemporary
Stella Blues Café	★★★★½	Mod	American
Central Maui			
Maalaea Waterfront Restaurant	★★★½	Exp	Seafood
Mama's Fish House	★★★½	Exp	Seafood
Manana Garage	★★★★	Mod	Nuevo Latino
A Saigon Café	★★★	Inexp	Vietnamese
Upcountry Maui			
Haliimaile General Store	★★★★★	Mod/Exp	Hawaii Regional

Restaurant	Overall Rating	Cost	Cuisine
MAUI'S BEST RESTAURANTS BY REGION *(continued)*			
Molokai			
Maunaloa Room	★★★	Mod	Hawaii Regional
Molokai Pizza Café	★★★	Inexp	Pizza
The Village Grill	★★	Mod	Island
Lanai			
Blue Ginger Café	★	Inexp	Island
The Formal Dining Room, The Lodge at Koele	★★★★★	Exp	Contemporary
Henry Clay's Rotisserie	★★★	Mod	American
Ihilani	★★★★½	Exp	Mediterranean

More Recommendations

Best Oceanfront Restaurant Five Palms, 2960 South Kihei Road, Kihei; (808) 879-2607

Best Brew Pub Fish & Game Brewing Co. and Rotisserie, 4405 Honoapiilani Highway, Kahuna Gateway Shopping Center; (808) 669-3474

Best Deli Caffe Ciao in Fairmont Kea Lani Maui, Wailea; (808) 875-4100

Best Late-Night Restaurant Lahaina Coolers, 180 Dickenson, Lahaina; (808) 661-7082

Best Al Fresco Lunch Cafe Jacques Northshore Restaurant, 120 Hana Highway, Paia; (808) 579-8844

Best Local Plate Lunch Sam Sato's, Wailuku Millyard complex; (808) 244-7124

Best (Fish and Other) Tacos Maui Tacos, Napili Plaza, Napili; (808) 665-0222

Restaurant Profiles

Maui

Aloha Mixed Plate ★★★

ISLAND | INEXPENSIVE | QUALITY ★★★ | VALUE ★★★ | WEST MAUI

Beachfront, 1285 Front Street, Lahaina; (808) 661-3322

Reservations N/A

When to go Sunset or lunch

Entree range $3–$14

Payment V, MC, AE, DC, D

Service rating ★★½

Parking Free, but limited in front

Bar Full service

Wine selection Limited

Dress Casual

Disabled access Adequate

Customers Islanders and tourists

Lunch and dinner Daily, 10:30 a.m.–10 p.m.

Setting and atmosphere Can't beat it—beach- and oceanfront gardens (next to the Old Lahaina Luau gardens), shaded by huge trees. The bar has a shed roof, though, in case of blessings (showers).

House specialties Coconut prawns are the prize-winning pupu (appetizer). The plate lunch, on paper plates, is also popular. If you can't swing the price of a luau, you can get the flavor at least with a Hawaiian plate, featuring such local favorites as kalua pig and cabbage, Korean barbecued beef and short ribs, laulau, lomilomi salmon, macaroni salad, and two scoops of rice, followed by *haupia* (coconut pudding) for dessert. Small appetites will be appeased with a miniplate of shoyu chicken or the other plate lunch specials.

The Bay Club ★★★★

CONTINENTAL | EXPENSIVE | QUALITY ★★★★ | VALUE ★★★ | WEST MAUI

Kapalua Bay Hotel, I Bay Drive, Kapalua; (808) 669-4650;
www.kapaluabayhotel.com

Reservations Highly recommended

When to go Sunset

Entrée range Dinner $21–$38

Payment V, MC, AE, DC, JCB

Service rating ★★★★

Parking In adjacent lot

Bar Full service

Wine selection Good

Dress Resort attire
Disabled access Good
Customers Islanders and tourists

Dinner Daily, 6–9 p.m.

Setting and atmosphere The oceanfront location offers a superlative view through a wall of windows. Tables on the open-air deck fill up quickly, so it's best to make reservations and go early to catch the full romantic effect of sunset. Inside, the restaurant resembles a plantation-era beach home, with a fireplace near the entry, a piano, and a comfortable room with low lighting.

House specialties Dinner begins with crispy fresh lavosh served with salmon mousse. Caesar salad is prepared tableside. Main courses change seasonally but might include scallops and prawns with white truffle risotto and veal demi-glacé; half a roasted duck with butternut squash or grilled rack of lamb with Molokai sweet potatoes and pineapple-starfruit chutney.

Other recommendations The day's fresh Hawaiian catch can be prepared Mediterranean style (with tomato concasse, lemon, capers, parsley, garlic, and anchovies, in white-wine butter sauce) or Oriental style (with shiitake mushrooms, scallions, cilantro, and soy and sesame oil sauce). Maui bouillabaise features Kona lobster and local fish. Try seasonal specialties like pohole fern shoot salad in spring.

Summary and comments Shuttles run from Kapalua Bay and the Ritz-Carlton Kapalua, to the Bay Club, but the most pleasant way to get there when staying at Kapalua Bay Hotel is to walk, strolling along the palm-shaded path beside the picturesque bay and beach. Diners may charge checks to their rooms in either hotel.

BJ's Chicago Pizzeria ★★★

ITALIAN AND PIZZA | INEXPENSIVE | QUALITY ★★★ | VALUE ★★★ | WEST MAUI

730 Front Street, Lahaina; (808) 661-0700

Reservations Suggested
When to go Sunset, for the oceanfront view
Entrée range $8–$25
Payment MC, V, AE, D
Service rating ★★★
Parking Paid nearby lots
Bar Full
Wine selection Limited

Dress Casual

Disabled access Fair

Customers Tourists, Islanders

Lunch and dinner Sunday–Thursday, 11 a.m.–11 p.m.; Friday and Saturday, 11 a.m.–midnight

Setting and atmosphere Second-floor, Lahaina waterfront view.

House specialties Deep-dish, Chicago-style pizza so good that local folks brave the Lahaina traffic to come into town to get it. Pizzas include shrimp thermidor and barbecued chicken as well as cheese and tomato, veggie, and ham with pineapple. Appetizers, such as spinach and artichoke pizzadilla and Charleston-style crabcakes will get you started.

Other recommendations Pasta dishes, salads and sandwiches are other choices to wash down with a wide choice of microbrewery beers.

Summary and comments When you need a pizza fix, come here. It satisfies, with standard and creative choices and a sunset view Lake Michigan just can't match.

Chez Paul ★★★★½

FRENCH | EXPENSIVE | QUALITY ★★★★★ | VALUE ★★★★ | WEST MAUI

Highway 30 (6 miles south of Lahaina), Olowalu Village; (808) 661-3843; www.chezpaul.net

Reservations Highly recommended

When to go Dinner seatings

Entrée range $29–$39

Payment V, MC, AE, D

Service rating ★★★★★

Parking Free in adjacent lot

Bar Full service

Wine selection Good; wine cellar

Dress Resort attire

Disabled access Good

Customers Islanders, a few tourists, celebrities

Dinner Daily, seatings at 6:30 p.m. and 8:30 p.m.

Setting and atmosphere "Centrally located in the middle of nowhere," proclaims chef/owner Patrick Callerac, and he's right. But it's only six miles to Lahaina and absolutely worth the drive to savor the cuisine of this bright, personable chef, formerly executive chef at the Ritz-Carlton, Kapalua. His approach is classic Provençal with an island touch. You might smell the garlic wafting in through your open car window if you drive past this little blink-and-you'll-miss-it roadside restaurant at Olowalu, a wide spot in the road and most unlikely setting for a great French restaurant.

House specialties Don't miss the homemade duck pâté, a great starter before entrées such as fresh Kona lobster, fresh fish in champagne sauce, or slow-roasted duck in cassis sauce. The desserts to die for are crème brûlée baked in a Maui pineapple and banana cobbler with coconut ice cream.

Other recommendations This is the place to satisfy yearnings for classic French dishes—escargots, warm goat cheese salad, coq au vin, tournedos with peppercorn brandy cream sauce, and crêpes suzette prepared at your table.

Summary and comments It's so tempting not to move your car from its Maui resort parking space, but this cozy (14 tables plus banquettes and a private room) restaurant is definitely worth the short drive from Lahaina.

David Paul's Lahaina Grill ★★★★

CONTEMPORARY AMERICAN | EXPENSIVE | QUALITY ★★★★½ | VALUE ★★★ |
WEST MAUI

127 Lahainaluna Road, Lahaina; (808) 667-5117; www.lahainagrill.com

Reservations Highly recommended
When to go Early or late to avoid the 7 p.m. crowd
Entrée range $29–$39
Payment V, MC, AE, DC
Service rating ★★★★★
Parking On street or in adjacent lot
Bar Full service
Wine selection Extensive, many by the glass
Dress Resort wear
Disabled access Good, separate wheelchair access
Customers Islanders and tourists

Dinner Daily, 6–10 p.m.
Setting and atmosphere This hopping bistro in the middle of the Lahaina action has two dining rooms and a private, intimate room for Chef's Table dinners for up to eight. Diners may also eat at the bar. Soft pastels and flowers restore a measure of calm to the somewhat hectic atmosphere.

House specialties David Paul's signature dish of tequila shrimp with firecracker rice competes with the kalua duck with reduced plum-wine sauce, seasonal vegetables, and Lundberg rice for first place on the dinner menu. Kona coffee–roasted rack of lamb boasts a full-flavored Kona coffee–Cabernet demi-glaze served with garlic mashed potatoes.

Other recommendations The vegetarian eggplant Napoleon and the Maui onion–crusted seared ahi with vanilla bean rice and an apple cider soy-butter vinaigrette are light enough to reserve room for dessert—a luscious pie of raspberries, blueberries, and black currants with whipped cream, or decadent Hawaiian Vintage chocolate cake with chocolate mousse and macadamia nut caramel. If you just can't decide what to order, try the chef's tasting menu at $74 per person.

Entertainment and amenities Thursday through Saturday evenings, a jazz pianist plays and sings.

Summary and comments If you'd like a quiet little table for a romantic dinner, ask for Table #28, #29, or #34. These tables for two are tucked into an out-of-the-way corner of the restaurant, where you can check out the action in the dining room, but the action can't check you out. David Paul's awards include *Honolulu Magazine*'s Hale Aina Award, received six years in a row for Best Maui Restaurant.

Gerard's ★★★★

CONTEMPORARY/ISLAND/FRENCH | EXPENSIVE | QUALITY ★★★★ | VALUE ★★★★ |
WEST MAUI

Plantation Inn, 174 Lahainaluna Road, Lahaina; (808) 661-8939;
www.gerardsmaui.com

Reservations Recommended

When to go Dinner

Entrée range $29.50–$39.50

Payment V, MC, AE, DC, D, JCB

Service rating ★★★★★

Parking In nearby lot

Bar Full service

Wine selection Excellent, 10 wines by the glass

Dress Casual resort attire

Disabled access Good for garden-level dining, adequate via a back entry for in-house dining

Customers Tourists and Islanders for special occasions

Dinner Daily, 6–9 p.m.

Setting and atmosphere Located in a plantation-style inn, Gerard's has the feel of a gracious home, with flowered wallpaper, stained glass windows, and candle lamps inside and a lushly planted lanai outside.

House specialties Diners rave about the calamari sautéed with lime and ginger and the shiitake and oyster mushrooms in puff pastry. Though chef/owner Gerard Reversade changes the menu, some dishes stay constant—confit of duck cassoulet and the roasted snapper with star anise and savory in orange-ginger emulsion. Homemade tropical sorbets are refreshing, but there is an assortment of rich desserts for you to choose, as well as a cheese plate with pear and a glass of Ulupalakua raspberry wine.

Other recommendations Start with ahi tartare and taro chips or pasta with shrimp sautéed in hazelnut oil. Move on to something imaginative, like pork loin with rhubarb compote, roasted banana, and coconut curry sauce.

Summary and comments In the years since Gerard's opened in 1982, Reversade has incorporated lighter sauces and tropical ingredients into traditional dishes, evolving his own Hawaiian-French blend. Over the years his traditional French cuisine has been adapted to Island taste, so that sauces are lighter and hints of Island flavors and ingredients show up. He has been featured on PBS's *Country Cooking* and the Discovery Channel's *Great Chefs of America*. The wine list repeatedly receives *Wine Spectator*'s award of excellence.

Haliimaile General Store ★★★★★

HAWAII REGIONAL | MODERATE/EXPENSIVE | QUALITY ★★★★★ | VALUE ★★★★½ |
UPCOUNTRY MAUI

900 Haliimaile Road, Haliimaile; (808) 572-2666; www.haliimailegeneralstore.com

Reservations Highly recommended for dinner

When to go Anytime on weekdays

Entrée range Lunch $7–$22; dinner $22–$39

Payment V, MC, DC, D, JCB

Service rating ★★★★½

Parking In adjacent lot

Bar Full service

Wine selection Good, many by the glass

Dress Casual

Disabled access Adequate, via ramp

Customers Islanders and tourists

Lunch Monday–Friday, 11 a.m.–2:30 p.m.; mini-menu, 2:30–5:30 p.m.

Dinner Monday–Friday, 5:30–9:30 p.m.

Setting and atmosphere Chef/owner Bev Gannon's Hawaii Regional Cuisine is famous throughout the Islands, but you'll still feel as if you've made a discovery when you search out the restaurant, located in the middle of vast Upcountry sugarcane and pineapple fields, partway up the slope of Haleakala. Once a plantation general store, the large, airy, casual and occasionally noisy room is now a creative dining destination.

House specialties The crab boboli is legendary for lunch, while for dinner, check out the fish preparations, as they vary every night. As an appetizer, sashimi Napoleon, a crispy wonton layered with smoked salmon, ahi tartare, and sashimi and served with a spicy wasabi vinaigrette, is always in demand. Rack of lamb Hunan-style keeps Islanders coming back for more. House-special martinis include the Upcountry, with pineapple juice, triple sec, and coconut rum.

Other recommendations Paniolo ribs done with a secret lime barbecue sauce and coconut seafood curry are also popular. As pastry chef, Gannon's daughter Theresa whips up chocolate macadamia-nut caramel pie, coconut cream cake, peanut butter pie, and pineapple upside down cake. Kids will find not only their own menu for food, but also a kids' cocktail menu. How about a Green Gecko (kiwi soda) or a Baby Blue Whale (lemonade with blue oranges)?

Summary and comments Chef Gannon was one of the two women among the founding members of the Hawaii Regional Cuisine movement. Winner of numerous awards, Gannon has started a cooking school of her own. Participants sign up for a weeklong immersion in the hows and whys of Hawaii Regional Cuisine, complete with farm and winery tours, a dinner in her home, and a stay at Sugar House, a plantation manager's home restored as an inn for her students, private parties, and special occasions. The Gannons also run a catering service and Joe's Place (named for her husband) at Wailea, a casual restaurant at the tennis complex with unexpectedly good dishes.

Hula Grill ★★★★

HAWAII REGIONAL | MODERATE | QUALITY ★★★★ | VALUE ★★★★½ | WEST MAUI

Whalers Village, 2435 Kaanapali Parkway, Kaanapali; (808) 667-6636; www.hulapie.com

Reservations Recommended for dinner

When to go Anytime, but it's best on the open lanai at sunset

Entrée range Lunch $8–$16, dinner $16–$29

Payment V, MC, AE, D, DC

Service rating ★★★★

Parking Validated, in shopping center garage

Bar Full service

Wine selection Good, 10 wines by the glass

Dress Casual

Disabled access Good

Customers Tourists and Islanders

Lunch Daily, 11 a.m.–10:30 p.m. (Pizzas, salads, and sandwiches are served through the day in the casual Barefoot Bar.)

Dinner Daily, 5–9:30 p.m.

Setting and atmosphere Hula Grill is oceanfront and center at Kaanapali Beach Resort, in the Whalers Village complex. This Hawaiian plantation–style beach-house setting is charming and comfortable, with two distinct dining options—the interior dining room for dinner, with nostalgic decor of warm koa wood paneling and Hawaiiana memorabilia, and the outdoor Barefoot Bar, on a roofed lanai with some umbrella-shaded tables set right in the sand, for drinks, lunch, or light dinner. During the day you'll see the parade of passing beachgoers walking along Kaanapali's promenade that borders the golden beach; at night flickering torches light the path.

House specialties With menus crafted by another originator of Hawaii Regional Cuisine, chef Peter Merriman, even the cheeseburger is special at Hula Grill. For starters, try kulua pork or scallop and lobster potstickers served in bamboo steamer baskets. The signature item in the dining room is mahimahi crusted with macadamia nuts, among five fresh fishes nightly. Some diners swear by the Steak Kiana, a filet with shiitake mushroom cream and lilikoi butter.

Other recommendations This is a great place to cool off and enjoy a casual lunch, maybe a warm focaccia roasted vegetable sandwich with grilled eggplant, tomato, Maui onion, mushroom, and cheese—one of the best preparations of this Italian sandwich—or a chicken focaccia sandwich with Monterey Jack, roasted poblano pepper, avocado, and tomato-chile aïoli. These and the pizzas topped with Puna goat cheese, fresh spinach, tomato, and mushrooms come crispy hot from the kiawe wood-fired oven.

There's a formidable cheeseburger, fresh fish sandwich or plate, Indonesian gado-gado salad with peanut dressing, and a fresh Island version of fish and chips. You might want to share Hula Grill's famous dessert—a homemade ice-cream sandwich, made with two chocolate macadamia-nut brownies, vanilla ice cream, raspberry puree, and whipped cream.

Entertainment and amenities It's easy to slip off the beach for a Lava Flow, a piña colada–like drink made with fresh coconut, pineapple juice, and rum and topped with a strawberry "eruption," during happy hour, when a guitarist and vocalist entertain from 3 to 5 p.m. Hawaiian musicians return during dinner hours from 6:30 to 9 p.m., and hula dancers sway at table-side around 7 p.m. every night.

Summary and comments Chef Merriman was instrumental in founding the Hawaii Regional Cuisine movement, and his expertise is reflected in Hula Grill's fare. The restaurant can accommodate large parties and weddings of up to 350 people.

IO	★★★★½

HAWAII REGIONAL | MODERATE | QUALITY ★★★★½ | VALUE ★★★ | WEST MAUI

505 Front Street, Lahaina; (808) 661-8422; www.iomaui.com

Reservations Recommended

When to go Sunset for great views

Entrée range Dinner $23–$58

Payment V, MC, AE, DC, JCB

Service rating ★★★★½

Parking Free in lots next door and across the street

Bar Full service

Wine selection Carefully chosen to complement the food; by-the-glass pairings suggested for entrées

Dress Casual

Disabled access Adequate

Customers Tourists and Islanders

Dinner Daily, 5:30–10 p.m.

Setting and atmosphere Sunset views are exceptional from the outdoor tables set amid tropical plants on a beachfront lanai. But the three-island ocean vista is also fine from the airy, artful interior of this intimate café, where the decor of light woods and stainless steel is like a frame for the decorative glass—two huge see-through murals of aqua-tinted glass etched with underwater scenes to resemble an aquarium and ceiling lights made like bouquets of glass flowers.

House specialties "Fresh new Pacific cuisine" sums up the fare. The emphasis is on really fresh fish, required for dishes such as Island carpaccio—paper-thin slices of raw fish dressed with a citrus herb vinaigrette, extra-virgin chile oil, and sea salt, sprinkled with pink peppercorns and powdered pink shrimp shell. Several Hawaiian fishes are featured daily in a variety of preparations, including one that delivers fish medallions crusted with sesame-coconut-lemongrass paste, accompanied with fresh hearts-of-palm salad and spicy cold soba noodles, mango dressing, and sweet-beet vinaigrette. For a little cultural fusion, try the silken purse appetizers, steamed wontons stuffed with roasted peppers, mushrooms, spinach, macadamia nuts, and silken tofu, served with a jalapeño-scented tomato sauce and basil-yogurt puree.

Other recommendations A cut beyond the steakhouse, IO's grilled filet mignon comes with roasted garlic cloves, oyster mushrooms, and pothole fern shoots with herb-butter escargot in a veal demi-glace sauce. For dessert, try "Island Dreams"—an ice cream made of carmelized Maui pineapple, coconut, and goat cheese, with an almond ginger tuile.

Entertainment and amenities Live jazz is featured at 505 Front Street Thursday through Saturday, 9 p.m. to midnight.

Summary and comments Executive chef/owner James McDonald, voted best chef on Maui, also owns and operates PacificO next door, reviewed below, and The Feast at Lele, a sophisticated luau held beachfront at sunset next door on the opposite side, with food prepared at IO's kitchen featuring the cuisines of four Polynesian cultures (see Nightlife, page 341). McDonald's eight-acre vegetable farm in Kula supplies the eateries with some of their fresh ingredients.

Kai Ku Ono   ★★★½

HAWAII REGIONAL | MODERATE | QUALITY ★★★ | VALUE ★★★★ | SOUTH MAUI

2511 South Kihei Road, Kihei; (808) 875-1007; info@kaikuono.com

Reservations Recommended for large late groups

When to go Anytime except Sunday and Monday

Entrée range $20

Payment V, MC

Service rating ★★★★★

Parking Free self-parking in lot

Bar Full service

Wine selection Limited

Dress Casual

Disabled access Adequate

Customers Resort guests and residents

Breakfast Daily, 8–11 a.m.

Lunch Daily, noon–3 p.m.

Dinner Daily, 6–9 p.m.

Lounge Daily, 5:30–11 p.m.

Setting and atmosphere This casual, open-air bistro is the ideal surf-side hangout when you are hungry and thirsty, whether alone or out late with the gang.

House specialties Fresh local catch of the day (ahi, mahi, ono, or monchong), homemade pasta, fresh Maui garden salads.

Other recommendations Every Wednesday night is prime rib night.

Entertainment and amenities Breezy, kick-back tropical setting full of local ambience, with a choice of bar seats, couches, or tables for 2 or 20.

Summary and comments For 18 years, this beach café has attracted hungry beachgoers, surfers, entertainers, families, and singles who enjoy good food well served.

Kimo's ★★★

STEAK AND SEAFOOD | INEXPENSIVE/MODERATE | QUALITY ★★ | VALUE ★★★ |
WEST MAUI

---

845 Front Street, Lahaina; (808) 661-4811; www.kimosmaui.com

Reservations Recommended

When to go Anytime; to sit outside in the upstairs dining room, go early—it's first-come, first-seated

Entrée range Lunch $7–$11, dinner $15–$26

Payment V, MC, AE, DC, D, JCB

Service rating ★★★½

Parking Limited on-street or use Lahaina Center lot and walk a couple of blocks

Bar Full service

Wine selection Good, 8 wines by the glass

Dress Casual

Disabled access Access to the main dining room upstairs is inadequate for wheelchairs, but seating is available downstairs in a secondary dining area near the bar.

Customers Tourists, some Islanders

Lunch Daily, 11 a.m.–3 p.m.

Pupu Daily, 3–5 p.m.

Dinner Daily, 5–10:30 p.m.

Bar Daily, until 1:30 a.m.

Setting and atmosphere This two-level restaurant is a casual place where it's easy to drop by for lunch or for a cocktail downstairs at sunset before heading upstairs for dinner. Kimo's takes full advantage of its oceanfront setting, with an open lanai perched one story above the rocks and lapping waves. At night, torches cast flickering shadows on the spreading limbs of a monkeypod tree. You can order from the full menu or a lighter menu at the bar, which seats 22 downstairs.

House specialties Kimo's fresh catch is done several ways, but Kimo's Style, baked in garlic, lemon, and sweet basil glaze, is a favorite. At lunch, fresh fish tacos will fortify you for an afternoon of swimming or shopping.

Other recommendations Beefeaters swear by the prime rib, but there are also seafood dishes like Tahitian shrimp, with garlic and cheese. Try a lighter lunch, such as the veggie sandwich of Maui onions, fresh tomatoes, sprouts, cheese, and avocado, and then you can afford to top it off with the dessert that sailors swim to shore for—the original hula pie, a wedge of vanilla macadamia-nut ice cream in an Oreo cookie crust, topped with fudge and whipped cream.

Entertainment and amenities Kimo's swings on Friday and Saturday nights from 10 p.m. to midnight, when live rock-and-roll music enlivens the night. Hawaiian music is featured weekdays with dinner, 7–8 p.m.

Summary and comments Local diners voted Kimo's, in the heart of touristy Lahaina, Maui's best restaurant. Kimo's entrées come with a Caesar salad, carrot muffins, sour-cream rolls, and steamed herb rice, so you don't go broke ordering à la carte. Generous portions and fairly priced food of a consistent quality make this one of the better Lahaina view bars.

Longhi's ★★★

MEDITERRANEAN/ITALIAN | MODERATE | QUALITY ★★★ | VALUE ★★★ |
WEST MAUI/SOUTH MAUI

800 Front Street, Lahaina; (808) 667-2288; The Shops at Wailea, Wailea Resort; (808) 891-8883; www.longhi-maui.com

Reservations Recommended for dinner

When to go Anytime

Entrée range Lunch $8–$16, dinner $28–$80, except for lobster at $55

Payment AE, V, MC, DC, D, JCB

Service rating ★★★

Parking Free valet at dinner in Lahaina, free self-parking in adjacent lot in Lahaina and Wailea

Bar Full service

Wine selection Extensive, many Italian wines and 3 house wines, 20 by the glass

Dress Casual

Disabled access Good for downstairs dining

Customers Tourists and Islanders

Breakfast Daily, 7:30–11:30 a.m.

Lunch Daily, 11:45 a.m.–4:45 p.m.

Dinner Daily, 5–10 p.m.

Setting and atmosphere Both Longhi's locations have ocean views in open-air settings and casual surroundings. The second floor in Lahaina has additional tables open to the tradewinds.

House specialties Nobody wants to stop at just one appetizer, even if it's as good as the grilled portobello mushrooms with goat-cheese pesto. Follow up with shrimp Longhi, a classic served since the restaurant's opening night more than 20 years ago. Plump white shrimp are sautéed in butter, lemon juice, and white wine, then combined with fresh Maui basil and tomatoes and served on garlic toast. Fresh fish prepared with white wine and garnished with grapes is another specialty.

Other recommendations The in-house bakery prepares oven-fresh cinnamon buns, macadamia-nut rolls, coffee cakes, quiches, and cheesy jalapeño and pizza bread. Pastas made on the premises and fresh salads are available both at lunch and dinner. Desserts include macadamia-nut pie, cheesecake, or strawberry mousse cake, though you may prefer to order a special chocolate or Grand Marnier soufflé in advance.

Entertainment and amenities Live bands play music for dancing upstairs on Friday nights in Lahaina, from 9:30 p.m. to closing.

Summary and comments Created in 1976 by "a man who loves to eat," Bob Longhi, these restaurants are a family affair, with son Peter the general manager and daughter Carol O'Leary an executive chef. The restaurant has repeatedly received *Wine Spectator*'s Award of Excellence. Longhi's has an all-verbal menu, which can prove irritating or exciting, depending on your mood.

Maalaea Waterfront Restaurant ★★★½

SEAFOOD/CONTINENTAL | EXPENSIVE | QUALITY ★★★★½ | VALUE ★★★ |
CENTRAL MAUI

50 Haouli Street, Maalaea; (808) 244-9028; www.waterfrontrestaurant.com

Reservations Highly recommended

When to go Sunset

Entrée range $18–$54

Payment V, MC, AE, DC, D, JCB

Service rating ★★★½

Parking Free in upper level of adjacent condominium garage

Bar Full service

Wine selection Extensive, 30 by the glass

Dress Resort attire

Disabled access Adequate, via elevator

Customers Islanders and tourists

Dinner Daily, 5 p.m.–closing

Setting and atmosphere Remodeled in 1998, this elegant oceanfront restaurant has textured pale-green walls, white tablecloths decorated with candles and tropical flowers, and scenic Island paintings on the walls. Outdoor dining on the deck is lovely on a balmy night, but bring a sweater if the tradewinds are brisk.

House specialties Depending on what the fishermen bring in, five or more different kinds of fish are served daily in your choice of nine preparation styles. This means there are always 45 or more choices to make while you nibble on homemade bread slathered with the house's special beer-cheese spread or watch the tableside preparation of your Caesar salad.

Other recommendations Besides rack of lab and prime rib, Maalaea Waterfront features game, such as venison, pheasant, or ostrich, as a daily special. For dessert the white chocolate blueberry cheesecake will satisfy any cheesecake aficionado.

Summary and comments Maalaea Waterfront Restaurant is a family endeavor, opened in 1990 by the Smiths: Bob, the chef; Gary, the manager; and Rick, the detail man. Their success is evidenced by the support of local patrons—the restaurant has repeatedly been cited the best in seafood and service by *Maui News* readers.

Mama's Fish House ★★★½

SEAFOOD | EXPENSIVE | QUALITY ★★★★½ | VALUE ★★★ | CENTRAL MAUI

799 Poho Place, Kaau; (808) 579-8488; www.mamasfishhouse.com

Reservations Highly recommended

When to go Anytime, but sunset is most romantic

Entrée range Lunch $25–$44, dinner $31–$49

Payment V, MC, AE, DC, D, JCB

Service rating ★★★★

Parking Valet or adjacent lot

Bar Full service

Wine selection Excellent, half a dozen by the glass

Dress Casual resort wear

Disabled access Good, but it's a distance from the lot

Customers Tourists and Islanders

Lunch Daily, 11 a.m.–2 p.m.

Pupu Daily, 2:30–3 p.m.

Dinner Daily, 5–9:30 p.m.

Setting and atmosphere You'll find Mama's in a rambling, open-air beach house, at the end of a gecko-patterned walkway beside the ocean, with cool green lawns and shady coconut palms out front. A wooden bar and wooden paneling inside are made of tropical almond, monkeypod, and mango wood. It's a perfect place to while away an afternoon over a Mai Tai Roa Ae—a fresh-fruit-and-rum concoction like originated by Trader Vic years ago—or to sample other retro drinks: Singapore Slings of Raffles hotel fame, Zombies, and Scorpions.

House specialties Fishermen get credited by name on the menu for catching the fresh fish of the day, so the fish is always top-notch, whether you have ono, ahi, uku, or opah. Preparations include sautéed with garlic butter, white wine, and capers; grilled with Thai red curry; fried with Maui onion, chilis, and avocado; or served with honey-roasted macadamia-nut-lemon sauce. A signature dish, Pua me hua Hana, features sautéed fish with fresh coconut, tropical fruit, and Molokai sweet potatoes.

Other recommendations To sample island-style cooking, try a laulau, pieces of mahimahi wrapped and baked in ti leaves with mango and coconut milk and served with tender, moist kalua pig and poi. Another imaginative entrée with local flair is crispy kalua duck with mango-mui glaze served with baby bok choy and wild rice. The New York steak is Big Island–grown, a local treat for beef lovers.

Summary and comments The open-air, Polynesian atmosphere of "Grandma's Living Room" draws residents to hang out, listen to vintage Hawaiian music, and snack on pupu rather than ordering a pricy full meal.

Manana Garage   ★★★★

ISLAND NUEVO LATINO | MODERATE | QUALITY ★★★★ | VALUE ★★★ |
CENTRAL MAUI

33 Lono Avenue, Kahului; (808) 873-0220

Reservations Recommended

When to go Anytime

Entrée range $14–$24

Payment All major credit cards

Service rating ★★★★

Parking Free in adjacent lot

Bar Full

Wine selection Good

Dress Resort wear

Disabled access Good

Customers Mauians, tourists

Lunch Monday–Friday, 11 a.m.–2 p.m.

Dinner Daily, 5:30–9 p.m.

Setting and atmosphere Bright purple and yellow umbrellas outside on the lanai are a hint of what's inside this café with indoor and outdoor tables on the ground floor of an office complex. Droll "garage" touches support the name—old license plates, crackled green safety glass on the bar top, a mechanic's tool stand for the hostess, and a corrugated steel garage door on one wall hiding the private dining room. But it's very much a front-of-the-house kind of place, zesty and modern, with lots of bright colors, from the walls to the table wear, and sparkling with Murano glass lights.

House specialties A creative cuisine borrowing from Brazil, Pureto Rico, Cuba, Mexico, and Venezuela offers something refreshingly different among Maui dining spots. Paella is a house specialty, saffron rice with fresh fish and traditional shellfish. Many dishes are familiar but with a novel twist—for example, the pulled-pork adobo, with hints of orange, clove, cumin, and Ancho chile in its rich, dark taste, or ahi ceviche, with avocado and coconut milk and a hint of Tahitian poisson cru in addition to the traditional lime, cilantro, chile, tomato, and onion. A sweet potato–praline pound-cake ice-cream sandwich might be your choice to conclude this feast, or dulce de leche strawberry trifle.

Other recommendations Quesadilla con queso for real, with homemade tortillas and mild Mexican cheese and served with a selection of salsas, from mild to hot-hot, makes an irresistible starter. Or try them stuffed with adobo barbecue duck and sweet potato, or chiles and cheese. Fresh fish chimichangas come with tomatillo sauce, guacamole, wasabi sour cream, and greens.

Summary and comments Chef Tom Lelli risked adding a lively new dimension to the cultural mix of Maui flavors and came away with a winner, now run by co-chefs Eddie Santos and Scott Idemoto.

PacificO   ★★★★½

HAWAII REGIONAL | EXPENSIVE | QUALITY ★★★★½ | VALUE ★★★ | WEST MAUI

505 Front Street, Lahaina; (808) 667-4341; www.pacificomaui.com

Reservations Recommended

When to go Sunset

Entrée range Lunch $9.50–$15.50, dinner $26–$54

Payment V, MC, AE, DC, JCB

Service rating ★★★★

Parking Free in lot across the street

Bar Full service

Wine selection Excellent

Dress Casual

Disabled access Adequate, but it's a long way from the parking lot

Customers Tourists and Islanders

Lunch Daily, 11 a.m.–4 p.m.

Dinner Daily, 5:30–9 p.m.

Setting and atmosphere The outdoor terrace is hard to resist, with tables and umbrellas set close to the sea. Inside, ceiling fans spin lazily and windows are open wide to the ocean breezes and the three-island view.

House specialties The Pan-Pacific menu features one of Maui's best lobster values ($36) for an innovative dish—two tails poached in ginger butter and served with lobster coconut sauce.

Other recommendations Fresh catch comes crusted with macadamia nuts and coconut; seared and served over home-grown greens with avocado, salsa, goat cheese, and macadamia nuts; seared with Asian spices and curry vinaigrette; or crusted with chili-lime panko crumbs and topped with macadamia nut–banana hollandaise, with a side of flambéed bananas. The melt-in-your-mouth dessert of pineapple lumpia and macadamia nut ice cream is a beautiful blend of texture and taste.

Entertainment and amenities Live jazz after dinner, Thursday through Saturday, 9 p.m. to midnight.

Summary and comments The same chef/owner, James McDonald, also owns IO, the hip modern restaurant next door, and The Feast at Lele luau, also a beachfront neighbor.

Plantation House Restaurant	

CONTEMPORARY | MODERATE | QUALITY ★★★★ | VALUE ★★★ | WEST MAUI

Plantation Course Clubhouse, 2000 Plantation Club Drive, Kapalua Resort; (808) 669-6299; www.theplantationhouse.com

Reservations Recommended for dinner

When to go Anytime; lunch or sunset for the smashing view

Entrée range Lunch, $8.50–$16; dinner, $22–$54

Payment V, AE, MC, DC

Service rating ★★★

Parking In adjacent lot

Bar Full service

Wine selection Extensive

Dress Casual

Disabled access Good, drop off at front door

Customers Golfers, tourists, and Islanders

Breakfast and lunch Daily, 8 a.m.–3 p.m.; light menu 3–5 p.m.

Dinner Daily, 5:30–9 p.m.

Setting and atmosphere High above the shoreline, diners in this not-your-average golf club restaurant can admire sweeping views of moody Molokai, wind-whipped blue ocean, green fairways, and the rest of Kapalua Resort through windows open to cool upland breezes. The decor is a blend of swanky and casual, as befits the well-heeled golfers, with lots of rattan and tropical woods setting off a large mural of pineapple workers in the Kapalua fields. A double-sided fireplace creates a warm glow to ward off any evening chill up on the lower slope of Puu Kukui.

House specialties Fresh fish comes dressed for dinner in many styles, including an Oscar with asparagus, crab meat, and lemon butter sauce, and a Venetian choice with shrimp, baby fava beans, green beans, and pine nuts. Vegetarians can substitute tofu for fish in any of the featured preparations or request other meatless entrees. A full roster of eggs Benedicts tops the breakfast/lunch menu, including one that could stretch your fusion limits—Cajun-style ahi sashimi Benedict with wasabi hollandaise.

Other recommendations Hungry duffers will find substantial fare like lamb shanks and mashed potatoes, "surf-n-turf" with Australian lobster and filet mignon, and pork tenderloin.

Summary and comments Chef Alex Stanislaw created an inspired and varied menu deserving of the spectacular setting, merging Mediterranean flavors and island ingredients. It's a refreshing alternative to the other resort restaurants down below.

Roy's Kahana Bar and Grill and ★★★★
Roy's Kihei Bar and Grill

HAWAIIAN FUSION | MODERATE/EXPENSIVE | QUALITY ★★★★ | VALUE ★★★ |
WEST MAUI/SOUTH MAUI

Kahana Gateway Shopping Center, 4405 Honoapiilani Highway, Kahana; (808) 669-6999; Piilani Village Shopping Center, 303 Piikea Street, Kihei; (808) 891-1120; www.roysrestaurant.com

Reservations Highly recommended

When to go Anytime

Entrée range $24.50–$32.50

Payment V, MC, AE, DC, D, JCB

Service rating ★★★★½

Parking Free in shopping center lot

Bar Full service

Wine selection Excellent, 10–15 by the glass

Dress Casual

Disabled access Good, via elevator to upstairs restaurants in Kahana

Customers Tourists and Islanders

Dinner *Roy's Kahana:* 5:30–10 p.m., *Roy's Kihei:* 5:30–9:30 p.m.

Setting and atmosphere The new Kihei eatery and the established Kahana Roy's both offer the same creative fare, with little difference between them except geography and setting. (The Kahana restaurant is on the second floor of a small shopping complex. The Kihei restaurant is a new separate building in a small shopping center.) Both are guided by Corporate Chef Jacqueline Lau with 20 to 25 specials nightly, and both have the distinctive Roy's touch.

House specialties Since items change so rapidly, you never know what you'll find, but everything is made with the freshest local ingredients with Euro-Asian accents. Appetizers like Szechuan baby-back ribs or Roy's shrimp and pork spring rolls with hot sweet mustard and black-bean sauce set a spicy scene. Lemongrass-crusted shutome (swordfish) reflects a touch of Thailand, with sticky rice and basil peanut sauce. Hibachi-style salmon and blackened ahi are signature entrées.

Other recommendations The left side of the menu is made up of Roy's signature dishes, prepared the same throughout the chain, down to the garnishes. The right side reflects the in-house chef's daily inspirations, which lean more toward Hawaiian than Asian flavors. If they're serving poke in a martini glass with aïoli and avocado, get it for a silky, rich appetizer. Or try the dim sum "canoe" for two, a sampling of the traditional Asian treats done up with Hawaiian ingredients.

Summary and comments You really can't go wrong with Roy's Hawaiian fusion brand of cuisine, dishes that are exciting and rarely disappointing. The young master chef Roy Yamaguchi is himself a genius in the kitchen but has an even rarer skill to pick and train other chefs to guide his many restaurants in more or less the same vein. He has won so many awards that it's difficult to track them to his specific restaurants. *Gourmet* magazine's Top Tables, *Honolulu* magazine's Top 20, the James Beard Foundation, and many others applaud this imaginative and energetic chef, who has more than 30 restaurants worldwide.

A Saigon Café ★★★

VIETNAMESE | INEXPENSIVE | QUALITY ★★★★ | VALUE ★★★★★ | CENTRAL MAUI

1792 Main Street, Wailuku; (808) 243-9560

Reservations Recommended, especially for dinner

When to go Anytime

Entrée range $6.75–$17.95

Payment V, MC, AE, DC, D, JCB

Service rating ★★★★

Parking In adjacent lot

Bar Full service

Wine selection Limited

Dress Casual

Disabled access Good

Customers Islanders and a few tourists

Lunch and dinner Daily, 10 a.m.– 8:30 p.m.

Setting and atmosphere Sit at the low wooden bar or choose a Formica table or booth for lunch and dinner in this basic, white-walled restaurant minimally decorated with Vietnamese lacquered art. A gold Buddha greets guests at the door, ceiling fans whir overhead, and the TV might be on at the bar. It's a low-key place that can be difficult to find because there is no sign.

House specialties Start with cha gio (fried spring rolls)—little deep-fried bundles of ground pork, long rice, carrot, and onion wrapped in rice paper; the waiter will show you how to roll them in romaine lettuce with mint leaves and vermicelli noodles, then dip them in sweet-sour garlic sauce. Among any number of in-demand Vietnamese entrées, one of the most delicious is garden-party shrimp dipped in a light batter, deep-fried, and served with sautéed ginger and green onions on bean sprouts and lettuce (with rice on the side).

Other recommendations With 92 items on the menu, it's hard to make a choice. Green-papaya salad is a favorite accompaniment. For lunch, the noodle soups—with seafood and chicken, calamari and shrimp, wonton, and other ingredients—provide a big bowl of steaming goodness. The several rice-in-a-clay-pot dishes feature chicken, catfish, shrimp, or pork.

Summary and comments Everybody loves A Saigon Café, and regulars admire proprietor Jennifer Nguyen as well. Nguyen opened the restaurant in January 1996, but the restaurant's sign is still stored in a box somewhere. The sprightly, hard-working proprietor says, "We've been so busy, we've never gotten around to putting it up!"

Sansei Seafood Restaurant and Sushi Bar   ★★★★★

JAPANESE FUSION | MODERATE/EXPENSIVE | QUALITY ★★★★½ | VALUE ★★★★ |
WEST MAUI/SOUTH MAUI

The Shops at Kapalua, 115 Bay Drive, Kapalua; (808) 669-6286
Kihei Town Center 1881 South Kihei Road, Kihei; (808) 879-0004;
www.sanseihawaii.com

Reservations Highly recommended

When to go Anytime for dinner and later

Entrée range $16 –$38

Payment V, MC, AE, D, JCB

Service rating ★★★★

Parking In shopping-village lots

Bar Full service

Wine selection Extensive, also array of sakes

Dress Resort attire

Disabled access Adequate

Customers Islanders and tourists; late-night karaoke crowd

Dinner Daily, 5:30–10 p.m.

Late night Tuesday–Saturday, 10 p.m.–2 a.m.; karaoke Thursday and Friday from 10 p.m.

Setting and atmosphere Booths and tables fill up fast in the intimate 120-seat Kapalua restaurant, which includes a sushi bar and cocktail lounge area. The newer Kihei location, in a shopping complex along busy Kihei Road, has proved to be a hit as well. Restaurant decor blends a bit of Japan with a Maui plantation look, echoing the blend of flavors—Japanese with Pacific Rim influences. Samurai pictures decorate the walls, and the sushi bar, with its scalloped awning, could have come from Tokyo (as some of the sushi chefs did).

House specialties There's no end to Sansei's creativity, matching Eastern ways with Western flavors and vice versa. The dishes are some of Maui's tastiest. Try a lot of dishes and share. With sushi this is easy, and Sansei offers up delicious tidbits, from crab and mango salad hand rolls to spider rolls with soft-shell crab to bagel rolls with smoked salmon, Maui onion, and cream cheese. The family-style concept applies to entrées as well. Pass around the house special: Peking duck breast with shiitake potato risotto. Other favorites: Asian rock-shrimp cake, Japanese calamari salad with greens in a crispy won ton basket, and nori ravioli of shrimp and lobster.

Other recommendations Come early (before 6 p.m.) and get a 25 percent break on the tab for food and sushi. Come late (after 10 p.m.) and enjoy more dining specials along with laser karaoke. Pay attention when the waiter describes nightly specials like asparagus tempura and fresh fish preparations, or try shrimp tempura fried in a light-as-air batter, or a grilled fresh mahimahi on Kula greens. The Granny Smith apple tart is a pure American finish to any meal.

Entertainment and amenities Sansei's karaoke after 10 p.m. on Thursday and Friday draws a happy crowd at both restaurants.

Summary and comments Big-name Maui chefs gather at the casual restaurant set unobtrusively in the Kapalua Shops. The launch of a Kihei restaurant is good news for South Maui patrons who used to have to drive an hour each way to indulge in Sansei's Kapalua treats. Chef/owner D. K. Kodama says his menu reflects the way he likes to eat, with playful flavors and bits of this and that.

Spago at Four Seasons Resort Maui ★★★★½

CONTEMPORARY | EXPENSIVE | QUALITY ★★★★½ | VALUE ★★★ | SOUTH MAUI

Four Seasons Resort, 3900 Wailea Alanui, Wailea; (808) 874-8000;
www.fourseasons.com or www.wolfgangpuck.com

Reservations Highly recommended

When to go Sunset is spectacular

Entrée range $36–$42

Payment AE, V, MC, DC, D, JCB

Service rating ★★★★★

Parking Complimentary valet or self-parking in covered hotel lot

Bar Full service

Wine selection Extensive and international, prices varied

Dress Resort attire

Disabled access Good, via elevator

Customers Hotel guests, other tourists, and Islanders for special occasions

---

Dinner Daily, 6–9 p.m., bar open 6–11 p.m.

Setting and atmosphere Casual but elegant, Spago's interiors were completely redone in a contemporary version of Asian design, featuring stone and wood and Asian art. The new bar and lounge enjoy big ocean vistas of Wailea Beach and the entire length of Wailea's coastline.

House specialties Famed Chef Wolfgang Puck fuses Hawaii and California cuisine to create dishes such as whole moi fish steamed Hong Kong style with chili, ginger, and baby choi sum. Roasted Cantonese duck is prepared with Maui white pineapple, star anise, and tempura scallions. Desserts with tropical flair include lilikoi crème brûlée and mango upside-down cake with lilikoi sorbet.

Other recommendations Starters include a spicy ahi poke served in sesame-miso cones. Or try the fragrant Thai coconut soup with Kahole farmed lobster, kaffir lime, chile, and galangal (mild ginger). Sweet Upcountry corn is stuffed into agnolotti pasta with spring leeks and thyme.

Summary and comments Four Seasons has transformed the former signature restaurant Seasons into a Wolfgang Puck restaurant, Hawaii style. The first of its kind in the Islands, it's a hit with the southern Californians who frequent this hotel and any diners interested in seeing what a master chef will do with Island ingredients and multicultural influences. Bryan Geisser is the sommelier. Puck has also created his first children's menu for this Spago (pizza, grilled cheese and fries, chicken fingers, and spaghetti). Free shuttles operate between all Wailea hotels.

Stella Blues Café   ★★★★½

AMERICAN | MODERATE | QUALITY ★★★½ | VALUE ★★★½ | SOUTH MAUI

Azeka II Mall, 1279 Kihei Road; (808) 874-3779; www.maui.net/~stelablu

Reservations Recommended

When to go Anytime

Entrée range Lunch $6–$13; dinner $16–$21

Payment Cash

Service rating ★★★

Parking: Free, shopping center lot

Bar Full service

Wine selection Good, bottled and by the glass

Dress Casual

Disabled access Good

Customers Residents, visitors

Breakfast Daily, 7:30–11 a.m. (until 2 p.m. Sunday)

Lunch Daily, 11 a.m.–5 p.m.

Dinner Daily, 5–10 p.m., plus late-night light menu and drinks until midnight weekdays, l:30 a.m. Friday and Saturday

Setting and atmosphere Stella Blues, once a little vegetarian lunchroom, has moved up and out, taking over a large, modernistic place just up the street and expanding its menu to three meals of "New American comfort food." With curving walls and warm Mediterranean colors, the new site has an exhibition kitchen surrounded by a bar where diners can watch chefs at work, and an outdoor lanai.

House specialties The menu takes a something-for-everyone approach with an extensive list of "small plates" ranging from hummus to crabcakes, served from 5 p.m. to midnight; plus pastas, pizzas, fresh fish, and something special to try: Maui-grown beef, in burgers, steak sandwiches, and steak-end-eggs. Vegetarian roots are still evident in dishes like vegetarian shepherd's pie and tofu curry. For dessert, go light with tropical sorbets or rich, with lilikoi cheesecake or brownie à la mode.

Other recommendations If you're pining for breakfast that doesn't cost $20 or more and isn't the same old buffet, drive in for smoothies and espresso drinks, lox and bagels, or the choice of hungry dawn-patrol surfers, loco moco (hamburger patty with two eggs, rice, and gravy over all). You can build your own omelet or savory tofu scramble, not to mention eggs with cheese and jalapeños. Takeout and catering are also available.

Summary and comments Some things actually change for the better, and Stella Blues' popular lunch formula shows every sign of success on a much broader scale. If you've wondered how the average Maui resident manages to survive in a world of resort prices, this is how: good grinds, good wines, plenty of choices, and affordable prices.

Molokai

Maunaloa Room/Kaupoa Beach Village Molokai Ranch ★★★

HAWAII REGIONAL | MODERATE | QUALITY ★★★ | VALUE ★★★ | MOLOKAI

The Lodge at Molokai Ranch, #8, Maunaloa; (808) 660-2725;
www.molokai-ranch.com

Reservations Recommended

When to go Anytime

Entrée range $15–$28

Payment AE, MC, V

Service rating ★★★★

Parking Free in hotel lot

Bar Full service

Wine selection Good

Dress Resort wear

Disabled access Excellent

Customers Resort guests, visitors

Breakfast Monday–Saturday, 7–10 a.m.

Lunch Daily, 10 a.m.–4 p.m. (light menu)

Dinner Daily, 6–9 p.m. plus pasta buffet on Wednesday and Asian buffet on Sunday

Setting and atmosphere Inside, the decor follows a Hawaiian ranch theme with wooden tables, chairs with pineapple print seats, and wagon wheels chandeliers with electric candles. Views from an open-air deck stretch three miles over horse pastures and open ranchland to the blue sea. Deck chairs are metal with woven fiber seats and backs that sport the Molokai Ranch steerhead logo.

House specialties Chef Irwin Kudoba describes his menu as Molokai Regional because as many ingredients as possible are island-grown and the flavors reflect Molokai's populace and traditional dishes. The à la carte dinner menu has been limited to steak, fresh fish, and tofu with roasted vegetables. Starters include kalua pig lumpia (a Filipino version of spring roll) with tropical chutney and seared ahi on Asian slaw. This is one of the few menus that feature fresh opihi (a crunchy limpet that is a vanishing delicacy) as an appetizer. Entrées change according to what's fresh, but Island fish are bound to be included—one recent preparation was ahi steamed Asian-style with ginger, cilantro, and onions, as well as sweet peppers and asparagus, with a tangy soy-peanut oil sauce.

Other recommendations Plate-lunch style meals are available for take-out in the Paniolo Lounge. For breakfast, lunch, and dinner, diners can opt to catch a shuttle down to the Kaupoa Beach Village camp and eat in the open-air, ranch-style cookout pavilion. Food is cooked and served buffet style with common seating at long tables under roof by the sea. It's good, fresh, and plentiful for appetites sharpened by the ocean breezes and ranch activities, and fun, especially for kids. For lunch, the grills are busy with fresh fish and burgers; for dinner, it's grilled fish and steak. Omelets are made to order on Sundays. This is worth doing at least once even for nonranch guests.

Summary and comments It's a shame the Maunaloa Room has retracted from its original gourmet approach, because it was creative and very good. But the core of the Molokai Ranch experience is outdoor activities and family fun. After dinner, it's a pleasure to relax in the Great Room, with its enormous stone fireplace, and listen to acoustic Hawaiian music strummed and sung by a ranch paniolo (cowboy). If you're lucky, a hula dancer might join in the evening's entertainment.

Molokai Pizza Café   ★★★

PIZZA AND SANDWICHES | INEXPENSIVE | QUALITY ★★★½ | VALUE ★★★★ |
MOLOKAI

15 Kaunakakai Place, on Wharf Road; (808) 553-3288

Reservations Not accepted

When to go Anytime

Entrée range $4.50–$13

Payment Cash

Service rating ★★

Parking Adjacent lot

Bar None

Wine selection None

Dress Casual

Disabled access Good

Customers Locals and tourists

Lunch and dinner Monday–Thursday, Sunday, 10 a.m.–10 p.m.; Friday and Saturday, 10 a.m.–11 p.m.

Setting and atmosphere This clean, air-conditioned café with booths and tables is a Molokai family kind of place, often decorated with artwork and thank-you cards by schoolkids. Some of the Formica-topped tables are set in a quieter area at the front of the restaurant, and guests are welcome to bring their own wine or beer to enjoy with dinner on the outside lanai.

House specialties Fresh fish is served at market price when available. Wednesday nights a Mexican menu featuring burritos, fajitas, tacos, and nachos is added for variety, and Sunday nights prime rib is the draw.

Other recommendations You can order pizza by the slice, order a Molokini pizza for a single person, or get a big one to go or to share in the café. Chicken dinners come with rice or fries and veggies. Sandwiches, pasta, salads, and frozen yogurt are also served.

Entertainment and amenities Strolling musicians are hired for big private parties and sometimes for special holidays.

Summary and comments Eventually everyone stops by the Pizza Café. Kids hang out here after school, and tourists stop by for a slice of pizza, as it's one of the few places that serves food as late as 10 p.m. on weeknights, 11 p.m. on weekends.

The Village Grill ★★

ISLAND ECLECTIC | MODERATE | QUALITY ★★★½ | VALUE ★★★ | MOLOKAI

Maunaloa Highway, Maunaloa Town; (808) 552-0012

Reservations Recommended

When to go Anytime; 5–6 p.m. for the early-bird special; it gets busier later

Entrée range $17–$24.50

Payment V, MC, AE, DC

Service rating ★★★

Parking Adjacent lot

Bar Full service

Wine selection Adequate, with several wines in a reasonable price range

Dress Casual

Disabled access Good

Customers More tourists than Islanders, but a good mix

Dinner Daily, 6–9 p.m.

Setting and atmosphere Remodeled in 1998 by Molokai Ranch, the former Jojo's Cafe still sports a historic bar, but it now has a bronze countertop with a lariat design. The restaurant has a Western feeling, with light fixtures sporting Western-design shades, and saddles and cowboy pictures on the wall, but most people prefer to sit outside on the screened deck to enjoy the stars above this quiet little town.

House specialties Good, filling entrées, like prime rib, New York steak, and pizza are flavored with locally grown herbs. There's always a fresh catch of the day that can be ordered sautéed, broiled, or Cajun style, plus lobster and king crab. Try a "sky-high pie" for dessert: a mound of vanilla-, macadamia-, and coffee-flavored ice cream in a graham-cracker crust with custard, strawberry, and chocolate sauces.

Other recommendations Wok-seared Asian stir-fry, with veggies, shrimp, and scallops, and baby-back ribs impart a Molokai flavor. A local favorite for dessert is lilikoi (passionfruit) and coconut cream pie on a macadamia cookie crust made with a layer of haupia (coconut pudding), glazed with passion fruit, and topped with whipped cream and toasted coconut flakes.

Summary and comments Much of the fun here comes from cooking your own entrée on a stone grill brought to your table. Dinner in this small-town restaurant makes you feel as if you're rubbing elbows with the local folks, even though tourists are likely to be sitting at the next table.

Lanai

Blue Ginger Café ★

ISLAND ECLECTIC | INEXPENSIVE | QUALITY ★★★ | VALUE ★★ | LANAI

409 Seventh Avenue, Lanai City; (808) 565-6363

Reservations Large parties

When to go Anytime

Entrée range $5.50–$13.95

Payment V, MC

Service rating Self-serve

Parking Street

Bar Full service

Wine selection Limited

Dress Casual

Disabled access Good

Customers Islanders, travelers

Breakfast Daily, 6–11 a.m.

Lunch and dinner Daily, 11 a.m.–9 p.m.

Setting and atmosphere Set in a little wooden plantation building in Lanai City's main square. Diners pick up their orders from a counter and eat at tables with plastic cloths in this plain and simple alternative to Lanai's fancy hotel restaurants.

House specialties Try the tasty vegetarian breakfast omelet that comes with rice, or order fresh-baked apple turnovers or cinnamon rolls. For lunch, the bacon-cheddar cheeseburgers are better than Big Macs, but you might want to try the island soup called saimin, a generous steaming bowl of noodle soup garnished with sliced fish cake, green onions, and shredded egg. At dinner, sautéed mahimahi with capers, onions, and mushrooms is the signature dish. Top it off with an ice-cream dessert. Blue Ginger serves Dave's ice cream, made in the Islands with local ingredients.

Other recommendations Banana or blueberry pancakes accompanied by cappuccino are great for breakfast. For dinner, try a local plate with a choice of teriyaki beef, katsu chicken, or hamburger with gravy, plus rice and macaroni salad.

Summary and comments This has been a Lanai hangout owned by the same family for years. Blue Ginger and the little deli called Pele's Other Garden, located across the park, are the best independent restaurants around the square in Lanai City.

The Formal Dining Room, The Lodge at Koele ★★★★★

CONTEMPORARY | EXPENSIVE | QUALITY ★★★★½ | VALUE ★★★ | LANAI

Lodge at Koele, Keomuku Drive, Lanai City; (808) 565-7300; www.lanairesorts.com

Reservations Highly recommended

When to go Anytime for dinner

Entrée range $42–$46

Payment V, MC, AE, DC, JCB

Service rating ★★★★★

Parking Valet, hotel lot

Bar Full service

Wine selection Excellent

Dress Jacket required

Disabled access Adequate

Customers Hotel guests and other visitors

Dinner Daily, 6–9:30 p.m.

Setting and atmosphere The mood is relaxed and refined in this room, which looks out onto the lodge's huge backyard—reflecting pool, wide green lawns, and forested slope beyond. A fire in the fireplace lends a romantic touch. But the emphasis is on enjoying a truly fine dinner at the place some patrons consider the best in Hawaii.

House specialties Hawaii-born Chef Mark Tsuchiyama works magic with fresh, local ingredients in imaginative dishes such as these starters: orange-scented venison carpaccio on arugula with a drizzle of port syrup and white truffle oil; or ahi and hamachi tartare with potato galette, crème fraîche, chive oil, and beet essence and two caviars (Iranian and Californian). Stuffed pheasant with polenta and black trumpet mushrooms and seared Lanai venison with sugar peas, morels, parsnips, and pancetta with huckleberry sauce reflect the woodland setting.

Other recommendations If you're a fan of lobster, the Keahole (Big Island–grown) lobster with morel ragoût paired with lobster soufflé might be hard to resist. But keep dessert in mind—pineapple-guava parfait on coconut ladyfingers with baked pistachio meringue, for instance, or banana and chocolate tart with crème fraîche ice cream. The chocolate Dome (chocolate bavarian cream with Grand Marnier crème brûlée on chocolate chip–macadamia nut genoise) speaks volumes about chocolate in the hands of a master.

Entertainment and amenities Dinner music, often traditional Hawaiian songs, or classical musical scores, drifts in from the adjoining lobby. You can extend what is sure to be an expensive evening by relaxing in the lobby after dinner with a snifter of brandy in front of a crackling fire. Just be careful not to spill the $175 Remy Martin Louis VIII, which tops a list of after-dinner drinks that includes sweet wines, cognacs, armanacs, calvados, ports, madeira, and sherries rivaling the selection in some French airport duty-free shops.

Summary and comments This could be the perfect place to pop the question, with the intimate atmosphere in this quiet dining room. Tables are far enough apart to whisper, and the food is delicious. No wonder The Formal Dining Room keeps winning high praise.

Henry Clay's Rotisserie ★★★

AMERICAN COUNTRY | MODERATE | QUALITY ★★★½ | VALUE ★★★★ | LANAI

Hotel Lanai, 828 Lanai Avenue, Lanai City; (808) 565-7211; www.hotellanai.com

Reservations Highly recommended

When to go Anytime

Entrée range $12–$28

Payment V, MC; guests of all 3 island hotels can charge to their rooms

Service rating ★★★

Parking Hotel lot; many people ride a shuttle from the other 2 hotels

Bar Full service

Wine selection Good, especially California wines, many of which are available by the glass

Dress Casual

Disabled access Adequate

Customers Tourists and Islanders

Dinner Daily, 5:30–9 p.m.

Setting and atmosphere Two fireplaces create a warm glow on knotty pine walls, oak floors, and a granite-topped bar. Rich floral tapestries in mauve, green, and gold, Island scenes by Lanai artists, and outdoor lanai seating add to the old-Hawaii country charm. Diners can watch the chefs and rotisserie action through a display window into the kitchen.

House specialties The chef/owner, Henry Clay Richardson, came from New Orleans, so his ragin' Cajun shrimp and "almost Grandma's" gumbo taste like the real thing. The restaurant is recognized for rotisserie chicken and wild game, including venison, quail, rabbit, and duckling, as well as fresh Hawaiian fish.

Other recommendations For a bit more Southern zing, try seafood jalapeño pasta or eggplant Creole. Everything is made from scratch, so you can't miss by sampling the pâté, clam chowder, or pecan pie.

Summary and comments This is the best dinner value on the island, considering the cost comparison with the luxury hotel restaurants.

Ihilani ★★★★½

MEDITERRANEAN | EXPENSIVE | QUALITY ★★★★½ | VALUE ★★★ | LANAI

Manele Bay Hotel, 1 Manele Road, Lanai City; (808) 565-7700; www.lanairesorts.com

Reservations Highly recommended

When to go Anytime

Entrée range $32–$40; vegetarian menu, $28–$32

Payment V, MC, AE, DC, JCB

Service rating ★★★★★

Parking Valet

Bar Full service

Wine selection Extensive

Dress Jacket optional

Disabled access Good

Customers Tourists and visitors from the neighbor islands

Dinner Tuesday–Saturday, 6–9:30 p.m.

Setting and atmosphere Fine china, silver, and lace-clothed tables under hand-blown Italian crystal chandeliers set the elegant mood in this formal room, with views of pool and sea.

House specialties Seafood and Mediterranean flavors rightfully dominate the menu in this hotel restaurant perched on a cliff by the sea.

Other recommendations A nightly set menu of six or seven courses can be ordered paired with wines for $95 or sans wines for $65 per person. Prices may change according to what is featured. You might begin with oysters, then sample Maine lobster with shiitake mushrooms, proceed to pan-fried ahi, and savor a main course of roasted duck breast in red wine port sauce with Molokai sweet-potato puree and sautéed endive. Next, a selection of cheeses and walnut bread is served, plus a dessert selection followed by Hawaiian Vintage Chocolate and other sweets.

Summary and comments This is the kind of dining experience that is more than just grabbing a bite to eat. Expect to take several leisurely hours to do all the courses justice.

Part Nine

Shopping

Made-on-Maui with Aloha, and
Other Tropical Shopping

Made on Maui? Or Bali, or in Laguna Beach, Paris, or China. You'll find goods from all over the world for sale in Maui's burgeoning retail market and the resulting shopping centers that continue to spring up everywhere. Who will buy all these wares? They're hoping that you will, and other visiting shoppers throughout the budget ranks, particularly free-spending young Asians, as well as the folks who live here.

Gone are the days when Mauians could buy only what the plantation company store had not yet sold, at whatever price the proprietor wanted to charge. Direct-mail catalogs were more than a burden in the mailbox then. As tourism replaced the plantations, retailers slowly realized visitors want to shop when on vacation, and not just for T-shirts and gimcracks but for finely made Island arts and crafts. Shopping on Maui soared from dismal to extraordinary as the island attracted an increasingly well-heeled crowd, especially the Japanese who are bound by tradition to bring home *omiyagi* (gifts) and who prize the famous brands of European and American designer boutiques. Smart-shopping Americans found there's no better place to buy cool resort wear than a cool resort destination. The people of Maui benefit from the bigger retail market tourists help them create—more goods are available at better prices nowadays, and more residents are able to buy them. The retail boom on Maui rests partly on the advent of mainland chains and discount stores that never bothered with the Islands until waves of Japanese visitors proved to be a lucrative market.

The best reason to shop on your Maui vacation is to find goods that just aren't readily available elsewhere. The Aloha State is known for high costs, understandable since most of the goods, and the buildings that contain them, are imported. But its low sales tax of 4 percent makes purchases more palatable. Besides, there's no going home empty-handed after an enviable trip to Hawaii, and you can't stay in the tropical sun all day every day. So get ready to shop.

Rule #1. When you're after something widely available—plumeria jewelry, aloha shirts by your favorite purveyor, retro hula girl lamps, or something as basic as half a papaya for breakfast—comparison shopping will pay off. That papaya? The price of half a papaya with a piece of lime one summer morning, surveying Kaanapali Beach Resort restaurants along the promenade, varied from $2.99 to $4.99 in just a quarter of a mile. That purveyor? The price of Tommy Bahama's silky resort togs, never low, varies according to whether the shop you're in has them on sale, often up to 50 percent off. The Tommy Bahama's store at Shops at Wailea is not the place to find a bargain, although it has way more selection and probably sets a price maximum.

Rule #2. When you fall in love with something unique but big—antiques, art, or a must-have collectible—get it, even if you are on vacation in Maui and will have to arrange to get it home. That's not difficult in a place with lots of pack-and-ship stores, catering to lots of people in the same dilemma.

Buyin' Hawaiian

Local arts and crafts are flourishing. Finding them is often as much fun as buying them. Local wares sold by their makers dominate the frequent crafts fairs held throughout the Islands. Hawaiian product stores are proliferating (some are listed below). Occasionally, you'll find local things among the cheap imports in tourist-zone kiosks and souvenir stores. You can find local books, music, aloha wear, and other goods at favorable prices in the national chain stores such as Costco, Longs, Sears, and Borders and the local resort sundries chain, ABC stores.

Hawaii's indigenous products range from inexpensive to astronomical in price. They include foods like macadamia nuts, coffees, teas, wines, tropical jams, syrups and honeys, candies, and real Maui potato chips; soaps and cosmetics with tropical ingredients and fragrances; fiber arts made of coconut leaves, lauhala, pandanus, and other natural materials; wearable art such as hand-painted silks, swimwear, aloha-print shirts, baby clothes, totes, bag tags, dresses, glasses cases, even golf-ball bags; Hawaiian books and music; warm-weather designer clothing; high-tech windsurfing gear and surfboards and equipment; furniture, bowls, and boxes hand-made from tropical woods; one-of-a-kind Hawaiian appliquéd quilts, sewn only with permission of the family that created the design; and jewelry including gold heirloom jewelry, Niihau shell jewelry, koa wood jewelry, plumeria flower jewelry, and the South Pacific black pearls that dominate Lahaina shops.

One solution to the nice-but-not-too-nice gift dilemma is packaging. Buy some affordable soaps or foods and bed them in a colorful piece of aloha fabric or natural fiber inside a lidded *lauhala* (woven fiber) box. Then tie it with fiber ribbon and decorate it with a shell. Gifts are sold prepackaged this way, too.

Hawaiian heirloom gold jewelry, Victorian name bracelets, and other pieces in an arcane style created for 19th-century royals are the precious gifts of choice for special occasions in the Islands. Heirloom jewelry pieces include medallions, pendants, watchbands, link bracelets, rings, and earrings for men as well as women and they are sold at jewelry shops and at jewelry counters in other stores. Prices vary by gold weight and creative design. Most women in the Islands wear at least one oval gold bracelet ornately patterned and bearing their Hawaiian name, or their Western name translated into Hawaiian, in black enameled script. Mothers may wear their daughters' bracelets until the girls are older; many women wear them by the armload. Many bracelets never come off. A bracelet might cost anywhere from $250 for a simple pattern on a thin band to $1,200 or more for a complex design on a big band. This is a subjective purchase based on design, but do shop around enough to satisfy yourself that the price is fair for what you want. Shop for a bracelet early in your trip, to allow time for sizing and name engraving. The case samples are inscribed "Kuuipo," meaning "my sweetheart."

Where to Shop

It's hard to avoid shops, beginning with the lobby stores in resort hotels, where stylish, high-quality resort clothing, swimsuits, and shoes can often be found, and ending at the airports, where gift shops actually have local gifts and fresh tropical flowers.

Maui has become a favorite place to buy art while on vacation, and the galleries are numerous and exceptional. South Maui has acquired its own branches of favorite stores, galleries, and restaurants popular in West Maui, a long 45-minute drive away from Wailea. Even without billboards (not a Hawaii species), we know you can find local versions of national chain stores on your own, so we've mentioned only the larger shopping complexes and some nonchain stores worth attention. Expect slightly higher prices on some items, even at Wal-Mart. Hilo Hattie's stores, crammed with matching bold-print aloha wear, are everywhere, and they will find you if you don't find them. But that's not all there is.

Below are some stand-out places to find local arts and crafts and other goods. The first group features specialty storefronts, galleries, and the like; the second includes shopping complexes with multiple stores, both independent shops and national and international chains.

Specialty Shops

West Maui

Gold Fantasy

Location 3350 Lower Honoapiilani Road (Kahana area)
Phone (800) 411-9495 or (808) 661-6288
Hours Monday–Saturday, 9 a.m.–5:30 p.m.
Description Master goldsmith Robert Cohn works in platinum as well, does custom orders, and displays his own works. If you have a pearl in your pocket, see what he can do with it.

Hawaiiana Arts and Crafts

Location Cinema Wharf Center, Lahaina
Phone (808) 661-9077
Hours Daily, 10 a.m.–8 p.m.
Description Hand-made arts and crafts by some of Maui's best artisans, including raku pottery, woodcrafts, and woven baskets.

Honolua Store

Location Office Road, Kapalua Resort
Phone (808) 669-6128
Hours Daily, 6 a.m.–8 p.m.
Description Historic plantation grocery store features books, gifts, and clothing, along with groceries and beverages.

Lahaina Mail Depot

Location Wharf Cinema Center
Phone (808) 667-2000
Hours Monday–Friday, 10 a.m.–4:30 p.m.; Saturday, 10 a.m.–1 p.m.
Description Send those purchases packing here—shipping, materials, FedEx, UPS, and mail-a-coconut services.

Lahaina Printsellers

Location Three stores in Lahaina: 505 Front Street, 1013 Limahana Place, and in Whalers Village
Phone (808) 667-5815

Hours Daily, 10 a.m.–10:30 p.m.

Description Premiere vendor of vintage prints and etchings, antique maps of locations around the world, sea charts, early Hawaii maps.

Mr. Wine

Location 808 Wainee Street, Lahaina

Phone (808) 661-5551

Hours Monday–Saturday, 11 a.m.–7 p.m., closed Sunday

Description More than 600 boutique wines, champagnes, and sparkling wines, including those premiums ($15 and up) kept in the 55°F wine cellar. Hawaiian microbrews and cigars are also available.

Sandal Tree

Locations Whalers Village and Hyatt Regency Maui shops, Kaanapali; and Grand Wailea Shops in South Maui

Phone Whalers Village, (808) 667-5330; Hyatt Regency, (808) 661-3495; Grand Wailea, (808) 874-9006

Hours Daily, 9 a.m.–10 p.m.

Description Best collection we know of sandals of all sorts for women and men, from fancy rubber beach slippers to strappy dancing shoes, and manly topsiders and strapped sports sandals. Plus: kids' wear, socks, handbags, backpacks, and even a hat or two.

Central Maui

Gallerie Ha

Location 51 Market Street, Wailukku

Phone (808) 244-3993

Hours Daily, 1–5 p.m.

Description Ha is the studio gallery for artist Pat Masumoto, who paints papayas, cats, and montages of female figures, among other things. Visit the gallery's Web site, **www.gallerieha.com.** Ha means "breath of life" in Hawaiian, not "ha-ha" funny.

Hoaloha Wood Heirlooms

Location Kaahumanu Shopping Center, Kahului

Phone (808) 873-0461

Hours Monday–Friday, 9:30 a.m–9 p.m.; Saturday, 9:30 a.m.–7 p.m.; Sunday, 10 a.m.–5 p.m.

Description Heirlooms features Hawaiiana and Polynesian merchandise, including koa bowls, jewelry and accessories, dolls, quilts, hula implements, ukulele, artworks, and carvings.

Kaukini Gallery

Location Kahakuloa Head, northwest coast

Phone (808) 244-3371

Hours Daily, 10 a.m.–5 p.m.

Description More than 100 local artists' paintings, prints, jewelry, ceramics, fabric arts, and wood works are displayed and sold in this handsome gallery, a modern plantation–style yellow house that stands alone by the road in an incredibly scenic remote setting. Huge wood sculptures welcome you in the gardens, while affordable to pricy creations compete for your attention inside. Look for bracelets of woven gold-and-silver wire echoing mariners' knots, linen dish towels silk-screened with Hawaiian botanicals in natural colors, and jewelry set with black pearls alongside precious stones. The artist/proprietress, who opened her first shop seven years ago on the porch of her grandfather's ranch house up the road, built the gallery three years ago.

Moonbow Tropics

Locations 300 Maalaea Road, Maalaea, and 36 Baldwin Avenue, Paia

Phone (808) 243-9577 and (808) 579-8775 or 579-8592

Hours Monday–Saturday, 10 a.m.–7 p.m; Sunday 10 a.m.–6 p.m.

Description Men seem to be comfortable shopping here, browsing through classy aloha shirts and other clothes for men and women, as well as other appointments to the tropical good life, including CDs. Stores include one by the Maui Ocean Center and two on Paia's main shopping street, Baldwin Avenue.

Precision Goldsmiths

Location 16 North Market Street, Wailuku

Phone (808) 986-8282

Hours Monday–Friday, 9 a.m.–5 p.m.

Description Tasteful inspirations by master goldsmith Brian Thomsen, who can create something just for you. For a preview, visit **www.precision goldsmiths.com.**

Sig Zane Designs

Location 53 North Market Street, Wailuku

Phone (808) 249-8997

Hours Monday–Friday, 9:30–5:50; Saturday, 9 a.m.–3 p.m.

Description Distinctive men's and women's clothing, plus fabric for interiors, in bold Hawaiian graphics and striking colors by Hawaii designer Sig Zane.

South Maui

Kii Gallery

Location The Shops at Wailea

Phone (808) 874-1181

Hours Daily, 9:30 a.m.–9 p.m.

Description A remarkable collection of brilliantly colorful studio glass sculptures of all hues, sizes, and shapes, sharing the space with turned wood art objects and unlikely Greek marble statuary, bronze lamps, and the like, by American artists.

Dolphin Galleries

Location The Shops at Wailea and Whalers Village, Kaanapali

Phone (808) 893-1000

Hours Daily, 9:30 a.m.–9 p.m.

Description Jewelry and art, some familiar, some extraordinary in well-designed galleries where "just looking" is a pleasure. Modern cloisonne set in gold, kinetic gemstone rings, and dolphins galore are among the works.

Kihei Wine and Spirits

Location 300 Ohukai Road, Kihei

Phone (808) 879-0555

Hours Tuesday–Friday, 10 a.m.–6 p.m., Saturday 10 a.m.–6 p.m., closed Sunday and Monday.

Description A selection of more than 500 wines, premium liquors and liqueurs, Hawaiian microbrews, gourmet foods, and cigars.

Noa Noa

Location Shops at Wailea and Whalers Village, Kaanapali

Phone (808) 879-9069 and (808) 661-2056

Hours Daily, 9 a.m.–5 p.m.

Description Women's tropical clothing batiked in Indonesia to order for this Island chain, from Polynesian-inspired graphics and designs, in natural light fabrics and rayon.

Serendipity

Location Kaahumanu Center, Kihei; Shops at Wailea; Lahaina Cannery Mall

Phone (808) 871-1116

Hours Daily, 9 a.m.–5 p.m.

Description Women's dresses and other clothing in the form of colorful Indonesian imports, in tropical-weight rayon and other breezy fabrics and styles just right for Maui moods, including silk sarongs. Also for sale are Javanese teak furnishings and accents. Serendipity's owner does the design and buying.

Upcountry Maui

David Warren Gallery

Location 3625 Baldwin Avenue, Makawao

Phone (877) 572-1288 or (808) 572-1288

Hours Daily, 10 a.m.–6 p.m.

Description This small, eclectic family gallery is dedicated to the late David Warren, who painted scenes of the lovely place where he lived, Upcountry Maui, abloom with blue jacaranda trees, and human figures dancing, often hula. Warren died suddenly in 1998, and his wife, sons, and friends took over the gallery, selling his works and their own, including handcrafted placemats and fine woodcraft, as well as framing and jewelry. The gallery is online at **www.davidwarrengallery.com.**

Tropo

Location 3643 Baldwin Avenue, Makawao

Phone (808) 573-0356

Hours Daily, 10 a.m.–6 p.m.

Description Guy things—men's designer aloha shirts, of silk and other fine fabrics, name-brand tropical wear, and tasteful informal clothing; also books, jazz CDs, Swiss Army knives, binoculars, accessories, and Crabtree and Evelyn cosmetics.

Hana

Hana Coast Gallery

Location Hotel Hana-Maui

Phone (808) 248-8636

Hours Daily, 9 a.m.–5 p.m.

Description Visit here to see the exquisite collection of Maui artists' works as you might a small museum, because it's that committed to the culture and it's that good. Oil, watercolors, woods, feathers, stone, prints, glass, and fibers are among the media used to interpret the beauty of Hana and Maui by famous and lesser-known artists in artworks, furniture, and jewelry. If you want to purchase some excellent local pieces for your collection, don't miss this one. Visit **www.hanacoast.com** for more information.

Hasegawa General Store

Location 5165 Hana Highway, Hana

Phone (808) 248-8231

Hours Monday–Saturday, 7 a.m.–7 p.m.; Sunday, 8 a.m.–6 p.m.

Description An old-fashioned general merchandise store, so beloved that a song was written about it. Founded in 1910, this family-run store sells necessities and some frills for residents of and visitors to faraway Hana. There's a good collection of Hana-related music and books.

Molokai

Big Wind Kite Factory

Location 120 Maunaloa Highway, Maunaloa

Phone (808) 552-2364

Hours Monday–Saturday, 8:30 a.m.–5 p.m.; Sunday, 10 a.m.–2 p.m.

Description Kites of all shapes, sizes, and designs, some made on site; plus imported gifts. The friendly owner provides free kite-flying lessons (at an adjacent open field) with "no strings attached."

Lanai

Akamai Trading

Location 408 Eighth Street, Lanai City

Phone (808) 565-6587

Hours Monday–Friday, 9 a.m.–6 p.m.; Saturday, 9 a.m.–5:30 p.m.; Sunday, 9 a.m.–4:30 p.m.

Description This general store has an interesting selection of Island necessities, souvenirs, gifts, and locally made jams and jellies.

Gifts with Aloha

Location Seventh Street, Lanai City

Phone (808) 565-6589

Hours Monday–Saturday, 9:30 a.m.–5:30 p.m.

Description Made-in-Hawaii gifts, including resort wear, koa-wood products, scented candles, books, hand-quilted pillow covers.

Shopping Centers

West Maui

505 Front Street

Location Front Street, Lahaina

Phone (808) 667-2514

Hours Monday–Saturday, 10 a.m.–9 p.m.; Sunday, 10 a.m.–6 p.m.

Number of stores and restaurants 25+

Description Oceanfront boutique mall at the quieter southern end of Lahaina. Unusual storefronts feature made-on-Maui products, spa cosmetics, clothing, souvenirs, gifts, and there are several good waterfront restaurants, including IO and PacificO. Live jazz is played here on Thursday, Friday, and Saturday nights. Visit 505 Front Street online at **www.hio hwy.com/f/fiveofiv.htm.**

Lahaina Center

Location 900 Front Street, Lahaina

Phone (808) 667-9216

Hours Monday–Saturday, 9 a.m.–10 p.m.; Sunday, 9 a.m.–6 p.m. (store hours vary.)

Number of stores and restaurants 30

Description Stores feature aloha wear, gifts, sundries, apparel, T-shirts, swimwear, children's apparel, jewelry, and microbrews. Free hula shows are held Wednesday and Friday, at 2 and 6 p.m.

Whalers Village

Location 2435 Kaanapali Parkway, Kaanapali Beach Resort

Phone (808) 661-4567

Hours Daily, 9:30 a.m.–10 p.m.

Number of stores and restaurants 60

Description Upscale European and American boutiques, jewelry, scrimshaw, Hawaiian koa furniture, gifts, art galleries, island apparel, and general goods are all available here. Waterfront restaurants include casual outdoor cafés like Hula Grill and Leilani's. Free hula performances are held at 7 p.m. nightly, except on Tuesday and Thursday. Visit the village online at **www.whalersvillage.com.**

Napili Plaza

Location 5095 Napilihau Street, Napili

Phone (808) 665-0546

Hours 9 a.m.–9 p.m., market until 11 p.m.

Number of stores and restaurants 17

Description Napili Plaza has a supermarket; informal plate lunch, pizza, sub, and taco eateries; a coffee store that roasts its own beans; a jewelry store with Hawaiian heirloom jewelry, watches, and the husband-and-wife designer team's own creations; a day spa; and a mailing-services store where you can mail a coconut postcard, hand decorated, for only $7–$8 postage.

South Maui

Azeka Place Shopping Center

Location 1279 and 1280 South Kihei Road, Kihei

Phone (808) 879-5000

Hours Daily, 8:30 a.m.–10 p.m.

Number of stores and restaurants 50+

Description That traffic snarl at the southern end of Kihei is due largely to this shopping conglomeration of specialty stores, markets, and restaurants serving residents and visitors.

Kihei Kalama Village

Location 1941 South Kihei Road, Kihei

Phone (808) 879-6610

Number of stores and restaurants 60

Description Collection of more specialty stores and restaurants, including Tuna Luna, an artists' collective selling local arts and crafts that may have the gift you're seeking. Also try Pua's Lei Stand, which sells fresh flower lei and Hawaiiana, including made-on-Maui products. Kalama Tropical Treasures offers another stash of fabric, wood, and other gifts and will ship them for you.

The Shops at Wailea

Location 3750 Wailea Alanui Drive, Wailea Resort

Phone (808) 879-4474

Hours Daily, 10 a.m.–10 p.m.

Number of stores and restaurants 25+

Description This new $24 million cluster is the swankiest shopping center you're likely to find anywhere. Four restaurants offer alternatives to hotel dining: Longhi's (American food), Tommy Bahama's Tropical Cafe (attached to a clothing and home store), Cheeseburger, Mai Tai's and Rock 'n' Roll, and Ruth's Chris Steak House, not to mention Honolulu Coffee Company's Cafe Wailea, which opens at 7 a.m. (8 a.m. on Sundays) with espresso drinks and breakfast breads. Retail vendors include Tiffany's, Mont Blanc, Moschino, Gucci, Celine, and the like, along with the Gap, Banana Republic, Tommy Bahama's Tropical Emporium, and local clothing firms Crazyshirts, Noa Noa, Serendipity, Reyn's, and Blue Ginger. Martin & McArthur features Hawaiian koa furniture and other wood crafts. Galleries include works ranging from Wyland seascapes to extraordinary glass, jewelry, and sculpture at Dolphin Galleries and Kii Galleries. In sum, you'll find resort wear, upscale boutiques, gifts, art, wood crafts and furniture, toys, camera shops, sundries, ice cream, and beach wear. Watch for special events like food festivals. Every Wednesday, you'll find restaurant specials and live entertainment, fashion, and art events.

Piilani Village Center

Location 225 Piikea Avenue, Kihei

Phone (808) 874-8900

Hours Daily, 10 a.m.–10 p.m.

Number of stores and restaurants 25+

Description This new shopping complex, built for a newly created Kihei neighborhood, describes itself as the place visitors shop when they actually need something—groceries, haircuts, lattes, dry cleaning, beach wear, music, smoothies, medical services, photo printing, video rentals, and the like. Lightening Bolt Maui surf shop includes Patagonia sportswear and some exotic imports among the array of bikinis, board shorts, rash guards, and coverups required for young beachgoers. Another great place for dinner is the new Roy's Kihei Restaurant specializing in East/West Island fusion cuisine, Maui's third restaurant masterminded by chef Roy Yamaguchi. It's located just off Piilani Highway on the southern end of Kihei.

Central Maui

Queen Kaahumanu Center

Location Kaahumanu Avenue, Kahului

Phone (808) 877-3369

Hours Monday–Friday, 9:30 a.m–9 p.m.; Saturday, 9:30 a.m.–7 p.m.; Sunday, 10 a.m.–5 p.m.

Number of stores and restaurants About 75

Description This is the island's principal mall, recently redone, and a good place to get a sense of the scope of goods available on Maui. Several of the local stores have other outlets in the resort shopping centers, such as Serendipity, which sells Indonesian clothes and furniture. Department stores (including Macy's, which bought the Island store Liberty House), books, gifts, toys, cards, jewelry, cartoon logos, coffee, shoes, apparel, photo processing, movies, and restaurants are included here, along with frequent community events.

A Final Option

Don't want to go anywhere to shop? Need a clone to do your shopping for you? Here's a service that might work for you: Maui's Personal Shopper provides personalized, door-to-door services, such as grocery shopping, document delivery, home care, and errands by the hour. Call Kevin Reiss, (808) 667-0662 or (808) 870-6889, or visit **www.mauispersonal shopper.com.**

Part Ten

Entertainment and Nightlife

You Came to Maui for the Nightlife?

You must be misinformed. Wait, don't go away. Actually, there is life after sundown on Maui, but it isn't always what you might expect. It may even surprise you.

If you came to Hawaii to escape the ordinary and experience something new and different, even exotic, now is your chance. The Islands of Hawaii were once an independent kingdom, and nowhere does that legacy seem clearer than in music and dance. Even in this age of mass media and world culture, Hawaii has its own popular music and star performers, its own cultural dance and theater tradition based on the chant, its own language and legends, its own style of dress and casual speech, and its own killer cocktails, headlined by the mai tai.

Islanders don't pack up their native sounds and moves until a cultural holiday comes along. Hawaiian music is the daily music of choice for a lot of people of all ages, and many kids today take hula classes at some age or another, much like piano class elsewhere. This is not to say you'll find only Hawaiian entertainment on Maui, Molokai, and Lanai. But you won't find it at all in most other places, so this is the best chance to sample it. Hotels usually feature live Hawaiian entertainment sometime during the day, and some of the clubs star popular contemporary Hawaiian musicians and singers, often with a bit of sensual hula thrown in. Plenty of clubs, mostly in Kihei and Lahaina, feature rock and pop music live for dancing and late-night fun.

The Islands are full of gifted musicians and singers, such as Maui's Kealii Reichel, Willie K., Amy Hanaialii Gilliom, Hookena, Makaha Sons of Niihau, the Peter Moon Band, Robbie Kahakalau, and Na Leo Pumehana, to name a few. Check the *Maui News,* or the free *Maui Times* and *Maui Weekly,* for dates and venues.

It doesn't take much originality to go to the Hard Rock Cafe and get another T-shirt, but you can, right on Front Street in Lahaina. Or, you can seek out what makes Maui different from other islands.

A few caveats: The legal drinking age is 21. Keep in mind the State of Hawaii has tough drunk-driving laws (the legal blood-alcohol limit is 0.08 percent) and police set up roadblocks on weekends and holidays to check the sobriety of motorists. If you drink, don't drive; take a taxi.

Most Maui nightlife action is centered in Kihei and Lahaina, where a variety of clubs draw crowds, and the action picks up and gets interesting after 10 p.m. Some biker bars in Kahului and Wailuku have become all the rage with unlikely patrons—holiday Boomers on rental hogs.

The state's best live theatrical production runs nightly in Lahaina: *Ulalena,* a *Cirque du Soleil*–inspired, must-see rendition of Hawaii's fabled history at the high-tech **Maui Myth and Magic Theater.** The diversity of the percussive band alone is worth the price of a ticket.

Otherwise, nightlife is limited to hotel lounge acts (some quite good) and commercial luau, and yes, you should certainly attend at least one luau during your stay. The best, in our view: **Old Lahaina Luau, The Feast at Lele,** and **Wailea's Finest Luau** at the Marriott Wailea Beach Resort, which features world champion fire knife dancer Ifi Soo.

If your timing's good, you may see Willie Nelson (who has a home on Maui), the Beach Boys, or even Tony Bennett at Maui Arts and Cultural Center, and for a lot less than on the mainland. It's just a question of when you will be there. Maui Arts and Cultural Center, the crossroads of lively arts, features a diverse year-round schedule. Check out who's there when you are at **www.mauiarts.org.**

Someone's always strumming a ukulele or singing a Hawaiian song at **Kaanapali Beach Hotel.** Maui's "most Hawaiian hotel," celebrates **Aloha Friday** not only every Friday but every day of the week in song and dance; the hotel employees' choir even created a local Kahili award–winning compact disc, *E Hoomau I Ka Pookela.*

The attractions are stellar, up on the roof at the Hyatt Regency Maui Resort and Spa, where at the three-times-nightly **Tour of the Stars** astronomers show guests how to find astral phenomena by peering through high-powered, computer-operated telescopes to scan Maui's incredible night sky. After finding the Big Dipper you may see the rings of Saturn, the moons of Jupiter, the Southern Cross, and other timely celestial sights, or look into the beyond, to distant stars and new planets. This popular after-dark activity began a decade ago and continues to attract stargazers and junior stargazers up to the roof at 8, 9, and 10 p.m. nightly. On weekends the late-night Tour of the Stars, popular with honeymooners, starts at 11 p.m. and includes chocolate-dipped strawberries and champagne.

The Maui Ocean Center may not be at the top of your mind as a hot nightspot, but after sundown, big pelagic fish like sharks show their nocturnal side at the **Aquarium After Dark;** it's safer than the night dives certified divers do.

SEA ADVENTURES AFTER DARK

Night Dives

And, no, we don't mean biker bars. This after-dark-on-Maui adventure is for certified divers, only. Take a night dive off Maui with Mike Severns, a biologist, underwater photographer, veteran scuba diver, and author of *Molokini Island, Hawaii's Premier Marine Preserve.* On Wednesday nights he leads two-tank night dives to the reefs off Maui where you can see what really goes on after the sun goes down. The abundance of underwater nightlife will surprise you. Eels, manta rays, and big fish come out to play and hunt along with lobsters and nudibranchs.

A rare treat is offered only on certain nights in the spring, when Severns leads a few divers to watch the coral spawn. Coral is a living organism, and there are only a few places, the Great Barrier Reef in Australia, for one, where you can see it propagate.

It's "a beautiful and unearthly sight," says Severns. "Hundreds of coral colonies release orange globes that rise to the surface in curtains, then they break apart and spawn."

Contact **Mike Severns Diving** at P.O. Box 627; Kihei, or phone (808) 879-6596.

Dive at Dusk

Ed Robinson takes you down at dusk on two-tank dives to watch crabs, shrimp, lobsters, octopus, the Spanish Dancer nudibranch, and the nocturnal reef fish.

"Dusk is a unique time of change for the reef animals," he says. "Some perform mating rituals, others display feeding activity, and some are easy to approach as they become sleepy."

Call **Ed Robinson Diving Adventures** at (808) 879-3584.

It's not the same as the real thing, but **Hawaii Experience Domed Theater** on Front Street, Lahaina, presents a 40-minute nature film on the Islands from 9 a.m. to 11 p.m. daily on a three-stories-tall, 180-degree screen.

Nighttime, when it's cooler, is the right time to play tennis on Maui. You can play after dark on world-class courts on Maui at the **Wailea Tennis Club** (phone (808) 879-1958), which has 14 courts, including 4 lighted for night play, or **The Tennis Garden** at Kapalua, with 10 plexipave courts, 4 of them lighted for night play (phone (808) 669-5677).

Techies on a break can surf the Web at Internet cafés all over the island and at Maui resort hotel business centers; most offer hookups, some, like Marriott Wailea Beach Resort, have in-room keyboards.

And the bright lights of Waikiki are only 30 minutes away by jet, in case you need to hear more than the sound of surf and wind in the palm trees.

You did come to Maui to relax, didn't you?

Big-Time Performers

Sooner or later, entertainers from elsewhere come to Maui to perform, as diverse as rock's Melissa Etheridge, country's Crystal Gayle, New Age music guru George Winston, Prince, and the New Shanghai Circus, all of whom appeared on-island recently.

The **Maui Arts and Cultural Center,** the island's premiere venue in Kahului, has a lively schedule of Hawaiian and other entertainment. For information call (808) 242-7469 or visit **www.mauiarts.org.**

SUNSET ON HALEAKALA

Everyone goes up the volcano at sunrise, but sunsets on Haleakala are just as spectacular. And less crowded. After the sun sinks in the Pacific, you can watch the moon rise over Haleakala, another surreal act of nature, and then the inky black night sky shines with a million points of light. Bring a sleeping bag, you may not want to leave. You can crash at the park's nearby Hosmer Grove Campground, often full of other starry-eyed campers.

There's a reason the U.S Air Force maintains its Maui Space Surveillance Site up here on Haleakala, and it isn't only to monitor spacecraft (ours and maybe theirs). It's off-limits, but otherwise the night is yours up here. To reach the summit, take Haleakala Highway 378.

Molokai and Lanai after Dark

If you're staying on Molokai or Lanai, bring a good book and your iPod, or plan to revive the lost art of charades. Resorts sundry stores usually have some beach-reading, old paperbacks, last month's magazines, and day-late city newspapers from the West Coast, as well as the *Maui News.* The major hotels provide a daily fax version of the *New York Times* if you want to stay abreast of current events. The resort libraries are often libraries in name only, with shelves full of gilt-edged leather-bound books, mostly in German, bought by the yard from interior decorators. Maui does have a Borders (call (808) 877-6160), two Waldenbooks (call (808) 661-8672 or (808) 667-6712), and the Old Lahaina Book Emporium (call (808) 661-1999), with hard-to-find and collectible Hawaii books.

You may get lucky on Lanai, where a monthly **Visiting Artist** lecture at the hotels may produce a famous artist, writer, chef, or other celebrity while you're there. (See below.)

Molokai's East End has a bar or two where *pau hana* (work's end, like TGIF) is celebrated over beer and *pipikaula* (beef jerky) and, sometimes, a loud boogie band or even local entertainer Darrell Labrado, whose "Shaka Da Moon" gives a faint hint of nightlife on a tropical island. Be careful which pretty lady you ask to dance or you may get more than you thought. Molokai is noted for its drag queens, transsexuals, and *mahu* (boys raised as girls, a Polynesian tradition that still endures in some families).

When you grow tired of watching the cows graze on the 54,000-acre Molokai Ranch, there's little to do except sip your cocktail and enjoy a long, leisurely dinner and your companion. After sundown, which is the big event on Molokai's West End, there's usually somebody, either a thirsty local cowpoke or a bored out-of-towner, to talk story with at the bar at **The Lodge at Molokai Ranch.** On Molokai, if the lights are out at Kaunakakai's **Mitchell Pauole Stadium,** home of local softball games, your next best shot at nightlife is stargazing, an old Polynesian pastime, considered excellent since night skies in the mid-Pacific are clear and distracting ground lights nearly nonexistent. On dark nights a local astronomer sometimes invites Molokai Ranch guests to probe the galaxies.

Finally, if you are really desperate for diversion, there are always movies—on demand in your hotel room, in video rentals, at multiplexes on Maui (in Lahaina, Kahului, and Kihei) and even Molokai (in a new Maunaloa town theater) and at the restored 1930s **Lanai Theatre,** which also features live programs and special events.

Lanai's Visiting Artist Program

Perhaps you've seen the picture of King David Kalakaua and Robert Louis Stevenson sitting on the beach at Waikiki. The author is telling stories, regaling his majesty with bon mot. Or maybe the image of Jack London describing the voyage of the *Snark* to Queen Liliuokalani. The *tusitala,* or storyteller, was always held in high regard in old Hawaii. Visitors were always welcome, especially if they had a good story to tell, and Hawaii, the most isolated populated place on Earth, developed a grand storytelling tradition that continues today on Lanai.

To this former black hole of arts and culture comes now the literati and glitterati of continental America to share their talents in a retro version of royal turn-of-the-century parlor games.

On Lanai, you can plan your vacation with, say, Carlos Barbosa-Lima, the classical guitarist. In the beginning, pickings were slim since few outside Hawaii had ever heard of Lanai ("Where, exactly, is it?" Pulitzer

Prize–winning author John McPhee asked.) Now, this small gathering has grown to become the year-long Lanai **Visiting Artists Program.** Poets, musicians, writers, actors, chefs, and others are invited to share their talents in a casual living room atmosphere. You may step out on the verandah and find yourself in the company of the pianist Eduardus Halim, jazz singer Cleo Laine, drama critic Sheridan Morley, screen-writer Terry George (*In the Name of the Father*) or Ron Maxwell, direc-tor of *Gettysburg*. Others include humorist Dave Barry, actress Elke Sommer, and John Loring, author and Tiffany & Co. design director.

"We never had anything like this on this island before," said Kurt Mat-sumoto, the hotel's former general manager and creator of the event.

All events are free to hotel guests and Lanai residents. To check Visiting Artists Program at The Lodge at Koele, visit **www.lanai-resorts.com** or call (808) 565-7300.

Dinner Shows

Note: Look for show ads in Maui's myriad tourist magazines. Some are worth $10 a person off your tab.

Kupanaha

Location Kaanapali Beach Hotel, 2525 Kaanapali Parkway, Lahaina
Phone (808) 661-0011
Show times Tuesday–Saturday, 4:30 p.m.
Length 3 hours
Cost Gold Circle seating, $79; general seating, $69; teenagers, $49; children, $29
Food 3-course dinner
Beverages Mai tai, wine, beer, soft drinks, coffee
Description and comments The name Kupanaha is Hawaiian for magical and mystical. Illusionists Jody Baran and Kathleen Pomeroy pre-sent a magic show based on Hawaiian legends about Kekaa, the Black Rock, that's Kaanapali Beach's famous landmark. Keep an eye on this cast of magicians (if you can); this fast-paced family show features sleight of hand in a good dinner show.

Ulalena

Location Maui Myth and Magic Theater, 878 Front Street, Lahaina
Phone (877) 688-4800 or (808) 661-9913

Web site www.ulalena.com

Show times Tuesday–Saturday, 6 p.m.; additional shows Tuesdays, 8:30 p.m.

Length 90 minutes

Cost Adults, $45; teenagers, $35; children, $25

Discounts None.

Type of seating $10 million, state-of-art theater with stadium seating, features live Hawaiian chant and music with 8-channel surround sound

Food Snack bar in lobby

Beverages Beer, wine, soft drinks, juice, coffee

Description and comments Best original, creative show in Hawaii. Excellent entertainment. A *Cirque du Soleil*–style production by the Montreal troupe blends island myth and fact in a culturally keen live theatrical performance. If you go to Maui, you must see *Ulalena*.

Warren and Annabelle's

Location 900 Front Street, Lahaina

Phone (808) 667-6244 or (808) 667-MAGIC

Web site www.warrenandannabelles.com

Show times 2 shows Monday–Saturday, 6:45 and 8:15 p.m.

Length 3 hours

Cost $45 general admission (adult or child), $73 includes two cocktails and pupus, $79 includes two cocktails, pupus, and dessert

Discounts Coupons offering a 20 percent discount are available in hotel lobbies

Type of seating Table seating for pupus and cocktails. Intimate 78-seat theater (stadium seating) for show. First come, first served.

Food Unless you order pupu, everything is à la carte. Pupu menu includes spicy crab cakes, coconut-battered shrimp, chicken satay, and crab-stuffed mushrooms. Desserts include chocolate truffle cake, crème brûlée, deep-dish apple pie, and New York–style cheesecake. Vegetarians should request alternatives in advance.

Beverages Tropical drinks, specialty drinks, beer, wine, soft drinks, juice, coffee.

Description and comments "Close-up" magician Warren Gibson performs sleight-of-hand tricks in the cozy theater with Annabelle, a piano-playing ghost who takes requests.

Before- and After-Dinner Lounges

Major resort hotels on all the islands offer good Hawaiian music, jazz, and a place to dance or relax with an after-dinner drink and enjoy the evening. Here are the best.

WHERE TO FIND THE PERFECT MAI TAI

Bright as a tropical moon, smooth as summer surf, rich as old Lurline passengers, cool and fresh as green limes, the mai tai is Hawaii's favorite drink. One sip and it's paradise. Or, should be. Most mai tais served in Hawaii today are too strong, too sweet, and, at $7 and up, too expensive. Some taste like gasoline, others like cough syrup. They burn the throat, produce terrible headaches, and generally give Hawaii a bad name. These tacky concoctions have little in common with a real mai tai and should be avoided at all costs. Some variations on the original theme are excellent because they don't alter the basic ingredients. The classic mai tai is an unforgettable cocktail, an icy Jamaican rum and fresh lime juice drink with a subtle hint of oranges and almonds and a sprig of fresh mint for garnish. Now, that's a mai tai. Where you sip a mai tai is almost as important as the ingredients. This tropical drink always tastes better in a thatch hut on a lagoon with coco palms lining the shore.

Here's where to find and enjoy the best mai tai on Maui today:

The Bay Club, Kapalua Bay Hotel, Maui Maui may be the Chardonnay capital of the Hawaii (all those ex-pat California wine-bibbers) but you can find a great Mai Tai at the newly renovated Bay Club overlooking Kapalua Bay.

The Lodge at Molokai Ranch, Molokai At the end of a hot dusty trail ride on the Molokai Ranch, nothing tastes finer than a mai tai on the lanai of the Lodge at Molokai Ranch overlooking the back 40 (thousand acres) as an orange sun sinks into the blue Pacific.

Hula Moons, Marriott Wailea Beach Resort, Maui Surrounded by memorabilia of the 1930s, this nostalgic shrine to poet Don Blanding, who created Lei Day in Hawaii (celebrated every May 1) is the ideal watering hole to sample tropical cocktails like Missionary's Downfall or Tropical Itch.

Maui

Hula Moons, Marriott Wailea Beach Resort (808) 879-1922. Nostalgic bar filled with old photos and vintage art with live Hawaiian music on weekends.

Tsunami, Grand Wailea Resort (808) 875-1234. High-tech disco with dressy couples dancing to DJ Top 40 tunes. Loud, noisy, and fun, on Friday and Saturday nights from 9:30 p.m. to 2 a.m.

Molokai

The Lodge at Molokai Ranch, Maunaloa Room (808) 552-2791. After a hard day on the ranch kick back with other dudes at The Lodge watering hole, where the view overlooks pastures that run to the Pacific. Live Hawaiian music Friday, 6–8 p.m. and Saturday, 6:30–8:30 p.m.

Hotel Molokai (808) 553-5347. New Hula Shores restaurant and bar features live Hawaiian entertainment seven nights a week from "about 6–7 p.m., sometimes until 9 p.m., just depends."

Lanai

Hale Aheahe Lounge Manele Bay Hotel (808) 565-7700. The lounge features pianist or Hawaiian music most evenings.

Lanai Theatre 465 Seventh Street, Lanai City; (808) 565-7500. Live local performances, including school plays, art programs, movies, and special events.

The Lodge at Koele (808) 565-7300. Hawaiian music most evenings in the Great Hall.

Nightlife

Profiled Clubs and Nightspots

Maui shows signs of a burgeoning nightlife industry. You can find late-night amusement on Lahaina's Front Street, but don't expect a scene elsewhere. The legal drinking age is 21.

Below are the island's hotspots, grouped by region. Clubs come and go; schedules and formats change often, as determined by which places are hot or not. Check with your hotel concierge for up-to-the minute details.

MAUI NIGHTLIFE		
Name	**Description**	**Region**
Dick's Place	Billiards bar	South Maui
Hapa's Brew Haus	Bar with live bands	South Maui
Hard Rock Café	Music-themed restaurant and bar	West Maui
Jacques Northshore Restaurant	Restaurant and bar	Central Maui
Life's A Beach	Beach bar with dancing	South Maui
Manana Garage	Latino-themed restaurant and bar	Central Maui
Maui Brews	Restaurant and bar with dancing	West Maui
Mulligan's on the Blue	Irish pub	South Maui
Sports Page Grill and Bar	Sports bar	South Maui

West Maui

Hard Rock Café

INTERNATIONALLY KNOWN MUSIC-THEMED RESTAURANT

Who Goes There 18–50; tourists, music lovers, T-shirt collectors

900 Front Street, Lahaina; (808) 667-7400; www.hardrock.com

Cover None

Minimum None

Dress Casual

Beverages Beer, wine, mixed drinks.

Food available Pig sandwiches, pot roast, grilled fajitas, burgers, and barbecue chicken.

Hours Dining: daily, 11:30 a.m.–11 p.m. Bar: Sunday–Thursday and Saturday, 11:30 a.m.–12:30 a.m.; Friday, 11:30 a.m.–1:30 a.m.

What goes on Live entertainment on Friday, 11 p.m.–1 a.m.

Comments Same place, different artifacts.

If you go Expect a wait to eat.

Maui Brews

10,000-SQUARE-FOOT EATERY AND CLUB

Who Goes There 18–35; postgrads, whale-watchers, beach boys and girls

900 Front Street, Lahaina (behind Hard Rock); (808) 667-7794

Cover None

Minimum None

Dress Casual (no swimwear or tank tops)

Beverages Beer, wine, mixed drinks.

Food available Pizza, steamed clams, pasta, taro rolls, steak, and sandwiches.

Hours Daily, 11:30 a.m.–2 a.m.

What goes on Hip hop on Tuesday; salsa on Wednesday; local entertainment on Thursday; disco on Friday and Saturday; and an open-mike night on Sunday. Maui Brews Night Club is open 9 p.m.–2 a.m. The restaurant is open 11:30 a.m.–2 a.m. daily.

Comments Dining and dancing available at this island bistro with a thatched-roof bar. The full bar features more than 30 beers, 16 on tap.

If you go Dinner reservations are suggested.

Central Maui

Manana Garage

THE MOST WONDERFUL RESTAURANT IN THE MOST UNLIKELY SPOT

Who Goes There Locals, foodies

33 Lono Avenue, Wailuku; (808) 873-0220

Cover None

Minimum None

Dress Casual

Beverages Margaritas, Mexican beer, wine, soft drinks, juice, coffee.

Food available Nuevo Latino cuisine.

Hours Monday–Friday, lunch starts at 11 a.m; dinner is served nightly from 5 p.m.; the bar stays open late.

What goes on Manana Garage draws mostly local crowd for cheap lunch (starts at $6.95) and dinner, as well as for live music and dancing at night. Off the tourist path, it is popular with foodies seeking innovative Latin American cuisine like paella, guava-tamarind salmon, roasted vegetable enchiladas, and fresh fish chimichangas.

Comments On the ground level of an office building in Kahului, this gearhead-inspired bistro with open-air outdoor dining (so you can watch cars cruise Kaahumanu Avenue) delivers meals as exciting as its mechanically inclined interior. Central Maui's spiciest restaurant and bar offers Latin food and hot flamenco guitar music, à la Gypsy Kings and Mana, until 11 p.m. weekends. There is indoor and outdoor seating at tables or the bar.

If you go Reservations are recommended for those going to dine but not to dance.

Jacques Northshore Restaurant

INDOOR AND OUTDOOR BISTRO AND SOCIAL HUB

Who Goes There Sooner or later everyone goes to Jacques, the perfect tropo bistro, but it's known as a surfer hangout

120 Hana Highway, Paia; (808) 579-8844

Cover None

Minimum None

Dress Surfer casual (T-shirts, board shorts, slippers, lots of tan skin)

Beverages Beer, wine, soft drinks, juice, coffee.

Food available Fresh seafood, salads, sushi, for lunch and dinner.

Hours Daily, 5–10 p.m.

What goes on You can dine inside (at a fish-themed sushi bar) or out, (on an open-air lanai with bandstand offers after-dinner dancing under the stars), and no matter where you are at Jacques, you are part of an in-crowd of North Shore surfers, unreconstructed hippies, and wandering haoles. It's the best place to see and be seen by the sea.

Comments Off the beaten path for tourists, this is the local hangout for windsurfers with jazz on Monday nights, Hawaiian music on Aloha Friday, and lively fun every night; the food's good, too. Seating is available indoors and outdoors under a banyan tree in the tropical garden.

If you go Be prepared to make new pals in old Paia town.

South Maui

Dick's Place

BILLIARDS BAR AND RESTAURANT

Who Goes There Pool players, families until 10 p.m., sports fans

2463 South Kihei Road (next to Denny's), Kihei; (808) 874-8869; www.mauibars.com

Cover None

Minimum None

Dress Casual

Beverages Beer, wine, mixed drinks.

Food available All you can eat snow crab on Monday, fajitas on Wednesday, and fish on Fridays.

Hours Daily, 11 a.m.–2 a.m.

What goes on Pool on 8 regulation-size tables, satellite sports on 11 big-screen TVs, and games in the video arcade.

Comments This bar strives for a *"Cheers*-like atmosphere," Maui-style. Happy hour with free pool is held weekdays, 5–7 p.m. More fun and games than great food.

If you go Great place to shoot pool, eat nachos, drink cold beer, and enjoy an evening out on Maui. On NFL Sundays, expect to meet sports fans whose team loyalty may surprise you, as well as local and imported pool sharks.

Hapa's Brew Haus

LOCALS-MEET-TOURISTS ISLAND HANGOUT

Who Goes There 21–35; celebrities, locals, and visitors

41 East Lipoa Street, Suite 4A, Kihei; (808) 879-9001

Cover $5

Minimum None

Dress Come as you are

Beverages Beer, wine, mixed drinks.

Food available Pizzas, burgers, and sandwiches.

Specials Ladies' Night every Thursday

Hours Every day, 4 p.m.–2 a.m.

What goes on Nightly entertainment featuring a variety of live bands (Willie K on Monday), dancing, bikini contests, and comedy acts.

Comments Hapa's has fallen somewhat from local favor, but is still a lively spot to see good Hawaiian entertainers. Hotel and restaurant workers go later, after shifts.

If you go Go before 8:30 p.m. to enter free.

Life's A Beach

BAR AND HANGOUT WITH MEXICAN OVERTONES

Who Goes There Beachgoers, partiers

1913 South Kihei Road (Next to Foodland), Kihei; (808) 891-8010; www.mauibars.com

Cover None

Minimum None

Dress Casual

Beverages Beer, wine, mixed drinks, $1 mai tai, 50 kinds of margaritas.

Food available Burgers, appetizers, Mexican, kids' menu, daily specials.

Hours Daily, 11 a.m.–2 a.m.; kitchen closes at midnight.

What goes on Nightly live entertainment, Karaoke on Sunday, open mike on Monday, and a daily happy hour, 4–7 p.m.

Comments A regular watering hole with cheap drinks and food that won't break your budget; real working people go here for pau hana.

If you go Get ready to party with locals in Kihei over one-buck mai tais.

Mulligan's on the Blue

IRISH PUB

Who Goes There Locals, tourists, resort workers late (after their shifts at the golf course)

Wailea's Blue Course Clubhouse, 120 Kaukahi Street; (808) 874-1131; www.mulligansontheblue.com

Cover None

Minimum None

Dress Casual

Beverages Guinness and 24 other international beers, wine, Irish coffee, mixed drinks.

Food available Breakfast (all day), lunch, dinner.

Hours Daily, 8 a.m.–1 a.m.

What goes on Nightly live music and dancing; Sunday nights host a traditional Irish jam session, 7–10 p.m., followed by dancing.

Comments 200-seat indoor/outdoor restaurant with genuine Irish flair, is, as advertised, the only place to have rowdy fun at night in Wailea. Lawn settings can be arranged for weddings and special parties.

If you go Wailea nightlife is an oxymoron. Mulligan's by day doubles as the Blue Course Clubhouse, and after dark may either be a full-tilt boogie scene or a bore. You never know what high tide will bring; Guinness is far more dependable.

Sports Page Grill and Bar

SPORTS BAR LIKE BACK HOME

Who Goes There Are you ready for some fearless spectators?

2411 South Kihei Road, Kihei; (808) 879-0602; www.sportspagemaui.com

Cover None

Minimum None

Dress As you are

Beverages Beer, wine, mixed drinks.

Food available Burgers and hot dogs, sandwiches, plate lunches, babyback ribs; Sunday NFL special breakfast. College and pro football games start early in the morning in Hawaii (which is in its own time zone, Hawaiian Standard Time), so you can catch almost all the action before noon and spend the day at the beach.

Hours Daily, 11 a.m.–1:30 a.m. (7 a.m.–2 a.m. NFL Sunday)

What goes on Games on a big-screen TV and 17 little ones; 2 satellite dishes provide a full sports roster. Pool tables, video games, and foosball also available.

Comments Heavy pupus and sandwiches, burgers, chicken wings. This is Kihei's sports center every Sunday in football season. Games start in the morning in Hawaii due to time difference on mainland.

If you go Be careful which team you cheer—the big, nasty guy full of Bud Lite behind you roots for the other side.

Appendixes

For fun, we include here a quiz about Maui to test your knowledge before you go.

For ease of use, we provide three separate indexes: one devoted to accommodations, a second devoted to restaurants and nightclubs, and the book's general, or subject, index. In all three, bold text indicates the profile for applicable entries (hotels, condos, B&Bs, attractions, beaches, golf courses, restaurants, nightclubs, and such) or a summary passage in order to steer you toward passages containing descriptions, contact information, ratings, and prices.

THINK YOU KNOW MAUI?

So, you've made it to the end of this *Unofficial Guide?* Let's see what you learned. Answer all 15 questions correctly and win an autographed photo of Don Ho. Okay, just answer the questions. The correct responses are on the following page.

1. **Maui is located**
   a) off the coast of Los Angeles
   b) in the North Pacific
   c) in the South Pacific

2. **True or False:** Honolulu is the most remote city and Hawaii the farthest islands from any continent on the planet.

3. **Hawaii has**
   a) 4 islands
   b) 8 islands
   c) 132 islands

4. **The last monarch of Hawaii was**
   a) King Kamehameha the Great
   b) Queen Liliuokalani
   c) King Kalakaua

5. **The mai tai, the classic tropical cocktail of Hawaii, was invented by Trader Vic Bergeron in:**
   a) Hawaii
   b) Tahiti
   c) California

6. **The official state bird of Hawaii is**
   a) a California sea gull
   b) a Canadian goose
   c) India mynah

7. **A Loco Moco is**
   a) a crazy person
   b) something to eat
   c) a Hawaiian male

8. **Rainbows occur on Maui**
   a) only at sundown
   b) when it rains
   c) when they are turned on

9. **Is Maui closer to Tokyo or to Washington, D.C.?**

10. **Aloha means**
    a) hello
    b) good-bye
    c) with love
    d) all of the above

11. **Maui No Ka Oi means**
    a) Maui is the best
    b) Maui is kosher
    c) Maui is okay

12. **Maui onions are sweeter than Vidalia onions, true or false?**

13. **Maui Nui is**
    a) the big kahuna of Hana
    b) the islands of Maui, Molokai, and Lanai
    c) ancient game played with iliili stones

14. **The first European to set foot on Maui was**
    a) British explorer Captain James Cook
    b) French explorer Admiral Perouse
    c) Spanish explorer Magellan

15. **Kahului is**
    a) a Filipino dish of roast goat
    b) the Hawaiian word for driving while intoxicated
    c) Maui's airport

QUIZ ANSWERS

1. b) in the North Pacific
2. True
3. c) 132 islands
4. b) Queen Liliuokalani
5. c) California
6. b) a Canadian goose
7. b) something to eat
8. b) when it rains

9. Tokyo

10. d) all of the above

11. a) Maui is the best

12. True

13. b) the islands of Maui, Molokai, and Lanai

14. a) British explorer Captain James Cook

15. c) Maui's airport

Accommodations Index

Restaurant and Nightclub Index

Subject Index